Divine

Messages

A Journey Through the Workbook for Students in A Course in Miracles

Divine

Messages

A Journey Through the Workbook for Students in A Course in Miracles

By

Revs. Paul and Deborah Phelps

MiraclesOne Foundation

ISBN - 978-0-6152-0239-6

*We dedicate this book to all those who still suffer from believing
that they are alone and friendless. Most certainly, we are not!
Within these pages we hope that you will receive guidance, as we did, on how to
personally experience this eternal truth for yourselves.*

*I wish to thank the Holy Spirit for bringing Deborah into my life. The Guide she
follows is strong and constantly reminds me of a better way. She is truly a
spiritual leader who quietly leads the way. Without her hard work, dedication to
Holy Spirit and to her own awakening, I do not think this book would have been
completed in a timely manner.*
Thank you Deborah for your gifts to me. I love you.

*My embrace of gratitude to the Holy Spirit for the holy relationship that Paul
and I share so deeply as we always put God first in our lives together. His
steadfastness and devotion to shining the Light of Healing to all the unhealed
places in his mind has always been an inspiration to me.*
You are my mirror, my partner, love and friend.
I love you with the Love of God. Thank you for Who you are.

*And lastly, we are deeply grateful to Holy Spirit and Jesus for all the help that
They have given to us. We are grateful and relieved for finding the Light and the
Voice of God within ourselves, for now we know without a doubt that
we are not alone.*

Table of Contents

Journal Entries on Workbook Lessons

Divine Messages

A Journey Through the Workbook for Students in A Course in Miracles

For 365 days, Revs. Deborah and Paul Phelps allowed their minds to be open to the Voice of God and to receive His messages. By simply utilizing their daily life situations as conversation topics with the Holy Spirit, they found that their healing increased by the simple act of practical application of the ideas of forgiveness in *A Course in Miracles*. These personal messages were written daily and now shared with many.

Since 1980, Rev. Deborah Phelps has been in touch with the Divine. At 16, she embraced the practice of meditation which led her to many spiritual and light-filled experiences. In 1994, *A Course in Miracles* came into her life, thus deepening her awakening and healing journey as she continued to listen and honor the Divine Voice within.

In 2003, she joined with her ministerial partner and husband, Paul. Paul had also experienced many Light episodes and heard the Voice of the Holy Spirit. Since the late 1990s, through his meditation practice and study of *Conversations with God* and then *A Course in Miracles*, he too had experienced a tremendous amount of healing in his life.

Together, Deb and Paul have created a unique God-Centered partnership of support, love, honor and respect. For one year, they shared together a journaling process of receiving healing messages from the Holy Spirit. This one year was specifically dedicated to reading, practicing and journaling on the Workbook for Students in *A Course in Miracles*.

With honesty, willingness and openness, both Deb and Paul allowed the Holy Spirit to bless their minds. Sometimes in the daily process they received insights on current or past situations and sometimes direct Love Letters from the Holy Spirit or Jesus. Sometimes they presented their struggles and the willingness to forgive and thus see differently. And sometimes they simply had wonderful spiritual experiences with the Light, Voice or Feeling of Love's Presence. In a sense, it is their authentic journaling and healing process that you will see with each day's journal entry.

We hope that what you find in our Divine Messages will truly inspire you. But do not let it stop there for we encourage you to take it one step further by creating your own inner dialogue with Holy Spirit for yourself. Whether you use our Practical Application Series or Illumination Journal, or your own journal, take the time to be with each A Course in Miracles reading and ask the Holy Spirit what meaning it has in your life in this present moment. It is a tremendous gift that you receive and give to yourself and to the world when you connect with the Divine within.

Namasté,

Deb
Paul

Do not hide suffering from His sight, but bring it gladly to Him.
Lay before His eternal sanity all your hurt, and let Him heal you.
Do not leave any spot of pain hidden from His light, and search your
mind carefully for any thoughts you may fear to uncover.
For He will heal every little thought you have kept to hurt you and
cleanse it of its littleness, restoring it to the magnitude of God.
T-13.III.7:3-6

Divine Messages

16

Journal Entry on Lesson 1

Nothing I see in this room [on this street, from this window, in this place] means anything.

And so I begin my journey into the training of my mind. Today, I begin to lay the foundation for miracles to light my way Home. With the idea of "nothing I see means anything," I could be tempted to either exclude an item or purposefully choose an item for the practice periods. Instead, I am to apply the lesson to what I see surrounding me whether it is inside or outside, whether I am attached to it or not. All that I see has no meaning. That idea could even make me scratch my head, "What do you mean nothing I see means anything?" when I see it and can touch it and can experience it in so many ways. It is not for me to argue the fact or continue to be puzzled but instead I am to be open and willing to the idea presented today. Jesus reminds us of the same in the Introduction to the Workbook. And so today, I will apply this indiscriminately to all that I see, neither excluding nor singling out. I accept that this idea encourages me to wipe the sleepers from my eyes and to stretch my mind a little more today. I am grateful that I have made the choice to begin again. The moment is now and I gladly accept it.

My last name and the family clan that it is associated with does not mean anything *because* it is not who I really am. The surroundings and environment that I live within does not mean anything *because* it is not where I really am. The world that we live on and its man-made and natural disasters that seem to shockwave around the planet do not mean anything *because* none of it is really happening in Reality right now. This may be difficult to believe because to the body these experiences feel very real. The body and everything that it seems to experience is just a dream that we are dreaming as the Son of God.

In Reality right now, we *are* a spiritual being of white Light who is pretending that he has fallen asleep and is dreaming a terrible dream. He is dreaming that He has become a physical body and that terrible things can happen to it and, that he is no longer the Son of God. As we begin to open up to the experiences the Workbook Lessons set forth, the Holy Spirit will begin to show us the truth about ourselves. He will begin to give us glimpses of the white Light of our True Selves and the corresponding state of peace that we are in right now, in Reality, as the Son of God. When this begins to happen we will begin to recognize that everything we think we are experiencing with the body is just an illusion. These experiences are a happy time for the Son of God who has fallen asleep. It is a time of great celebration and joy that echoes throughout Heaven because, the Son of God has begun to awaken and return to his rightful Home.

∞∞∞∞

Journal Entry on Lesson 2

I have given everything I see in this room [on this street, from this window, in this place] all the meaning that it has for me.

I have given everything I see in this room all the meaning that it has for me because everything I see triggers a past memory. If we recall what I shared with you in yesterday's Message, everything we see and experience with the body is not real. It is an illusion. When we walk into the room of an unfamiliar place and we see something that we haven't seen before such as a framed photograph of a family sitting on a shelf, we will have one of two responses. We will have a response of happiness or joy or one of sadness or regret.

These responses are coming from our own past memories and experiences. In the past, we had some kind of experience with a family situation and depending upon what kind of experience that was we formulated a meaning out of it for ourselves. Then, we parked that definition of that situation into the back of our minds for later retrieval. Down the road different sights, situations and experiences may trigger the retrieval of that memory. The memory is brought forth and the definition or meaning that we have placed on that particular situation is used to help formulate and supplement the meaning that we are giving to the current situation being experienced. This memory leapfrog effect tends to go on and on as we go about living our lives.

This is the perception of the ego. This perception is like a dark cloak that is drawn about the body to cover it in darkness and block out the Light of Reality behind it. The mind must be trained to let go of the way it is seeing the world right now, so that restoration of True Sight may be restored. That is why we undertake the Workbook Lessons. It is to help us train our minds to let go of what we think we are seeing now and exchange it for something else.

As we practice the Lessons our minds will begin to let go of the illusion of darkness that surrounds us. The glimmerings of the Light of Reality will begin to break through bringing forth tidings of gladness and joy for the beholder. For this is the time that the shackles placed upon the mind are being released and fall to the ground, as the Light of Heaven illuminates the mind and washes away the darkness with the sinlessness of the Light of Christ, your True Self. The Voice for God will begin to speak to you and guide you along your way. Listen to Him well, for He is your Friend Who will walk you gently and easily from the darkness into the Light. Amen.

With today's Lesson, I had the feeling of bestowing blessing upon each item my eyes came in contact with. In a sense, "Thank you and I bless you on your way; you are no longer required in my mind." I have a choice in what I can perceive and know once I relinquish the meaning of what I have on anything that I come into contact with. I am a clean slate, what can be written on my heart now is what the Holy Spirit would have for me. The yearnings will have now ceased and I will accept the gift of His Love to be etched in my mind in Light. This Lesson and the following may seem small but yet they are mighty in their significance as I learn each day to release the past perceptions and accept what is now. Now is all there is. Now is all there ever will be. I come to You today Father with a choice for my freedom by the outstretched hands open to receive and remember Your Love.

∞∞∞∞

Journal Entry on Lesson 3

**I do not understand anything I see in this room
[on this street, from this window, in this place].**

If everything I see is then devoid of meaning and understanding, how can I make a judgment? How can I respond? I cannot. It is my past that attempts to serve as a guide, an unfit one at that. I can only trust that the Holy Spirit will share with me all that I need to know. He will always lead me to perfect peace. Today Holy Spirit, I am open to Your meaning and understanding, to Your Voice of Truth that will always lead me Home. The Light of Heaven is behind everything that I see and so I relinquish all that I have used to block its' illumination of my mind. It is the blocks to Love's presence that will be removed each time I offer my mind to You. The blocks are my understandings and meanings that come from the fearful, ego mind. Each time I give my meanings to the Holy Spirit, I will receive a miracle, a shift in perception to one of Love. I am grateful in this today. I do not have to understand anything that I see, for You will do it for me. Thank You for the miracle of Love. Amen.

Journal Entry on Lesson 4

These thoughts do not mean anything.
They are like the things I see in this room [on this street,
from this window, in this place].

In the training of my mind, today's exercise is building another mind "rep." I practice the Lesson as indicated because I know that it will assist me in increasing my "spiritual muscle." Just as in physical exercise, the benefits of my mind training will not be seen until I have been working at it for some time. Muscles do not appear overnight but they continue to build just as my spiritual muscle will continue to build with each day's repetition. The daily Lessons continue to lay the foundation for the healing of my mind. Today, I will choose any thought that comes into my mind, seeming "good" or "bad" and attempt to judge it not and use what Jesus has presented for me. I am grateful that I have the willingness to follow the Lesson as provided, trusting that it will achieve its' goal.

All the thoughts that you are used to harboring within your mind create darkness in one way or another and block you from seeing the Light beyond. Make no assumptions that one thought or another is an exception from the application of today's Lesson. If you are not seeing the Light then you are creating darkness with your mind. The Light will come in the place where you rest in no thoughts. Ask the Holy Spirit to help you with this. He will help you to experience the gap where the Light will flash through for a moment and illuminate your mind. At the perfect moment He will help you to get to the experience of the Light or to the experience of hearing His Voice speak to you. Be patient and loyal to the Lessons and the experiences will come in time.

∞∞∞∞

Journal Entry on Lesson 5

I am never upset for the reason I think.

Today's Lesson gifts me with a mindfulness of what is occurring with my thoughts. I do not have to spend the time figuring it out at this point, why I am feeling upset, angry, afraid or the like. I just have to be willing to notice and be observant of what is there in my mind that is causing me some form of distress. With Jesus' gentle voice, I can achieve this goal today. I will learn as I continue to progress that all upsets are equal in their disturbance to my mind. I may know this already and know their causes if I have been practicing the Lessons for some time, however, today I will be in the present moment with the Lesson. I will search my mind, apply the idea and trust that all that I need to know will be provided for me.

If I am not afraid to be late for work for the reason I think, afraid to commit to a project for the reason I think, or feeling depressed for the reason I think, then what is it? The ego presents us with reasons for feeling fear in all of these situations and you may notice that the fearful thoughts are always based on something that has happened in the past, or something that we are afraid may or may not happen in the future. This is the game the ego plays with the mind to keep it distracted from paying attention to fearful thoughts and to letting them go by turning inward to the state of Peace. The state of Peace is inside the mind beyond all these thoughts in the stillness. This is where Peace will reveal itself to you with the Holy Spirit's help. This is where Reality will be revealed to you with the Holy Spirit's help. The ego doesn't want you to know about this place so it keeps your mind busy and distracted with fearful thoughts about everything that seems to be going on around you and outside of you in the world. If we're paying attention to the ego's distractions in the outside world by seeing, hearing and feeling things we're failing to discover the truth that is hidden inside of us.

Journal Entry on Lesson 6

I am upset because I see something that is not there.

It is amazing how much is contained in the mind as I contemplated on today's Lesson. As a few items came to mind to apply the idea, many more followed. Soon I had the realization that there must be thousands of latent thoughts in my mind of some sort of upset or grievance. People or situations that I had not even thought about in years appeared in my mind, and with each one I applied, "I am upset because I see something that is not there."

Today I will use the Holy Spirit to assist me in clearing out the drainpipes of my mind by letting go of each upset that comes to me. It does not matter if the upset seems miniscule or immense as Jesus tells me in the application of today's idea, that all upsets are equally disturbing to my mind. There are no small upsets, period. If what it is there in my mind brings me out of peace, then I need to remember that it is because I have made some sort of judgment. I have made my own conclusions, my own observations or my own opinions of what is occurring or not occurring. Today, I am devoted to letting the gunk of upsetting thoughts be flushed up and out so that peace is restored to my mind. And I thank You Holy Spirit for being the Ultimate Plumber!

∞∞∞

Journal Entry on Lesson 7

I see only the past.

So the Light begins to dawn as my mind wakes up to this Lesson. I put aside all that I have known before from doing this Lesson in the past. I look at this Lesson with new eyes and follow the instructions mentioned. It is the past that fills my mind and creates the judgments that are there. I could question all of this and suggest that well, how else would I know how to drive a car safely, or fix a meal, or work on a computer? There is a line that Jesus uses after the monologue about the "cup." "You would have no idea what this cup is; accept for your past learning. Do you, then, really see it?"

This reminds me of some words a friend spoke not too long ago about how he looks at his wife. He tries to see her and actually everybody for the first time, each time. It really is a gift to give myself today. To look at all that I see and not see what I want to see in a particular person, place or thing. Looking at the world for the first time, each time, just as an innocent, like a baby. I can be in awe and wonder and in love with everything I see, couldn't I if I was as a mere infant? Everything would be fascinating, the garbage can, the diaper, the flower, the shiny jewelry, each face that I come into contact with. So this Lesson today gives me quite an amount to contemplate upon as I move through the day. I need new ideas about time, Jesus is correct in that. And so I approach this Lesson as if I have never seen it before. I follow it and allow the gifts to shower forth. Amen.

∞∞∞∞

Journal Entry on Lesson 8

My mind is preoccupied with past thoughts.

Once again it is in the observation of my thoughts that amazes me as to how much goes on within my mind. Even as I sit still, practice the Lesson and meditate on its' meaning afterwards, I can still experience the "monkey mind" chattering away. My mind indeed is preoccupied with past thoughts. Thoughts of tasks that I need to complete later in the day, or during the next week are still based on past thoughts. Even the comparisons of perhaps times when I had not completed the tasks on time and how painful it was to me when I had not are past thoughts.

This really is the retraining of my mind and through each time as I make a pass around the Workbook Lessons, year after year, I am open to that retraining today Holy Spirit. I know what You have for me and that is the perfect peaceful Presence of mind. So today, I consciously slow down; I take the time to relax in Your peace, maintaining my focus on the present moment. As a thought comes into my mind's view, I will release it simply. The great strength in this is that I can do this anytime I choose. It does take practice to keep my mind focused on the Truth. Even if I have been meditating for many years, I am open to another golden nugget of learning to be in the space of stillness. In the silence I will hear You speak to me, offering me a new way to live my life. It is a way of peace and tranquility in accepting the Now moment. Slowly breathing in and slowly breathing out, being in the moment, I will receive a tremendous gift; a gift that I have bestowed upon myself.

∞∞∞∞

Journal Entry on Lesson 9

I see nothing as it is now.

Let's play an imagination game for a moment. Let's sit still and observe the room that we are sitting in right now for a moment. Note the table or the chair, the window or the framed picture on the wall. You may see a television or a telephone or some books. In general, observe and note the room you are sitting in now. Then close your eyes and see the room in your mind. Then with your mind look at each one of those items again remember the table, now change the table into a cloud. Move your attention over to the chair and change the chair into a cloud. Continue doing this with each of the items you observed in the room until the entire room in your mind has been changed to a cloud that surrounds you. Hidden behind the cloud is the Light of Reality. The Light is everywhere behind the cloud. It can be perceived by the mind as a white Light or as a golden Light depending upon how far toward the Light you can go. Just like we used the mind to convert each of the items into the cloud, we use the mind to create the items in the first place.

This is all done at an unconscious level of magnitude that the human mind cannot understand. This is the ego part of the mind. Anything that the ego part of the mind miscreates is the same as the cloud that surrounds you and blocks the Light from beyond from coming through. The Light is really there and you can perceive it but we must continue to practice training our minds to let go of the habit of seeing the projections of the ego mind. These Lessons are moving us in the direction of doing that. Eventually the Light from beyond will begin to pierce through the cloud towards us and we will begin to perceive the Light with our conscious minds. Eventually as we continue to clear the clouds away more and more we will come to understand and become aware that we are the Light that we perceive which comes from our Source, Who is within us. Thank You Father for Your gift of Light to us which will help us find our way Home. Amen.

∞∞∞∞

Journal Entry on Lesson 10

My thoughts do not mean anything.

After awhile as I practiced this morning's meditation, I started to feel myself become a little irritated and impatient. I began to feel this way because I would observe a thought about a situation at work come to mind, and then I would say to myself, "My thought about this situation at work does not mean anything." Then, I would let it go with my mind and turn my mind's attention toward the nothingness beyond where the Light comes from and wait for the Light to come. But what would happen is that an image would show up in my mind about something and my mind's attention would leave its' focus on the nothingness beyond and focus on the image, again I would say, "My thoughts about this image do not mean anything." and I would let it go again and turn my mind's attention to the nothingness beyond and wait for the healing Light to come again. Then, something else would pop into my mind, a memory about something, another image, a fearful thought. Each time these things would distract my mind's attention from being still and waiting in the nothingness from beyond them to redirecting my attention on to these things that were popping up. This seemed to happen over and over again and I felt like I was having difficulty to settling into the peace into the nothingness beyond and staying there.

All of these thoughts, images, memories and situations are things that the ego mind pops up into our attention to distract us from resting and waiting in the nothingness beyond. It is in the nothingness beyond where we want to settle into. The space where there are no thoughts. In the stillness is where the Light of peace will come and flash into the mind and illuminate the body with the release of healing peace. This is the goal to find the place where the Light of our True Self reveals Itself to us. Remember to ask the Holy Spirit for help with this process. He will help you to move beyond the clutter of the ego mind and will raise you up to Him, Who is our Source. Thank You Holy Spirit for Your help. We love You and we love each other and our Father. Amen.

Today I focus my mind to the thoughts that come into the mind's view and willingly release them. As I do this, I realize that through this process, it is setting the foundation for a meditation practice. By being observant of my thoughts and recognizing their lack of meaning, I am letting each one go as a bubble rises to the sky. When I was first learning meditation many years ago, that was one of the images that I used to assist me with keeping my mind focused in the present moment by imagining each thought as a bubble gently lifting and being carried away. In essence, the Lesson is doing the same. I am watching the procession go by with the knowledge that as I practice this exercise that it will help me to let go of my previous way of thinking and believing. This will allow me to be in the Now moment. This also plants the seeds for a beneficial practice of stillness. It is a gift that I give myself once again today when I join with Him in practicing these Lessons.

∞∞∞∞

Journal Entry on Lesson 11

My meaningless thoughts are showing me a meaningless world.

Today's idea is a depressing thought for me because it means that all the things that I have come to cherish and value in the world as things that make me happy really aren't true. I think it makes me feel sad because there are some things that I do not want to not be true. I think it's even more difficult to feel a sense of freedom and happiness when I have forgotten the experience of the peace of the Light that comes with the letting go of the world. The Holy Spirit tells me that these depressing thoughts are really hidden thoughts of anger because the ego wants to make true what is not true. It is a trick of the ego to keep me trapped in the belief that anything in the world would make me happy. It will not.

Forgiveness is the only appropriate response to anything I think I see or cherish in the world of illusion. The gifts that lie beyond will come and set me free as I truly forgive with the Holy Spirit's help the things I think are making me happy in the world. Each thing that I think I am enjoying in the world can be a hook if I am not careful. If I have any sense of dependence on anything in the world to make me happy then I am hooked by the ego belief system. For example, if I think that I need to have some ice cream to help me to feel happy then I am hooked by the ego belief system. If I think I need to live in a nicer home to be happy then I am hooked by the ego belief system. If I think I need to have a nicer car then I am hooked by the ego belief system.

When we are hooked by the ego belief system and then follow that guidance and obtain those things, we eventually discover we're not truly happy in the long run. It's not lasting. Underneath there is hidden anger. This is what eventually leads to the feelings of depression. It's because we thought we had the solution to the problem. We achieved what we believed was the solution to the problem and then we come to find that it really wasn't the solution to the problem.

This is the cycle of the ego thought system. It has been going on since the beginning of time itself. This is a great time of joy for us for we are learning the tools of dismantling this tragedy upon the mind of the Son of God. Forgiveness is the most blessed tool given to the Son of God to help him break free of the chains of the dreams of the cycle of life and death, of pain and terror, of misery and hell for the Son of God. None of it is true and none of it has happened but the Son of God who you are will not realize this until the illusion is forgiven and atonement accepted. So remember the only appropriate response to any thought that disturbs your peace or ego hooks on things in the world is forgiveness. In those moments immediately invite the Holy Spirit to join with you and to help you to forgive what you think you are seeing, what you think will make you happy because it will not. Only the recognition and personal experience of your True Self will truly make you happy. These will come as forgiveness is practiced and the dreams of illusions are healed in the mind of the Son of God.

Thank you Jeshua for this message. We love you. Amen.

Journal Entry on Lesson 12

I am upset because I see a meaningless world.

I can look at the news today and quickly be reminded of the world that I think I see. Within a few minutes, I can see an angry, fearful, crazy world. This all based on my past experiences of what I think a "bad" world is and what I think a "good" world is. My childhood memory images might have taught me the same and so carried forth until this moment. If I close my eyes in meditation and allow the Holy Spirit to show me deeper into all of this, then I can realize first that I give everything that I see all the meaning. Secondly, I can decide to follow His lead and allow Him to show me the Real World of Heaven.

Once I can see the result of my decisions and projections, I can see that I am manipulating the world into what I want based on my beliefs. Are my thoughts of fear and judgment? Do I then see a disappointing world? Are my thoughts of kindness? Do I see a caring world? When I recognize that my thoughts control what I believe about the world then I can take responsibility for those thoughts. A world devoid of meaning cannot upset me. The only world of meaning is God's Real World. In the space of eternity are all my dreams fulfilled, all peace restored, all wanderings ended. At Home with my Creator with the hearth of His Love is the only place to repose. In the stillness, I commune with Him and listen to His Word. He is the meaning to my life as He extended His Holy Love to bring forth Perfection.

∞∞∞∞∞

Journal Entry on Lesson 13

A meaningless world engenders fear.

The chalkboard of my mind stands before me, the fear is there that if I do not chalk up my thoughts and ideas then I will be left with emptiness so deep and dark that I will never be rescued. This is the fear that a meaningless world engenders. My ego mind uses all the projections and illusions to fill the slate in its' insane protection that I will not experience that God has forgotten about me, that He has abandoned me and left me alone to wither and die. I take matters into my own hands this way because of this fear.

All of this is all further from the Truth. The Truth is that in relinquishing all the meaning that I have placed there I will have cleared the space to permit my Heavenly Father to shine His Love ever so brightly in my mind. I will know the facts that I have not been abandoned at all. I have always been kept safe in His Arms. My mind in meditation can do the same. As I begin to quiet my mind, thoughts creep in to pad the space. In my practice then, I simply allow each thought to be acknowledged and dismissed. I wait for God. God will come to my holy mind because He is in my holy mind. Releasing the fearful, judging thoughts increases the vastness of the experience of God. Here, I abide in Joy. His Voice speaks to me and I am content.

Let Me speak to you in these moments when you feel afraid of the world that surrounds you. Know that you are not alone in My Love. The world that you see is nothing but what you have made up in your mind for your fear of Me is so great. Come now and listen to what I say to you, there really is no need to fear My Love. My Love is what will save you from the darkness that you perceive. Look upward towards the Light and the pit of despair leaves you. Focus on the Light within you for it is My connection to you. Embrace that connection for it will lead you to Me. It is a golden cord, a path that will assimilate you to your Home here in Heaven. The ego has deceived you in thinking that it will offer sure protection from Me. It is only afraid of its' own demise. I offer to you so much more than the ego could. I offer you a peace that is indescribable with mere words. These words are but symbols and what I have to give you lies beyond symbols of limitation. Love, Peace and Joy are without limits.

Come to Me in the space of silence and you will know the truth of what I speak. Take the time whenever you begin to feel distracted by the world and its' issues for I am here in the stillness of your mind. There is an everlasting abundance of Truth for you to experience this day. Permit yourself the occasions to train your mind to think with Me. I will never leave you comfortless. My Love surrounds you always and forever.

∞∞∞

Journal Entry on Lesson 14

God did not create a meaningless world.

Today's idea can be a difficult one to accept indeed. Like a match that flares up into a bright angry flame when it is first lit, the ego often flares up when it is first introduced to this idea. It often creates a chain reaction as if it were lighting a pile of matches, like dominoes, one match lights another and lights the whole pile of matches until one large flare up. But like the pile of matches that suddenly flare up, they settle down into a slow steady burn until the match is gone. This tends to be the pattern of healing that we all go through when we're introduced to new ideas that challenge the belief system that the ego has taught us.

Everything you see, hear, touch and feel around you and including your body is not real. It is a dream, just like dreaming a dream when you are asleep at night which can seem very real while you are dreaming the dream. Then suddenly you wake up and recognize that you are only dreaming. The dream is gone except for the memory of it. The characters in the dream are gone. The situations and events that you were experiencing in the dream are gone. They vanish because it was only a thought that you made very real in your mind. The same thing is happening on a much larger scale to the Son of God.

Imagine for a moment that you are God's creation. Everything He has been given to you. Imagine that you are one vast Mind melded with His. With that Mind imagine that you could fall asleep, forget who you really were and begin dreaming that you are something that you are not. You begin dreaming that you are in a place where time exists and things can change from good to bad, bad to good, large to small, small to large, life to death and death to life. This is what is happening, and you think you are experiencing it all around you. It is only because of the incredible power of the Mind that God has given you that you are able to create a dream that seems so real around you. Had it not been for your Father's immediate response to this problem that you created within your mind, you could have been caught in this dream forever. But He gave you a way out, a way to awaken from the dream in the same instant you began to dream of being exiled in hell. He gave you the Holy Spirit Who is the tool of forgiveness. He is the miracle that comes to illuminate your mind when you open up to the reality of Spirit within you.

The Light of Truth will illuminate your mind and heal the darkness you have brought upon yourself little by little as you open up to It. The little healings from the Light will compound and grow and begin to give you glimpses of reality beyond the dream that you are dreaming. When this begins to happen it is then that today's Lesson will truly begin to become meaningful to you. There is another World, another Reality that exists beyond the one that you are now dreaming. To begin having experiences of the Reality that lies beyond continue to practice letting go as the Lessons set forth. Wait for the sparks of Light to come and illuminate your mind as you begin to practice your silent meditations. The Light will come by resting in the silence. This is the asking. The Answer has already been given. Thank you for your dedication.

Love, Jeshua

ꝏꝏꝏ

Journal Entry on Lesson 15

My thoughts are images that I have made.

Disney creates this grand illusion that if you go there you are going to be happy. They spend all kinds of money on hiring the best people, the best imagineers so they call them. These imagineers create spectacular effects and illusions from their thoughts and imaginations. There is only one message to behold from all the experiences that Disney creates for its' audiences and that is "This is not it." There is no effect, illusion, image, or experience that will give you happiness and fulfillment within the dream except the illusion of awakening itself. Forgive all things that you think you should be doing. Forgive all things that you desire to do again because you think you had a good experience in the past with it. Forgive them and let all your desires go except the desire to be reunited with God, except the desire to be reunited with peace, except the desire to know true joy once again. Make these your one goal. They are one and the same. Let the strength of true joy illuminate your mind and body. Ask the Holy Spirit to allow the experience of true joy and indescribable happiness to come to you for an instant so that you may understand the direction and the goal of this entire Course.

The curtain is drawn to the Truth and so my play is presented before it. I am the writer and the director of this play. I choose the characters, the sets, the music, the comedy, the tragedy, and the drama. In this production, the thoughts I think are brought forward into seeming reality on the world's stage. The scenes may shift, the acts spanning years, but it all consists of my own thoughts making the images and stories as I go. With the Holy Spirit's help, I can close the curtain on this production and lift the veil to see the Light. Each time I come to Him, the story I write becomes the story that He would write for me. In Heaven there is thunderous applause when I partner with Him. God is the producer of my life for He extended Himself in Love and the Son came forth. With today's Lesson, I simply take the objects that surround me and with willingness see that all that is there are illusions. As real vision comes, the images will begin to fade and the Light radiates ever so softly. I am drawn to the Light. It is the Light that fulfills me for it is God that is my only fulfillment.

Holy Spirit, partner with me now to release the grand illusion and open my mind to the true Light of God. In the silence I hear Your Voice, always loving and soothing, reminding me of serenity and peace. This is what I would have in my life now. Amen.

ᴏᴏᴏᴏᴏ

Journal Entry on Lesson 16

I have no neutral thoughts.

It is said that on average the human mind has 60,000 thoughts a day. It is also said that each of these thoughts are miscreative; meaning they are creating an experience that is not of God. If we see something such as a vehicle passing by in front of us, the image of that vehicle was created by our thoughts on some level. The sounds coming from the vehicle as it passes by are created by our thoughts on some level. The image of our bodies, the feelings that they seem to feel, the tastes and smells that they seem to experience are all a result of our thoughts on some level. When we see, hear, and feel these experiences they draw our attention to them and away from the reality of the Light of Heaven that surrounds us. Furthermore, when we close our eyes and go inward and we listen to the Voice of our thinking thoughts again we are being distracted from allowing the awareness of Love's presence to reveal Itself to us. This is why it is said that we are at war with God. We as the Son of God are using our holy mind to imagine that we are experiencing everything that we are not.

We are having a bad dream. We are dreaming that we are not God's only creation but instead we are a human in a small fragile body capable of dying, full of limitations. The Reality of Heaven lies beyond all these dark thoughts and the thoughts of Heaven are our own. But in order to begin to experience the Reality of Heaven we must train our minds to let go of all these thoughts. The 60,000 thoughts that we have a day is a habit. Thinking thoughts is a habit of the ego mind. By practicing the exercises in the Workbook Lessons we are changing this habit and developing a new one. As we progress through the Lessons we will practice more and more of letting go of this habit of thinking and allowing the awareness of the Reality of the Love that surrounds us to be restored to our awareness. It is there all around you right now. That is why eventually you will begin to have light episodes and encounters with the Voice of God speaking to you.

This is the beginning of the restoration of the awareness of your direct communication with God Who speaks to you all the time. As we practice the Lessons we will practice more and more letting go of our thoughts and being still in the silence; being at peace in the silence. As we wait for the Holy Spirit to help us with the process of being still and resting at peace in the silence, He will help us to have the experiences of the glimpses of Reality that surrounds us all the time.

Thank You Holy Spirit for Your help. Thank You Father for creating us. And thank you brother Jesus for your messages that help us along the way. Amen.

∞∞∞

Journal Entry on Lesson 17

I see no neutral things.

My prayer today my Father is to enter the state of real aliveness and joy. I do this through the recognition of today's idea that all things that I light my eyes upon are projections of my own thinking. I do not see neutral things because my thoughts are not neutral. I have decided what all things mean to me and judge them accordingly to the beliefs that I carry within my mind. These core beliefs may be of unworthiness, lack or limitation, unloveability, but mostly fear. They are subtle there in my mind. If I allow these core beliefs to project upon the screen then my experiences here in this world will be that of seeming proof that I am unworthy, unlovable and the like.

As I shift my perceptions with the Holy Spirit and devote myself to miracle-mindedness, I can see that there is much more beyond all of this. There is true joy and love, true worth in You. I am an unlimited being of Light because Light is all I am. The Light is Your Love, my Father and now each thought will become a prayer only to the awareness of Love's presence. I do this through the practice of mindfulness as I go about my day, as thoughts enter my mind I can be aware that they are not neutral and invite the Holy Spirit to purify each one. Today is my day that I drop the chains of judgment and permit true perception to set me free. My freedom lies in You and only You. Amen.

Today's thought is a joyous one indeed because it tells us that it is possible to escape from the world you made. Doesn't it feel good to be told that there is something far better to behold than the world you've seen thus far? Doesn't it feel good to have found a way to unravel your mind and have the truth be shown to you at last? At last we have found a way to begin to release our mind from the darkness that it has shrouded upon itself for such a long time. The Light of Forgiveness will begin to come flashing its holy Light into your mind and washing away all iniquities that have been placed upon it. The Light begins to heal the mind in little doses gently cleansing it of the darkness twinkle by twinkle, flash by flash, until the memory of God and His Son has been restored.

Patience is due the Holy Spirit's Light of Forgiveness for He knows the way. His way is gentle and loving and peaceful. His way gently lays the carpet before you leading you to God. You are God's Son, His holy creation and you will come to know this once again in His gentle and loving way because He has said that it will be so. God has not forgotten His beloved Son and He holds you in His arms and wills for you to know that this is so. He loves you and you love Him. In your Oneness Love is extended, creation is extended, gratitude is extended, peace is extended, joy is extended to each other forever, God's world without end.

Thank You Father for us. We love You. Amen.

ᵒᵒᵒᵒᵒ

Journal Entry on Lesson 18

I am not alone in experiencing the effects of my seeing.

My Dear One,

Join with Me today to look upon the world and see truly the Love that is there. The world you see now is the world of the ego. It is fear brought forth from your thoughts. When you align your thoughts with Me, I gift you with True Perception. True

Perception is looking upon the world and seeing the Light of Innocence. The harsh edges begin to fade and a softening occurs as you open your mind to My Presence. I give you the gift of spiritual sight, the gift of Christ Vision. I see you as the perfect Lamb of God that you are. The lamb is just a symbol I share with you today in helping you each time in recognizing your innocence. You have forgotten so many times that you are innocent and that you are loved by Me. I bring you reminders of Who you really are.

Do not deny the strength that is there for you in your Father. Do not be afraid of His Love and Power for it is your Love and power. You have the power to decide upon the goal that you would see. Select peace by selecting the idea of your freedom. Release and do not bind. Be free in your Father's Love. Those that surround you are yes, images that you have made, yet each one is a symbol to you of healing. Let forgiveness shine in your heart today and let it help you release all the edges of pain from your holy mind. Let Me help you through this process. That is My function, that is why I am here. You do not have to do anything alone. I am your Wise Friend. Picture me as you will in whatever way is helpful to you. I will speak to you from beyond the form that you choose. It doesn't matter what the form is for it is not the form where the message arrives but from far beyond. The Message is simply of My Love for you; My Love for the Sonship.

There is only One Mind and that is why you are not alone in experiencing anything that you see. Now join together with the One and see the truth that yields to you. There is no need for genuflecting before your Father, He welcomes you wholly and with open arms. Surrender simply to Love and My direction. You can confide in Me; you can trust Me. Let go of all that binds your mind, all the petty thoughts, all the past, all the situations that seem difficult for you, the relationships, the jobs, whatever it is let it be left with Me today. Love is powerful and you are that Love. Remember Love today and always. I am with You. Amen.

Journal Entry on Lesson 19

I am not alone in experiencing the effects of my thoughts.

"I am not alone in experiencing the effects of my fearful thoughts about myself or others or situations and events," means that on some level everyone else is experiencing the effects of those thoughts too. If I believe in the fearful ego thought that I am unworthy of something, or some experience, not only do I experience the effects of that fearful projection but so does everyone else at an unconscious level. This includes your mother, your father, brother, sister, and friend. This includes people you work with and people you don't know. Others are entertaining these fearful ego-based thoughts as well. In turn, you too are experiencing the effects of their thoughts as well on an unconscious level.

Everyone is doing this all the time at an unconscious level. Becoming aware of this and working with the Holy Spirit to shift out of this habitual ego-based thinking is part of the plan of the Great Awakening to the Spirit that you are. The fear of the lack of time, money and health are all ego-based thoughts designed to keep your attention diverted from experiencing the thoughts of God right now.

As you allow Holy Spirit to help you learn how to let go of your focus on the projections of the ego mind, you will begin to experience the Light of Reality that lies beyond all of the dark projections that you see in this world. Experiences of the Light and Peace will begin to be experienced from the world around you, and in your mind, as you begin to awaken the illusion of darkness around you. Your awakening from the dream of the cycle of life and death will begin to accelerate when this begins to happen.

Be patient, and continue to practice forgiveness with the Holy Spirit every time you feel disturbed. Forgive all your fearful thoughts as much as you can. None of them are true which is why they must be forgiven. In time you will begin to experience the world of darkness around you slowly vanish away as the Light of Heaven that surrounds you begins to reveal Itself more and more. This is the experience of the process of removing the blocks of the awareness of Love's Presence.

How happy are we to be joining with our mighty companions. Gratitude is due to each and every one of us for we all must work together in order to return to the awareness that we are at Home. We are there right now in joyful Love with our Creator and with each other and our dear Friend, the Holy Spirit.

Thank You Father for Your help. Amen.

∞∞∞∞

Journal Entry on Lesson 20

I am determined to see.

My determination is strong today my Father, for I truly want another way to see my life and the world. Each day Your Lessons provide me with deeper reflections into what I think is real and what truly is. My determination and my willingness is one. I do dare go where I have not gone before; to seek the Real World, to seek a new frontier, to embrace my trek into the Light. The Light is my freedom; it is my radiant Self revealed. And this is an adventure that I gladly embark upon today.

Now, the journey of my soul's intent is there before me and I make the confident statement of today's Lesson. As I travel along with Holy Spirit, the way is made straight. I do want to be happy.

I do want joy. I do want peace. I do want to remember only Love. With each circumstance today I will allow the Vision of Christ to light the way. What more could I want today for You are beside me? I do not have to travel far at all to realize where You are. You are within me. Heaven is within me, it is not a far off place within the sky and stars. Heaven is here and now. My purpose is to remember You, to be steadfast in my beliefs, to arise with certainty to all the lessons presented to me today, to persist in regarding my brothers as One in the same with me and simply to acknowledge my strength in the Love of Truth.

Thank You Father for this affirmation of Your Love. Amen.

∞∞∞∞

Journal Entry on Lesson 21

I am determined to see things differently.

Anger is easily hidden by the ego through habitual distractions of the world. It plays little games with your mind. It shows you things that you think you want or need to be happy, and then it tells you that you cannot have them for one reason or another. Guilt is the ego's main weapon in these situations. It uses memories from the past or laws of the world to tell you that the pursuit of joy would be wrong. If you pursue the things that you think will bring you joy without consulting the Holy Spirit first, turmoil is the only gift that the ego has to offer you at the end of the road.

The internal confusion and conflict that is associated with this tug-of-war that the ego cleverly presents always leads to internal frustration and anger. The projected feelings of being held back and restricted by others, the world and yourself are projections of your own unconscious ego beliefs projected out onto the world so that the hidden anger within yourself seems to be coming from somewhere else. The slight irritations are often quickly repressed

42

by diverting your attention elsewhere. If the pain is too acute then the anger often comes out and is projected onto another, again diverting your attention away from the fact that the anger is coming from within your split ego mind.

Again, I remind you to be vigilant of your feelings. Ask yourself often, "How am I feeling right now?" Ask the Holy Spirit to help you identify how and what you are feeling in that moment. Stop whatever you are doing, step back from the situation and turn inward into your mind where the Holy Spirit resides and ask Him, "Holy Spirit what am I feeling right now? How should I respond to this situation?" Then be silent, be still and wait for His answer to come. It will be the peaceful answer. It is the only answer to the situation that you want. Anything else would come from the ego and, as I have said, the only gifts that the ego has for you is pain and turmoil. If you are feeling anything other than perfect peace in any moment, then the ego is having an influence on your body experience.

It is quite possible to walk this world in perfect peace and joy all the time. It takes vigilance, discipline, willingness, practice and patience but it can be done with the Holy Spirit's help. Every answer He gives you is an answer of forgiveness and moves you into the direction of perfect peace. Do not assume that you know what true forgiveness is, you do not. He knows the way, let Him lead you and you will be led to joy. It will be done because it is Father's Will. Allow the Light of the miracle to heal your mistaken beliefs for you. The Holy Spirit will help you to do this. Peace be with you. Thank you for helping me with this message.

∞∞∞∞

Journal Entry on Lesson 22

What I see is a form of vengeance.

Nothing in this world is eternal my Father, but You. I look about me and see the miscreations of my mind. I thought that by separating from You that I could make a world that was better than Yours. One in which to hide in shame from my guilt of leaving You. But I could never leave. None of what I have made here in this world matters, to You it does not even exist. All that I see are really holographic images being projected from my mind giving me the illusion that I have another life. My True Life is still in Heaven. I have not gone astray as I have thought. I am safe at Home. And even with this miscreation, You do not deny me Your Precious Love. You gently awaken me from the dream of separation with a whisper of my holiness. The words gently arouse me as I listen more deeply each day. I am awakening to Who I am. I am embracing my radiant Self.

My Child, come into My World of Love. Leave behind these false images and come into the glory of Oneness. Your Divinity is a gift as I extended Myself to you. You have all the Love, Joy, Peace and Power that I have for you are Me. Remember this in everything that you do. You can change your world experience by simply changing your thoughts. Place your thoughts in my care and see the beauty that together you and I can create. Be gentle and loving with yourself as each moment passes. Remember to come to Me to envision the Eternal and to lay aside the perishable. The Truth indeed will set you free. Amen.

∞∞∞∞

Journal Entry on Lesson 23

I can escape from the world I see by giving up attack thoughts.

Today we are going to practice being vigilant of feelings that disturb our sense of peace and joy. We are going to practice monitoring the effects of our thoughts in order to backtrack and identify the fearful attack thought itself. When we notice that we are feeling disturbed, remember to pause for a moment and ask yourself, "What was the causing thought that came up that created this effect of disturbing my peace right now?" Ask the Holy Spirit to help you to identify the exact causing thought. The causing thought will be some form of fear. It may be anger, regret, guilt, shame or fear itself.

These thoughts are injected from the ego mind into your thought stream to create the effects of pain which is the opposite of peace. You do not recognize yet that the ego actively does this at an unconscious level in order to disturb your peace. Fear is how the ego maintains itself. It's how it keeps the projections going. Remember, the projections of the ego mind result in everything that you see, feel, hear and touch around you. None of it is real and you can use the mind to begin to let it go right now. This is why we undertake mind training. We have passively allowed the ego to inject these miscreative attack thoughts into our mind since time began.

Our belief in them miscreates the experience itself through our unconscious projection. As we practice identifying and letting go of each of these attack thoughts and allowing Holy Spirit to replace it with peace, we will begin to experience more and more peace in our lives. This will continue until the whole illusion dissolves into Light and we awaken to the Reality of Who we really are. The Holy Spirit will teach us how to do a new kind of projection. We can project Light and perceive the Light with our spiritual sight. The Light is a reflection of Who we really are. It will open up a new world into our sight. This will be the beginning of the restoration of the memory of God to your mind. This will be a joyous time for all of us for the loveliness of Heaven that lands upon perception matches no other experience that you have had before. Love and joy will fill your heart. Glee will fill your mind and a smile will come to your face. Thank You Father for helping us. We Love You. Amen.

∞∞∞∞

Journal Entry on Lesson 24

I do not perceive my own best interests.

With today's Lesson, I find Jesus very correct in saying that *"I do not perceive my own best interests."* As various situations crossed my mind, even more outcomes rose to the surface as well. And, as he states in the Lesson they were often contradictory. It came down to; I do not know what is right for me, for anyone else for basically I know nothing. Actually, knowing nothing is a great place to be for at that point of realization I can be in a stance of non-judgment. I can step back and allow the Light in me to step forward and lead the way as only the Holy Spirit can do. I may not think that I am attached to certain outcomes, but as these situations crossed my mind, some had a feeling of tension associated with an outcome that came to mind. Perhaps the thought at times may be, "It must be this way for I will accept no other." By releasing an outcome to a situation, I am then not resolving it on the level of the ego but I am allowing the endless possibilities to flourish. It may be a possibility that I had not even considered, but yet reaps spectacular rewards. The only reward is the feeling of deep peace that occurs when I join with the Holy Spirit. That is my job in any situation that arises, to bring all thoughts, including desired outcomes to Him. When I set the goal before me of simply peace, then peace is what I will gladly receive despite all the many factors in a situation. Today, my Father, my goal is peace for I know that is indeed in my own best interest.

When I look at the vehicle that I drive, lately I have been having this reoccurring thought that I would like to get it replaced or repaired. The vehicle is a little beat up now because I have had it for awhile. A little bit of rust, some dents and scratches here and there, and the dirt is beginning to show its older age. I think to myself it would be nice to get a new vehicle because I don't have the money to clean it up. There is an underlying thought of shame involved in owning the vehicle in such condition.

The fearful thought comes up that it is a reflection of who I am and what kind of person I am. The conflicting thoughts and scenarios come up in my mind about the vehicle from time to time, "I should do something to fix it but I can't because I don't have the money." or "I should buy a new vehicle but I can't because I don't have the money." These kinds of thoughts about this situation are the types of conflicting thoughts that the ego brings up for us time and time again.

There is an underlying whisper from the ego that if I were to make a change with the vehicle, I would feel happier and I would find my salvation. Then it turns around and gives me the conflicting thought that says, "But you can't do this." It tells you salvation is within your grasp here but you can't have it.

The important thing to remember here is that I do not perceive my own best interests unless I have consulted with the Holy Spirit. I do not know whether changing the vehicle or not is the best thing to do but the Holy Spirit inside of me does. I am being reminded that if I have a reoccurring conflicting thoughts about any situation coming up in my life over and over again, to take the time to sit down with Holy Spirit and truly ask Him for some guidance on the situation. I spend days on and off worrying about and being conflicted in my mind about the situation. Why then would I not spend a few days talking with Holy Spirit about it? This is the insanity of the ego. The ego does not want us to discover the Spirit within us. This is what it does. It keeps us distracted from going within and discovering our Guide and Who we really are.

The Spirit within us is connected with the Mind that knows the solution to all things, every problem and situation that could ever come up. If we truly want peace in our lives then we must begin to let go of the old ways, and turn to Him Who knows the answers. He will gladly give them to us and guide us along the way to a sense of peace and joy and freedom that we have not experienced before. Thank You Holy Spirit for helping me with this message. Amen.

ooooo

Journal Entry on Lesson 25

I do not know what anything is for.

I looked at the dresser in my room and said to myself, "If that dresser is not for holding clothes, then what is it really for?" I had a memory of a pet that I used to own come to mind and I thought to myself, "I miss that pet and wished that I had shown it that I loved it just a little bit more." This feeling of regret made me wonder, "What is this really for?" I then decided to let these thoughts and memories go in my mind and turn inward and be open to what Holy Spirit had to say about them.

What happened next was that I saw a flash of white Light wash my mind and body with a healing release of peace and the answer came, "Hiding the awareness of the Light of Love's Presence is what they are for." Everything that we see around us represents darkness because it hides the Light behind it from shining into our awareness. Our ego mind unconsciously projects the images of the things that we see around us similar to the way a movie projector projects the images of film on a movie screen. When the movie projector is turned off the only thing that remains is a white screen. This is the same idea of the experience that we will begin to have as we begin to let go of the unconscious ego projections within our mind. The images will begin to go away and we will begin to experience the white Light of Love that surrounds us. We will begin to experience that we are the Source of that Light and that there is a Source that gives us that Light from within.

Thank You Father for Who we really are. We love You. Amen.

ɷɷɷ

Journal Entry on Lesson 26

My attack thoughts are attacking my invulnerability.

Through Your Holy Lesson today, Father, I am learning that it is my own thoughts that are the source of all my discomfort. I came to believe in limitation instead of the unlimited Love that I am, always surrounded by Your sure protection. My awareness today of my thoughts that lead me down a road of anger, depression and the like help me to understand and relate the stories that I am making up about myself and the world around me. My mind can rapidly make assumptions and experience reactions and that is when I allow the fear or the ego to be in control. It is fear that holds me in that place of mistrusting You. I feel that I can handle it better or that You will lose my file and forget to assist me.

I have had this experience many times in my life. I permitted the fear to take charge and make decisions all based on not trusting that You indeed will provide for me. Saying "no" to the ego is saying "yes" to the Divine Creative Source within me. I do not have to control all the outcomes to all situations. I can come to the place of quiet when my mind begins to rattle with desired outcomes. All desired outcomes are outcomes that indeed attack my true Eternal state. Coming into the sanctuary with Holy Spirit, I can release the list of proposed outcomes and allow Him to soothe my troubled mind and propose a new outcome. His outcome will always be of serenity and Oneness. Today, I can give up these attack thoughts and listen to His Voice Who will replace all the thoughts with thoughts of God's Love. That is truly what I want. That is my goal for today, to realize my Eternal Oneness with Him. Amen.

Just before I awoke this morning, I had a rather lengthy and vivid dream. The dream was informational because the symbols and situations in the dream brought to my awareness memories of things that I am afraid of or will happen. When I first reflected on the dream and the series of fearful thoughts that it arose for me, the overall peaceful state that I was feeling began to shift into an unpeaceful state. I began to become concerned that the Holy Spirit was attempting to give me messages through the dream to help me to brace myself for an outcome to a situation that I am afraid might be happening in my life right now. After a few minutes of looking at this I then began to realize that the ego must be involved here because each of the symbolic situations in the dream included something that I was afraid was going to happen as a result of past behavior. I began to recognize how Holy Spirit was helping me with these things because today's Lesson is the perfect lesson for me to apply to each of the fearful ideas that came up in the dream and so I did. I welcome this dream now and I feel grateful to the Holy Spirit because I feel that I have given the tools to help me to heal and let go of these unconscious fears that I have been harboring in my mind.

I intend to continue to work with these attack thoughts by applying the ideas in today's Lesson toward them because I really do want to exchange the unconscious fear for peace. The fear is very subtle, a little worry here, a little concern there, little things just enough to put little ripples into the stillness of peace. Each attack thought adds another ripple to the surface of the calm waters and it is each of these ripples that I want to heal forever in exchange for perfect peace with the Holy Spirit's help. Thank You Holy Spirit for this opportunity to work with You today. You truly are my personal Friend and I am coming to know that now. I appreciate the little nudges that You give me throughout the day. I appreciate the waves of peace that You give me when I see the flashes of Light. I appreciate the little promptings You give me to help me to extend Love to others. I feel like You are really helping me and I want You to know that I really appreciate it. Thank You for helping me. I love You and I love the feeling of getting to know my Friend. Amen.

∞∞∞

Journal Entry on Lesson 27

Above all else I want to see.

When I reflect upon what I am being asked to practice today, I have to ask myself to take a good honest look at these questions, "How much do I really want to experience the gift of Christ Vision?"; "How much do I really want to experience the gift of seeing God's World?" and "Am I really willing today to give the Holy Spirit the few moments of time of thought each hour in order to receive the most blessed and joyful gifts that He has to offer to me today?"

He is waiting to illuminate our mind with the gifts of Heaven upon our asking. We need but be willing to let go of our grasp on the world around us just for a day. Can we give God a day, today for a change? We are normally engaged in the habit of dedicating the day to the ego by seeing and living in the world around us because we believe that it is not possible to see another world.

The ego has trained our minds to believe this and has very carefully kept the other world hidden from our awareness in

51

darkness. I assure you that it is very possible to see the world of Light that surrounds you if you but begin to practice to let it go with your mind. This is the aim of practicing these lessons to begin the process of letting go of the world you think you are seeing and experiencing around you with your mind.

As you begin to let go of the shackles of darkness that you have placed upon your mind you will begin to experience Light and peace and joy. Each experience will undo the shackle of darkness and heal the mind in little increments. Today is a day of the practice of surrendering the world you have made in exchange for the World God created. Imagine yourself succeeding with the goals of today's Lesson when you start your day. See yourself saying today's idea in every situation that you can imagine you may encounter as you go through your day today. This would be a recipe for success.

Thank You Holy Spirit for this message. Amen.

"There must be another way," the phrase that birthed not only the Course, but also many a Course student. I know for myself after going through yet another difficult time with depression, the Course was a Light shining in the darkness encouraging me that there was indeed another way. With today's Lesson, my determination to see becomes deeper each time I approach another year of the Workbook Lessons. In the darkness that I perceive, I desire to look upon the Light. Above all else I want to see. Everything that I see around me is not what would bring me the happiness that I seek. And that's being honest with myself, even now.

Happiness is not found in material possessions, relationships, educational degrees, money and the like. Happiness is only found within when I remember my connection to All That Is. Above all else I want to see. Above all else I want to remember. Above all else I want to experience my connection with God. Thank You Father for the gift of spiritual sight and for the Holy Spirit Who is there to gently remind me of what I truly want to see. I affirm that today as often as I can recall and I will step up to the plate and make my intention reality. I want to see because I want to be happy. I want to see because I desire peace. I want to see because I am only an extension of God's Love and I am deserving of remembering my union with Him. Holy Spirit, be my Guide today and lead me in each moment with the Vision of Christ. Amen.

ooooo

Journal Entry on Lesson 28

Above all else I want to see things differently.

One of the key sentences in today's Lesson is, *"The light you will see in any one of them is the same light you will see in them all."* Jesus is telling us, that if we can let go enough with our minds what we think we are seeing, that the Light of Heaven will reveal Itself to us. He's trying to tell us that we can do this right now! We can choose to allow the Light of Heaven to reveal Itself to us, right now. When it happens, it is unmistakable. We begin to experience the glimmerings of Heaven in sparks of white Light.

This is the beginning of true perception of the Vision of Christ. The Vision of Christ begins to reveal Itself to you from beyond all things that you see now as the flashes of white Light, the sparks of white Light. As you continue to let go with your mind, the experiences of this miracle become brighter and stronger. Healing is brought with these experiences every time. Joy and happiness and hope are brought with the experience every time. Peace begins to fill the body every time.

When this begins to happen we begin to understand the purpose of the universe around us, because we begin to recognize that the purpose of the universe around us is to hide the truth of the Light that lies beyond. The reflections of the Light that you perceive are coming from your eternal Christ Self. You are the Holy One that you are beginning to perceive. Be patient and do the Lessons well, and in time, the Light of Truth will begin to reveal Itself to you. It will be a joyful time for all of us indeed.

Thank You Holy Spirit for helping us with this message. Amen.

∞∞∞

Journal Entry on Lesson 29

God is in everything I see.

Today's Lesson helps me to practice looking beyond the images, the things, and the people that I see. God is behind everything because He is in everything that I see. It comes to my mind today that I want to be reminded of this in all my interactions whether it is with other people or simple inanimate objects. God is the True World that I will see when I release the blinders which are my projected fears. There is nothing to fear for God is with me. He is in me and in everything that I see. What more could I want but to recognize His presence? I am not alone.

If God is in everything that I see then I am truly surrounded by the Love of God. He has not abandoned me and left me "for dead" as the ego has slyly whispered to me. It is my own fears and guilt once again that have projected images of darkness and loneliness away from Him. This is not so. Behind these shadows there lies the Light, ever the beacon Home. It stands in strength for it stands in God.

All these images, the people and places that I see, are as a flimsy curtain, they just seem to be 3-dimensional with form and sound. The Light shines strongly from behind this curtain and at times I can see the holes poking through, those glimpses of the Truth.

These are the times when I give all fear thoughts to the Holy Spirit and Truth is revealed. The ego's story does have holes in it because it is not wholly the truth. The only Truth is my holiness and it is revealed as I come to Him. Father, today I embrace the fact that You are with me. I am not alone for You are in everything that I see. As I remember, it will bring me peace. As I remember, it will increase my joy. As I remember, it will bring me Home. Amen.

If God is in everything that I see, then God must be inside of me. If God is inside of me, then there must be a way of reaching down inside of myself with my mind, to see and experience God. God goes with me wherever I go, because He is inside of me. God is communicating with me all the time, but I cannot hear His Voice because I have blocked it out from my awareness by paying attention to the sights and sounds around me. The way to reach down inside of you to see God and to hear His Voice speak to you, is to be silent and still. This is why we practice the Lessons. They are helping us to let go of the thoughts that busy our minds all through the day. These thoughts block the awareness of the Light of God, and the Voice of God that illuminates our minds. The way we let go of the busy thoughts is to rest in the stillness within. He will come and meet us there in the silence. We need but have the willingness to meet Him partway; to go within and be still, and rest in the silence. It is there He will come and greet us and say, "Hello, my friend." It is then that you will begin to know God.

It takes time and practice but it is well worth the journey. The experiences that will begin to come as a result of your practicing will begin to release your mind from the shackles of the world. It is here where your salvation will be found. For it will never be found any place else. It is here where you would begin to discover Who you really are, The Christ, the Holy Son of God Himself. Amen.

∞∞∞∞

Journal Entry on Lesson 30

God is in everything I see because God is in my mind.

There is a place you can go within your mind and actually meet God. It takes dedication and practice to find Him but He will come if you try. If you sit and be still, letting all of your thoughts go and have an open mind He will come and reveal Himself to you as the Light. He will also come and speak to you. This is an experience that surpasses no other. In that moment you will recognize that God is within you and goes with you wherever you go. You will never feel alone again because you will always know from that point on that He is with you and that you can turn to Him in any time of need.

You will probably notice resistance to this idea of finding God within. The resistance is a delaying maneuver from the ego. Stilling your mind of all of the ego's chatter and resting in the silence of peace waiting for God to come and reveal Himself to you is one of the most difficult ego resistances to overcome. The ego does not want you to discover God within yourself because it does not know of God. The ego thinks that it is God. The idea that there is something else is a threat to the ego's existence which is why the unconscious resistance comes up. Anything that disturbs your peace from perfect stillness is resistance.

We will continue to practice stilling our minds and letting go of the ego chatter and having an open mind in exchange for peace. In time, we will all master this task and free ourselves from the shackles on the mind of God's Son. This is a joyful time for all of us right now, because we are all joining together in a mighty crusade to undo the tragedy that has not been brought upon the mind of God's Son. Keep in mind that all of this is an illusion, it is just a dream and it is not happening. In fact, it never happened at all. This is too difficult for the ego mind to understand. Faith and trust would be in order on this reminder.

God the Father has blessed us all. He has not forgotten us, although we have forgotten Him temporarily. He has not forsaken His Son. He remembers His Friend well and always will because *you* are His Will. You are His Kingdom, the Kingdom of Heaven. *You* are His Joy. *You* are His Home. *You* are His Son created in perfect Holiness just like Himself. *You* are His Friend and He is yours eternally. Heaven sings joyfully for the Union of the Father and His Son forever without end. Amen.

∞∞∞∞

Journal Entry on Lesson 31

I am not the victim of the world I see.

The ego is a precarious thing. It wants to divide and separate to keep going the illusion that God's Son does not exist. Projections of anger and guilt are among its most powerful weapons. Remember that anytime you point at someone else out of anger that you have three other fingers pointing back towards yourself. Let this be a reminder that the projections of your perceptions are coming from yourself. The attack that you seem to be projecting onto another is really being projected onto yourself. You are not the victim of the world you see because you made it.

On some level you are doing this to yourself with your own thoughts. The thoughts are coming from the split mind of the ego and they are not real but yet you believe they are so. Attack is never justified in any form. Its only goal is to increase pain for yourself and others in order to keep the belief in separation going. Complete surrender to the guidance of the Holy Spirit is the only way to restore sanity to the mind that attacks itself with anger.

If you are experiencing anger you are insane and it will bring pain upon yourself. The only way out of the pain is to engage in the process of forgiveness with the Holy Spirit. You must hand the situation over to Him so that He can help you to release yourself from hell. Do not keep the illusion going by embracing anger or projecting guilt but instead replace it with a desire to be at peace. Make peace your one goal always and the Kingdom of Heaven will be restored to your mind in a holy instant. Anytime that the ego tempts you with a situation that will disturb your peace immediately call upon the Holy Spirit for help.

Remember the prayer that I have given to you in the time of need:

> *"I am here only to be truly helpful. I am here to represent Him Who sent me. I do not have to worry about what to say, or what to do because He Who sent me will direct me. I am content to be wherever He wishes knowing He goes there with me. I will be healed as I let Him teach me to heal."* T-2.V (A).18:2-6

∞∞∞∞

Journal Entry on Lesson 32

I have invented the world I see.

Whatever happens to me in this world, I have created it. What a statement to make and it is true. Can I go back and look at all the situations in my life and agree with this? I can, however, it may seem hard to do so especially if I have experienced some difficult or traumatic situations. What I focus on I attract. Have I focused on the idea of unworthiness? Then those situations are what will come as witnesses to that belief that I have about myself.

When I can take responsibility for my beliefs, my thoughts, my words and my actions, then I can take responsibility for changing them as well. It is for me to become mindful in every aspect of my life. Do I really need to make snide comments under my breath when someone upsets me? Or do I need to take the perceived behavior by that person immediately to the Holy Spirit for forgiveness and a healed mind?

I find the more that I take each thought, opinion or judgment that I may have about another to the Holy Spirit then I am releasing myself from my self-imposed bondage. And when I take responsibility for my thoughts, I own it and I do not make excuses for what I have said or done. I have done it based on my perceived beliefs about myself and it is up to me to change those thoughts. No more excuses for what I do or say because now there is another way. However I may choose to view it, it could be "What Would Jesus Do?" or it could be simply turning it over to the Holy Spirit for healing. That is my function here to forgive and to let go of everything that occurs.

Holy Spirit, I am open to healing my mind in this area today. I understand through You today, that it is my own thoughts that invent the world I see. It is my own fear thoughts that claim my victimhood in this world. Today, I release all thoughts to You for Your gentle cleansing. And today, I will claim my birthright as a Son of God. I am wholly blessed. I am changing my mind about my mind. My openness is there for you, my hands are open to receive your Love and closed to the ego's messages of pain. Be in my mind Holy Spirit and assist me in creating only Love this day. Amen.

∞∞∞∞

Journal Entry on Lesson 33

There is another way of looking at the world.

How happy are we who see the world of joy. This is what we are striving to achieve, to experience the shift in perception where we begin to see the other world, my brothers and I. This is our journey together as we practice the Workbook Lessons. It's a happy and joyous world to see indeed. The Lights that begin to illuminate your mind begin to free you from the shackles of the world, one link at a time, one flash equals one link. Each flash is the flash of healing. They heal the links in the shackles one at a time.

There is another world to behold with the spiritual sight in your mind than the world you see now. You can experience this spiritual seeing either with your eyes open or closed. It does not matter. However, because of the current state of your undisciplined mind you will find it easier to experience the shift in perception with your eyes closed. When the eyes are open at this stage of development, the undisciplined mind is too easily distracted by the things it sees. The mind has not detached itself from its beliefs from the things it sees and values for the Light of True Perception to come into its awareness. So that is why it is helpful to close the eyes because it removes unnecessary distractions while we practice stepping back and letting go of the world with our minds as we go within.

Although, you do not want to rely on this technique solely to restore your vision, it could become a crutch thus delaying your ability to see while your eyes are open. It is time for us to begin to practice detaching ourselves from the world we see during the day while we walk about and do the things we need to do. There is a way to go about your day in a detached observer mode. Have an open mind and just be an observer for something new to come into your perception while you observe the illusions that are presented to your eyes throughout the day.

As you practice remaining in a peaceful detached observer mode, shards of light will begin to reveal themselves to you. You will begin to perceive golden sparks of light around things, white sparks of light. These are light episodes. They will not persist; they are merely reminders of Home. But they will persist as long as you need them to help you to remember Who you really are. They are the symbols of the Christ that lies beyond all illusions. They are the reminder of your Home and of your Father's call to you to return. These are the experiences that are part of the gifts from God to help you to find your way Home, to forgive the illusion and to awaken from the dream.

Thank you Jesus for this message. Amen.

ooooo

Journal Entry on Lesson 34

I could see peace instead of this.

I think that most of the time when we think about the word "peace", what comes to mind is that it is a "feeling" that we experience. But notice the words that Jesus chose to use in today's lesson, "see peace" not "feel peace". The reason for this is that peace can actually be perceived, or seen, by the mind. It is a gift that the Holy Spirit has for us; a gift from God Himself. When we practice sinking down and letting go during meditation, there is a place in our mind that can be discovered where a white Light flashes into and illuminates our mind. This is an experience of the Vision of Christ. When the experience comes, it also happens to bring with it the "feeling" of peace as well.

Whenever anything comes into my mind that disturbs my peace, today's Lesson tells me just what to do. Simple it seems, but I can truly see peace if I choose to do so. There may be situations that I encounter as I go about my daily life, the difficult phone calls to make, the co-worker who never seems to change, the ex-spouse who always has a digging comment or two, the cashier in the grocery store who chooses to converse with the bagger instead of paying attention to my order, the persistent floor attendants when I walk into Best Buy, the forgotten birthdays, the disagreement with a family member, the friend who talks incessantly about themselves and never listens to me, and so on, and all the others that may cross my path in a course of a day.

In this lesson, Jesus tells us that we could see peace instead of what we are currently seeing. What is that I am seeing? I think I am seeing the present moment but what I am seeing is the past in disguise so in fact I really am not seeing anything but a shadow of fear. This brings pain; this brings the disturbance of my peace. And so, with each situation that comes to me, I can let go of what I think I am seeing and choose to see how the Holy Spirit sees and this through His Eyes of Peace. I know that I do not have to do all of this alone. Holy Spirit is always there with me. I can recognize that I am not at peace and then relax, let go of any tension that I may feel and gently allow the Holy Spirit to take my hand and lead me back to the sanctuary of peace. It is my own thoughts that cause the disturbance in my mind and so it is my thoughts in which I need to work with Holy Spirit on.

I can do this in various ways. Perhaps in an exercise of being mindful, I could use a notebook and jot down any unpeaceful thought that comes into my mind throughout the day. I can use this as an experiment for just one day and truly see what thoughts come into my mind that brings a lack of peace.

As I write each thought that comes in, I can also write that I am willing to release these thoughts and feelings to You, Holy Spirit. I then become open to an experience that truly will bring me comfort and serenity. This mindfulness exercise can either be continued in that way or then I could do this process within my own mind. Either way it is doing as Jesus has suggested many times and that is to be vigilant of my thoughts. We are indeed much too tolerant of our mind wandering. Today, I make the conscious effort to replace all my distressing feelings for the experience of peace with the Holy Spirit's assistance. This is my goal today, my Father, to see peace everywhere I can. Amen.

Journal Entry on Lesson 35

My mind is part of God's. I am very holy.

This list that Jesus invites us to make in this Lesson can become very long as I contemplate how I see myself. When I practice this exercise, it comes to mind that the images that I have made about myself are ones of separation. It is either I am better than another or less than another. Neither is correct because we are all one and holy in the mind of God. Because of my core beliefs built from the ego's fear base, I do not recall seeing myself or anyone else in that Light of God.

This world is a world of separation and division. That is what the ego desires. Conquer and divide. Even as I go through the laundry list of beliefs that I hold about myself, Jesus reminds me that no matter what I have come to believe about myself, *"My mind is part of God's. I am very holy."* The more I can release the blindfold of the false images of myself; the more I will embrace my radiance.

As I practiced this Lesson, descriptions that I had never even thought of had come to mind. At first in wonderment about those, I did not focus on them for if I drew my attention to any of the descriptions then the ego's voice would be the one that I attended to. In allowing each description to pass by, just as a train of railcars passes by, I stay on track with Holy Spirit's conduction of the truth of my holy nature. I am a part of God, my mind is holy and so am I. I open my mind today to affirm my identity with my Source. I welcome in all the attributes of God in which I share. In meditation I softly heard Karen Drucker singing, "I am holy, holy, holy. I am whole." This repeated a few times and it was my message from Holy Spirit of where my focus is today and that is in remembering my holiness. That is what I am. That is what you are. For that is the truth and there could be nothing else.

Journal Entry on Lesson 36

My holiness envelops everything I see.

"My holiness envelops everything I see." As I internalized this message today, I felt the Light within me move forward within my being with an intensity of desire to extend outward. As I looked around the room and repeated the Lesson, I felt the profound Love for all pour forth. This is what my holiness is. It is the truth of Who I am.

In being created in the image of my Creator, I possess all the creative powers as He does. I have the ability to create and extend all that I am and that is Love. There is nothing that I cannot do through Him. He is my pillar of strength. The Light around all that I see is the blessing of Who I am. I would not want it any other way. I bless my innocence. I forgive all that I thought I had made in this little small self personality made by the ego. All of what I think I see through the ego's eyes is that of separation and abandonment from God.

God has never left me, it was I that left or hid from Him. He gently takes my hand and says, "You need not hide any longer for what you are hiding behind is an illusion." I pull back the curtain in the land of illusions, just as in the Land of Oz, and I see that I am just as everyone else. I am part of the Sonship. Illusions hide the truth of God's Son.

In remembering my holiness, I am remembering it for everyone. Our connection is clear. Our connection is all there is. These times are now times of quiet expectation. The only expectation is to hear the Holy Spirit's Voice speak to me. His words will only bless. Is that not what I now strive to do with my own words? I want peace to prevail in my life and so the mindfulness comes into play again. If I am in a conversation with someone, have I come to bless or curse? It is the practice of stepping back and allowing Him to step forward, letting my words be chosen for me. Let my words be that of enveloping the world in holiness. Let me remind another of their holiness. It is easy to make reactionary statements and these come from the place of fear no matter how it is disguised with anger, sadness or judgment. But, it is easier to stop and become quiet and ask, "What would You have me say?" My prayer is to let only words of Love come forth from me for I am the vessel of God's Love. It is "walking the talk" or "talking the walk" whichever you prefer. And I prefer to speak only Love this day.

∞∞∞∞

Journal Entry on Lesson 37

My holiness blesses the world.

We are like blind mummies walking around the world in our sleep. We think we are seeing with our eyes but we are not. The Light of Christ inside of you calls to you to see another world within your mind. The Christ within you has another world to show you within your mind. But in order to see it you have to continue to practice letting go of the world you see now and open your mind to the vast domain hidden inside of it. It is very carefully hidden in the darkness by the ego. But the Holy Spirit will help you to discover the new world.

Miracles are seen in Light and the Light is perceived in your mind by allowing your mind to shift to the use of its spiritual perception, or spiritual sight. Spiritual perception also includes shifting to spiritual hearing within the mind. The Voice of the Holy Spirit will speak very clearly to you in restful place of silence. These truths, these gifts, are waiting there to be discovered by you. These gifts are a part of the fortitude of gifts that are waiting for you to discover within your mind. These gifts are so abundant, so healing, and so joyful that they surpass all other gifts that the ego of the world would give to you.

My gifts are gifts of Love and Love always heals. Love always blesses the perceiver and the receiver whether they realize it or not. The ego's gifts always separate. Their means, their goal is to crucify your holiness. You give them the power to do this at an unconscious level. As you turn to the Holy Spirit for help with each of the temptations that the ego offers you in the world the Holy Spirit will help you to make the right choice to choose the correct path, the path of peace. Remembering to ask Him for help with everything, any decision you need to make is the trick, the key to success. Is it so hard to remember to ask Him to give you the keys to Heaven? He gives them freely, He wants you to be happy, and He wants you to discover your path of highest joy and aliveness. Would you accept these gifts of Him and join with Me as a savior of the world? Your holiness blesses everything in the world. To read this is one thing, but to experience it is another. This is the gift that God has given to you. When will you be ready to accept it again? I love you too My Son.

∞∞∞

Journal Entry on Lesson 38

There is nothing my holiness cannot do.

Deep inside each and every one of us is a very holy place. It is the place where the Holy One resides. It is the altar of God Himself. You can find this place through the practice of being very still, letting go of all your busyness and resting in the silence. Ask the Holy Spirit to help you find this place where the Spirit of God resides within you and He will surely come. The Light within you is so joyful and so healing that the experience surpasses all others. It is the experience that will begin to help you to awaken from the dream and enter into the awareness of the Reality of Who you really are. The Voice of God will speak to you from this place and you will begin to remember your Friend once again. What a joyous experience this is! Set your intentions with the Holy Spirit on discovering this place within yourself. It is your purpose for being here. It is the freedom that you seek. It is the joy that you seek, to discover Who you really are once again.

When coming across any situation in my life, today's Lesson is knowing that no matter what seems to be occurring, the situation does not surmount my holiness. My holiness is all that I am; it surmounts all. My holiness invites no order of difficulty. All that I see is the same. My holiness is my gift from the Creator. Miracles, forgiveness, peace all show the power that lies within my holiness. I can change my thoughts about the world, about situations, about people. My holiness can shine forth and my world will change because I have now aligned my thoughts with the Holy One in the sanctuary of stillness.

ooooo

Journal Entry on Lesson 39

My holiness is my salvation.

In practicing the ideas for today's lesson, we are practicing the monitoring of our thoughts. As we step back from the world today, we practice monitoring for unloving or fearful thoughts that enter our minds. Anytime we experience a sense of worry, fear, distress, sadness, or frustration and anger, we want to pause for a moment and choose peace instead. We want to pause for a moment and ask Holy Spirit to heal these unloving thoughts, to free our minds from the fear they bring in exchange for a peaceful mind. This is the process of forgiveness.

We behold the problem in our mind, we ask Holy Spirit for His perception of the problem, and then we pause a moment to receive His new perception of the problem. We give each problem to the Holy Spirit and we ask Him to heal it for us in our minds so that peace may be restored to the mind of God's Son. The Holy Spirit has the answer to every problem but He cannot give it to us unless we really take the time to pause for a moment to receive His answer. We easily get caught up in worrying about the problem we are beholding but we forget to set it down for a few moments and to ask Holy Spirit what does He think about this situation, then to wait and be vigilant for His answer. He will answer us immediately. But are we truly trying to see it? To hear it? To receive it? That is the practice. It will come if we really want it. Do not be fooled by the joys of the ego world. Step back. Let Peace lead your day today. Let Peace be your guide today. Let Peace be your friend today. Make Peace your companion today. Consult with Him in your mind in every moment and in every situation and follow His guidance. Surely, peace, a quiet sense of joy and serenity will be given to you this very day.

∞∞∞

Journal Entry on Lesson 40

I am blessed as a Son of God.

You are blessed as My Son in every way. You can know where happiness abides for it abides in you. Know that peace makes its home in your innocent nature. You are My Son in Whom I am well pleased. Be content in knowing that I bring you a sense of calm and quiet to soothe your weary mind. When you are afraid or worried, bring all your perceived problems to Me and I will provide the one and only true Answer. It is the Answer of Love; Perfect, unconditional Love.

You are blessed My Son. Be confident and walk in certainty as you go about your day. Remind yourself often of your birthright, for in your remembrance, you will find the peace you so seek. Lay all your guilt and pain into My bag that I hold outstretched to you and I will close the bag to fear, remove it and show you the sanctuary of peace where the living waters flow. In these waters, be you cleansed of all that you thought you had ever done. It is not so. It is gone. This is a time of purification for you. You are on the right track. Follow the guidance of mindfulness in every moment with every thought that is not of Love. With the unloving thoughts, bring them gently to Me. Do not leave one speck of fear behind. I will gladly take all that you are willing to give. I have a glorious gift for you and that is the gift of serenity. Allow serenity to be placed upon your forehead and the worry that is there will dissipate and disappear. Peace is restored. Be assured of this that I will never leave you comfortless. I am with you always.

Walk your day in Peace for you walk your day with Me.

Amen.

∞∞∞∞

Journal Entry on Lesson 41

God goes with me wherever I go.

Today's Lesson is wonderful indeed. It gives us specific instructions on how to meet the Christ hidden within us. This is the personal experience we are all seeking while we walk in our slumber. This is it! This is the way to discover the truth about ourselves and the world around us. None of it is real but the discovery of the Light of Christ within us is very real indeed. Let us delay our awakening no longer and put forth all of our efforts towards discovering this prize of all prizes, this gift of all gifts; to begin to discover and experience the truth of Who we really are!

Hallelujah! Hallelujah! Hallelujah! Heaven and the Holy Spirit waits earnestly for our willingness and our efforts to meet Them part way. They and the angels will surround us and support us, lifting us the rest of the way to discover the deepest secret of all time. This is a time of celebration, a time of joy for we are at the threshold of healing all of our sadness, all of worries, and all of our pain at last!

Would you allow the Holy Spirit to help you come in and take a peek just for an instant, a Holy Instant? Trust your Guide Who knows the way; He will help you with His little loving nudges, His little loving promptings. He will help lift you up and find your way Home. Reality will begin to illuminate your mind in little sparks of white Light, or little stars piercing holes through the veil of darkness in your mind. Sometimes the experience will be greater than this. Little footsteps are all we need now to walk the path which will lead us to the greatest discovery of all time, the treasure chest of the Light within us. This discovery will bless us with the gift and understanding, that God goes with us wherever we go.

∞∞∞∞

Journal Entry on Lesson 42

God is my strength. Vision is His gift.

How happy are we today to be learning how to receive the wonderful gifts God has for us. The Twinkle in His Eye and the Smile on His Face will light up your mind and bring joy to you when you hear His Voice speak to you. There is nothing in this world that will ever satisfy you or heal you from its angst and worries. The answer to all of your problems whatever they may be is found within. There is only one place to go to receive the solution to every problem that confronts you in this world. That place is within. It is here we are learning the steps on how to let go of the world we perceive, so that we may allow our minds to shift into alignment with the Christ Mind that resides within each and every one of us.

The Christ Mind is very holy. It is pure and it is happy. It is you! It is you in your right mind. It is a joyful discovery indeed to find this shift, this change in perception; this gift that God has given to you. The Holy Spirit will help you to find it. He is truly with you, although you cannot see Him. He is right here with you, right now, fully aware of everything that is going on in your life. He's waiting anxiously for you to ask Him to help you. Ask Him as often as you can for He will help you to discover the many wonderful gifts God has given to you. Each of them not only blesses yourself but everyone else around you. Only the gifts of God are capable of setting you and the world along with it free. This is the place of salvation; to discover the many gifts hidden deep inside of you. Let us continue our practice of letting go in the silence of meditation, so that the gifts of God may begin to be bestowed upon us at last.

God is my strength. Vision is His gift.
Peace surrounds me always.
All that I have is given to me by God.
Peace is awaiting my open mind.
To truly see, I let go of my own sight.
There is nothing my holiness cannot do.
Love abides in me.
God gives only of Himself and what He gives is Love.
Let me see with the eyes of Christ.
Let me love with the heart of God.
God is my rock, my resting place.

I do not have to do it alone, for God is with me.
Step by step, I reach new heights of my awareness.
Let gentleness come to me.
The Holy Spirit speaks to me all through the day.
I am holy, holy, holy.

Be in the presence of the One.
Light the light of forgiveness in all hearts.
Shine away all fear in my brothers.
Rest in Him Who knows.
God gives freely.
I accept my freedom in Him.
Rise above and see the Love.
The gift of forgiveness warms all hearts.
When I heal, I am not healed alone.
I join with my brothers who are One with me.
Gratitude is given God for all that He has given me.
In Him is my strength. I choose to see.

∞∞∞∞

Journal Entry on Lesson 43

God is my Source. I cannot see apart from Him.

The reason we cannot see apart from God is because we are in God. We are a part of Him and He is a part of us. In Reality, there is no need for perception of any kind because all is One and the same, a formless Love extending and creating Love forever. The ego world is made up of projection and perception of everything you see, feel and hear around you. The idea of giving up perception is a fearful one for the ego indeed, because it means that it would cease to exist.

In Reality, the ego does not really exist at all. It is merely nothing more than a dream, a tiny mad idea in the mind of God's Son that "didn't happen" for a moment. Because nothing in the ego illusion is really real, everything that you value and cherish within it will always lead you to a sense of emptiness, a feeling of loss and a feeling of disconnectedness. Eventually you always have the feeling that something is missing, that you haven't found it yet and you will ask the question, "What is it? What am I looking for?" The answer to that question is, you are looking for God.

In the back of your mind there is a distant memory of the reality that you are God. You have forgotten this temporarily but the call to return to God from the Holy Spirit will not allow you to forget completely because that is His task. Father created the Holy Spirit the instant you forgot Yourself to help you find your way home. It is not "seeing" that you seek; it is "being". You miss the experience of "being" God's Son. You miss the experience of the blessed relationship that you share with your Father. You miss the song of Love that you sing to the Father and that He sings back to you in harmony with All That Is forever and forever.

This is what you are seeking. The sparks of Light hidden within your mind will begin to show you the way Home. Each spark of Light lays out the path before you. Each flash of Light contains a glimmering of the memory of God. It will naturally draw you Home because it begins to heal your mind. It begins to restore peace to your mind. It begins to restore the memory of Love to your mind and it is naturally attractive to you because it contains the memory of who you really are. The miracle not only blesses you but it also blesses everyone around you. Ask the Holy Spirit to help you to find the spark of Light within your mind. The joyful ending to the journey will begin to come indeed. It will be a joyful time and a time of celebration because mind of God's Son is beginning to awaken at last. Hallelujah! Hallelujah! Hallelujah!

∞∞∞

Journal Entry on Lesson 44

God is the light in which I see.

It is quite possible to have an experience of conscious contact with God. It is quite possible to see God right now. It is quite possible to hear Him speak directly to you very clearly right now. This is because He resides within you and He goes with you wherever you go. For the untrained mind that busies itself with thoughts about the world around it, it is impossible to reach the Light of God. But the mind can be trained however, to settle down and sink past all of the busy thoughts to the place within our minds where there are no thoughts and we rest there in peace, waiting for the Light of God to illuminate our minds. The flash of white Light is unmistakable when it comes.

When we rest in this quiet place of peace and wait for the Light to come it is our invitation to God to reveal Himself to us. As we practice finding and resting and waiting in this place of peace, we will soon discover the most wonderful gift of all; that God resides within us and that we can experience Him anytime we want. It takes a lot of determination and practice to find Him but I assure you He is there and it is well worth the effort. The discovery of the Light within yourself is unmistakable because many aspects of God come with the illumination of the mind at the same time. This is because what your sight beholds is Love and Love can only heal. Your body will experience a sudden shift into a state of peace higher than you have ever experienced before. You will suddenly shift into a feeling that everything is ok. Joy and happiness will fill your heart. Your body may suddenly heal of any ailments that it may have.

As you practice opening up to the Light within your mind you will eventually discover that you can use it to heal yourself and anyone else at the same time. However, you must come to me first and ask me when to perform these miracles because I am in charge of the Atonement and I alone know what's best for you in every circumstance that you may encounter in the plan. This is important to remember. You have discovered a most wonderful gift within yourself, however, you do not know how to use it properly yet. This is why you must ask me first. I will manage the miracles for you so that everyone may benefit in the most efficient manner possible. If improperly used, miracles can scare people. They can drive them further away from the Light into darkness if misunderstood.

This has happened many times throughout the ages. This is why we must be careful in its application. We want to help our brothers awaken to the Light of Joy within them, not to frighten them. Gentleness, humility and humor are wonderful tools for delivering the message of the Light. Remember to center yourself in peace and listen to my voice only as you share the message of the Light for I will tell you exactly what to say and how to say it, just as I am doing right now. Be careful, be careful, be careful. Gentleness, compassion, patience, mindfulness are all in order in delivering the messages of God to His Children. Purification is always needed first and purification is always a slow, loving, tender, healing process because Father would not awaken His Children abruptly. He helps them to awaken tenderly, lovingly, sweetly. He whispers in His Children's ears to help them awaken them from their dreams of hell. Thank You Jesus for this message.

∞∞∞∞

Journal Entry on Lesson 45

God is the Mind with which I think.

In the section in the Text, "This Need Not Be" Jesus explains to us about our mind. It is our choice what we would think at any given time. If we are depressed, sad, and anxious or feel guilty, we can realize that it need not be.

In this section in Chapter 4, he says:

> T-4.IV.2. *I have said that you cannot change your mind by changing your behavior, but I have also said, and many times, that you can change your mind. When your mood tells you that you have chosen wrongly, and this is so whenever you are not joyous, then know this need not be. In every case you have thought wrongly about some brother God created, and are perceiving images your ego makes in a darkened glass.* **Think honestly what you have thought that God would not have thought, and what you have not thought that God would have you think.** *Search sincerely for what you have done and left undone accordingly, and then change your mind to think with God's. This may seem hard to do, but it is much easier than trying to think against it. Your mind is one with God's. Denying this and thinking otherwise has held your ego together, but has literally split your mind. As a loving brother I am deeply concerned with your mind, and urge you to follow my example as you look at yourself and at your brother, and see in both the glorious creations of a glorious Father. (Bold mine.)*

With today's exercises, I am moving away from all the conflict, comparison and competition thinking that the ego would keep me preoccupied with at any given time. I am journeying inward into the sacred sanctuary with the Holy One and realize my own holy nature. I *can* change my mind. I *can* change the thoughts that I think with my mind. I *can* decide to be dedicated to practicing mindfulness. Do I want to feel at peace today? If I do, then I will monitor my thoughts and give each one gladly to the Holy Spirit. As I go about my day I can ask myself, am I thinking what God would think in this situation? With this person? About myself?

My mind is very holy and I can access the holiness and the real thoughts. I take the time today to be still, to rest in Him, to appreciate the thoughts that I can think with Him when I have the willingness to do so. He will enter my mind and bring a quiet serenity that is most welcome. I am Home in my holiness. It does not have to feel foreign to me no longer. I accept the truth of Who I am, God's glorious Son. I am joined with Him in Heaven now as I share in His thoughts. I am indeed grateful that I have the means, the Holy Spirit, as a Friend to walk along the road with me.

ოოოჂ

Journal Entry on Lesson 46

God is the Love in which I forgive.

In the stories that I have written for myself, either I am the guilty one or others from my past and present are guilty. I have condemned them and myself. With this Lesson, I learn that God has not condemned anyone for He knows only Love. It does not matter what scenes I have written in the script for myself or others, the scenes of anger, abuse, fear, depression, deceit and the like. What is only true is that God's Love is there blessing me always. In the practicing today, I am releasing the chains that have bound me to guilt in myself and others. In using, *"God is the Love in which I forgive you,"* I am recognizing and affirming that through God there is only Love to see in all of us. Love does not attack nor condemn. It simply lifts me up to my rightful place in Heaven where I have always been. In these dark shadows of the stories I have made, I do not see the truth. I have hidden in the pain and anxiety thinking that it was the only way to live. It is not where I wish to live now. I remember that I only live in God. The mindfulness of forgiveness with anyone today continues to remove the barriers that keep me from Love. If Love is what I want, then it is Love that I will instill in my practice today. It is the practice of honesty with the thoughts in my mind about others or myself, then stopping and joining with the Holy Spirit to offer only Love to us all. In this, we are all blessed.

Today's Lesson is a wonderful Lesson indeed because as we practice it and apply it into our lives, we will discover that it contains the keys to freedom and peace. In the ego world it is not difficult to create a laundry list of people in our mind who we have some type of grievance with. Remember that any form of grievance or irritation or fear that we may have in association with anyone that comes to mind is of the ego. The ego wants us to see separation from each other because this is how it keeps itself going. This is how it keeps your mind dwelling in the realm of fear and hell. By keeping your mind busy with the busyness of the world around you and the fearful relationships that you perceive that you have with others is the way the ego continues to surround you with darkness. The darkness blocks from your awareness that you and your brothers are One Light. You and your brothers are the Light of God because God created you Himself. And in His creation of you, He created you *exactly* like Himself.

In Reality, this is the only thing that is really true. Right now we are experiencing un-reality which is the darkness that surrounds us. But the reality of the Light of God, who we really are, can be experienced *now* if we choose to attempt to do so. We can go within our minds and be still. And as we be still within, we can continue the practice of forgiveness, or the letting go of the ego's illusions around us. As we continue to practice the process of letting go of the illusion around us, the Light of God, your True Self, will begin to spark through the veil of darkness that you have surrounded yourself with. This is when you will begin to free yourself at last. We thank the Holy Spirit for His help for He will take your hand and guide you and help you along the way as you go through this process.

Journal Entry on Lesson 47

God is the strength in which I trust.

There is an old teaching that when someone catches on fire, they should immediately think to themselves, "Stop, Drop and Roll." This concept can be used as a helpful memory aid to help you to remember how to respond to any situation that seems to cause you concern. As you go about your day remember to monitor your thoughts. Remember to be vigilant about the thoughts that you are thinking. "Stop" and ask yourself, "Is this particular thought that I am thinking right now causing me any worry or concern in any form?" If it is, then "Drop" into peace.

One of the key phrases that Jesus shares with us in today's Lesson is *"try to reach down."* He literally is inviting us to practice sinking down and relaxing into peace. If you practice this right now, where you close your eyes and just sunk down with every breath that you exhale, you would notice yourself becoming more and more relaxed. You would notice more and more that you are sinking into peace. This is the technique that he is asking us to use to discover the place of Heaven inside of us. After you do this for a few moments, it may feel that you have come to a point where you cannot sink down any further into peace. This is not true, keep going because it does not end. If you keep trying, you will notice that you can sink further and further down into peace with each practice session. As you continue to practice this, you will discover that as you sink down further into peace you are approaching the realm of God. And as you rest in this peaceful space, you will eventually discover that He will reveal Himself to you. This is a most wonderful gift and treasure to discover within yourself. When the discovery is made you will "Roll" in laughter, happiness and joy.

The beginning of Today's Lesson reminds me that for many years I thought I could run my own life. What a joke that is now as I review this idea of *"God is the strength in which I trust."* In the past, I had every situation planned out and indeed was angry if the planned outcomes were never achieved. I was attached to what I wanted and other people, places and things had better cooperated because it was all about me. This person needed to respond in a certain way and do certain things and if they did not then I retaliated in some form either overtly or covertly; the same with other situations. I walked around with the black spot of blame and fear within my heart. Trusting God was a foreign concept back then. But now, as I rely on Him to provide the means for a happy and peaceful life, I can see that people and situations that come into my life are for my highest growth and learning. No longer do I dwell on what should happen or try to control it, instead I simply trust that what God has planned is for the higher good of everyone involved. They are all lessons presented for myself.

As I release my hooks into expectations, there are no longer the resentments. There is a saying that goes, "Expectations are pre-meditated resentments."

If I simply trust in my Father, then only joy will be the outcome. Peace will be the outcome. I have been blessed with wondrous gifts when I have released all that I believe should occur in my life. The Holy Spirit always leads me Home. His Voice will only lead me there. It is for me to stop and listen to what the message is there for me and then gladly follow it. This does not mean that challenging situations do not continue to occur in my life, but it does mean that now I do not have to depend on my own strength, my own answers to resolve them. That is the Holy Spirit's job. He has all the answers, if I am willing to hear them. Many gifts can come out of the most difficult situations. I have found that those gifts include a dedication and devotion to a continuance of mindfulness and the practice of forgiveness. Through this, I will come to the sanctuary of peace more often. For this, I am grateful.

ooooo

Journal Entry on Lesson 48

There is nothing to fear.

It's amazing how many fear thoughts can appear in the mind in a course of a day. Let's even take a smaller segment of time such as an hour. It could go something like this: fear that the roads are snow-covered and icy; will there be an accident; will the car even start; will I be late for my appointment; I need to make that difficult phone call to that friend to answer "no" to their request and what will they say; the heating bill just came in and will I be able to pay it; where will the money come from; what if I don't get the job; what if I do get the job; what if...what if...what if...

Indeed how our minds can rattle on and on and on. As today's Lesson states, *"The presence of fear is a sure sign that you are trusting in your own strength."* In just the above examples, underlying it all is a sense of wanting to control the outcome to any of the situations. What vested interest do I have in, say if my car doesn't start and I am late for an appointment? What does that feel like to me? It may arouse a sense of anger and frustration for I have it set within my own mind that I need to be at a certain place at a certain time. I have made the plan and I have not allowed Holy Spirit's plan to enter. The sense of anger and frustration stem from fear since there is either the presence of love or the presence of fear. And fear, the Course tells us, is not real.

In this particular example, if indeed the car does not start and I am running late for an appointment, the best thing to do is to put the entire situation into the Holy Spirit's hands for His Answer. It is a lesson for me to go to peace instead of pieces. Was I really going somewhere today anyway? Nothing is what it seems to be. The phone call to a friend to deny a request is truly not about the request on the surface. It may be a lesson in following my guidance and being confident in following the said guidance with no excuses or regret or fear of acceptance or withdrawal of love. Nothing is as it seems to be.

I have nothing to fear when I rely on the Divine within. God's strength is there and when I am aware that there is nothing to fear then I have remembered God is present in my life. I trust and let go and allow Him to lead me. Today's Lesson is a lesson in mindfulness. I am to use the idea in every situation immediately as soon as I am aware of a disturbance to my peace. I am willing today to let go of everything that I have known and allow Him to lead. I will always be led in the right direction, the direction of Home.

∞∞∞∞

Journal Entry on Lesson 49

God's Voice speaks to me all through the day.

There is another Voice within your mind that can be heard which is different from the voice that you have been listening to all of your life. All of the thoughts that you think now, all of the words that you hear in your mind when you talk to yourself in your thoughts as you go throughout the day are coming from the voice of the ego. When we were born into this world, we were born into the realm of the ego. In the realm of the ego, the ego has many voices that block us from hearing the Voice of God Who is speaking to us all the time. But we cannot hear Him if we are paying attention to all of the distractions in the ego world.

For example, if you see a vehicle driving down the street, you are paying attention to a distraction of an ego voice that is speaking to your eyes. It is saying, "Hey, look at me. I exist as this vehicle that you think you are seeing." I assure you that it is not really there; it is just an illusion. What is actually happening is that the projection of the image of the vehicle is blocking you from seeing the Light of God that lies beyond it. Another example of a type of distraction that the ego voice presents to us, would be the same as the one I mentioned before where we listen to ourselves think as we go throughout the day. The ego voice in our mind that we listen to all through the day is saying, "Hey, listen to me. I am alive because you can hear me speaking to you in your thoughts." What it is really trying to do is to get you to believe that the body you think you are walking around in is real. But I assure you it is not. It is just another illusion, another distraction that the ego is using to block you from the awareness of the reality of the Light that you are.

As we continue to practice letting go of the images we think we are seeing in the ego world and the voices that we think we are hearing in the ego world, we will begin to have experiences with the Truth of the Reality that lies beyond all of it. God the Father is speaking to us all the time but we are unconsciously blocking this experience from our awareness by paying attention to the many voices of the ego world. The way to begin to free our minds from being captivated by the distractions of the ego voices is to sink down into silence and to *listen to the silence*. When we first begin to practice listening to the silence within our minds we will probably discover an uneasiness at first. It may feel uncomfortable. This is the resistance of the ego.

The ego does not know of God and therefore does not know what you are attempting to do when you stop listening to its voice. It is disturbing for it because it threatens the ego's very existence. As we practice sinking down and being very still and listening to the peace of silence, we begin to approach the realm of God's world. This is a very holy place within yourself. This is where the altar of the Light and Voice of God resides. As we practice listening and resting in this place of silence, this is where the Light and the Voice of God will reveal Himself to you. When it happens, it is unmistakable. Holy and blessed are you who begins to discover the Christ, the Holy Son of God within yourself.

∞∞∞

Journal Entry on Lesson 50

I am sustained by the Love of God.

In a day of feeling very ill, I was at first anxious and felt guilty because I could not follow through with the commitments that I had scheduled for the day. I tried to figure out what remedy, natural or over-the-counter, would make all the symptoms go away. In looking at my thoughts when the symptoms started, I could not find the defining "a-ha" thought that caused this seeming ill effect. That disturbed my peace more. I find as I go through these symptoms that it is an approach of gentleness that I need to take with myself. I do not need to sit and continue to analyze why I am feeling as physically bad as I do when the day before I was perfectly healthy. That is the ego that wants to analyze and keep me distracted. As this Lesson indicates, "*Put not your faith in illusions. They will fail you.*" This means to me to let go of trying to find the "right" solution either through searching my mind or using magic pills.

As the Lesson continues, "*Put all your faith in the Love of God within you; eternal, changeless and forever unfailing.*" I can resolve everything that I am feeling by remembering my Source, my Creator, and my Comforter. In this connection, none of these illusions... *ill*-usions exist. I am not sick; I am perfect. My mind then need not dwell on what is wrong with me but rather remember only the Truth. In quiet space with the Holy Spirit, I can give to Him all of what I am feeling; the guilt, the anxiety, the sense of helplessness, the sadness and the physical symptoms. I can stop ruminating about it all in my mind, "Why has this occurred?" and just drop the focus on the physical and focus on what He would have me know. My sustentation comes only from God. As I write this, I feel a lightening of the burden and an invitation to rest in Him.

As I continue to reflect on the idea of sickness, I am reminded of a later Lesson in the Workbook. It states that *"Sickness is a defense against the truth."* The truth being that I am as God created me. So to be blunt here, what do I do in the meantime when I am lying in my bed or crouching in the bathroom? I talk with the Holy Spirit and ask if there is anything that I could know from this experience and if so, reveal it to me at the appropriate time. I do not have to be angry with myself for missing appointments, or angry that I am sick or fearful of the level of illness. I can simply "go with the flow" and allow Holy Spirit to soothe my forehead and take care of me in the most gentle, loving way. I do not need anything outside of me to replace that Love from God. If I just simply rest in Him, all needs are met; all difficulties are taken care of. I can truly rest in peace.

ooooo

Journal Entry on Lesson 51

Review Lessons 1-5

My Dear One,

You are now beginning to step out of the fog that has held your mind in the theatre of past pain. The glimmer of Light is beginning to appear in your mind as you come to know and realize that everything that you think you see in this world is not really what you think you see. The projections of your fearful thoughts have kept you blind to God's World. It will no longer. The dawning has come. You are releasing yourself each day from the self-imposed chains. These thoughts that you have are not your real thoughts. They are not the thoughts that you think with God. They are merely fillers in your mind to keep your mind distracted and away from your Father. These thoughts of fear hide the Light, cover the connection that you have with your brothers, and shroud you from knowing your true Home in Heaven.

You know this, you are feeling this. You know that now there is another way of looking at all you see. There is another way of looking at the world. The hooks of pain, anger, accusation and fear no longer have to be your friends. Let those go in your mind and give all those thoughts to Me. I will purify all your thoughts and return to you peace for peace is what you truly want. Any upsets that you may have bring them to Me with your willingness and you will see that they are not what they appear to be. You are indeed never upset for the reason that you think. Your upset is always coming from the past. It is time to let it go and relieve that heavy burden.

There is no need to continue to carry any baggage along the road with you. Indeed a teacher of God travels lightly and everyone is a teacher of God. And so as you enter into the holy sanctuary with Me, lay upon the altar all that troubles you and let yourself feel the freedom, the breeze of fresh air that comes along with laying the burden down. The more you try to possess or control; the more distress. I am here for you always. I speak to you always. Listen to My Voice for it is the only Voice that will give you the guidance that you need. Do not pay attention to the voice of the ego, either yours or another's. Many have set themselves up as gurus telling others that they have all the answers, that they can only see it their way, for they are the ones that are enlightened. This is not true. You need no other. I am the only Teacher that you need. Trust in Me. Can I still speak through others? I certainly can. And when I do you will feel a sense of peace. That is how I speak to you, with peace, certainty and confidence. I do not guilt you, or frighten you into making another choice. I simply offer the alternative choice out to you. It is always your decision. I will not invade your free will. The voice of guilt and fear is the ego's voice and it is a voice that demands. You are in mind-training to strengthen your trust in Me and to listen to what I say to you for it is only the Truth.

In this Course, you will see many times that you are told to come to Me with everything, not to leave one spot of hurt behind. I am your Friend, I am here to outstretch My hand to you and walk with you along the way and to carry your burdens for you. Allow Me to decide for you. All that is needed is a simple statement, "Decide for me," and it is done. Peace will be felt at the moment of your release. Walk through your day today knowing that you can align your thoughts with God and that you can let go of a thought system that has only hurt you. God will always surround you with His Love. In Him is your sure protection always. In Him, there is only Love.

∞∞∞∞

Journal Entry on Lesson 52

Review Lessons 6-10

The Holy Spirit wants us to be happy. The questions that we need to honestly ask ourselves are "Do I want to be happy? Do I really want to feel peaceful and to be in a state of peace all the time? Do I want to feel happy? Do I want to feel truly joyful? Do I want to have a sense of an inner peace and inner quiet joy that cannot be disturbed by anything? Do I really want to live a life that gives me this kind of experience?"

It's easy to allow the shenanigans of the ego world to lead us into believing that many of its things will bring us happiness. The ego has many clever facades going on in the world. The ego is constantly sending out the message, "If you do this, or have this experience you will be happy." It tells us that the experience would bring us happiness and joy or perhaps even a sense of peace. But when we fall for these illusory temptations we discover every time that it leads to nothing. They always lead to a dead end and a sense of inner disappointment and issatisfaction and even anger hidden on some levels. This is because we have attempted to make the illusions of the world real.

We have forsaken Heaven for something much less. We have given up our ability to see truly the Reality of Heaven. And this is what pains us. It is the repetitive falling down and down again that pains us. It is the forgetting and the not learning and accepting the lessons of dead ends as a fact that pains us. Sooner or later however we will have had enough of the pain and we will begin to decide that there has to be another way. And we will begin to turn to the Holy Spirit for help. The Holy Spirit will gladly give it to us. Monitor your mind very carefully all through the day and be vigilant of all of your fearful thoughts even the ones hidden behind the facade of the ego's happy faces. They are nothing more than masks that hide the intentions of the evil behind them. The ego does not want you to be happy. Listen only to the Voice of the Holy Spirit. Talk with Him about everything. Ask Him about everything including the things that you think will bring you happiness. Question everything with the Holy Spirit and ask Him to decide for you and it is done.

The past has been held within my mind bringing forth all the witnesses to the beliefs that I have held in that past. The beliefs of unworthiness, guilt, fear, unloveability and the like are all being seen in the present moment.

When I look at another, when I engage with that person in conversation or in a relationship, I am not truly seeing them as they are, the holy Child of God. What I am seeing instead is a projection of all the pain that I have held within my own heart. Their actions, their words are merely the result of the messengers of fear that I have sent forth. If I truly want to be happy, then I need to let go of the past and live in the present moment. My upset is only what I have created in my mind and I am willing now to let it go. Holy Spirit, I offer to you all my thoughts of upset, of the past, of all that I think I see. I know that there is another way and I gladly choose to accept that way now and to receive Your Wisdom and Understanding and Your Peace. Amen.

∞∞∞

Journal Entry on Lesson 53

Review Lessons 11-15

"What is the meaning of life?" We've heard this question before, so many have contemplated and try to conclude even further, "Why am I here?" According to the Course, there was a tiny mad idea when the Son of God forgot to laugh and hence the ego and the meaningless world that we experience. The good news is that at the same instant, the Holy Spirit entered into our mind as our Guide back to the remembrance of God. How many times have I myself put forth, "I want my life to have meaning."

Today, I remember that all meaning, true meaning comes from the Father. I have chosen otherwise by being caught up in the ego's ill effects. Because the "ego quite literally is a fearful thought" then anything that I think with the ego will resonate of fear. The world I see, the situations that I find myself in, the people that I interact with, all will reflect some speck of fear that I hold within my mind. Even being here in a body reflects the fear stemming from the ego. If I am depending on anything in this world, then I am depending on just a hologram. Can I really depend on what I see around me? The people, the places, the things? It is only in God that I can place my trust. It is only in God that I can depend. I have the connection to God within me for He placed it there. I can give up the idea of these fearful, insane thoughts and align my thoughts with Him. Think only with Him.

Indeed, I could but do I want to? Am I perfectly fine in what I am experiencing on a daily basis? Am I really experiencing peace as I go about my day? Do others irritate me? Do I feel judgmental at times? The thoughts of fear weary us, and that is what judgment is, what irritation is, withdrawal of love is, a wearisome way of living our lives. I can choose again. I can choose a way of life that does give meaning and purpose to my life and that is choosing with the Holy Spirit. He will define the meaning of life if I so allow Him. I have a mighty purpose and that is to forgive the meaningless and to remember the meaningful. It is for me to apply this to every situation that I experience in my life. This *is* a course in practical application. I could get caught up in intellectualizing and discussing the principles, but what good are ideas if I do not put them into action. Today, I make the commitment of truly remembering to forgive all thoughts of judgment, to relinquish all desires to correct a brother, to release all thoughts of fear to the Holy Spirit, and to actually walk my day living the Course and not just to talk about it. Today, I make the dedication to the vigilance of my mind.

As we go about our day today let us remember that everything we see is not real. It is difficult to believe this when we have not experienced a glimmer of the Reality that lies beyond. Everything you see in the world is a projection from your unconscious mind. We don't realize that we are projecting illusions for us to see with our eyes because it is happening from the unconscious part of the mind of God which you are a part of. When we came here and were born into this world we forgot who we really are. This is why our lives seem to be constantly filled with strife and challenges.

Unconsciously we recognize that there is something wrong, there is something askew. But the conscious mind pushes that problem, that conflict to the back of our mind away from our awareness. The conscious mind busies itself with trying to find the solution to the problem by using things of the world to make itself feel happy. This is what we call the ego. All of it is a distraction, a delaying maneuver to prevent us from letting go of everything we think we are seeing and believing in, in exchange for allowing reality to come into our awareness. The only purpose for the world is to forgive it and to recognize that everything we see in it is an illusion.

This is difficult to accept and understand at first because the ego part of the mind has placed so much value on the world. This is why we need the help of the Holy Spirit. If we allow ourselves to let go of everything that we are experiencing and ask the Holy Spirit to show us His world, to show us Reality, He will help us with that process.

As we practice working with the Holy Spirit and allowing Him to help us to let go of illusions He will bless our minds with many gifts. He will begin to show us glimpses of Reality, glimpses of the Light of Heaven in our minds. We can see the Light of Heaven with our mind, with our eyes open or our eyes closed, it does not matter. It is easier at first to practice with our eyes closed because it removes many of the distractions that the ego uses to prevent us from placing our attention fully on the Holy Spirit within our minds. It is here where illumination takes place. It is here where the Voice of God, the Voice of the Holy Spirit will begin to speak to you and explain the truth of Heaven to you. His Voice is very clear and unmistakable andyou will know it when you hear it for the Light and the Voice that speaks to you always speaks of peace, always reminds you of Who you really are. We are the Children of God and because we are the children of God, we can only be like God in Reality. Anything other than this truth is just an illusion, a lie, a deception and it is not real.

Let us remind ourselves today as we go through the day to say to ourselves, "This is not real." It will help us in the process of letting go and opening up to the gift of true forgiveness that waits for us in our minds. The Holy Spirit will help us to find the gift. Thank You Holy Spirit for helping us and thank You for our brothers and sisters who are One with us. And thank You Father for our Holy Self. We are all One in Heaven forever without end. Amen.

∞∞∞

Journal Entry on Lesson 54

Review Lessons 16-20

To our dear friends near and far who have inspired this prayer to Spirit. It is our gift to you.

Holy Spirit,

Today the word "determination" is in the forefront of my mind. I understand that I alone am responsible for my thoughts and what they project outward seeming to deceive me that this world is real. My desire is to share only my real thoughts, the thoughts that I think with You, to everyone and everything. It is the real thoughts of God's Love that bring me the peace and the safety that I desire.

There are times that I feel overwhelmed and feel that I cannot quiet my mind. In these instances, I merely remember how You are always with me and that is as a quiet, gentle presence in my life. So in these times of busyness, I remember to be gentle with myself too as You are with me. I remember to appreciate the now moment and live in that now moment. Everything that needs to be done will be done in perfect timing. My lesson now is to accept the living and breathing moment, the moment that is in front of me. When I do not, that is where the ego monkey chatter comes to play in my mind and fill it with the decisions that I need to make or have made, the future that I want for myself, the pain of daily living in a situation that I may be in or desperation about my past. I give all of these to You, Holy Spirit for Your Love and Gentleness of Being. You are my Quiet Strength. If I don't feel that I can come into the quiet with You, I can accept where I am, knowing that it will soon pass. I can focus on You as best as I can, forgiving myself that I have not lived up to my own expectations. A moment or two is all that is needed for my connection to You.

If I get wrapped up in the illusion, and think that the outside world will bring me joy, it is ok. I will remember when I remember. The time for self-flogging is over. The time for all criticism and doubt is over. The time for determination is now. There may be times that I feel alone in all of this, but ever so quietly in the back of my mind I do hear Your Voice reassuring me that I am never alone. It may even come in ways that I do not expect such as a book that I am led to pick up and read, an honest phone call with a friend, an email of outpouring sharing with another, or a song randomly played on the radio. I do have the willingness, even if it seems as just a speck. A speck is all that is needed for me to experience my liberation from the ego. I know that You dear Spirit will only take me as far as I am willing to go. I know that in the depths of my soul I am willing even if it seems that my mind is undisciplined and unfocused right now.

I know that my heart yearns for God for the Call to God is very strong within, and I know this intellectually. At times bringing it into the feeling level seems so difficult. But I do trust You Spirit. I trust that You are indeed working with me even now as I pray this prayer to You. I may feel a sense of peace when I am finished or I may not, but I do trust that You are there and that You support me every step of the journey. If I have to remind myself a hundred times today that I am not alone and that You are with me, I will do so. If I have to journal my feelings and fearful thoughts all throughout the day, then it is what I must do. Give me the way that is absolutely perfect for me, the way to work hand in hand with You. I affirm that freedom does lie in what I give to You however small it may seem, I am still releasing it into Your Loving Hands.

Dear Spirit, I want to remember peace and joy in my life. I know that it is there waiting for me to embrace it. I need Your assistance in bringing it into the forefront. I know that I am Light and the Light never dims for its radiance can be seen forever. I want to embrace my radiance again. I want to know You again. I want to be in a place of gratitude again. I affirm right here and right now that it is done and that it is so. You are my Light, my Way, and my Rock. You are my Oak Tree firmly rooted in the ground. I come to rest with You, my dear Inner Teacher, to be shaded by Your Protection and Love. Teach me what I need to know. And as I learn from you, I will share and demonstrate it to the world.

I am holy, I am blessed, I am Love. Amen.

∞∞∞∞

Journal Entry on Lesson 55

Review Lessons 21-25

What is real or unreal? Only the Holy Spirit can judge for me. What I have believed to be real for so long is not. Illusions upon illusions have kept hidden the Truth of the Light of Heaven. With my forgiveness I can begin to see the glimmer of God. The practice of forgiveness on a consistent basis is vital. If I do not wish to be frightened by my thoughts of the past or hurt and pain any longer, then forgiveness is the answer.

If I do not like to see the diseases and horrors of the world, then forgiveness is the answer. If I do not seem to have a peaceful life, then forgiveness is the answer. It is up to me to decide what I will allow in my mind and what I will not. The practice of forgiveness is just not for seemingly "big" occurrences, it is for every occurrence, every situation, and every thought that is not of God's. It is to make a habit of vigilance and mindfulness, letting go of opinions and judgments.

While I am here in this world, I do not know what to think that is why the Holy Spirit is in my mind to assist me. The healing of God's Son, who is me, is all this world is for. It is for me to remember that this world does not exist in the eyes of the Father. My own thoughts of separation I have used only to attack myself and make a world not of God and therefore not of complete Love. But Love can return to my awareness. I can feel peace, safety and joy when I make the decision to forgive and allow the Holy Spirit to "decide for me." It is through my own determination to see things differently that I will create the habit of forgiveness in my everyday life. What have I to lose by trying? I have nothing to lose but everything to gain by recognizing my fearful thoughts and releasing them to the dawn. The Light of God is my world. The Light of God is my joy.

ooooo

Journal Entry on Lesson 56

Review Lessons 26-30

As we practice sitting in silence with a still and open mind, the awareness of the borderland will begin to approach and shift into our awareness. As we allow ourselves to be still we move into alignment and up the ladder in prayer where our perception will shift into another reality. This is the land of Light. We will notice when it begins to approach our awareness because we will feel an "awareness shift" beginning to happen. Do not be afraid of this, allow it to happen. When it happens fully, at first we may feel disoriented. It is because everything we know now which is upside down in our perception begins to be corrected.

The shift into the Light of the borderland is a shift into the realm that approaches the gates of Heaven. Much healing and purification begins to occur very quickly here. The mind is prepared very quickly for Heaven. For when we allow this to happen we are quite literally preparing to step into the awareness of Heaven. This is a joyful time because it is healing. Pain is replaced with peace. The mind is illumined and we become healers as we are healed. It is here that the awareness that minds are one becomes known. True Forgiveness is taking place when we allow our mind to shift into this realm. All teachers of God come here to aid in their teachings in the world before the final step Home is taken. This is what we are approaching and attempting to reach with our mind. It is not something that we do; it is something that we allow to happen because allowing is merely allowing God to take His natural course. It is allowing ourselves to settle into the inheritance that Father gave to us when He created us. This is the meaning of accepting Atonement for ourselves. It is merely an allowing to occur as we wait in silence and expectation for the awareness of Heaven to come and illuminate our minds. Much healing takes place when this begins to happen. What a joyful, joyful, joyful time this is indeed! For this is the time of enlightenment for the Son of God. The gifts of Heaven are ready and rush to meet Him in their abundance as they bless His holy mind when He awakens from his dreams of exile.

∞∞∞∞

Journal Entry on Lesson 57

Review Lessons 31-35

In the movie "The Matrix" there is a scene where the character Morpheus begins to explain to the character Neo what the Matrix is. Morpheus shares, "The Matrix is the world that has been drawn down before your eyes. You see it when you wake up in the morning, you feel it when you go to work, and pay your taxes. It is the world that has been used to imprison your mind. But unfortunately I cannot tell you about it you have to experience it for yourself to begin to know the truth and so I offer you a choice, a choice which is yours on whether to experience the truth or not." *(paraphrased)* Neo chose the red pill in the dream because he truly wanted to experience the truth. Inside he knew all of his life that something was wrong but he couldn't quite put his finger on it. Because in his heart he was seeking the truth he was answered and so his friend Morpheus came along. Morpheus had already awakened from the dream and explained to him that there is something else and that there is a way to experience that something else. Morpheus knew that Neo's mind was imprisoned in the ego thought system and he also knew that Neo could free his mind by making a choice. Morpheus helped him to realize that something else was possible. And through his sharing forgiveness began to happen.

Once we begin to open our minds and believe that something else is possible we begin to forgive and things begin to happen. Morpheus is symbolic of our friend Jesus who is telling us exactly the same things through *A Course in Miracles*. The world we see and experience around us is not true. It is an illusion. It is not real just like the Matrix was. He is also telling us that if we really want to experience that it is not true, there is a way to do that. He reminds us over and over again to go within our minds, be still and sink past our busy thoughts. This letting go of the world around us is forgiveness. He gives us a very simple solution to a very big problem. Be still and sink down into the silence of peace within your mind and ask the Holy Spirit to show you the Light of the Real World. This is opening up to the experience of True Forgiveness.

Like Neo, in order to have this experience you have to really want it. If you want it, it will surely come. The face of Christ will come and illuminate your mind and begin to free you from the prison that you have placed upon yourself. This discovery of the truth is a joyful time indeed. For the dark shackles that have been placed upon the mind to keep it ensnared in the dreams of hell begin to be loosened at last. The end of the dream will begin to come much more quickly now. And the Son of God will begin to remember how to begin to hasten his pace back towards the gates of Heaven. The rays of Light extend outward in welcoming arms to receive God's Son and to embrace his awareness with these loving arms of Love, helping him to remember who he really is and where he is right now in Heaven forever. He has not left his Home but he will not remember this until he begins to believe that it is possible and he begins to forgive all that he sees now.

∞∞∞∞

Journal Entry on Lesson 58

Review Lessons 36-40

It is affirmed for me five times of my holiness in today's Lesson. In this grouping of the Lessons, Jesus is obviously trying to get his point across about the truth about me and that is that I am holy. I may have carried guilt around with me for many years of past things that I have done. All is forgiven for there is only love. It is for me to release my own gun to my head that I have held for so long. The ammunition is guilt and fear and for so long I have pulled the trigger, releasing pain into my being. But there is another way.

I no longer have to continue to punish myself. I can be free, right here and right now. Accepting the truth of who I am is accepting my holiness and my safety in God. It is from God that all things are possible. And it is possible that I am blessed, because it is true. My holiness is not defined by pain and guilt; it is defined by my innocent nature as God's created one. I cannot accept this until I accept this.

If I have been struggling for a long time with my many "sins", stacking and counting them up one by one, over and over, I have indeed kept my mind in the past, hoarding the guilt in the cold halls in the cave that I have carved out of madness. But the Light does come, it is already here. I am led out of the cave of my pain with the Hand of the Holy Spirit as I release each token of guilt.

As I come forward into the Light, I see that all that I have cherished is now vanished. The Light assures me of Who I am in God. I am never alone and do not need to feel alone. I do not have to return to the cave of insanity. Rather, I can choose to accept my holiness, right here and right now. I can do this with every speck of fear that enters into my mind and choose the holiness and relinquish judgment.

As this Lesson states, "*My Father supports me, protects me, and directs me in all things. His care for me is infinite, and is with me forever. I am eternally blessed as His Son.*" This is the truth, there is nothing else.

When we take time to talk with the Holy Spirit in our mind either during meditation or in journaling, He often helps us to get in touch with the unloving images and stories we have made up about ourselves in the past. They tend to come up more easily during a journaling process because there is a flow, a rhythm that you get into when working with the Holy Spirit.

As you write, He seems to give you "downloads" of thoughts while you are writing down the previous thought. This helps the flow of thoughts keep going, to get you in touch with the things He would have you get in touch with. He does this because He knows that these memories and beliefs about yourself need to be excavated from your mind. He helps you to dig up the unholy thoughts and beliefs that have been taught to you by the ego thought system so that you may turn them over to Him for healing by the truth of the Light that resides within you.

The stories that you have made up about yourself are not true. What is true is that you are a holy Child of God. You are a Light that extends forever with God. The Light that you are has been blocked from your awareness by the darkness of the ego thought system but It cannot be abolished forever because the Light that you are comes from your Source, your Father forever. It is impossible for your Light to be extinguished by the darkness because it is not God's Will. And nothing opposes the Will of God. We are thankful for that indeed. We thank You Father for Who You are and we thank You for our holy Selves because of Who You are. We are One and Eternal with You in Heaven forever, Your World without end. Amen.

∞∞∞∞

Journal Entry on Lesson 59

Review Lessons 41-45

When we see the Light of God flash into our minds and we hear His Holy Voice speak to us from within, we begin to recognize where our true Home lies. Our true Home lies within the peace of God Who walks with us wherever we go. He is our Source and He is our Strength in all things that we do. His Light will show us the way. His Voice will give us direction when we need it. He has the

Answer to all of our problems and choices we need to make. He is our Guide and He is the One Who will guide our lives so easily if we but rely and trust in Him Who goes with us wherever we go. Vision is His gift to us. It is the strength that we can call upon in a time of need. Peace, assurance, wisdom, certainty, confidence and joy will be given to us whenever we call upon Him in time of need. Ask Him and trust Him to give them to us when we think we need them. His blessings are as sure as Heaven Itself. Joy and happiness is all He wills for His Son. Thank You Father for Your gifts to us. Amen.

∞∞∞

Journal Entry on Lesson 60

Review Lessons 46-50

What do I have to lose if say, I took the next 15 minutes to forgive every unloving thought, every judgment that enters my mind? How about an hour? I have nothing to lose and everything to gain. I could then expand that to even longer periods of time, several hours, an entire day. And if there is a moment that I do not forgive, when I remember I can begin again.

This Course *is* a course in practical application. If I want to truly absorb the principles in my life then I trust the strength of God to help me to forgive all that I see and all that I think about. When I forget, I will be reminded to remember. As I remember, my mind experiences true freedom. It can be done; I can begin to train my mind to forgive at an instant. I can practice in short periods of time and then expand them outward. All it takes is my determination to want to live another way. I am called to forgive; His Voice speaks to me of my greatness and of His Love.

When I listen, deeply listen to what His Voice has to say, then the practice becomes easier and easier. I do not have to trust in anything but Him. Trusting in myself, my ego self has only brought an agenda of pain. The only thing that I give up is the pain when I forgive. The only thing I receive when I forgive is peace. I am ready today to have a quiet mind, a mind at rest. And so Holy Spirit, I ask Your assistance, Your guidance throughout my day. I know that it is through my forgiveness that I will be saved and the world along with me. I know that my strength comes from You and in You solely that I can place my trust. I have nothing to fear for You are with me every step of the way. And You will only take me as far as I am willing to go. My heart is open, my willingness is present. Lead me to the higher ground, where I am centered in peace. I affirm that I have accepted the idea of practicing forgiveness and will do so as I am able. Thank You for Your sure Guidance and Direction. Together, I know that the Light of God will be seen.

∞∞∞∞

Journal Entry on Lesson 61

I am the light of the world.

If you have ever asked yourself, "What in this life will bring me my highest joy and fulfillment?" or "What life can I live and perform as a service that will help me to feel happy all of the time?" The answer to these questions lies in discovering the great secret that today's Lesson will lead you to. Discovering the spark of Light within your mind will be the greatest discovery of your lifetime. It is the discovery of Who you really are. You are the light of the world, not a body.

When you discover the light within yourself you will also begin to learn that you are beginning to perform miracles the same way that Jesus did. The Holy Spirit and Jesus will work with you when you begin to discover the light within yourself. They will help you to discover the light. Remember to ask them for help. Also remember to ask them when you can perform miracles. They will let you know and will help you in your times of need. You will discover that letting go of illusions with your mind and sinking down and opening up to the light within yourself is the process of rising up the ladder of prayer to the awareness of the Christ that you are. This awareness is the miracle. The glimpses of the Christ that flash into your mind are the experience of true forgiveness of all illusions for an instant, a holy instant.

As you practice sinking down and opening up to the light within yourself, the Holy Spirit will help to raise you up the rest of the way to the experience your Light. The Holy Spirit knows the way and knows how to help you but you must remember to ask Him to help in everything you do and ask Him to help you to discover your Light. When you are ready, He will reveal the truth to you and you will begin to know that you are the Light that you perceive. Each encounter with your Light will bring an experience of healing, joy, peace, and a knowing that will bless you with a calm inner peace as you go about your day. This is what we are all after, to discover the truth about ourselves. To begin to awaken to the reality of Who we really are, the Christ, the Holy Son of God Himself.

ooooоo

Journal Entry on Lesson 62

Forgiveness is my function as the light of the world.

In Chapter 17, in the first section, "Bringing Fantasy to Truth" we are reminded that *"When you try to bring truth to illusions, you are trying to make the illusions real, and keep them by justifying your belief in them. But to give illusions to truth is to enable truth to teach that the illusions are unreal, and thus enable you to escape from them."*

And so it is for me to bring the darkness to the Light. That is my function; that is why I am here. It also states in the Course in Chapter 9 that *"To forgive is to overlook."* But how can I do this with various situations in my life when they may seem to be so insurmountable? With my awareness and my willingness I can bring every situation to the truth. It is as I am ready. When I am ready to let go of the sense of weakness, strain, and fatigue from my mind, I will understand what forgiveness will do for me. When I am ready to allow the fear, guilt and pain to be washed away, then I will know and accept peace. It is entirely by my own choice. What is it that I choose right now?

The dedication to one's healing is important. How much do I want to heal? How much am I willing to let go? Am I willing to release the hooks of attachment to the outcome? When I can release, I can experience peace. I can experience the freedom that forgiveness offers me. This can be done. It is possible.

"Tolerance for pain may be high but not without limit." That means when I have come to a point where I can no longer take the emotional stress of what is occurring in my life, I will open up to another way of living. That is when I forgive and become willing to truly walk with the Holy Spirit.

I went through this myself over a month ago. A day or so of anger occurred that really not only interrupted my peace but seemed to disrupt my life. I experienced what I needed to experience. I had not been in that place of anger in a very, very long time. Anything that anyone could say or what I could read that was Course-related meant nothing to me in the moment. I had to be where I was and as I was ready, I opened myself up to looking at the situation differently, which was also looking at myself differently. This included forgiving myself for not being as "spiritual" as the ego told me I wasn't being. So it prompted me to take my spiritual dedication to a deeper level. For many years I have taken the idea of practical application of the Course very seriously. And so, why not now?

And that's what I did. How many teachers of God admit when they have merely made a mistake? It is perfectly fine to make a mistake and then to move on. It is our own devotion to reprimand and punishment and pain that keeps us from moving forward. When I embrace the innocence that I am as the Holy Spirit sees me, overlook all that I see and seem to experience, then the happiness, the true happiness of the Father enters into my life. I have felt and experienced this in the last month. And how is that? By applying exactly as it all states in the Course, following my specialized curriculum sent to me by the Holy Spirit. Not cursing what has happened in my life but blessing each situation as an opportunity to forgive, heal and move forward into the Light. Many situations in my life have occurred over the years, the "trauma dramas" so to speak, the ones that the world would stand judgment on.

However, if I stay stuck on the questioning of why did this happen, why did that happen, O, I should have done this differently, or not, because of this such and such happening my life is ruined. This is not the truth. I am not what has happened to me. I am not the tragedies. I am God's Child Whom He loves and has never abandoned. All the experiences that I have had lead me to the greater truth if I so allow them. It leads me to God. All things are lessons that God would have me learn. Curse them and I curse myself. Bless them and I am free.

That is my function today, forgiveness as I am the light of the world. I would remember this because I indeed want to be happy.

∞∞∞∞

Journal Entry on Lesson 63

The light of the world brings peace to every mind through my forgiveness.

It is up to me to save the world, save myself, and save my brothers. What? Sounds like a tall order, huh? It is actually completed easily as I forgive. Each time I forgive I bring us all closer and closer to the recognition of Home. Each time I let go of judgments I experience peace. It comes to a point of appreciating the peace that I feel and truly wanting it to pervade my life all the time.

I will remember to take time today to enter into silence with Him, allowing the Holy Spirit to so guide my thoughts. I need do nothing but allow Him to show me what forgiveness can do. I no longer wish to distort the world but to see it truly, to see it through the Eyes of Love.

A Prayer From the Text –

Forgive us our illusions, Father, and help us to accept our true relationship with You, in which there are no illusions, and where none can ever enter. Our holiness is Yours. What can there be in us that needs forgiveness when Yours is perfect? The sleep of forgetfulness is only the unwillingness to remember Your forgiveness and Your Love. Let us not wander into temptation, for the temptation of the Son of God is not Your Will. And let us receive only what You have given, and accept but this into the minds which You created and which You love. Amen. ~T-16.12

∞∞∞∞

Journal Entry on Lesson 64

Let me not forget my function.

Today I am prepared in knowing that as I go throughout my day that all my decisions are very simple. My decisions will either lead to happiness or unhappiness. Which do I want? Each phone call, each interaction with another, each task I complete, each judgment, I am choosing whether to be happy or not. I can choose to be right in what *I* believe, what *I* think should occur or I can choose another way of looking at the world which is through the lens of freedom. Forgiveness offers me freedom. Forgiveness offers me joy and a peace of mind. I choose not to remain blind today and I have been blind in my unforgiveness.

Instead, I can learn a joyous lesson, a lesson that is not of limitation but one of liberation. Safety lies in my forgiveness. I no longer have to control outcomes or hold foolish expectations for myself or for others or for situations. I can let go, and yes, let God. The way *is* open; it *is* certain. It has been given me by God my joyous function, simply to be happy. This is only achieved through forgiveness. There is no more need to catalog the sins of my brothers or of myself. I am forgiven already in the Eyes of God. He sees *only* Love in me as He created me to be. I no longer need to continue to learn through pain. I can remember that to change the world, I merely change my thoughts about it. I forgive it.

Today, I have the mind discipline to remember my function, to remember that to forgive *is* to be happy. I gladly remember that now. My day will be filled with opportunities for true happiness through true forgiveness. And through this is the recognition of that this Light in me I am radiating will awaken It in all.

ထၜထ

Journal Entry on Lesson 65

My only function is the one God gave me.

The idea of the old junk drawer came to mind today. You know that drawer, all the little what-nots and whatcha-ma-callits and even yes, old keys. Yes, you know those keys, the ones to the car that you sold 15 years ago, the keys to locks that you don't know even know where they are, your old high school locker combination, old apartments and homes; all the old keys cluttering up the drawer along with everything else. All these only hold keys to the past, the memories of experiences that are now faint.

Today, I am offered another key that I have carried along with me all this time and did not even realize that it was in my possession. This key of light will open the door that I have held shut in my mind and I will see that the darkness that I thought was behind this door is gone. It never existed but in my mind. What the Holy Spirit has for me is only to help free me from possessing and obsessing about the old keys in my hand. Through His guidance, the way is made clear for me. Behind the door is only peace. It is for me to *"Accept this key to freedom from the hands of Christ Who gives it to you, that you may join Him in the holy task of bringing light."* T-14.II.7:8.

That is what forgiveness is. It is the key to peace, the key to happiness. With this awareness, I will be motivated to clean out the junk drawer that is in my mind. It takes persistence and determination to gently toss away the old, blessing it for what it was and what it has meant, appreciating the lesson and moving forward. As I remove each unneeded thought, the golden key of peace will shine more radiantly. I will appreciate it more. I will want to use it more. And so I shall.

∞∞∞∞

Journal Entry on Lesson 66

My happiness and my function are one.

Let us remind ourselves today that there is only one way to find true happiness and that is found by going within. The ego part of our mind is very good at presenting us with illusions that we think will bring us happiness. It is all a facade to continue to delay us and distract us from remembering to go within. Let's practice observing our thoughts and beliefs today, especially the ones that become our happy goals. Let us practice being truly honest with ourselves and recognizing that the ego's happy goals never really do bring us the experience of true happiness. For example, the ego may teach us that we love to go to a particular restaurant to have a meal. The ego may teach us that the food is wonderfully prepared there and the atmosphere is fun. The ego may teach us that pursuing another job with a higher wage will bring us happiness. The list goes on. Let us recognize that these are delaying maneuvers of the ego.

The Holy Spirit within us is the only one who knows the way; the correct choices we should make. He is the only one who can lead us to truly happy experiences within the dream while we awaken. Let us remember not to substitute the ego's happy goals with the goal of finding your Friend the Christ within yourself and following His direction. When we discover our Friend within ourselves, we will discover a gift of happiness that is automatically given to us in that holy instant. The moment that we truly let go of all illusions within our mind is the moment of true forgiveness. Forgiveness brings us the experience of the Voice for God, the light of our Friend, happiness, certain direction and joy. This is the experience that we are truly seeking to find within ourselves and in our lives. The experience of knowing that we are not alone and that we have a Friend who is with us and will help us to have a happy life.

Let us remember to work with our Friend the Holy Spirit today to help us practice mindful observance of the seeming happy goals the ego offers us today. Perhaps it would be even helpful to write them down as we go through our day so that at the end of the day we could review them and remind ourselves one last time that none of these could ever replace the gift of happiness that comes from finding the light and guidance of our Friend that resides within us. Holy Spirit, please help us to remember how to find You now. Thank you. Amen.

∞∞∞

Journal Entry on Lesson 67

Love created me like itself.

If you are suffering from some form of addiction, it is because you have identified yourself with the wrong creator. The ego mind teaches us that our parents are our creators and therefore we are destined to be like them. This unfortunate belief has been the cause of extreme pain for countless numbers over the ages. The ego mind can see its own unworthiness in the images of the parents it has created. And in that unworthiness belief it has decided that it too is unworthy of God. It has decided that God is punishing itself and therefore will take on the responsibility to continue to punish itself on behalf of the Creator. This insane idea has been the source of great pain, anguish and distress for the Son of God. This is a core belief in the distorted idea that you have been separated from your Creator because you are unworthy of His attention and love. This belief has been a tragic blasphemy and attack upon the Creator and His Son indeed. Nothing can be further from the truth.

You who suffer from these beliefs and ideas about yourself are suffering because you have identified with the wrong father. This is a tragic story indeed but fortunately for you it is not true. You have discovered the Light of Christ within yourself and so you know these things are not true. The problem you are having is that you do not want to believe that it is true. You still want to use the addictions to continue to punish yourself so that you can attempt to make the untrue true. When will you truly decide to lay down your hammer and nails that you are using to crucify yourself on behalf of me? You clearly misunderstand the message of the crucifixion which I have taught you, my brother. Lay these weapons of mass destruction down, these toys you use to punish yourself in an attempt to make yourself worthy of Me. And some and join with Me in a walk of happiness and peace and joy forever. It is not necessary to believe in these ideas anymore because they are simply not true. There are false ideas, false beliefs about Who You really are. Lay them down and come and find the blazing Light within you now.

Come and walk into the Light in your mind within Me now and discover Who You really are. Your face will light up with the joy of Christ inside of you when your mind allows this truth into your awareness. It will be free of its shackles once and for all and nothing but joy will flood the mind. Light and radiance will wrap about you and shine the Love that you are from you and out into the world around you to wash it away in the Love that you truly are. You are Love because that is Who created you. Teach only Love for that is what you are. Come and find it within you now so that you may know this is true once and for all. God has blessed you because you are God.

∞∞∞∞

Journal Entry on Lesson 68

Love holds no grievances.

What really surrounds us right now is Light and Peace and Joy and Love. Unfortunately most of us spend most of our time believing in the darkness that surrounds us. Seeing the people, the places and the things that surround us, going here and there, doing this and that, is an engagement in the belief of darkness. None of it is true but the ego mind wants to hang onto it. The ego mind wants to hold onto the belief of darkness so that it may block out the Light from its awareness. It does this very well for it does not know the Light because it is not Light itself. The ego is made of darkness because it is darkness itself. Fear is darkness period.

The Light that shines forth from your true Self surrounds you all the time and you can catch a glimpse of it now if you like. You can try to behold the Light within yourself so that you may recognize it as your Light if you want to right now. The way to do that is to follow my instructions as I have given to you in the Workbook Lessons very carefully. Spend time with them. Soak with them. Think about them deeply. Think about each word carefully. I have chosen my words very carefully to help you and to help myself for I am not complete without you. It is just as important for me to help you to awaken as it is important to you. I am helping you to help yourself but it is your choice whether you want to help yourself now or later or not. You can delay yourself from awakening as long as you like. You can wallow in pain as long as you like but eventually you will choose to return to God. I invite you to continue to practice doing that now. The Light of Christ is within you. Finding it will save you and others thousands of years of the illusion of pain and suffering. Would you not have this gift for yourself now? Practice imagining yourself in Heaven right now. Practice opening up to the awareness of the Light that you really are right now and I assure you that it will begin to happen because it is the Father's Will for you, it is my will for you and it is your will for you. God has blessed you. Would you accept your blessings and inheritance now?
Amen.

When I look at what "grievance" means to me, what comes is the idea that I have had an attachment to a desired outcome, or an expectation of some sort. When someone or something doesn't do as I had planned, then I have resentment and anger, a grievance. Also, if I am in the space of judgment, then I am holding a grievance. The more that I walk the middle path of non-judgment and release all attachments; the more I can experience peace, the more I can experience that I am truly safe and held in the Arms of God. The more that I practice this and feel the results; the more I want to continue the practice. I am attached to this world. I have expectations and judgments all the time, even if I do not recognize it. That is why I see the world as it is. I can see beyond the world to the truth within. I can experience the truth here and now. It is a serene way to live my life. That is what I truly want. I want to walk about my day and truly sense that all is well, all is as it is to be. It is a process of acceptance and allowing.

With my willingness, I accept the truth and allow the Holy Spirit to lead. As I step into His guidance, I step into and embrace my radiance. As I practice each day, it continues to build the foundation; the foundation of Love that strengthens me and so surrounds me always.

∞∞∞

Journal Entry on Lesson 69

My grievances hide the light of the world in me.

This is a very important lesson today. It defines the goal of the Course. The goal of the Course very specifically is to get you to a point where you have a personal experience with God. With enough effort and willingness you can actually have an experience where you see and hear God personally. We have the ability to do this anytime we want. It does seem difficult and it does take a lot of practice to get to that personal experience but it is well worth it. It is the goal of the Course and it is the goal of your life. Nothing we may pursue in the world is more important than accomplishing this one task that Jesus asks us to pursue today. He wants us to discover our Friend inside of us. He wants us to discover personally our Friend, God inside of us.

Do you really want to meet God? Do you really want to see and know and hear Him talk to you? Would you like to be able to go to a place where you can sit down and have a personal conversation with a Friend Who will always be there for you? Who will always be your Best Friend? Who will always help you to feel better about yourself? Who will bring so much joy to you in your experience with Him that you could not even imagine it? The keys to finding this most wonderful personal encounter are being given to you in today's Lesson. Ask yourself very honestly how much you really want to meet your personal Friend, God. How far are you willing to walk through the clouds today to find Him and to have Him lift you up? Would you walk a mile today? A hundred miles? Or perhaps a thousand miles through the clouds to find Him? At some point He will lift you up. Would you like to find that point today?

∞∞∞

Journal Entry on Lesson 70

My salvation comes from me.

Today's Lesson is about addiction; addiction to anything in the world that we think would complete us or make us happy. And we know in the world, it seems that lives have been made chaotic with addiction. Today, we are offered another way. It is a way of resisting the temptation of "God replacements." It is our own mind that has caused us the pain that led to the addiction to people, places and things.

Our mind has used guilt to form the foundation of pain but our mind can be used to build a foundation of healing. When I can realize that I am in control of my thoughts and when I have the awareness what my thoughts have done, then, I can take responsibility for my thoughts. As I take responsibility it is the little willingness that I possess that will allow me to move forward into releasing all that guilt has taught me. I enter into a time of self-forgiveness with the Holy Spirit leading the way. This time of forgiveness leads me Home. It points me in the direction of truth. I can no longer blame nor make excuses that outside events, things, and people have caused my painful experiences but instead point me inward to my Friend Who will help me to understand the sickness of my mind.

Through the Holy Spirit and the forgiveness work, little by little I move through the clouds and into the awareness of my role as savior of the world. It does not matter what I have been through, what I have done. What matters now is that I am determined to see things differently and that I am devoted to a new way of life. A life of trusting in the strength of God instead of my own strength is the practice to maintain now. With strong determination I gladly say, "My salvation comes from me. Nothing outside of me can hold me back. Within me is the world's salvation and my own." And I know it can be done.

ooooo

Journal Entry on Lesson 71

Only God's plan for salvation will work.

Do you still have experiences where you decide to go somewhere and engage in an activity that you think will make you feel happy but in the end discover that it really does not? This is because you have placed value on the valueless. The ego offers you many gifts of happiness in the dream of illusions. Each time you pursue the ego's gifts you will always be left with a sense or feeling of sadness and unfulfillment because you have not fulfilled your part in God's plan for salvation. You have chosen to fulfill your part in the ego's plan for salvation which leads you nowhere. The ego wants to keep you stuck in the dream of illusions and fantasies and beliefs that anything outside of you could ever bring you the experience of true happiness. The Voice for God inside of you wills for you to awaken from the cycle of hell that you have brought upon yourself.

Renounce everything that you see and hear around you in the world of illusions and ask Father Himself what He would have you do, what He would have you say, and where He would have you go because this is the only way to begin to feel happy and fulfilled in the dream while you awaken from the dream. It is fulfilling your destiny. It is fulfilling your role and why you came here, to be truly helpful. Sit and wait in silence to hear His Voice speak to you and guide you in what He would have you do. This is where your fulfillment and happiness lies within the dream. This is your purpose for being here.

This is a joyful moment indeed when we begin to learn how to truly do this, to truly hear His audible Voice speak to us. Refuse to hear anything else including your thoughts but His Voice speak to you personally. This is what we all are really seeking to find, to know His will for us and for us to fulfill our purpose for Him and our brothers who sleep in the dream of illusions with us. This is how we walk with God and our brothers in our awakening to joy and freedom.

∞∞∞∞

Journal Entry on Lesson 72

Holding grievances is an attack on God's plan for salvation.

Accept Who you are, My dear One. The truth is now known to you so all that is left is to merely accept your Divine nature. Looking into the mirror will only show you the illusion that you created and as you look you will already begin to have one grievance upon another about the illusion of the body that you made. Let that go. That is not who you are, it is not who your brother is. The body is the ego's device in hiding the truth from you. Do not listen to its weak and feeble voice, it may seem strong, but it is truly weak. I alone can sing to you of your brilliance because I alone created you. You are unlimited in what you can do; it is your mind that believes in limitation.

Be free today! Be free everyday in knowing that you can release your mind with your forgiveness. This brings complete peace as this brings you Home. Anything that you do with the body will not do this for you. Vacations, new "toys", good food, and other perceived fun will not bring you peace. This does not mean that you cannot enjoy the world that you see, but it is important to release any attachment to the world for your complete happiness. You have come to a point where you realize that "This isn't it."

You feel it within your nature as you look upon the sun and sand and truly see that this is not where your happiness lies. This is why it does not hold the same excitement as it might have once long time ago. You see things differently now. You know differently now. You have chosen another way to live. It is a way of relaxing into the truth and simply sitting back and soaking in the Light of My Love. You are the Son-Light so let your Light shine everywhere you go, knowing that I go there with you. Sing to your brothers of the truth of Who they are as well as you will continue to teach yourself of this truth. "What is salvation?" you ask? Salvation is you opening the door to your brilliance. Walk on through and embrace your Self.

Remember to challenge yourself today and everyday to practice actually hearing the Voice of God speak to you. This experience is where your true salvation lies. Remember to challenge yourself to practice seeing the Light of Christ within yourself today and everyday. Beholding the Light of Christ within your mind is where your true salvation lies. This is when you will begin to truly free your mind from the grasp that illusions seem to have on it. Your freedom lies in letting go if just for a moment and allowing the Christ of your true Self to be revealed to you. This is the Holy Grail that you are seeking. To drink from the cup of Christ within you is to receive the gift of Eternal Life Itself. Your blazing white Light is so beautiful to behold. It is as pure as God Himself, pristine and holy in all aspects of your Creator. To gaze upon this is a reflection of your true Self and of Him Who created you.

> Thank You Father for the Light of our Innocence.
> Thank You Father for our Purity.
> Thank You Father for our Holiness.
> Thank You Father for our Eternal Joy.

For all of these we behold within us as we behold the reflection of Love that we all are, One with You forever without end. We thank You for Your Love and we thank You for Who we really are. We are not alone and friendless. Praise God forever and ever. Amen.

∞∞∞∞

Journal Entry on Lesson 73

I will there be light.

In today's Lesson, paragraph 5, sentences 3 & 4 stand out to me: *"Grievances darken your mind, and you look out on a darkened world. Forgiveness lifts the darkness, reasserts your will, and lets you look upon a world of light."*

Last night as we were celebrating the last night of our trip to Florida, I began to have thoughts in my mind that clouded my judgment. I had appreciated the time that we had spent together 24 hours a day. We spoke about the highlights of the trip: the ordination and commitment of a new minister which provided another opportunity for us as a recommitment for our own spiritual ministry, her friends that shared so deeply during the ordination ceremony, the healing journey that we have had together, and the time that we had to be alone afterwards to simply relax.

As we talked, I started to allow clouds to enter my mind as I began to think that upon returning home that we would be back to our regular routines and the seeming closeness and intimacy that we shared would somehow disappear. That somehow our lives would not be the same. In realization of course, I see that was a trick of the ego to make me believe that somehow that the time spent together on a trip was more significant than the time we spend at home. This is not true. Intimacy and closeness can be part of our lives at anytime and it has been. As I drowsed into sleep last night, I spoke with Holy Spirit and asked Him to reveal to me what I needed to know about all of this. This morning I realized that there were some residual effects from the cloudiness of last night. I still beheld grievances in my mind. As I began to share them out loud, at first it came in sparks of emotion.

As I tuned in with the Holy Spirit and asked His assistance which was in fact releasing the thoughts and feelings to Him, I began to feel grounded and at peace. I could see above the clouds just as we did in our flight to Florida. And so the Light had come to my mind. I began to see things differently. I began to see my own attachments to outcomes. I began to see my expectations. I began to see my fear; all of these from above the clouds of grievances. It was not a little gift. It was peace. It was the Holy Spirit working in tandem with me in the forgiveness process and the healing of my mind. The Light broke through the clouds and my mind was serene. I did not have to follow the storm that was brewing in my mind, the winds of change blew the storm away and calm was restored. It is in my trust-walk with the Holy Spirit in which I can place my faith. Everything is as it should be.

The Holy Spirit works with me where I am and with my willingness. I am in gratitude for my willingness to see things differently. How often in the past would my mind follow the storm and stay in the storm. How grateful now to be in the Light! Forgiveness casts out all grievances. I continue to commit myself today to forgiveness of all things for in its wake is only the Light of Who I am. It is my choice today. I can choose to be in hell or I can choose to say "Hello," to my Friend, the Holy Spirit who brings me the blessing of Heaven. Today, I choose the latter for darkness is not my will. I will there only be light.

ooooo

Journal Entry on Lesson 74

There is no will but God's.

In the movie *King Kong*, the beast is seen to be spending most of his time in a state of anger and rage because he is attempting to pursue what he perceives to be beauty in the world but he cannot obtain it. His persistence in pursuing beauty in the world only brings him constant irritation, rage and unpeace. In the end, the pursuit of seeming happiness in the world ultimately destroys him. This is the only message the ego has for us. It is that the pursuit of happiness and joy will ultimately destroy us in the end. This is not true but it is true that true happiness and joy lies not in this world. It is found within yourself. The only time during the movie that the beast is observed to be in a state of peace is when he is resting quietly in silence and is spending time gazing upon the light on the horizon. This scene is symbolic of the key to discovering true happiness within you.

Remembering this scene can help us to remember to go within, be silent and to ask the Holy Spirit to help us gaze upon the joyful light within. The Light will come and kiss the eye in our mind tenderly, lovingly. The eye within our mind will gaze upon beauty, upon true beauty and holiness within itself and understand the purity that it sees. It will understand the blessing of joy that it illuminates upon itself for a moment. It will understand that everything else is an illusion for a moment and that there really is nothing else worth pursuing in the outer world. The only thing that the outer world does in our pursuit of places, things, situations, and people of beauty is that it delays us from finding the correct place where we discover true beauty and peace within ourselves. The real gift is having the willingness to find the light of beauty within ourselves.

Ask Me to come and join with you and to help you to find and gaze upon the light of your holiness within yourself. I will be there to hold your hand and also I will be the Light that kisses your face with holiness when it comes. When this holy instant occurs, where we join in holy relationship to find the light within yourself you will recognize that My Light is your Light and your Light is My Light and that in reality we are really One Light. Embrace the Light within your mind for it is the way Home for you; returning you back to the awareness that you are Joy Itself right now in reality and that you have never really left your Home for the illusions that you think you are experiencing now. You are this Holy One. You are the Light that you will perceive; God the Father's one and only perfect creation, His Son Who lives with Him forever. Amen.

Alleluia, Alleluia, Alleluia. Praise God.

∞∞∞∞

Journal Entry on Lesson 75

The light has come.

As the sun rises on the horizon Holy Spirit, I embrace the new day dawning. It is a glorious day of commitment to the Truth and a day of dedication to the process of forgiveness. Anything before that had darkened my doorstep has now passed by. It is the choice that I make right now in this moment as I share with You. Today, I have the willingness and the patience to make the change, to shift from darkness to light. In total honesty I will bring to You, Holy Spirit, all the darkness that has been held deep within my mind.

As I release it to You, I feel a lightening in my entire being. I *can* be at rest in You. There have been times that I have dreamed of such darkness and have held such turmoil in my mind. I have allowed it to twist and contort me in pain. But now the light has come. The shadows are gone. I need them no longer. I put my complete trust in You that You will so guide me the rest of the way. There is nothing to fear for You are with me. You are my strength when I feel mine is waning. You are my joy when I have found no other in the world. You beckon me now to rest near the cool stream of forgiveness that runs through the green meadows of Your Love.

I feel restored in You as You guide me ever so gently along the path of Truth and Light. I have nothing to fear for I am now anointed by You in Love. It is a glad celebration as I return Home to partake in the banquet of Love, Peace and Joy. Today, I accept true vision each time I say, *"The light has come. I have forgiven the world."* This forgiveness I extend to others, including myself so that darkness may be banished from the mind of God's Son.

∞∞∞

Journal Entry on Lesson 76

I am under no laws but God's.

Looking at the laws that you believe you are governed by, nutrition, family, relationships, etc. only limits your potential. I have so much more for you than what you believe in. When you place your trust in Me, I will provide in abundance. Using the words, "I can't do that," prevents you from experiencing the true happiness that I offer you in every Now moment. With Me, say "I can," and it is done. Laws are but boundaries. This does not mean that you do not follow the laws of your land because I tell you that the world is an illusion. You still believe that you are in a body and you will draw challenges and lessons to you if you still believe it so.

The laws that I speak of are the limits that you have placed in your mind, the attachments that you have made to what is unreal. You think that these things will bring you peace of mind but it is not so. What is so is what I offer to you. Believe in the words, *"I am under no laws but God's,"* and you believe in something that is more powerful than the world you have made in your insanity. Listen to Me and only to Me and you will learn of the Love that I have for you. Lay aside the barriers you have built against yourself. Open the doors and windows and allow the breeze of

My Love to enter to refresh and renew you. Be free today. Be free in your mind by allowing Me to share with you the truth. This is unblocking the channel to Me. Sit and wait in silence. Allow the space to be there. Do not fill the air with your thoughts and words. Do not place a limit on the silence. Simply allow it to be. That is My word for you today. Be.

∞∞∞

Journal Entry on Lesson 77

I am entitled to miracles.

I claim my right today to miracles. Miracles are a natural part of my life. The shift into the perception of the Holy Spirit is always there as my willingness to open my eyes to it occurs. Temptations can come quickly to judge and make assumptions. I am not peaceful when I am in that space. So instead I can practice trading grievances for the miracles that I deserve, that truly belong to me because of who I am. I do not have to live my life attached to guilt, fear or pain of the past. I can be free of all of that today by simply reminding myself that I am entitled to miracles.

The ego would make it an arrogant statement meaning that I above all others are entitled. In reality, we are all One, we are all therefore entitled to the gifts of the Father. Accepting the shift into Love from the place of unease is a welcome gift. Throughout the day I may become hung up on seeming little irritations or large ones but all are equally disturbing to my mind. Peace is a wondrous gift as I accept the miracle and appreciate the higher awareness. In silence today, I affirm my entitlement and listen for His Word. I do not have to do anything but merely listen to what He has to say. My answers are already known, it is for me to reveal them through my willingness.

It is in the practice today, the affirmation and the silence and even the vigilance of grievances and its suitable affirmation replacement where I will find peace. If I forget, or follow the thread of temptation, when I remember I will initiate the practice again. No guilt needed, only willingness to accept the miracle as my very own.

oooooo

Journal Entry on Lesson 78

Let miracles replace all grievances.

The figure is clouded. I can barely make out the person because of all the judgments, grievances and expectations. It seems that this person has let me down, disappointed me, and even betrayed me. The feelings of hurt and pain and even anger are present. But, the willingness is there to release the clouds that seem to weigh me down, depress me so to speak, whenever I behold this person in my mind. I know that the darkness that I feel is heavy and is covering the truth of who the person is. Holy Spirit, I am willing to see this person differently. A faint memory comes to mind, a time in which this person glowed in the truth for a moment. Their words were sincere; their actions loving.

Holy Spirit, Thank You for showing me a spark of light within them. As I allow the light to expand and grow within the image I hold, I sense an uplifting in my being. My mind is not as foggy; the clouds begin to clear. I see only the innate goodness and kindness that is really there. I know that I do not have to accept the behaviors of this brother for it is their behaviors that hide the truth even from him. There is so much more to see when I forgive, when I allow the Holy Spirit to show me the true perception of Love. This is also who I am. All the dark feelings that I hold is not where the truth lies. It lies much deeper than the mists that seem to protect it. It lies only in God. My willingness to forgive has brought me the light of Love that I now behold in my brother and myself. I can rejoice in this. I can also remember to practice this as often as I can. Thank You Holy Spirit for providing the means and Your sure guidance in my liberation from fear. All is well. I am at peace.

∞∞∞

Journal Entry on Lesson 79

Let me recognize the problem so it can be solved.

Entanglement after entanglement, the problems seem to ensue like a knotted up wad of yarn; difficult to find the beginning or the end and all the pieces in between just an entire mess. That is the way life can seem with all the problems. As in the previous lessons, grievances and judgments are what keeps me feeling separate from my brothers, God and so too myself. That is the problem that I am recognizing today; the separation from All That Is. It doesn't matter if it seems to be on the surface a disagreement with a friend, a fender bender with another, or some other confrontation or even replayed images of the past.

All these keep me from focusing on the truth. There is only Oneness. There is nothing that divides us. We are still together, still on the same page. Look at situations such as family squabbles or even divorce. Those that loved one another so dearly turn into bitter enemies because in their mind they had not fulfilled the function that was expected of them. The unity of Love seems to then be covered over by the division of vengeance and attack. Instead vigilance is needed. Love does heal all wounds. Forgiveness restores me to the place of peace. It is the key to my happiness. The answer is merely to remember Love in place of the squabbles. These squabbles only want to enforce that one is right and justified and that one reigns supreme over the other. Love sees us as equals, as mighty companions on the journey. Thank You Holy Spirit for the lessons that I have received in the past, of remembering that separation is only a tool of the ego to further attempt to divide and conquer the Son of God. But it is not so, and it cannot be done for Oneness remains whole and complete and unfettered by anything. Let me join with my brothers today and see the miracle that they are to me. Let me accept the gift of healing. It is for us all.

"Then try to suspend all judgment about what the problem is. If possible, close your eyes for a moment and ask what it is. You will be heard and you will be answered." The answer I was surprised to receive was, "Discontentment".

Discontentment is the problem. There is always a feeling of discontentment in the world no matter what you do and no matter how many goals you accomplish. The feeling is that if I were to get that job over there, then I would feel happier and have a happier life. If I were to move into that bigger home, then I would feel happier and have a happier life. If I were to move to a nicer climate, then I would feel better and have a happier life experience. How many times have we come up with these kinds of inspirations, pursued them and accomplished them, then later come to the realization that something still is missing? Something still doesn't quite feel right. It's not quite perfect yet. And then we begin the endless cycle again.

Light is the only solution to the problem. There is nothing in the world that will give you fulfillment and contentment like the experience of finding the Light of your Christ Self within yourself. Once we find it, we intuitively know and understand that this is the solution to every problem of fear, worry, anxiety, tension, etc. that we encounter in our lives. Once we know it is there, how healing it is and how good it feels to go there, we know that we can go there anytime we want and have each of our pains healed one at a time, spark by spark. This is where we want to remember to practice looking. The Gift of Contentment and the Solution is found within.

Journal Entry on Lesson 80

Let me recognize my problems have been solved.

Say to yourself today, "I recognize that I am out of conflict; free and at peace." This reassurance helps me to know that my problems have already been solved. It is simply up to me to peer through the weeds to see that it has. That is what the problem is, merely overgrown weeds. The weeds of dissention, discontent, and the like keep me focused on what is wrong in my life and who may have wronged me. It holds me in isolation so that I cannot see, just as a much neglected overgrown yard. The weeds are the judgments, and guilt and doubts that I have held about myself and others.

As I turn over a new leaf and clear away the debris, clarity is restored to my vision. I find that I no longer need all these weeds of judgment. I now can live cleanly and come from a fresh perspective and truly see my Oneness with everyone. My problems have all been solved because there is only one problem, my belief in separation. In the garden of God, there is peace and unity. I rest now beside the gorgeous blossoms of my brothers, listen to the birds sing of my glory, hear the trickle of joy in the gently flowing stream. Peace is restored in this place for it is the place of God. I have been answered and now at last I feel the breeze of freedom restoring me to new life. Thank You Holy Spirit for the means to release my grievances to the Light of Forgiveness. My heart is full of gratitude and open honesty and now I see that I am Home in You.

ooooo

Journal Entry on Lesson 81

Review Lessons 61-62

The Holy Spirit's work is never done until He has cleared your mind of all the distractions you have placed upon it to prevent yourself from seeing your own holiness. The Holy Spirit sees you as you truly are. You are the light of the world and nothing else is true. You are not the body that you think you are. The body is merely an illusion that the mind is projecting upon itself to block itself from the awareness of its reality as the light. The body and the world you seem to be in is the darkness that is blocking you from your awareness of the light.

However, there is a way to train your mind to let go of the illusions of the world that it is projecting upon itself so that you can see the light of yourself that is shining beyond. The white light and all of its radiance and holiness is hidden within your mind but truly there. Search and search and search again until your find it with the Holy Spirit's help. In reality, you need do nothing but just let go of everything the mind wants to hang onto and wait for the Holy Spirit to show you the reflection of your True Self. The white light will show up suddenly in your mind like a spotlight coming from the darkness on the darkest of nights. This is the light of the Christ, your Christ Self that you will begin to see and begin to know as yourself the instant you perceive it.

Open your mind and wait for the Holy Spirit to show this to you, ask Him to show this to you, the true light of your Christ Self. Wait quietly in expectation of this holy gift to be shown to you. It is truly there and you will know it when you see it. It is the beginning of your release from hell. Open your mind to hearing His Voice speak to you. The audible Voice is unambiguous as well. It takes great willingness to hear the Voice; but is well worth it. It too will be the beginning of your release from hell. When these experiences begin to happen, it is a joyful, joyful, joyful time indeed! Celebrate, celebrate, celebrate because the Christ, the Holy Son of God himself, who you really are, is beginning to awaken from his slumber. Hallelujah! hallelujah! hallelujah! Praise God! Amen.

∞∞∞

Journal Entry on Lesson 82

Review Lessons 63-64

I have a function God would have me fill. It is to extend forgiveness so that peace may reign in the mind of God's Son. It is my choice to fulfill this function. When I do my life flows very easily. When I am caught up in anger, guilt, fear or pain I have no sense of clarity. When I am in this space I may use busyness, addictive behaviors, withdrawal, and the like to cover the feelings or somehow bring comfort to the discomfort. I may find it scary to really feel the feelings as they emerge. It is safe to do so. The Holy Spirit is there with me every step of the way. As I place my commitment in Him, He will assist me to see things more clearly, to become an observer to my life experiences, and show me the unhealed places in my mind.

All of this will be mine with my willingness to open to a new perspective, a new experience in my life. I do not have to feel afraid to feel the feelings. They are just feelings; they do not define who I am. Others in this world do not define who I am. The inner critic does not define who I am. Only God has the true definition of who I am. I am His Son. I am to believe ONLY what He says to me about me and the world; if I listen to the other voices then I can become confused, depressed and in conflict.

Listening to His Voice is the only means of providing peace to my spirit. As I continue to work on forgiveness on every thing that occurs, I see this ever more strongly. Let go and let God.

Let go of my projections and judgments and let God reign supreme in my life. No one will ever fulfill the function that I have set for them because it is set with control and fear in mind. God has set my function and that is forgiveness. I will bring peace to my weary mind when I do so for it is the constant strain of judgment that wearies me so. It is time to allow the light of forgiveness to be strong and stable in my life. It is the lighthouse of faith, the way Home to God. And this will bring us all as One.

∞∞∞∞

Journal Entry on Lesson 83

Review Lessons 65-66

My Child,

I have given you a function, a role for you. It is to be happy. Very simple. Be happy. Be happy in My Love by recognizing the illusion that seems to surround you. Drop the veil and you will see the Light of My Love. This is where your happiness lies, not in the folds of the veil that hide the precious Light from your sight. The Light is yours because it is who you are. Do not forget this. When troubles come to mind and they do because you do not yet fully recognize your Oneness, these troubles can be used to set you free. You will see with My help that they are not the Truth. Some days it may seem as if they are heavy on your mind, overwhelming you, keeping you from going about your daily routine and your function.

In these times, be gentle with yourself, love yourself, nurture yourself and know that all that comes your way is perfect for you, perfect in helping you remember your happiness and your function. You are not your troubles. You are something much more beautiful in My Eyes. I have given you everything because you are everything to Me. Hear My Call to you to awaken from the dream. Lift back the dark covers and arise, spring to life. It is the dawning of a new day, a day in which you accept your birthright, your function, your happiness. It is a joyous day indeed. But yes what of the sadness and other feelings you may feel. Feel them and then let them be. They are not needed for the journey. I will show you this each time you bring them to Me. I will help you recognize true happiness. And it is not outside of you. It is found only with Me.

∞∞∞∞

Journal Entry on Lesson 84

Review Lessons 67-68

Affirmations of Love

I am as God created me.
I am holy and innocent.
My existence is to extend Love.
I remember that my Creator and I are one.
Forgiveness leads me to my happiness.
As I let go of grievances, serenity fills my being.
All I see is an illusion hiding the Light of Truth.
Wherever I go there is God.
All that I need is already given.
Patience brings me to a deeper level of love.
I am the Son He loves.
I am worthy and deserving of His Love always.
Nothing that I do can change Eternal Love.
I remember the truth of who I am.
As I remember, the light begins to dawn and the wings of freedom stretch outward.
My brothers and I are one.
I choose to learn from all that approaches me today.

My curriculum may be set, but I choose the lessons that I want to learn.
I am open and willing to learn now.
My mind is given to You, Holy Spirit.
My heart is open to Love.
I hear the song of peace as I listen and contemplate deeply.
I am never alone for You are with me.
I float along the river of peace and know that I am always being carried.
Thankfulness fills my heart with every passing moment.
When I am in gratitude, I am celebrating what is now.
Now is all there is.
I accept that I am whole and healed.
I extend love to all.
I embrace my Divine Light.
I allow my Light to shine onward to bring my brothers Home.
Where there is peace, there is joy.
My Father and I are one.
I join with my brothers in the recognition of our True Essence.

I let go of all beliefs that I have held that have not served me.
As I forgive, clarity is mine.

There is nothing outside of me that will ever bring me happiness.
My joy is God's joy.
My life is His.
I gladly step back and let Him lead the way.
I am always led to my Divine Nature.
I am always Home.
I am Love.

ꝏꝏꝏ

Journal Entry on Lesson 85

Review Lessons 69-70

If my mind is preoccupied with something that has disturbed my peace, then that is a grievance. If my mind is preoccupied with worrying about how someone else is living their life, then that is a grievance. If my mind is preoccupied with how to accomplish some future goal that I think will make me happy, then that is a grievance. Anything and everything in the world that I use to busy my mind with fear, in whatever form it may take, is a grievance. Grievances stem from darkness. Darkness stems from fear. Fear creates the illusion of darkness around us which presents itself as the world we see and think about. The world we see and think about is a metaphor for darkness. We don't realize it but the world we see and think about is blocking us from the experience and the awareness of the Light. The Light is the other world we are trying to reach.

The Light is quite literally there for you to see and observe and experience. The Light is your salvation. Your salvation depends on you because it is your choice whether or not to stop allowing your mind to be preoccupied with thoughts of fear about the world around you, or to let them go completely until you allow the Light to come and illuminate your mind. When you allow the Light to come and illuminate your mind, you are allowing your mind to be cleansed of the illusion in little increments. When the Light comes it is the miracle. And the miracle collapses time moving you along your path of returning Home more quickly.

When you choose the Light, time is collapsed for you because you no longer need the lessons that would have been presented to you during the time interval that would have been present had you not chosen to open up to the Light. Ask the Holy Spirit to help you with this process of finding the Light within yourself. It is very simple to access once you get the hang of it. It may seem difficult for awhile but really all it takes is a willingness to try, a willingness to sit down periodically throughout your day and to let go of everything you now behold and open your mind to something else, to another experience that the Holy Spirit will gladly give to you. Your little willingness is all it takes to call upon the power of Heaven to come and bless your eyes with the Holy Light of Christ that will be seen.

The blessing of the Light of Christ that gently kisses your mind is a holy encounter indeed because it is an encounter with the reflection of your True Self. It is an experience with seeing and feeling a glimpse of your true reality. This is true seeing, to be able to behold yourself in your mind as the Light and to see the beautiful Great Rays shine forth from the Light that is yourself. You will recognize that it is your One Self. You will recognize that this Light you behold is the reality of everyone, and all the dark illusions you thought before about anyone and everything around you in the world will be peacefully washed away in the joy of the Light that you behold within yourself. Dear Son of God, I love you and *you* love Me. And so it is, forever without end. Amen. Praise God.

What a beautiful prayer you co-created with Me today, My beautiful Son. Reflect on this today. Remember this. Remember to practice it, to behold your Christ Self. This is the vision that will wash all things away and bring the end of time. This is what you are after. This is what you seek, to find your joy in Him, Who is your Source and your Creator, to remember Him once again, to remember your love for Him and His Love for you. This is the only thing that is really worthwhile seeking; the memory of God within yourself.

∞∞∞∞

Journal Entry on Lesson 86

Review Lessons 71-72

There is only one plan to follow and that is His plan. His plan may not be popular in the world, or well received by others. It may seem that I create enemies or lose others in my life. The time of people-pleasing comes to an end as I follow Him. People-pleasing is about creating my happiness on what is outside of me. It does not come from within. It is sacrificing who I really am to benefit somehow in the world. Such "benefits" could be: avoiding conflict with another person, maintaining acceptance and approval by others, or appearing to others as a generous and giving person. What if God has another path for me? He does. It is a path of peace.

When I am in alignment with what He wants and not what the world expects of me, then I am free. He only wants for my happiness and my freedom from my own self-attack. I do not have to sacrifice myself to please Him. His Love is already assured and there for me. If I place my value in the world then I will always be disappointed in so many ways.

When I go to make a decision without Him, there will always be someone in the world who will disagree with my decision and I will always have a sense of unrest and unhappiness. It does not matter what the decision is, some will agree, some will disagree. It is for me then to make all my decisions with the Holy Spirit for as I do I can be confident and secure in knowing that His decisions benefit all. It may not seem that way on the surface as once again others may agree or disagree. But as I place my trust in Him, I will know without a doubt that I am to follow His plan.

Others may not be asked to do what I am being asked to do for it is not His plan for them. I can be confident in knowing that only His plan for my salvation will work. Yes, together we have a collective plan of salvation, the light of forgiveness. However, I do have my special function here in the world that only I can fulfill. My specialized curriculum from the Holy Spirit will lead me through lessons that will eventually assist me to returning Home in my mind. If I hold grievances, I will not move forward quickly. I will seem bogged down in every way. Grievances will block His guidance from me and I will not see the way open before me. As I place all my ideas and opinions and judgments about what *should* occur outside of the circle, I can truly begin to see the beauty of what *is* there for me. The way before me will be clear, peaceful and obstacle-free. All that occurs will seem to fit perfectly in place. It will be smooth and easy.

Holy Spirit, You alone know what is best for me right now. I cannot make decisions on my own, for when I have it has only brought upset to my soul. I now place all my trust in You. I am dedicated to listening to Your Voice to tell me where I am to go, what I am to do and what I am to say and to whom. You will surely direct my footsteps so that all that I may do will be truly helpful to the Sonship. I am blessed with confidence and clarity in Your Word for me. Whatever seems to be going on outside I will give to You in exchange for Your peace. Forgiveness shall be my tool for awakening and all grievances will be laid aside. I do not have to sacrifice myself to come to You. I merely surrender my will and let Your will now be mine. Amen.

∞∞∞

Journal Entry on Lesson 87

Review Lessons 73-74

Today's Message is lovingly provided by our dear friend, Rev. Christine Anderson, O.M.C. Her website: www.revhappywoman.org.

You stand with Me in the Light. Feel My hand on your shoulder directing you, guiding you. You are walking through the Mind with Me. The Mind that we share with God is full of light. And you are light. You are God's delight. And as you walk about in the Mind with Me right next to you, if you should see a place of cloudiness or darkness, just remember that I can help you to walk through the cloud, through the darkness. Keep your hand in Mine, it is perfectly innocent that you would see these places. They cannot harm you. They are only illusions. It is good that you are seeing them with Me at your side for I will never judge them. I will help you to dispel the illusion which may show up as uncertainty or anxiousness or discouragement. You may not be sure of your next step. Just be in this step you are in now, just be with that.

And in that place, right where you are now, I will help you. You are mistaken by believing you could ever be separate from Love. A self-hypnotic trance so to speak. I will help you to come out of that trance state. It's only a state of mind. The clouds and darkness are nothing, just the smoke and mirrors of the ego. As you stand here in the Light with Me, standing in the Truth, and willing with me that there be light, the illusions will fall away. Look not to a seeming outer world to change for there is no "outer world". The change is in your mind. This is the place where the change or the shift will happen. I must stress this thought to you, stay in the Mind with Me. All that you see is in the Mind. Form is Mind-projection. If there is any displeasure or anxieties regarding what your perceptions are bringing to you, take those perceptions to Me for re-interpretation. And together in the Light of God we will witness their transformation. We will experience together only Light and only Love. Thank you for walking with Me and allowing Me to help you. Every misperception that you bring to Me is a gift. I need you as much as you need Me. Thank you for your willingness to awaken to the Light.

∞∞∞∞

Journal Entry on Lesson 88

Review Lessons 75-76

The music of my soul encircles the Light. Freely it dances under the Love of God. There is nothing that I need. All bonds are laid aside. All self-imposed chains fall away. What more could I want but my own freedom; freedom from the boundaries and rules of the world. Stepping in to the Light I see what is true, what is real. Seeing the Light in another is seeing the Light within me. It is this that I would behold today.

When I think otherwise, when my decisions seem to be those with the ego, the heaviness that I feel is because of my belief in what the ego tells me. As I listen to Holy Spirit, I lighten up, I feel weightless. It is as if I am floating gently away on a cloud. No cares, no worries; only in the bliss of God's Love. I can do this. I can speak intimately with the Holy Spirit about the heaviness that I feel, the worries and concerns laid upon my mind.

As I share with Him deeply I can feel the tension begin to melt away as I join with Him in holy silence. In the silence I will hear His Voice; I will feel His Love. The more that I practice this; the more that I want to have it present in my life. I can choose again, I do not have to live the way I had before. Through my open, honest communication with Holy Spirit I am healed. As I share with Him the pain dissipates. I have now recognized that all that I made real is truly unreal. What is real now comes to me in a glorious Light, the gift of God, the reflection of my Christ Self. Is this not what I want? Yes and yes again. And so gladly I come to You Holy Spirit to the Sanctuary of Peace within. It is where I want to stay, to rest, to be.

ᘛᘚᘛᘚᘛᘚ

Journal Entry on Lesson 89

Review Lessons 77-78

My miracle today is turning around and seeing the miracle that is in front of me. In the past, I had tightly clung onto the doorknob of the door that was closing behind me, while not being aware of the golden door of opportunity that lay open before me. Fear kept me from walking through the threshold in those times. I do not have to be afraid to step forward and away from my grievances and judgments that I hold about myself and others. The Great Rays of Light shine forth from the miracle. I step forward leaving my cloak of fear and pain behind. I am held in such Love, such Peace, and such Joy as I embark upon another change of mind. How can I move but forward into the everlasting arms of my Father? Do the fear, judgments, criticisms and pain really mean that much more to me? Do I really prefer to be right in every situation instead of accepting God's happiness for me?

When I can let go, I can experience so much more of the harvest of joy that is abundantly waiting for me. This can be in situations with jobs, family, friends, dreams and goals. I can release *my* outcomes, *my* expectations, *my* control of everything. No agendas, only Love. When others irritate me with seeming lack of truth or the face of facades, I can look within and ask the Holy Spirit what He would show me in these situations: My fear of not coming to the truth myself; My fear of honesty and intimacy with Him. I no longer have to hide from my Father for He only loves me.

There is no punishment for I have done nothing wrong. It is in my mind that I believed that I have sinned against Him. I was mistaken. I offer those mistakes to Him. He blesses and caresses me in Divine Embrace. Forgiveness, forgiveness and more forgiveness is the answer to accepting my happiness. Miracles are there, ripe for the picking. Their sweet nectar of joy quenches me of all my former beliefs. The true knowledge is revealed. I have never left the garden. I am Home and always will be.

oo◦ooo

Journal Entry on Lesson 90

Review Lessons 79-80

The ego plays its games over and over again until you don't get it. You never will be able to solve the ego's problems because the ego thought system in the split mind is designed to never be resolved. It is designed to sustain itself in conflict and chaos as long as it can. Conflict and chaos is what sustains the ego thought system. It is what appears to give it life but it cannot be life because it is a thought that was made. We are reminded time and time again to be mindful of the ego's temptations that are presented to you in life. The ego is always dangling a carrot before you in one way or another.

It's easy to be lured into the temptation of reaching for the carrot but the carrot is designed to never be grasped. It is important to have faith in this concept, to trust, to understand that this is so and to resist the temptation to leave your peace in exchange for reaching for the carrot that can never be found. The ego is designed to give you this resistance, this resistance to remaining in a state of peace. It is designed to lure you, your mind, your being, away from a state of peaceful being. It's what keeps the ego going.

Forgiveness is what heals; peace is the result. If you want to feel peaceful and happy all of the time then you must continue to practice forgiveness within your mind. Forgiveness is letting go of the temptation to being lured away from a place of just being happy, just being peaceful. Anytime you are feeling just happy and peaceful and a thought comes to mind that raises a problem or a question or a feeling of uncertainty, this is the ego bringing in a disturbance to your peace and happy being. This is the moment that you want to remember to ask the Holy Spirit to help you to forgive these disturbing thoughts and to let them go. It is important to practice this all the time from moment to moment. The ego is relentless in its desire to keep the Son of God in hell, to keep his mind caught up in dreams of sickness, pain and death.

This is not what your Father wills for you nor is it your will for yourself. You have found yourself caught up in a dream world in an illusion that seems to exist and seems to keep you separated from the awareness of your oneness with your creator and yourself. It's not really happening but to you right now it seems that it is and you feel like you are trapped in the dream with no way to get out. It feels like it is difficult to awaken from the dream and perhaps even impossible at times. It feels like it takes a long time to awaken. All of these deceptions are deceptions of the ego to keep the solution to the problem, the answer hidden from your awareness.

The memory of God has been placed inside of your mind. It has never left you and goes with you wherever you go. It is the miracle that you are seeking to find. You will know when you begun to find the miracle within yourself, the path to the memory of God when you have begun to see the sparks and the flashes of white light. That is the answer to the problem. That is the solution to every problem that you will ever encounter while you awaken from your dream of illusions. Everything you see and experience is an illusion with the exception of the light within your mind.

The light itself is an illusion of perception but it is true perception, a gift that God has given to you to help you remember your True Self, to help you begin to remember Who you really are and where you really came from. The Light will wash and cleanse your mind of all illusions as you continue to practice opening up and allowing It in to your awareness. The perception of the Light is the perception of True Forgiveness. It is the tool that the Holy Spirit uses with you to help you forgive illusions and replace them with the Light that will guide you Home. The light is a transition; it is a bridge to cross from one world to another. As you cross into the world of Light you will eventually experience another transition which is the transition back into your formlessness with the Creator Who is One with you right now in Reality. Your hopelessness has not gone unresolved. The answer has been given to you and is found and can be found with the Holy Spirit's help as the Light within your mind. It is here where you will begin to discover that you too are the Way, the Light and the Truth.

∞∞∞

Journal Entry on Lesson 91

Miracles are seen in light.

It is darkness when I feel the tension and anxiety in my chest and my mind is swirling with numerous thoughts that seem to be relentless. This seems so very real when it occurs, but it is not my reality. Tossing and turning at night with no sense of rest disrupts me but it does not disrupt Who I really am.

When these bodily and mental sensations are present it seems that they are truly transpiring and that I am experiencing pain and doubt, worry and concern, upset after upset. In this lesson, I am reminded that miracles are seen in light but not through which I believe they can be seen. These eyes within my body only see the illusion of darkness that seems to envelope me. I ask for a miracle. I ask for the light to dawn within my mind to bring me to the truth.

In these times of seeming weakness, I can look to the light as best as I can, allowing it to reveal the true power that lies in God, which lies within me. It may seem burdensome with what I am experiencing, be it loss, abandonment, anger, hurt, sadness, depression, but it can be revealed to me. As I am ready, I can turn my attention to the Holy Spirit just as I have done many times before. I know through my practice that all I need do is cast loose all of these thoughts to Him and my sanity is restored. I must be in a state of readiness, ready to give and ready to receive.

Holy Spirit, I surrender all the heavy thoughts that root me in the world of fear and today accept the strength of God, the power of God, the unlimited love of God, the certainty of the Father, the reality of Who I am, and the Light of truth. This is what leads me Home to You, not what I have made, not what I have replaced You with. I have been addicted to mere substitutes for Your Love. I have placed fear as my idol. But, nothing can take Your place in my life. Nothing in this world will ever bring me the solace and contentment that I have been rummaging for.

Once I realize this, I can forgive myself, forgive my brother and forgive You. I am the one that has placed these boundaries upon myself, only me. This does not need to be a declaration of guilt with these words but instead a declaration of my freedom. My spiritual eyes are open. I am grateful to You, Holy Spirit for taking this sojourn with me, using my experiences to aid my memory and to learn about the Love that is truly not of this world. I am humbled, yet I am blessed and will always be so. Amen.

∞∞∞

Journal Entry on Lesson 92

Miracles are seen in light and light and strength are one.

Dear Holy Spirit,
This morning I'm feeling afraid to listen to You. I'm feeling afraid to being open to listening to and receiving Your messages.

Dear Ones,

How wonderful it is to be hearing from you once again. You are such a blessed soul. Your heart fears no other but yourself.

What do you mean by that?

You are afraid to listen to your One Self. You are afraid to listen to your One Self because it means no more compromises. Only the ego would have you make compromises. In Reality, there are no compromises because you are an unlimited One Self as the Son of God. Everything has been given to you by your Creator, all power in Heaven and on earth.

You are not experiencing this now because you believe you are a body and a mind within that body. These are limits that you have placed upon yourself with the One Mind that God has given to you. You can choose to practice remembering the One Mind that you really are. The practice is in doing and being and practicing. It's the practical application of turning your mind inward toward the Real Mind of God that lies hidden within yourself and finding it and calling it forth to your awareness.

In doing this and practicing this, you are becoming a miracle worker, the same as I did in your past. Remember the past really does not exist but for now we will work within the parameters of the illusion because you believe in it. However, we are using it to transform your mind to the place that healing occurs. The illusion will dissolve before the light in little increments. You already know this. Keep doing it. Each time you call forth the light within your mind to heal the darkness, the darkness is washed away in little increments.

The accumulative long term effect is the dissolution of the illusion and the awakening of the mind of God's Son, who you really are. Go forth and be among the teachers of teachers and be a teacher yourself. The time of hiding for you is over now; call upon the strength within yourself and I will be there with you holding your hand as the light to help you along the way. This is your chosen journey. This is your choice; the one that you have called to yourself. Heal the fear with the Light within your mind and remember your Oneness with Me. Together we are joining in the great crusade of awakening the Mind of God's Son. This is a time of celebration for the Christ within yourself has begun to arise indeed. Your resurrection is beginning to come at last.

It is scary for me to hear these words. It is scary for me to think of walking a new walk for You, for I feel blind and blinded by the fear.

How delightful to be honest with yourself in this way. Your fantasies will need to be completely relinquished from now on. Call forth the light each time you feel yourself wandering off into the ego's fantasies and let them be healed by the light. Ask the Holy Spirit to bless you with more willingness to practice your mind training as you go about your day. Be willing to let go of everything with your mind more and more. Ask for help more and more and the help will be given to you. Do not rely on your strength alone. It is meaningless but call upon the strength of God within yourself to do it for you.

You are beginning to recognize how this works now. Let Him do everything for you. Let Him lead the way. You just need to remember to keep asking for the direction and the help and to be vigilant for His responses.

Open your eyes and see. Open your eyes and see. Open your eyes and see and behold the world you walk within. You hear the cries of the split minds around you. You see the cries of the split minds around you when you look and see with Me. Practice now this more. Look and see with Me and I will advise you on how to respond to those situations as they present themselves to you.

They are calling to you, would you hear them and answer their call? Would you join with me in responding to their perceived needs?

How holy are you who is the Son of God, the Christ Himself. God the Father has blessed us all, each and everyone of us. Look upon your brothers with the light of love within your mind and remember this and only this that shines within them always, eternally, forever and forever. Its reality will become yours. God has blessed and blessed and blessed again. Our task now is to help you to remember how to bless and bless and bless again as our Father does unto you and to all of His Children, forever. Amen.

J, I'm scared this feels like a mouthful.

It's ok. Don't let it rattle your cage. You can come out (chuckle). We'll be taking tiny steps. Just be with Me. It'll be okay. And it's going to be a lot of fun. You are going to have so much fun as you continue to surrender to Me. I love you my brother. You are so sweet and precious. I am absolutely thrilled with you as I am with each of my brothers. I love you all. And I cannot wait to help you all come Home. I am so glad that you are joining with Me to help Me in this in this great crusade of Awakening for us all. I love you Dear One. I love you Dear One. I love you Dear One. Let that echo in your mind. Soak with that. Be with that. Remember it. Believe in Me and believe in Yourself. You are a holy Son of God. How precious are Thee and We. Yea! Have a happy day!

∞∞∞∞

Journal Entry on Lesson 93

Light and joy and peace abide in me.

Holy Spirit, Last night while I was lying in bed with my eyes closed and being open to the light, I saw a flash of white light with the number 21 in the middle. Although I didn't understand what the 21 meant right away, I felt grateful for the example of what is meant by *"Miracles are seen in light, and light and strength are one."* The experience has given me the strength to continue to share what I am experiencing with regard to the light even though I feel afraid to share at times.

Early this morning when I woke up I was feeling a lot of fear about some of the things that came out in yesterday's message. In particular, I felt especially fearful about the word resurrection being used. Something felt out of place but I couldn't quite put my finger on it. I decided to get up and spend some time with the course to see if anything would come up to help me move to a place of feeling more peace.

I opened up the Manual for Teachers and turned to Section 21, titled, "What Is the Role of Words in Healing?" I hadn't read this section before so I was curious to see what it might have to say to me. By the time I finished reading the section I realized that You were speaking to me very specifically about what was going on with me and the message that came out in yesterday's Lesson. I felt grateful and reassured again that You were helping me along the way through this seeming difficult journey of awakening. It is scary for me to share some of the things that I am experiencing, some of the things that I am seeing and hearing. I am grateful to be reassured in this manner. It helps to give me strength and courage to keep moving forward with You to share the things that You would have me share for myself and for the others who are on this journey with me.

The standards of the world are so contrary to the things that are being taught in the Course and some of the experiences that I am having can be quite unnerving for me to share at times. It feels difficult to embrace the new and to let go of the old. I appreciate You helping me to understand that this is all for the process of healing and awakening. Although, as You said in the section that sometimes the words You share with us is to confront the teacher with a situation that appears to be very embarrassing to him. I appreciate the reminder that these are judgments that have no value and that it is ok for me to let them go and to trust the process. I appreciate the reminder to *"Judge not the words that come to me, but to offer them in confidence. They are far wiser than my own."*

Thank You for the vision of the nail and the storm while I reflected on this with You for You helped me to see ways that the ego is attempting to continue to crucify me with words and thoughts. I appreciate the reminder to forgive these and to continue to trust the words that You offer to me. I will continue to do the best that I can to listen to the words You offer me and to give them as I receive them and to let go of the fearful judgments I make about them as they come through. I will practice as best I can as You suggest in the section, *"He does not control the direction of his speaking. He listens and hears and speaks."* I can see now that I really do not know what is going on, I do not understand the big picture. I can see as You say, many of my reactions, *"Come from a shabby self-perception."* I can see, *"A major hindrance in this aspect of my learning is the Teacher of God's fear about the validity of what he hears. And what I hear may indeed be quite startling."* This is definitely what I often experience. I see things in the light and I hear messages that come through and I am really only afraid of what others will think about me when I share them. Oh Lord, what will they think of me now?

These things often confront me with situations that appear to be embarrassing, however, I see that they are to help me, and with that new perception, I feel grateful and a little more relieved for it is the healing that I truly want. The peace of mind and the awakening, that is my goal, that is all of our goal. I appreciate Your help in the training You have been giving to me to, *"Gradually learn how to let my words be chosen for me by ceasing to decide for myself what I will say."* I will continue to practice stepping back and letting Him/You lead the way.

Thank You Holy Spirit for Your help and thank You J. I truly love You and I love everyone else in this world with me. I appreciate how we are all working together to help us all go Home, help us all awaken to our Reality to the awareness of the Christ that lights the soul within us. Amen.

∞∞∞

Journal Entry on Lesson 94

I am as God created me.

"I am as God created me."

This is the truth of Who I am. There may be times though that the truth is not felt within my being. The experiences that I may have may not seem very holy or love-filled. But the good news is that I can choose another way. I choose that different way, the way of God, as I am ready. When I am really ready to set aside all the anxieties and outside circumstances causing my lack of peace, I will take the time to come to the Holy Spirit. I can use the affirmation of today, *"I am as God created me. I am His Son eternally."* to bring me to that place, the inner sanctuary in which I gladly join with Him. In this space of silence, as my mind begins to focus and all other thoughts are gently cast aside, the pregnant pause is there.

My experience may be different each time I enter into the sanctuary and it is always absolutely perfect for me at the time. All experiences bring me closer to the Source. The experience is indescribable. To describe it casts upon limits unto God, and God is unlimited. How can I define His magnificence, His glory, His Light that comes into my awareness bringing with it the Voice of Truth, the message of my innocence? I cannot. And so I just wait and listen and know that all is perfect. I will not fail because I have come with willingness and the desire placed upon my heart. I am open to receive and so I shall. Each time that I enter into this space, I feel the blessing, I feel the Oneness.

My personal experiences have been different over the years, at times I have experienced a flash of light in various colors at various times; other times I have experienced a golden arc of light that fills just about the entire internal field of vision; other times a crystal light of sorts that is expansive way beyond my mind and that is a little hard to explain; at times I have heard ancient lilting melodies carrying me Home; at times revelation and true communion with God; at times a complete feeling of peace and well-being coupled with utter joy; still other times a knowing or a vision or dream has brought me the exact message that I needed including through others; and at times my mind has wandered and wandered and experienced just the need to focus on an affirmation such as today's.

All is perfect in the experiences that I have. I do not regularly go into details about my experiences for in a sense I feel that I am trying to place judgment and form on something that just is simply formless and nonjudgmental. God' Love for me is unconditional. It is ever present. It cannot be denied. I deny my true Self when I believe in the falsities the ego has told me. These core beliefs of unworthiness and unloveability are now challenged by the awakening knowledge. How can I continue to believe in the ego's lies? I cannot. As I move along my journey, the more I learn, the less that I want to follow the ego, the more that I want peace ever present in my life. Today, I will use "*I am as God created me.*" as my personal mantra, my focal point in remembering my Home in which I have never left.

It is quite possible to see your holy Self today. As you practice sitting still and being quiet with your mind today remember that you are actually trying to have an experience of seeing your holy

Self as the Son of God. As you wait expectantly in the silence to see Yourself, It will be revealed to you as the white light that suddenly comes forth from the darkness in your mind's eye and illuminates your mind and body with peace. You will feel the blazing light heal your body and this is the place where you will hear the Voice of God actually begin to speak to you. The audible Voice is so clear in your mind you will be quite pleasantly surprised upon having the experience. In this moment, the truth about your real Self is suddenly being revealed to you in a holy instant. You will cherish this moment forever for it is the beginning of your release from hell that you have surrounded yourself with in the world that you seem to be experiencing now. The light of truth is hidden very carefully within your mind.

To the beginner, it may even be quite difficult to believe that it is even possible to experience another Self, another Reality. This is why we practice the Lessons as much as we can; to break through this ego defense and unwillingness to perceive the Light of Christ within ourselves. We need do nothing but practice being still and waiting expectantly to see our holy Selves be revealed to us with the help of the Holy Spirit. Ask the Holy Spirit within your mind to show it to you, to bring this experience to you. He is the designated Helper to help you bridge the gap between the world you made and the world God made. He is your Mediator, He is your Helper, He is your Guide. Be willing to meet Him part way, and then allow Him, and I emphasize, and allow Him, to take you the rest of the way. He will do the work for you. Once you have the experience, you will be surprised at how easy it is to let Him do the work for you. Be still with a quiet mind and wait expectantly for Him to reveal the beautiful Light of Christ within you. In that moment you will recognize that you are seeing your True Self. God has blessed His holy Son who reigns with Him forever united with His Creator in Heaven. Amen.

oooooo

Journal Entry on Lesson 95

I am one Self, united with my Creator.

Lately I have heard from others in regards to relationships such as friends, family, co-workers, lovers and spouses. There seems to be dissension and unease and upset. If I follow the ego's voice, I will believe that I am right and the other person is wrong. It is clear that unhappiness reigns when I follow the ego. This happens ever so subtly sometimes when I am not paying attention and holding watch guard over my mind. The ego slips in and then my peace vanishes. I want to hold on to grudges and judgments and be right vs... happy. When I can step back from the relationship in whatever form it comes, and find the place of love and for me it starts with compassion. I begin to open to seeing the other person not as an adversary but as another along the path and thus my teacher.

In this person, I may begin to remember stories of their life that they have shared, little nuances that point me to seeing where their core beliefs are held. And lo and behold, they mirror my very own core beliefs be it in unworthiness, abandonment or the like. Through this compassion I can see my brother in relationship in a whole new light....ah...the light. The unity that we share is shining brightly. We are not our behaviors. We are then simply here together, each learning what it is we are here to learn and awakening to the truth. I think I believe that there is separation and I even think I believe that I see it but in the realm of the Divine the oneness is all there is. My compassion turns to love and that is a truly wonderful place to be. It is because of a miracle, a shift in perception through my offer of forgiveness to the Holy Spirit. Today, I will be determined to sit quietly and allow Him to teach me all that I need to learn to be happy.

All the relationship busyness and conflict just keeps me distracted from seeing my Oneness with all creation and unaccepting of my limitless in power and in peace. When I let go of the attachment to the outcomes of what *I* want in the relationships and simply be loving, Heaven smiles upon me for I have remembered and acknowledged the Source from which I came. And so in these relationships I say to all my brothers, "*You are one Self with me, united with our Creator in this Self. I honor you because of What I am, and What He is, Who loves us both as One.*" The defenses are down and the love flows forth in the steady river of peace.

∞∞∞∞

Journal Entry on Lesson 96

Salvation comes from my one Self.

I can only see my one Self from the Home of Light which is in my mind. As I sit in contemplation reaching past the clouds of doubt, the eternal light shines in its strength. Whatever has gone before this moment in time does not seem to matter; only the brilliance of my soul matters. When I can come to this haven of happiness, I am using the power of my mind which was given to me in my creation. I am strong, all sense of weakness disappears, any physical malady that may be there (including my seeming hay fever) is gone as I rest in Him and hear His Thoughts of assurance and hope. I am saved each time I remember my Oneness in Him and my brothers. I certainly see the futility of conflicts with others, the simplicity of salvation in a loving embrace, the abundance that peace brings when I join with the Holy Spirit in my mind. All that I have craved or desired before is gone.

I had attempted to replace my Father and how can I replace perfection. That is what I saw today in my meditative experience, the perfection of All That Is. Everything leads me to remembering the extension that I am. I bless every opportunity, the love and the calls for love. I answer today with Love. I align my thoughts with

God and know that I am blessed and blessing, loved and loving, at peace and peace-giving, joyful and extending the joy of the Lord always and forever. Amen.

ΟΟΟΟΟ

Journal Entry on Lesson 97

I am spirit.

Let us gladly offer our little hindrances to practice today's hourly lesson up to the Holy Spirit for forgiveness. May we have an attitude of gratitude for being blessed with an opportunity to practice the Workbook Lessons with the Holy Spirit in our minds. We have seemingly been caught up in the prison of time and misery with no escape for ages. This is not really happening and yet we believe this is happening to us now.

The Holy Spirit, the spirit of peace within your mind is happy to join with you to work with you in helping you to awaken to the experience of the reality that really surrounds you right now in Heaven. The key to allowing this shift of the awareness of Heaven to come into your mind is to sit quietly as an observer with an open mind and to wait for the shift automatically to happen. You will feel the mind shift rise up from within yourself and automatically shift your awareness from this world to the awareness of the reality of another world. You will feel the light rising within yourself bringing with it joy and peace and an understanding of how simple this is. It is here where the Voice of the Holy Spirit will begin to speak to you very clearly. He will tell you how holy you are as the Son of God.

His Voice will speak to you of the gifts of Heaven that lie waiting for you in the borderland where the bridge is crossed from the unreal to the real. A smile will come to your face and a gladdening within your heart upon hearing His Voice speak to you in the silence. Practice listening to the silence within your mind today and from the silence the Voice of God will speak to you from the wellspring of the Source of life Itself. It is here that you will hear the loving words of your Father speak to you bringing with it a sense of peace and calm and a gladness that will fill your heart for the rest of your day. God, the Father has blessed us all and we return those blessings back to Him by offering our little hindrances gladly back to Him in thanks and gratitude and appreciation for His gifts to us. The peace of God reigns within us. Would we allow it to come forth into our awareness today? Glad tidings of peace and joy and happiness to us all. Thy Will is done. Would you have it be so today?

∞∞∞∞

Journal Entry on Lesson 98

I will accept my part in God's plan for salvation.

In taking a few days in retreat from the outside world living simply, it is the same as I sit in silent contemplation. Connecting with the Creator is simple living. It does not have to be grandiose, but just an allowing of quiet to enter into my mind. Of course I really do not have to go anywhere special to do just his as it is completed solely in my mind. In my mind is where all the rest and relaxation occurs, be it in a cabin in the woods or in the middle of a project in the office. Sinking past all the illusions of the world is where I find the truth and where I find my True Home.

Today, I am asked to accept my part in God's plan for salvation. What am I accepting except but peace? How do I perform my part? By my forgiveness of all that I think I see, all the past that I have believed in, all the worries of the future, all these I let go and are given to the Holy Spirit. This time that I dedicate to Him is for me. It is for my awakening, my peace of mind. The silence, the serenity that comes with devoting just the 5 minutes to Him is rewarding in so many ways. It helps me to step back in each time period and see that what I have been experiencing here in the world is not the truth. They are just stories, a play, a performance for the ego's amusement.

Each meditation I close the curtain on the ego's matinee and see backstage to the props and false scenery. The light comes up and shines all into my awareness. I have no attachments to what I see as this occurs for I see it all as it is, an illusion. I may not always feel this way as I go about my day with the daily stresses and challenges, however, when I can accept these precious moments more and more, these moments of truth, the stresses and challenges do not seem to hold this importance any longer I can begin to see the charade.

I am grateful that You, Holy Spirit, are with me, guiding me all the way. You show me the reality of truth and the falsity of the world. That is Your job and You do it well. I will continue to place my hand in trust to You for I know You lead me safely Home. Today, I accept my part in God's plan for salvation.

Complete forgiveness is surrendering to everything. Imagine what it would be like to go through a day and completely surrender yourself to whatever happens from moment to moment? To be completely present from moment to moment and holding into your awareness the presence of the Christ within your mind? Bringing that forth through the complete surrender and forgiveness of everything you think you want to see or do within the dream? How about trying a day of complete surrender to the Holy Spirit?

Try spending a day of having your attention towards the Holy Spirit in your mind as if He were right there with you looking with you, seeing with you, feeling with you, hearing with you and paying attention to what He would have you see, hear and do from moment to moment. Completely surrender to Him and let

Him guide your hands, eyes, body, and your thoughts today. Let Him show you what He would have you see, be, and do. Let Him make use of time for you. He knows how to do it well. He knows the best way. He knows the most efficient way to use time to help you awaken to your True Self, to help you awaken to the reality of the awareness of Love's presence that surrounds you right now.

Watch and see how He manages your time today. See the flow and be in the flow with Him. You will notice that He gives you the time for everything you need to do with ease. He will help you to do the things that are important to your awakening such as finding the time to do the hourly lessons.

It is here where you will begin the experience the awareness of Love's presence coming into your mind with the Light as you allow the Light to be raised up into your awareness. You will see it, you will hear it and you will feel it. The songs of Heaven are joyful ones indeed. The melodies of Home are a treat in contrast to the noises of the world you hear. Put forth your effort today in allowing all of this and more to be raised up into your awareness today.

Remember to join thanks and praise, appreciation and gratitude to Him Who helps you accomplish these goals today. Joy and blessings and good tidings to you today! Do not be afraid that you cannot accomplish this with Him today. Turn this fear over to trust, surrender to Him every fearful thought you have today and let Him take care of your day for you. He has a wonderful lesson plan for you for He is a wonderful Teacher and Friend indeed. Remember to trust and surrender and to forgive today. Be at peace, walk in peace, walk in trust, walk in complete trust, walk in complete surrender to peace today. Let every step you make symbolize your choice of stepping into peace in that moment. You may find it helpful to quietly say to yourself, "I am at peace," as you mindfully make every step today. Thank You Father for Your Love for us. Thank You for sending Him Who knows the way to help us. Thank You Father for Your Answer. Thank You Father for Your Holy Spirit. We love You and we love Him Who is One with us all. Amen.

∞∞∞∞

Journal Entry on Lesson 99

Salvation is my only function here.

Whenever I am sitting in my feelings, those pained emotions that are the seeming results of situations in my life, be it sadness, anger, upset, worry, concern, etc., I can choose another way. However, the prospect of another way may seem far-fetched or hard to reach in those moments as I am overwhelmed with emotion. I have found that it is easier to acknowledge the feelings rather than cover them or deny them. The ego, who reads the Course along with me, knows how to use it against me. Typically, it starts its opinions with the word "should" as in "I should be more spiritual than this," or "I should not feel this way," and on it goes. This is not allowing me to be in the present moment. In the present moment is where I will begin to heal. In the present moment I can acknowledge that yes, right now, I am not feeling peaceful or spiritual, instead I am feeling _____.

This feeling does not define who I am; it is merely a fearful thought. As I begin to recognize and become aware that I do not wish to continue the thoughts or experience the unpleasant feelings, this is where I am ready to invite the Holy Spirit into the moment. He assists me when I invite Him to do so. I am where I need to be. He does not rush me but instead works with me where I am. At this point, I unload all the thoughts and resulting feelings to Him, all the dark secrets and privately held thoughts. It brings a sense of release as I allow the words to flow whether it is in meditation or through the process of journaling.

It is the process of gently laying aside and offering to Him all that is not of peace. After I do this and once complete, my mind becomes ready to an experience of His peace. The stage is set with my willingness. I wait for the miracle. He gifts me with the beauty and radiance of His light, His words of wisdom or visions of serenity. I receive the comfort and understanding that I so desired when I experienced the pain. This is the process of forgiveness, this is my salvation. It brings me to the world of my Divine nature, the purity of Who I am.

Holy Spirit,

Thank You for the clarity that I receive whenever I turn to You. I am willing to lay fear aside and know myself as Love. Today, I see my completion in God, the unity that I share with Him and all my brothers, and the peace that surrounds my being. It is now that I can rest in the truth. I allow the light within me to shine ever brightly, guiding me to my rightful place in Heaven. I am only Love as God is only Love. Amen.

My Child,

Remember well these Lessons that are so healing for your mind. Practice them with diligence and fortitude. You are the Son I love so dearly. I have given you all power. Use your power to make your choice for peace, love and joy. Make your choice for Me. Let go of the darkness and allow your mind to be illuminated with the Light of Truth. It is Who You are, and that has never changed. Be One with Me always. Step into faith and all will be revealed. There is no problem that cannot be solved without the Answer I have given you. Trust in the Holy Spirit, He is your Teacher, your Guide and your Friend. Listen to Him well. He will never lead you astray. I love You eternally and hold that thought within your heart. Amen.

ΟΟΟΟΟΟ

Journal Entry on Lesson 100

My part is essential to God's plan for salvation.

Do not think that you are but a small player. You are vital to the plan. It is My will that you be happy. See now the image of the tomb at Eastertide. This is where you are to place all your wild beliefs about yourself, the upsets, the traumas, the judgments of self and others, all of it gets placed within the tomb. It is sealed and gone forever. What rises from within is the brilliant flash of Light and what was once a coffin sealed in doom has now become resurrected in the light. You are the butterfly emerging from the cocoon of darkness that has shrouded you for so long. See this now. Believe in this. You can be happy right here and right now. There is nothing to fear. My hand is outstretched to you. See me in the light of truth and take hold of Me. I am here for you always. Do not cry at my seeming absence. The Love always remains with you. The sadness you feel is because you have chosen to let go of Me but I remain with you. Arise and arise and arise again to radiance of your Divine Essence.

Be in the flow of love and compassion and forgiveness for this is your salvation. This is your happiness. The more you focus on blame and guilt, the more turmoil will enter into your mind. Arise right now and away from this heavy slumber, this nightmare that you have made. Wipe the sleep from your eyes for it is a sleep of sickness. Rise and walk, my Son for you are now amongst the Thoughts of God. These thoughts are only of complete Love. As you have faith more in more in what you do you will laugh at all you thought you were and joyfully smile at the nature of your soul. This you will share with your brothers, and they will come and follow.

See them now over the hill of the meadow, they run towards you, their faces of joy, their faces of peace, running to join with you, their holy brother. Together you dance and sing in the field of daisies, the symbol of your innocence. But look closely for they offer you a gift of lilies. It is the gift of forgiveness, a token of Love that will ever remain. Do not be hard on yourself any longer. Everything I have is yours and I gladly offer it to you. I will give you everything that you need. Trust in the walk of holiness. It is your walk of faith. I have called you to fulfill your part; will you not do it now?

∞∞∞∞

Journal Entry on Lesson 101

God's Will for me is perfect happiness.

No need to crucify myself for my birthright is happiness not the madness that I have made. The past need not have a grip on me. I can remove the crown of thorns and the nails from my hands. It does not matter what I have done in the past. What matters is right now. What would You have me do Holy Spirit? I release all my past to You, all the feelings that I have had about myself and others. I know that Jesus teaches me that *"the crucifixion was the last useless journey the Sonship need take and that it represents release from fear to anyone who understands it."* T-6.I.2:5. We can be so hard on ourselves for what we failed to do. However, we base it on what we know now, don't we? If we knew then what we know now...how many times have we said that? But we didn't know and so it brought us to where we are right now.

Bless the moment. Be in the moment. Do not strengthen the fear of your past; instead strengthen the love that you are. That is what you are here to teach. Remember that I said, *"Teach only love for that is what you are."* That is the message of the crucifixion. It is also the message of God's will for you. You are entitled to happiness for that is how your Father created you. Know that in the reality of your Spirit that you cannot even conceive of sin. Sin does not exist in the realm of God and so there is no punishment.

Allow the Holy Spirit to guide your life and you will know happiness. Remove the heavy burden from your shoulders and offer it to Him Who knows. Your freedom and your happiness lie in it. You are blessed my brother always and forever.

∞∞∞

Journal Entry on Lesson 102

I share God's Will for happiness for me.

When we rest in silence and wait with a still mind for the light of Christ to come forth and flash into our awareness, we are practicing our one function. The light of Christ that comes forth is like a beacon in the night. When we perceive this vision of Christ, It brings with It many gifts from God Himself. When the white light touches your mind, happiness is automatically given to you. Healing is automatically given to you in that moment. Contentment, joy, and peace are automatically given to you in that moment. You will begin to notice that your day will go smoothly, easily and happily from that moment forth for a period of time. This is because the Christ has arranged everything for you for your happiness. You will begin to understand how simple salvation is. Your function very simply is to practice stepping back and allowing the light to come forth in your mind to prepare the way for you automatically.

These are among the many gifts that the light of love within you waits to shower you with. Love has no limits or boundaries and nothing stands in the way of His gifts of happiness that He would have for you, His Son. All of these and more He would give to you right now. It is your choice whether you choose to accept them or not. Sitting still in silence is the only way that we can begin to allow this to happen; to allow the restoration of the memory of God into our awareness. This *is* the practice of miracle workers. These are the fundamentals of mind training that you must master in order to become a true miracle worker with the Holy Spirit and the Christ within yourself. Alleluia! Alleluia! Alleluia! The path has been set forth. Praise God for *A Course in Miracles*! The Christ has begun to awaken. The resurrection of the Christ is at hand. This is a time of celebration indeed. The Christ within each and every one of us is beginning to awaken at last. Praise God! Amen.

∞∞∞

Journal Entry on Lesson 103

God, being Love, is also happiness.

What do I have to be happy about? Everything! Happiness is what God is and what I am. And so that is my eternal nature. We have been taught by the ego to fear God and this was done by the traditional theology of the world. When I was younger, I questioned my beliefs, the training that I received. If God is Love and loved us so much, why would He damn us to hell? Ah, questions of youth that are the truth being spoke indeed. This is what this Lesson tells us today. We have nothing to fear. God is in fact Love and that is how we were created. We have made God in our own image which is an image of blame, guilt, fear, punishment and destruction when in fact, God is only Love. And that is the image that we were created in. What we have done with that glorious image is hide beneath the illusions of fear and doubt. We thought we had done something wrong, when God Himself calls to us to be at peace with Him in His Home. It is our Home as well. We have never left.

We do not have to justify ourselves, nor make ourselves bigger or better than anyone else here. No one is right and no one is wrong for only God's world is right. When I lay down my sword of judgment in whatever form it may take hold of today, I can embrace happiness into my life. I do not have to do anything except accept His vibrant Love. It is the Love that awakens me from the sleep of forgetfulness and allows me to remember that I cannot fail to seek the truth. For it is the truth of the One, that brings me happiness. I cannot seek outside the world for that happiness. It will never be found. It is only found within. That is where the Light of Christ dwells.

I do not have to win souls, I just have to be what I was created as, Love. Through my demonstration I set my brothers free. There is no need for God-fearing anymore. He tells us that He is joyous when we remember Him with Love. There is only unlimited Love. I can try to define it, or try to control it in some way but this is not trusting in the Divine and this is not True Love. True Love is freely held without conditions of any kind. When I believe in this then I am free. I can accept that God, being Love, is also my happiness.

∞∞∞∞

Journal Entry on Lesson 104

I seek but what belongs to me in truth.

Someone shared a story with me the other day about a man who found himself in distress out in the ocean. Apparently he had gone for a swim and got caught in the strong undercurrent which began to carry him further away from the shoreline. Despite his frantic efforts to swim back against the current, he found himself still drifting further and further away from the shoreline against his will. Apparently some dolphins had heard and responded this man in distress even when he didn't specifically call to them for help. He suddenly found himself surrounded by several of them. They began to swim around him in circles and gently guided him back to the shoreline where he belonged. What a beautiful story of love.

Have faith my dear brothers and be assured that the Holy Spirit hears all of your calls for love. He knows when you are in distress even when you are not aware of it yourself. Whether you realize it or not, He is constantly guiding you and carrying you through the dream of illusions. He is gently guiding you Home to your rightful place in Heaven with your Father. This is so because it is God's Will that this be so. You have nothing to worry about, ever. No matter what seems to happen in your life, be assured that you are being gently carried and guided by Him Who loves you.

It is His Will that you be reunited with your Father in Heaven and all of your gifts be restored to your awareness. He will not fail because nothing opposes our Father's Will for Us. His will is complete happiness, peace and joy for His Son forever. His Love is boundless and He wills that you know your love is boundless as well. He wills for you to be free and happy. So, be free and happy as you go through your day knowing that you are being cared for by Love Itself, the Creator of All That Is. He is your Father and you are His Son in Reality. Take solace in remembering that today. Spend time remembering how much you are loved by your Father in Heaven. Be open to allowing the Holy Spirit to show you the gifts He has for you. They are joyful ones indeed. The gift of light within your mind will deliver them all in one great flash. Thank You Father for Your gifts to us. We love You. Amen.

∞∞∞∞

Journal Entry on Lesson 105

God's peace and joy are mine.

Offer the gift of lilies today and I offer freedom to myself. In the past, I have withheld love from my brothers for I thought it would buy me something in return. What return could there be but pain when I offer fear? In offering love, I can see the purity of what lies beneath us all. Today, I desire the experience of God's peace and joy. To receive this experience, I merely offer peace and joy to all. It is a gift of no conditions, no limits that I have set up. I love freely and when I do, it returns to me a thousand fold. I let go of all expectations of what I believe love ought to be, what peace ought to be, what joy ought to be. It does not need to look or feel any other way than the way that God intended it to be.

The lilies are the fragrant symbol of my release from hell and into Heaven. I no longer have to crucify myself or others with thoughts of judgment, criticism or blame. I can listen instead to the Holy Voice within me, the Voice of my Friend, the Holy Spirit. He speaks to me of my gentle and pure nature. It is a nature of pure peace and joy that is reflected in Divine Love. Today is the opportunity to give completely without strings attached in any way. It is not, I will not give because no one has ever given to me. It is not I will only give to get. It is only that I give out of pure Love just as my dear Father has given to me. It is freedom to give truly out of joy. It is peace that I receive when I do so. All that I give is given to myself. Today, once again I embrace these thoughts and step back from my own ego constructs and towards the Light of Heaven. The Light of Heaven now dawns in my mind and Heaven rejoices as I accept the gifts of God. This is my own Easter time. I have resurrected from the tomb of darkness and have stepped into the Light.

∞∞∞

Journal Entry on Lesson 106

Let me be still and listen to the truth.

Be still and know that I am God.

Be still and know.....

Be still.....

Be.....

Today, I commit myself to time spent in stillness to listen to Your Voice speak to me. What words are needed except Your own coming into my awareness. I am open and willing to receive so that I may be Father, Your messenger to the world. I will not continue to follow the voice that leads me into hell, but instead the Holy One that leads me to my rightful place in Heaven. Today, I simply listen and put all my own words aside. Thank You, Father. Amen.

Practice being still today. Stop all the images that come to your mind. Stop all memories. Stop all the words so that no voice is heard within your mind. Listen to the silence and wait for the audible Voice of God to bless your ears today.

∞∞∞∞

Journal Entry on Lesson 107

Truth will correct all errors in my mind.

I am not what I conceive myself to be. I am something much more, much greater. This is what God's truth tells me of this day. I am created by the Thought of God when He extended His Holy Self to me in Love. And so I am Love. I do not need to look downward and away today but can hold my head high in confidence of the knowledge that I have received. My brother Jesus, who has walked before me, guides me now along this path of truth. The Holy Spirit is there as well ever lighting my mind at the perfect moment of surrender. Today, I surrender fear. I walk the path of non-judgment. I no longer assume but remember love. I begin each moment in my life fresh and clear and clean. There is no pass; there are no regrets. Those are of the ego. God desires that I be in the knowledge of the Eternal Now. When I simply love, I experience my freedom. Grace and peace are indeed mine.

Hidden within our minds, our very being, is the Light of Christ. This Light is very holy and pure. The white light can be called forth into your perception by letting go of everything you think you know now. When you let go of everything in your mind and wait for the light to come, the Holy Spirit will come forth and help you. The Holy Spirit is the light that you will see. This light is the light of truth. The light that you see and hear speak to you is the light and voice of your True Self. This is why it heals illusions.

Everything you perceive now with your eyes, with your ears, with your thoughts and beliefs is a symbol of darkness. It is dark illusions that you perceive now. When you allow the light to come forth in your mind, it washes away the darkness with its holy radiance. You will feel peace wash through your body as it is healed along with the world with you. You will know this inherently because knowledge comes with the light that you see. Understanding comes with the light that you see.

You will recognize that this is the one and only gift you need to begin to heal all things within your mind. You will recognize that this is the truth and that only this truth will heal all things within your mind. Rest with Him in silence, Who is One with you in reality, and allow Him to show you, to teach you how to do this. This is the work of the miracle healer. This is the work of miracle worker. This is the work of the teachers of God.

ꝏꝏꝏ

Journal Entry on Lesson 108

To give and to receive are one in truth.

This is the work of the miracle worker, to practice holding and placing your attention on one unified thought. It is here that you will come to understand that giving and receiving are one. You will come to understand that the light of gentleness is one, the light of joy and truth are one, the light of peace and happiness are one, and so forth. They are all aspects of creation. They are all aspects of Who you really are, waiting to be given to you to begin to restore your awareness to your reality as it is now.

Anything that you experience that is not of these things is the experience of darkness and darkness is hell. You are drawing the experience of darkness upon yourself with your own mind. It is your choice whether you choose to experience darkness or peace. Would you resist the temptations of the ego today by holding a unified thought to the forefront of your mind by placing all of your attention on it for as long as you can? Would you train your mind today to develop the habit of automatically focusing on the light that you are so that vision may be given to you? The Holy Spirit will help you to do this if you ask Him.

Hold the awareness of Him to the forefront of your mind today and practice seeing and listening to Him by having an open mind. It is here that the restoration of sight and hearing is accomplished through your openness to the Voice for God. All these things are already given to you. You do not have to do anything to experience them but to let go of everything you behold now. That is the key. That is the secret to success of allowing the light of the Atonement to come forth into your mind. It is to practice completely letting go of everything with your mind and surrendering with complete openness and waiting for the light of your Christ Self to reveal Itself to you in one holy moment. Wait, ask, and receive. Observe and wait for the light to come. Wait for the Holy Spirit to show it to you. Wait to hear His Voice speak to you. The clarity of each is unmistakable, unambiguous, and clearer than the clearest of days, and brighter than the brightest of nights you dream. Thank You God for Your holy gift to us.

ᴏᴏᴏᴏᴏ

Journal Entry on Lesson 109

I rest in God.

I rest in God.
I rest this day in perfect peace.
I rest the mind chatter.
I rest in the Light.
I rest in God.
I rest in quiet relaxation.
I rest with ease.
I rest in refreshing pose.
I rest in tranquility.
I rest by the cool stream waters.
I rest in God.
I rest in stillness.
I rest the mind of all its busyness today.
I rest in God.
I rest in joy.
I rest in gratitude.
I rest in willingness.
I rest in Love.
I rest in God.
I rest in simplicity.
I rest with the Voice.
I rest in the truth.
I rest wordless.
I rest in God.

ᴏᴏᴏᴏᴏ

Journal Entry on Lesson 110

I am as God created me.

How holy are you who is the Son of God. You and your brother's light shines steadily and brightly for all to see. The light you will see is unmistakable. Its clarity will surprise you when the experience comes. Let us put forth every effort in truly trying to see the light of our Christ Self today. This is what we are all seeking, to have the experience of seeing and knowing in that seeing *who we really are*. The Being of Light and its Great Rays shining forth in your sight is so beautiful to behold. The happiness and joy that you will feel inside upon finding the Christ within yourself will be immeasurable indeed!

Let us put forth all of our practicing and intentions today into accomplishing this one goal; to see ourselves as God created us. Let us be determined today to not let any temptation of irritation or anger or fear or worry or task or any preoccupation with thoughts in the mind, prevent us from seeing the Christ today. Sink down in silence, be still and see. Then sink down in silence some more, be still and see. Then sink down in silence and be still and allow yourself to see some more. Be determined to see. What you will see *is* the gift of salvation waiting to set you free. Thank You Holy Spirit for this message.

∞∞∞

Journal Entry on Lesson 111

Review Lessons 91-92

This morning at the 7:30 hour I was walking down a hallway at work carrying a cup of coffee when I remembered it was time to do the lesson. I told myself that when I got back to my desk I would take a moment to go within and complete the task requested of me today; one that has the potential to give me everything.

Then, all of a sudden, while sitting at my desk, I realized that it was already past the 8:00 hour and I had forgotten to complete my 7:30 lesson. The ego jumped in and told me that now I needed to make up two lessons; my peace was already ever so slightly being disturbed. I decided to go within and ask Teacher what He thought.

What came to me was that the habit of telling myself to wait until later, even if it was a few moments, was a delaying maneuver of the ego. He reminded me that I do not need to be in any "special" situation or surrounding to practice the lessons. If the world seems busy, I still can do them anytime, any place, if I really want to, even if it is just for a moment. I do not need to make a big deal or a big production out of doing them.

Complexity is of the ego. All that is really needed is to remember to pause, turn inward and practice remembering God for a moment. He will also remind me when it is a good time to practice the lessons; when there's a break in the action. I just need to pay attention to when He may be pointing out those moments. They will come in little inspirations.

Holy Spirit: "That isn't so hard now, is it?"
Paul: "No it's not. Thanks for making it easier for me."
Holy Spirit: "You're welcome."

ooooo

Journal Entry on Lesson 112

Review Lessons 93-94

Through my dedication today, I can truly welcome today's thoughts into my mind. I place the welcome mat outside the door of my mind and allow in only the loving thoughts of light and joy and peace. That is what will abide in my home, the mind, all of which is part of my True Home. In this, I remember how I was created; created in complete, unending Love. This Love is the foundation of my mind.

I choose to continue to build upon the foundation of Love. I allow myself to be guided by the Holy Spirit in all that I say and do, doing so with gentleness, patience and trust. It is time to spring clean and wash away the dust and grime of the ego with the Holy Spirit's gentle, cleansing power. The fresh breeze flows through the windows of my mind, clarity comes forth and purity is all that I know. I have all that I need. All that God is and has, is all that I am and have. It is simplicity in motion. It is appreciation and gratitude that I have for the One Who created me today.

∞∞∞

Journal Entry on Lesson 113

Review Lessons 95-96

Thank You for my One Self.
Thank You for the Light that sets me free.
Thank You for Your gifts to me, my brother.
Thank You Father for the wisdom that resides within me.
Thank You Father for Your holy gifts to me.
Thank You for the light that resides within me.
Thank You for the light of joy that I am.

Thank You for the light of peace that I am.
Thank You for the Voice that guides me along my way.
Thank You Father for Your many gifts to me, your gifts of eternity.
Thank You Father for being with me.
I am grateful to be getting to know my Friend in You once again.
I am grateful to be awakening in You and to begin to allow my heart to sing for You once again.
My ears have been deaf since time began, but Your holy sound of Love has called to me non-stop and now I am beginning to hear that call of Love You have for me.
Thank You Father for Your many gifts to me.

I love You and I miss You and I look forward to my awakening in Me and You and in my Brothers and Sisters once again where we all share happy, eternal life of joy and peace and happiness in You Who is our Home. Let me not dwell on the things of the ego world anymore, but instead, lie them down that I may find the peace that I rest with You, in You, always forever. May I always help my brothers to find Your peace that lies within them as it lies within me. The Light of our peace is so wonderful. I thank my brothers and sisters for the light of Christ that they extend to me and I am grateful to extend mine to theirs. In You, we find our holiness and we discover our innocence in You that has always been and has never changed.

Father, thank You for Your constancy. Thank You for the formless light of Love that we are. Thank You for creating us to be One with You that we may share in Your joy with us. We appreciate You Father and we love You.

Thank You Father for Your holy gifts to us, for us, Your one and only beloved Son Whom we share with each other and with You in Heaven forever. May our minds be silent now that we may find this place within ourselves where we dwell with You and Your eternal gifts forever. The sound of God's call to Love will never be silenced. Thank You Father for Your Love and for Your gifts to us. We love You Father.

The Light that You give to us that is our Source shines brightly and still because It *is* constancy and *You* are Constancy itself. We are secure in the pillars of Heaven because *You* are the pillar. *You* are our strength. *You* are our Source of Light that we are and we give back to You what You have given to us in everlasting peace and joy forever. Amen.

∞∞∞

Journal Entry on Lesson 114

Review Lessons 97-98

I am open to a new experience of myself. I am willing to accept that I am the Son of God, the spirit of Love. In accepting the certainty of myself, I can then welcome my part in the plan of salvation, the plan of happiness set forth by God for me, His Son.

Do I want to receive this gift? I acknowledge and affirm that I indeed do.

And so for me with these Review Lessons that I sit in quiet reflection, pondering on God's Word as it is given to me through my openness to receive. Few words are necessary to speak of this. It is time for me to truly hearken to the Holy Spirit's kind instruction.

Today, it is time to be at the ready, to take my place, my function, through my forgiveness of all that I see.

And I am willing to do that now.

∞∞∞

Journal Entry on Lesson 115

Review Lessons 99-100

A quote from the Text -

> *"Salvation is for the mind, and it is attained through peace. This is the only thing that can be saved and the only way to save it. Any response other than love arises from a confusion about the "what" and the "how" of salvation, and this is the only answer. Never lose sight of this, and never allow yourself to believe, even for an instant, that there is another answer. For you will surely place yourself among the poor, who do not understand that they dwell in abundance and that salvation is come."* T-12.III.5

And so my function is simply to forgive and as I forgive peace is mine. It is my job to perform in every moment. Remaining at peace is done by the release of all the people, places and things that I have created an attachment to. When I experience attachment, I am holding on to expectations and outcomes resulting in my fear and insecurity. When I place my trust in God, I am letting go of everything else that I have sought in this world to make me happy. I am accepting love. Only my function in loving forgiveness will achieve the happiness that I seek. Only God is what I seek and now remember. And so, today, with my goal as peace, my task is forgiveness and through this I recognize and accept my holy purpose.

∞○○○∞

Journal Entry on Lesson 116

Review Lessons 101-102

Remain focused on perfect happiness. If you remain focused on perfect happiness, everything that is not perfect happiness will be gently laid aside. That is what the tool of forgiveness is for, to assist you in sharing God's Will. This is what you truly want. You want happiness. You know that happiness cannot be found in the world. You have tried over and over to make it work. And you have seen over and over that it does not. Following the Holy Spirit's lead is the only way to live your life. I have told you this many times as your dear brother. You do not need to sacrifice or crucify yourself in large or small ways. I taught you that the purpose of all was to "Teach only love for that is what you are." Remember this, and you will indeed be happy.

What our Father has created cannot be undone. You can cover it with the veil of darkness, of illusions, of misperceptions but the Light of His Love however, is always there. It cannot be dimmed or blown out. It is the eternal flame of forgiveness. Your Father's Love shows you Who you really are. This is why you can indeed share in His happiness for you. This is why you can indeed walk the world in peace. Make the decision today and in every moment that you will follow His gentle lead. You do not have to be caught up in the web of raucous thoughts that pervade your mind. Let each one go and give them to the One Who knows and understands. He will purify each thought and a sparkling miracle will be received instead. You already know Love, for it is within you. Remove the barriers to Love and be free today.

∞∞∞∞

Journal Entry on Lesson 117

Review Lessons 103-104

Everyone has a light within themselves. It comes from our Source, our Life Force, our Creator. It is possible to learn how to see this light. When we are feeling down, perceiving the light will lift us up. When we are feeling that we are not in alignment with our life's purpose, perceiving the light will give us direction and certainty. When we are not feeling happy, seeing the light will bless us with joy. When we are feeling alone, the light will show us our Friend Whose Voice will speak to us and show us that we are not alone.

When we are not sure how to pray, our Friend will pray for us. When we are not sure how to perceive the light, ask and He will show us. When we are not sure which way to turn, our Friend will move our hand and point for us. When we are not sure what meal to choose, He will joyfully select it for us and joy will be ours. When we are not sure what career to pursue, He will give it to us and our joyful purpose in life will be fulfilled. When something ails us, the Light we perceive delivers healing and peace. These and many other gifts are automatically given to us when we learn how to perceive our light. The white light comes from our Source and this is all our Source knows how to do, He gives all to all. From limitlessness, limitlessness is given. Finding your Light, your Friend, is the same as finding your path of highest joy. Be a "Delight" by living your life in "The-Light".

∞∞∞∞

Journal Entry on Lesson 118

Review Lessons 105-106

Let my own feeble voice be still, and let me hear the mighty Voice for Truth Itself assure me that I am God's perfect Son. ~ Lesson 118

How true the words of stillness, the receptivity in my listening. All questions are answered by the Holy One in the silence as I come to know that I know nothing. My knowledge has been based in this illusory world. And so, I need not look outside myself for any understanding for the Eternal Truth remains within. As I enter the sacred sanctuary in my dedication to hearing His Voice speak to me, I remain calm, quiet, content, and ready to receive His peace. My mind is soothed with His healing balm of Love. I am anointed in His Holy Presence. I exchange the substitutes that I have formed from fear, judgment, anger and disbelief and embrace only peace, joy and happiness as my very own. No further words are necessary now. It is simply for me to *be still and listen.*

∞∞∞∞

Journal Entry on Lesson 119

Review Lessons 107-108

This message was received from Jesus in meditation ~

Perceiving the truth inside of you is the same as perceiving the white light of Christ. When we perceive the light of Christ we perceive the truth. We perceive the truth because the light that we see is replacing the illusions of darkness that we are seeing otherwise. This is why truth corrects all errors in our mind. Everything you see now with your eyes is an error. Everything you are thinking with your mind now is an error because it does not perceive the light of truth within yourself. You have chosen to block the awareness of the light of your Christ mind from yourself by seeing the world you now behold instead and then you have chosen to forget that you have created this illusion for yourself.

Your holy mind would have been lost in the dream of illusions had not your Father responded with the Answer, the Solution. When we ask to see the truth the Holy Spirit will show you the light of your sinlessness. This light that you see is a reflection of your True Self. Right now, if you were to take a look in a mirror you would see a reflection of your false self. The reflection that you see in the mirror is an illusion. You are not really a body made up of skin cells and hair, facial features, a skeletal system, organs, blood, fingernails, plasma and so forth.

There is another part of you that can be perceived, and I use the word "perceived" here instead of "see" to make a very important distinction between the two. When we use the word "see" it is often associated with "seeing with the body's eyes." This is not true seeing. What we are talking about here is learning how to use your spiritual sight. Your spiritual sight needs to be exercised within your mind. We have used the body's eyes so long for seeing that we have forgotten how to use our spiritual sight within the mind.

When we practice the lessons in the Workbook, we are practicing the transition from using the body's eyes to see to remembering how to see with our mind. We can see much more clearly with the mind than we can with the body's eyes. The gift of vision that the Holy Spirit offers for you is very vivid. The gift of light that He will show you about yourself is very clear. You will know it without a doubt when you see it because the light is like a bright beacon that suddenly turns on for a moment in the darkest of nights. You will be quite surprised when it happens for the first time.

So the question now is "How do we begin to practice perceiving this light within ourselves?" I would suggest starting with the "willingness treadmill". We need to make a commitment to ourselves and to the Holy Spirit to continue to practice exercising our willingness and desire everyday to perceive the light within ourselves. Are we really trying to allow the Holy Spirit to show us the light or are we paying attention to the thoughts, feelings and images that are coming up in our minds during our meditations. Refuse to see these. Refuse to pay attention to them and ask the Holy Spirit to show you nothing else but the light and wait for Him to do so. At the very least, you will settle into a place of peaceful quiet without the ego thoughts churning in your mind. This will be refreshing for you.

As you practice this opening up to perceiving the light within yourself, sooner or later it will begin to happen. You will begin to perceive the little spark. When you begin to perceive the little spark, perhaps you will say to yourself, "Aha, now I am getting a glimmering of what He is talking about." You will be well on your way when this begins to happen. This will be the beginning of the end of sickness for your mind for truth has begun to come to correct all errors within your mind. This is a wonderful gift to be giving to yourself. It is a gift of joy. It is the gift of giving and receiving at the same time. By allowing yourself to perceive the light, you are allowing yourself to receive the gift that God has given to you which is the awareness that you are His Light. By perceiving the light you are also giving to yourself because when you perceive the light all that is really happening is that the Holy Spirit, Who is the mirror that God gave to you, is reflecting the light that you *are* back to yourself. Thus you will begin to understand in that holy moment that giving and receiving are one in truth.

∞∞∞

Journal Entry on Lesson 120

Review Lessons 109-110

Let us practice remembering the importance of what we are trying to accomplish today. We are literally trying to hear God's Voice speak to us. From a place of silence, we will hear a Voice speak very clearly. It is unmistakable. Let us dedicate every half hour that we practice today to accomplishing this one goal. Let us sink down and listen in the silence for His Voice to speak to us; past all thoughts and vain imaginings. It is here where we will suddenly hear our Father's Voice speak to us telling us Who we really are.

Father, as I rest in You today, I reveal myself to You and allow You to reveal Yourself to me. It is in this resting place that I am open and willing to receive and remember my inheritance. My ears are willing to listen; my mind is quiet to receive Your Word, the Word of Love. This is my desire today. This is what I want. And so each time I pause and rest in You, I will know that no words are needed by me, simply a willingness to hear You. Your Word may speak to me as a voice, a knowing, an image, a phrase or a song. Whatever I receive from You shall be perfect because You are perfect. I will know all that I need to know when I practice the art of listening. And so even now, I stop and pause, to hear You. Amen.

ooooo

Journal Entry on Lesson 121

Forgiveness is the key to happiness.

When we think about the people in our lives that we could apply today's lesson to, I wonder how many of us find ourselves resisting the idea of applying it to those closest to us, to our loved ones? I wonder how many of us still find ourselves complaining to God or someone else about the status of our lives? For those of us who answer "yes" to these questions, perhaps today we could try something different, since what we have been doing does not seem to be working.

Perhaps we could start our day by telling God what we want and asking Him for help in achieving that goal. "Dear God, I want to be happy today. Would you please help me to have that experience? I want to have a happy day today." We could then practice going within for a moment, recite today's lesson, ask what to do next, then follow the inspiration that comes. This could be practiced every hour along with today's lesson. Then, to see how things went, at the end of the day we could spend some time with God again. We could tell Him all about our day, and perhaps, find ourselves thanking Him for all the gifts He gave to us.

In this lesson, I have seen how my mind has been in the space of unforgiveness, even if for just a little. There is no "just a little." I either have forgiven or I have not. Day to day activities can have me in this space very quickly whether I realize and notice it or not. In the first few paragraphs, I am told by Jesus what my unforgiving mind believes in. In the space of unforgiveness, the mind is in turmoil, conflict, constantly afraid to make a decision or a move, and looks upon all things and people and sees sin evident, basically, always in fear. There is no hope or peace when my mind has joined with the ego thought system.

The good news is that I can open up to the teaching of the Holy Spirit. Through my offer to Him of everything and everyone that I now perceive, I am uplifted and remember the Love that solely exists. Everything and everyone that comes before me is my lesson in love. I can rise in accepting that lesson, the perfect curriculum instructed by the One Who Knows. I can learn apply it as it states here, both an enemy and a friend. There are no differences here. Everything that I see is an illusion, an unforgiveness that I have brought forth from the separation from God. And so, as I release it all, I will pierce the veil and see the true Light emanating forth. Peace is restored. I do not have to be afraid for the Holy Spirit is with me every leg of the journey. Today, I become mindful. I will awaken and realize my eternal, perfect, innocent Self.

∞∞∞

Journal Entry on Lesson 122

Forgiveness offers everything I want.

I have been dealing with various emotions, turmoils, and conflicts as long repressed memories from the past have begun to surface in my mind. These "feelings" are a blessing, even if as I am going through them they do not feel as such. I can see how these deeply held "secrets" have continued to color different aspects of my life. Yes, there has been fear in exposing these secrets to my conscious mind. At times, it has felt quite frightening. At times, the tears have flowed for no apparent reason.

When I can come from the sane part of my mind, as now, I can see that all is there for my healing. I had asked the Holy Spirit to embark with me on the healing journey and bring to me what I need to know in a way that I can know and understand and forever be healed from it all. And that has occurred. With continued and consistent physical ailments, and recent nightmarish dreams, all that has taken place is there for the purification of my mind.

Today's Lesson, offers me yet another. *"Forgiveness offers everything I want."* So, if I do not wish to live my life in turmoil, the question "Did this happen to me in childhood? Or didn't?" is no longer valid. What's done is done. Certainly in the realm of the

Course, it has all been an illusion. It has been a deeply held belief that I have had that I could be harmed, exploited and remain now as a victim. So, in turning over all of these "beliefs" to the Holy Spirit, I can recognize that I am perfect and whole. I do no longer have to suffer in any way. I accept and learn from the lessons as they come. I have been reminded by the Holy Spirit and through others to be loving, compassionate and gentle with myself as I go through the process. Of course, all of that is what I would share with anyone else going through the same. Somehow, we never seem to take our own advice. I will accept it now.

Earlier this morning, I had to run a package to the Post Office. The gentleman who waited on me, and I use that term generously because he was indeed a gentle, joyful man, was bouncing with enthusiasm and love; he offered his assistance in such a caring way, it was unbelievable. He also made the comment at the end that to smile and go forth into the sunshine and choose to have a happy day. Interesting choice of words.....the clerk next to him asked with a little sarcasm, "Choose to have a happy day?" And I said, "Yes, it is a choice." He said the same and we both smiled at each other as if we both connected and knew in that moment that we were experiencing the Oneness of It All. That simple statement from him brought so much into my day for me to remember. I was grateful since I had forgotten with the focus on the bodily ailments of the day.

And so, with this lesson, *"Forgiveness offers everything I want,"* I am choosing what I want to experience. I can continue to be beset with the intensity of emotions that have risen or I can offer them all to the Holy Spirit for His perception of Love. Forgiveness will allow me to see the crystalline, pristine truth. The Light shines into my mind now as I stop for a moment to contemplate. It fills my inner field of vision just as the Course describes, *"an arc of golden light."* This Light that comes is my reminder of Who I am. I am so much more than anything that I have made up in this story of my supposed life. I am the Son of God. There is only perfection here. There is only Love here. And so in practicing forgiveness in all that I do knowing it brings me all that I so desire, I can truly hold dear to my heart that:

Today I have accepted this as true.
Today I have received the gifts of God.

And today, I will rest in God.

∞∞∞

Journal Entry on Lesson 123

I thank my Father for His gifts to me.

I find today that there is only quiet appreciation as I go about my day. There was a situation not too long ago in which I had become angry because someone was late in their arrival at the agreed upon time. (Ok, truth be told, it was Paul.) I had been journaling throughout the day and when I looked at my watch and saw the time, I proceeded to be ticked off as the hands ticked the time. "Well, now they are 5 minutes... 10 minutes... 20 minutes... half an hour late. How inconsiderate!"

In that moment the Holy Spirit inspired me to open up my pad and write what I appreciated about the person instead of the criticism and judgment that I was feeling. And so for a page and a half I wrote my gratitude for this person in my life; every aspect that I could think of, from their personality, to the talents and gifts that they possess, to the lessons that they had brought to me in the relationship.

As I wrote, I felt a definite lightening and shift in my whole posture. I found such profound love that it didn't matter anymore that they were late. As I completed the last few words, just then I received a phone call with his notification of his late arrival. All I could feel was a gentle love emanating forth. That love was the reflection of myself. This is the gifts that we receive when we give love. There does not have to be anything as a wall between us.

What defenses am I holding? What stance am I taking that keeps the separation between my brother going? Is it really worth it? Or, can I step aside and ask Spirit what I should do? The barriers between brothers can be so subtle that we aren't even aware of them. Today, I am more in recognition of what my barriers and defenses are. Being mindful of them with this awareness, I can go forth and extend the gifts of God and in giving I do receive. What is it that I am giving today? What is it that I am receiving today? The Holy Spirit is always there to assist me and remind me of all that I can do through Him, if only I stop and listen to His Word. I am grateful that I have chosen another way.

Thank You God for Your gifts to me.

∞∞∞∞

Journal Entry on Lesson 124

Let me remember I am one with God.

The practice of remembering God is not accomplished the same way that the ego has taught us. When we practice remembering God, we practice letting go of everything we seem to be experiencing now. We close our eyes and let go of what we seem to be seeing. We let go of the sounds that seem to be coming through our ears. We let go of the thoughts that seem to be speaking to us in our minds. And finally, we let go of the images that we seem to see coming and going in our minds. When we do all this and sink into the silence of nothingness we begin to allow opportunities for the Light of God to begin to reveal Himself to us.

This Light is also the Light of our brothers and our true Selves.

In this Light He also shows us images of our future and things He is guiding us to do. These messages always lead us to a happier dream experience. He is showing us the way out of the dream and, at the same time, reminding us that He is with us every step of the way. What a wonderful feeling that is!

In the Light we hear His loving Voice speak to us. Again, He is sharing information about our future and guiding us in what to do. In the Light we experience that we can heal ourselves and others from things that ail our bodies. In the Light we see and experience the reality of our true Selves reflecting back to us like the brightest of stars in the night sky. In the Light we feel an electric flow of peace and joy that suddenly flows easily through our bodies as if a light switch had been turned on. These are some of the many gifts He has in store for us. How joyful it is to experience these gifts from our Father and to realize that many more are coming with His Light that shows us the way.

∞∞∞

Journal Entry on Lesson 125

In quiet I receive God's Word today.

The affirmation for today tells you all that you need to do. There is no other message that I can relate to you. Take the time throughout the day to be still, be quiet and listen and receive My Word for you. That is all you need do. There is nothing else. Listen and hear my Holy One. Listen and hear. Hearken to this and you will have all that you need. Words are but symbols upon symbols and so they are meaningless in and of themselves. No more words are needed with lesson that is in your midst. Listen and receive My Word today.

∞∞∞

Journal Entry on Lesson 126

All that I give is given to myself.

My mind wandered as I meditated on this Lesson. Different situations, people and experiences came to mind....what I could say, what I did say or what I should have said. All the past projected into the future so I am not living in the now. As I focus on the now, what is it that I am giving? If I am focused on judgment, then judgment is what I give to others and myself. If I am focused on God's love for me, then that is what I give to others and myself. Do I not wish to be in a state of peace? Of loving harmony and brotherhood? Forgiveness does offer all of this. Do I want to be in a constant fearful state? Feel the need to control so that I may be happy? Do others need to change before I even think of changing?

It is *my* thoughts that need to be changed and now. Criticism, assigning guilt and blame, manipulation and control, isolation, etc., all I receive as I practice the same behaviors. And then in the past haven't I scratched my head at wondered why such things were happening to me?

If I practice otherwise, practice forgiveness with Holy Spirit, as Jesus speaks of, and I do now, I will experience a peace in my life that is true happiness and contentment. It is a mindfulness as I walk about my day. What thoughts am I sending forth to others in the world? To me? All these recent Lessons continue to help me to see past my perceptions and projections. I am in gratitude to know that I have Heaven's Help within me, the Holy Spirit, Who can see past it all when I cannot. He sees the light that is held within us, that spark of truth given to us by our Creator. It is Love, simple, complete Love. As I give this Love, I do give it to myself. Isn't this what I would prefer to have in my life on a daily basis? Indeed it is.

Journal Entry on Lesson 127

There is no love but God's.

"Seek not within the world to find your Self. Love is not found in darkness and in death." This quote has such deep meaning for me and with this lesson I find solace in the quiet with my Father. I have sought outside myself for replacements for His Love. They are not worthy replacements. I do not have to feel guilt or shame about that fact, instead I can allow the awareness to be present in my mind and then choose God. I can open my mind today and rest in His Love. I can allow the past to melt away and create a better present. I can embrace life and love everyone as I have been loved by God. I can allow forgiveness to be a beautiful fragrance in my life. I can appreciate, accept and love all my teachers who bless me as I walk through my days. Their lessons may seem challenging, but I accept my lessons with total gratitude. It is my choice where I place my value and today my value is placed on remembering my value in God. He only believes that I am loved in light, joy and peace.

∞∞∞∞

Journal Entry on Lesson 128

The world I see holds nothing that I want.

In meditation, images flashed by as if the ego was baiting or taunting me, "You mean this person has no value to you?" or "The new house you are moving in to has no value?" I would then respond as the lesson suggests with, *"This will not tempt me to delay myself. The world I see holds nothing that I want."* A calm quiet set in for a time and then once again the fleeting thoughts tickled my mind. My task was to stay focused on detachment from the world. Although in the world I certainly appreciate the people, places

191

and things that are present in my life. However, they are not what holds or defines my value.

If I focus on what is outside of me to "complete" me in some way, I will always feel disappointed and thus mistaken. It is for me to recognize my wholeness and my abundance that I have in God. My being here is to remember God and to assist the Sonship in remembering as well. The toys and the trinkets are worthless to me and defining happiness in them is also worthless. If I do, I am no better than a spoiled child who has everything but only wants more. The ego is never satisfied. A child only calls for love and freedom to love and not to be surrounded by the glittery distractions of the world. The ego wants to indulge the child. My Heavenly Parent knows otherwise and the Holy Spirit is ever present guiding me along the right path, the path of remembering. The child may certainly "act out" at times, but Holy Spirit is ever patient, always ready to take me another step as I, myself am ready. Today, I remove the bar across the door and allow in the awareness of my True Self, the Self so dearly loved by God.

∞∞∞

Journal Entry on Lesson 129

Beyond this world there is a world I want.

There is more to behold in my spiritual sight. The day before I came into the learning of releasing all value that I have held on this world; today, I attend to what truly is of value the world of God. I want no more than this. This Reality with God is all there is. Also today is the recognition of communication between God and the Son. *"Their language has no words, for what They (God and His Son) say cannot be symbolized."* Once again it is in the silence where I receive the greatest gifts. In the silence I move beyond the world that I see and experience to the world that I truly want. It is the direct experience, this knowing in the Divine communication as One. In the space of quiet timelessness, it is felt.

∞∞∞

Journal Entry on Lesson 130

It is impossible to see two worlds.

I am seeing the pieces of baggage that the ego has created in my mind to slow me down from honing in on fulfilling my purpose for being here. One piece of luggage has been flight instructing, another has been becoming a commercial airline pilot, another has been partying with my friends, another has been the desire for other life experiences, another has been triathlons, and the list of ego developed "luggage-habits" goes on. All of these are solutions my ego came up with to help me find happiness within my life. And when I achieved each one, the happiness never really did last.

Despite that, it still surprises me that I still find it difficult to let go of each piece of luggage. I still have to work at it. Not as hard as I used to but I still have to still keep turning things over, forgiving them and practicing the true desire to let them go. It's hard to have the willingness sometimes. I think because I didn't know of a better way; until now.

I am truly grateful for finding the light. Perceiving the light has really helped me to keep going. Each flash from the Light is gently helping me to let go of these things and at the same time is showing me an easier way, a gentler way, a happier way, a more peaceful way. Because of the light I know there really is no other way. I'm still learning how to get used to it, how to relax into that kind of lifestyle and letting go of the old lifestyle and allowing the new and unknown one to unfold in my life. It really is a building of a trust walk for me; to allow someone else, Holy Spirit, to guide and manage my life for me. Thank you Holy Spirit for helping us.

∞∞∞

Journal Entry on Lesson 131

No one can fail who seeks to reach the truth.

The image of the door in today's lesson reminds me of an insight I received from Holy Spirit many years ago. With this insight, it was the idea of letting go of something that did not serve me any longer, a needed change. However, it was one that I was ambivalent to make. With this decision it would seem that I would be leaving my traditional spiritual family and embarking into the yet unknown ACIM like-minded family.

In meditation I heard that the door lay before me open and yielding for me but my hand was still on the doorknob of the door that was closing behind me. The door open before me showed a fresh outdoor scene, one of fresh air, a new way to live. There was staleness in what was closing and I still hung on to it out of fear. Old ways are hard to let go of. We relish in these old patterns even if they do not serve us any longer. Lessons still come and go and continue to appear until we are ready to let go and change. As I received this message then, I realized that it was Holy Spirit's encouragement shining ever so brightly, leading me onward to the truth. I was seeking and He was allowing me to succeed. I did release the old spiritual family and transitioned into the new. A wise and grateful decision I had made.

Of course all these years later, it certainly does feel right to be exactly where I am now and to trust that I am where I am meant to be. I am on the journey and so is everyone else. We are all doing the best that we can. I do not need to question another's process, but simply allow them to be where they are at any given time. As they are ready, they too, will let go of the door that has closed behind them and step forward into the brilliant Door of Truth. It is not for me to force my brother's hand from the doorknob, no matter how much the door is falling off of its hinges, for even Holy Spirit would not do that. The Holy Spirit is ever patient in His Love. It can seem very tempting to want to change another, to point out their errors, to have them behave differently; to be right, but that uncomfortability that I feel indeed comes from the ego thought system. Projection makes perception. There is nothing to change but my mind about everything that I seem to experience. And so:

I ask to see a different world, and think a different kind of thought from those I made. The world I seek I did not make alone, the thoughts I want to think are not my own.

Today I seek and find all that I want.

My single purpose offers it to me.

No one can fail who seeks to reach the truth.

With this, I choose happiness instead.

∞∞∞∞

Journal Entry on Lesson 132

I loose the world from all I thought it was.

How weary we can make ourselves when we hang on to the worrisome thoughts from the past that never occurred. And then for good measure we add more worrisome thoughts about the future to weary ourselves all the more. There is no need to hang on to the images and the presentations of the ego from your past because it never happened. I know this is difficult for you to remember and to accept as true but I also am aware that you have begun to discover the Light within yourself that is beginning to show you the way out of hell for your mind. When you allow your split mind to attack and attack again after awhile when the pain becomes great enough what do you find yourself doing.

You find yourself retreating from the world to a place where you can spend some time undisturbed by its distractions. And you practice allowing the Light to come forth and wash your pain away. This is the gift of the miracle worker. I am so pleased with you when you practice this. It is a delight for myself and all of Heaven within you to be allowed to come forth and heal your split mind. The holy instant is the only way out. It is the practice of true forgiveness.

This is your task, your assignment, your purpose for being here. And you practice it so well. My dear Son, you are way too hard on yourself. Remember to practice being gentle with yourself by allowing the Light of gentle forgiveness to come forth and ease your soul with gentleness. The Light will do the work for you if you allow it to come forth. Salvation is simple. Close your eyes, be still and rest in the silence, waiting for the Light to come forth into your awareness.

As you continue to practice forgiveness it eventually becomes an automatic habit and the practicing gets easier, calling forth the Light becomes easier. Eventually you will no longer need to close your eyes. When the more advanced stages of your mind training is complete you will eventually allow the Light to be present in your awareness with joy all the time. This is the awakening process. Remember forgiveness, forgiveness, forgiveness is all you really need to practice. It's all you really need to do. That is the work of the miracle worker.

You asked me once, you asked me many times to teach you how to become a miracle worker like I was. This is it. You are learning how to become a true miracle worker. Calling forth the Light within your mind heals all things, the sick and the dead. You are getting it. Keep on practicing. Keep working on that willingness. Keep on. Keep on my brother. You are getting it. Hurray for all of us! God's Son is beginning to awaken at last. Amen.

∞∞∞

Journal Entry on Lesson 133

I will not value what is valueless.

The idea of choice comes to mind with this lesson today. I make the decisions of what I value or not value. Do I value time? Outcomes? Others? Do I make an idol of anything or anybody? The Course itself? The Course tells me that I weep each time an idol falls meaning that each time I have placed value, attachment or my happiness on something or someone outside of me and then I see that it will not or did not fulfill me, then yes, I seem to experience a sense of loss or grief over the so-called "idol." I believed my salvation lied in it or them. If I come truly with empty hands and an open mind as suggested today, I will be asking only for what can sustain me in truth. I then ask for what is of true value, that which is within me, my undeniable Divine nature, my connection with Father. I have everything of value in Him for it is already mine. I just need to recognize what I not of value and the beauty of Love will shine brightly forth and forever.

∞∞∞

Journal Entry on Lesson 134

Let me perceive forgiveness as it is.

It is very easy to catalog the "sins" and mistakes of another. With any one person coming to mind, even now, one can readily find their faults. Of course, I may see these faults or sins in another, see how they are wrong or their need to be punished, however, if I, myself have done the very same or similar, I proclaim my innocence. I make excuses or rationalize my behaviors. "They did ___ to me, so therefore...." However in the space of true forgiveness we allow a breath of freedom from the chains of fear to clear our mind.

As I stop and notice each unloving thought, each judgment or opinion, and even righteous behavior, all of it, I stop and use the wise affirmation of the day:

> *"Let me perceive forgiveness as it is. Would I accuse myself of doing this? I will not lay this chain upon myself."*

When I do lay the chains upon my brother, it is myself that feels its heavy weight. I never rest in this state. If I want peace and rest, and I do indeed, then I trust the Holy Spirit to assist me in the forgiveness process. I open to Him for a new way of seeing the person or situation. I perceive the goodness that is truly there.

Through my brothers so I return Home. Through my forgiveness of my brothers is my salvation.

∞∞∞

Journal Entry on Lesson 135

If I defend myself I am attacked.

Defend, attack; attack, defend ..... it can become a vicious cycle. It is similar to giving and receiving being as the same. What is there for me to really defend? If I am secure in all that I am, there is nothing to defend. However, I forget who I really am. Sure, there have been times in which I perceived attack and even times that I attacked back in my defense, but I do not have to stay in that state. I do not have to condemn myself for not being a "perfect" Course student or spiritual person. Situations happen, we have strong feelings and sometimes we express those strong feelings to others. We realize it was not the best response to make. We realize that there is indeed another way, as we are ready. No self-flogging necessary! Each time it does occur we can bless ourselves and the lesson it presented to us. We can remember to take the time to connect with Holy Spirit.

What can I do differently when this occurs? How can I continue to practice forgiveness? How can I step back from these kinds of situations? Holy Spirit, what do You suggest?

The plans that I make to "fix" anyone or anything always fail. Allowing Holy Spirit's plan into my awareness shows me the truth. His plan shows me that I do not need to defend or attack what is not real. That is why I do not need to continue to expend my energy in doing so. It only keeps me running in circles. With Holy Spirit, I lay down the sword and open to His insight of the hologram that I have mounted my defenses for. I see clearly!

Today, I am reborn in the recognition that I am the Son of God, His holy Child, created in perfect, eternal Love. I no longer need to defend against this knowledge nor make a false image in place of what is real. I can believe, accept and have faith in the Truth. Amen! Hallelujah!

Journal Entry on Lesson 136

Sickness is a defense against the truth.

In today's lesson, Jesus says that *"Healing will flash across your open mind."* What he is talking about here is the experience of perceiving yourself as a Vision of Christ. Remember, we are not bodies, we are spirit. The Holy Spirit has a gift for us to perceive within our minds. That gift is the perception of the flash of the white light of Christ. It takes a lot of practice to begin to learn how to perceive the Light of our True Self. When we perceive the Light, we are perceiving "the Light of Truth" which he also mentions in today's lesson.

When we first begin to open up to perceiving the Light within our minds, many of us will begin by perceiving little sparks of white light or flashes that look like stars. Some of us will have holy encounters with the Light of Christ and the Great Rays emanating from Him. Remember that these experiences are all a reflection of our True Selves. When they begin to happen, not only do we perceive the Light within our minds, we also begin to receive many other gifts from the Light at the same time as well. The brighter the light perceived, the more the gifts are experienced. This is why we practice mind training through the practice of the Workbook Lessons.

We practice training our minds to open up completely to the Light of our True Selves. As we learn how to do this we truly learn how to become miracle workers, miracle healers. Not only are we healing ourselves, the Light that we allow to come forth through us begins to heal the world and those around us automatically. This is because this is all the Light knows how to do, is heal. It heals everything that is not perfect like Itself. The Light is Love. It comes from our Source, our Creator, from All That Is.

When we experience the Light, we experience a release in the body of tension and angst that is suddenly washed away with the Light of Peace. We also experience a knowing and an understanding that the light we perceive is the Light of Truth because anything other than the Light is not truth. Our minds also experience a feeling of contentment and joy and a feeling that everything is okay as we allow the light into our awareness; our minds begin to heal and thus our bodies begin to instantly heal as well. This is why Jesus says in "The End of Sickness" section of the Text, "*If you but see the little spark, you will learn of the greater light, for the rays are there unseen. Perceiving the spark will heal, but knowing the Light will create.*" So let us remember to practice today asking the Holy Spirit to help us to begin to perceive the Light of Christ within ourselves as we wait in silence for His response. Amen.

∞∞∞

Journal Entry on Lesson 137

When I am healed I am not healed alone.

In order for us to truly learn what Jesus means when he says "*when we are healed we are not healed alone*" it is important for us to remember to commit and recommit ourselves to developing the habit of connecting with God. The practice of connecting with God is accomplished by having the willingness to periodically stop ourselves during the day, go within and listen to God. When we are silent and listening, observing with open minds, God's gifts begin to come to us. God's gifts come to us in many forms. We may receive thoughts or inspirations that contain the solution to a problem that may be going on in our lives at that time, we may see pictures or images in our mind, we may hear the Voice of the Holy Spirit speak to us, we may see words, we may hear music or songs, or we may see the Light of God Himself.

All of these gifts and many more come forth to heal us and the world along with us each time we take time to practice receiving His gifts. Jesus tells us in the Manual for Teachers that His gifts always benefit everyone. When we practice being still with an open mind and waiting for God to do something, something will just suddenly happen. We really we need do nothing but open up and receive His gifts.

Jesus:

This is the art of practicing True Forgiveness: letting go of all that we think we understand now and allowing God an opportunity to come forth in a manner that He chooses. He knows what is best for you in that moment of your life. He knows the best response, the perfect gift. The gift could be anything, absolutely anything. There are no limits to the gifts that He can give. Why would you limit yourself by going to Him with an expectation of a particular gift every time?

This is making a statement to Him that you know what's best and He does not. Surely you can see the absurdity in this ego thought process. Do not be hard on yourself. Remember that this is not really you, but you are practicing opening up to the other You. You are practicing allowing your True Self to come forth into your awareness to show you all the gifts that God has given to you. The Holy Spirit knows the best way for you and He will help you as you learn how to let Him help you. He knows what is best for you and for everyone.

So, let us remember to practice frequently today being open and receiving the many gifts He has for you. Practice letting Him surprise you with something new. Ask Him today to show you a new experience, something new that you haven't experienced from God before. Ask Him to surprise you with something fun and wonderful. Then let Him show you the gifts of Joy. And when they come, remember to thank Him for the gifts of Joy that you receive this day. Remembering to thank Him is important because it reaffirms in your mind that He is there, that He is with you and has given to you all that He has. It will bolster your faith in Him, in Me and in Him Who created all of us.

∞∞∞

Journal Entry on Lesson 138

Heaven is the decision I must make.

There is an important point in today's Lesson. "*Truth cannot come where it could only be perceived with fear. For this world be the error truth can be brought to illusions. Opposition makes the truth unwelcome, and it cannot come.*" It is not for me to cover my fears with thoughts of light and love. This is denial of the fear in a form that is not truly helpful to me. It is to be honest and authentic with the fear, and bring the fear to the Holy Spirit knowing that the truth is all that I want to remember. The decision for Heaven in these times is forgiveness of the illusions that I have made. In my decision, I am releasing all value I have placed on people, places, opinions, judgments, desires, the past, the future, the Course, everything. I am accepting the truth; the truth that Heaven is what I want, where I am, who I am. I no longer need to accept what I have made. It has truly never brought me happiness otherwise.

So, why not make the decision for Heaven today? Believing otherwise is hell. Holding any attachment to anyone, anything, any idea, any outcome is hell. I have allowed hell into my awareness by doing such. And so, all of this I gladly hand over to the Light of Truth with the One Who Knows. The Holy Spirit will illuminate my mind and show me that Heaven is indeed what I truly want. Peace is what I truly want. The recognition of Who I am is what I truly want. Love is what I truly want. And so I joyfully repeat the reminder for today, "*Heaven is the decision I* must make. I make it now, and will not change my mind, because it is the only thing I want."

Be committed today.

Be determined today.

Exchange hell for Heaven today.

Bring the darkness to the Light today.

Accept only Love.

ooooo

Journal Entry on Lesson 139

I will accept Atonement for myself.

"I will accept Atonement for myself, For I remain as God created me."

This lesson speaks about choice. This stands out to me today and in relation what comes to mind is the idea of "food" as an example. This is how the lesson works similarly. If I love pizza and there are two options laid before on a table, the other option being liver, to me, in my mind, there is no choice. In my certainty of my love for pizza, it is that I then eat for dinner. What is there to really choose in that moment? Nothing! *(Except of course if one really loves liver too!)* But if I don't, *(and this is simply to illustrate today's idea),* just as I do not like what I am experiencing here in this world.

Well, actually when I *realize* that what I experience in this world is not as palatable as the Love of God. I can see that I have no doubt and I accept my Oneness in God. And so today it is being focused on what is it that I accept in my life. There really is no choice between this world and God's. It is only because I have doubted the truth within that I think that this world would provide a hearty substitute. It is like using cheap margarine vs. real creamery butter.

Accept no substitutes today. "God is the real thing." Be certain in your truth. Accept that you are as I created you. You do not need to continue to place your search for happiness outside of you. This world you have made has a bitter taste, but yet you ignore the taste. Only My Love will clear your palate. Only My Love will fulfill and sustain you. Accept the truth that you are One with me, at One with all your brothers in certainty and in truth.

∞∞∞

Journal Entry on Lesson 140

Only salvation can be said to cure.

In today's Lesson Jesus is trying to help us understand that although we seem to be awake in the world, in Reality we are still dreaming. Remember in Reality right now, we are God's Son. If that is true, then the experience that we seem to be having as a body living in the world right now must not be true. This is why we call it an illusion. As God's Son, we are dreaming a dream that we are separate from our Creator, living a life in a body that is separate from everything else in a world that seems to be full of all aspects of Creation; love, joy, happiness, pain, fear, disaster, etc.

All of these things we experience here are an illusion. When we think we are experiencing happiness and joy in the world, we are not really experiencing true happiness and joy as it is experienced in Heaven right now with God; it is still just another illusion. This is how the delusional ego thought system keeps us trapped in the illusion. It has us thinking and believing that we are happy when we really are not. Why would we spend time seeking for something much greater if we think we are happy? The ego thought system loves this delusion because it delays us from even attempting to discover who we really are. It delays us from attempting to find the true Light of joy within ourselves.

Jesus points out in today's Lesson that if we find the Light within ourselves that the Light will begin to awaken us and end our dream of illusions. He also places a lot of emphasis today on the practice of discovering the Voice of God within ourselves. He points out that not only does the Light begin to truly heal our minds, but also hearing our Father speak to us through the Voice of the Holy Spirit will also heal our minds as well. Many of us have seen the Light and have heard the Voice of the Holy Spirit speak to us at some point in our lives already. When we recall these experiences we recall that they were joyful ones indeed. They are joyful because they bring the Light of truth and the Voice of Truth to our minds and dispel illusions that we seem to be experiencing every day. This releases us from all the things we believed in about the world.

One thing that is important to recognize, is that the ego does not want us to realize that we have a choice. We are capable of choosing to have these experiences any time we want. This is why we undergo the practice of mind training. We are learning how to let go of everything that we seem to be perceiving with our minds right now, and to open up to the experience of perceiving the Light of God and hearing His Voice speak to us. What a joyful and rewarding practice this is; to begin to learn how to truly carry on a personal relationship and conversation with God! No one will be left behind in learning how to do this because it is in God's plan for everyone to awaken from the dream. And because it is His Will, no one will fail.

All we need to do is continue to practice being silent and demonstrating a willingness, a desire to truly hear His Voice speak to us and to see His Light shine forth from the darkness in our minds. We practice laying aside everything that our minds desired except these two intentions, and then we practice resting in silence with an open mind, waiting patiently for God Himself to answer us. These are the gifts that we as miracle workers give to ourselves, and to the world, as we work with the Holy Spirit in accomplishing the goal of salvation for all.

ooooo

Journal Entry on Lesson 141

Review Lessons 121-122

When we open our minds and become receptive to seeing, hearing and experiencing through the Mind of the Holy Spirit, we begin to have experiences of seeing what the Holy Spirit sees, of hearing what the Holy Spirit hears, and experiencing what the Holy Spirit knows. We begin to have experiences that we are not an individual identity but instead that we are one with something else that is much larger. This Mind which the Holy Spirit is unified with, is hidden in another part of our mind and can seem tricky to learn how to access. This is because we have been trained by the ego to perceive its sights, sounds and thoughts for a long time.

It may seem difficult to learn how to let go of everything the mind now beholds and to open up to something new. But know that there is another part of your mind within your mind that can be experienced. It takes constant practice and a willingness to forgive and to let go of everything you perceive now in order to discover this other part of your mind. It is truly there, and as we learn how to be still and quiet our ego minds, the Mind of God will come forth into our awareness and our experience.

When these experiences with God begin to happen, it is a joyful time indeed. So, as we practice being still in silence and having an open mind, we wait with one intention, and that is to have the experience of God come into our awareness. This is something that we wait and allow to happen. It is not something we do. We simply practice waiting in silence with an open mind and allow it to happen.

While we practice, if we begin to listen to the chatter of our own inner thoughts or our mind begins to wander on images of past memories or on future events, we must remember to stop ourselves and to reaffirm our goal, "*My mind holds only what I think with God.*" We then re-focus ourselves by letting go of these thoughts, stilling our minds once again and waiting for God to respond to us in some way.

Forgiveness is the key to happiness and it offers everything we want. Remember to forgive your thoughts, your perceptions, your mind-wanderings and to simply let them go. They are meaningless. We also want to remember to not let the ego trick us into getting frustrated or angry with our mind wanderings. It's just a delaying maneuver. The ego's thoughts are meaningless. Just let them go and bring our minds back to a place of being still and waiting in silence for God to answer us. And when His response comes let us remember to thank Him for the help He has given to us.

∞∞∞∞

Journal Entry on Lesson 142

Review Lessons 123-124

During my meditation this morning I suddenly received a vision of a teenage African-American wearing brightly colored clothes. It reminded me of the unconscious fears that well up inside of me when I find myself in situations where I am in a mix of ethnically diverse people. Fears from unpleasant past experiences tempt me to want to distance myself from these situations. I realized that this is an example of unconscious thoughts, fears and beliefs that I do not think with God. These can only be coming from the ego who would have me continue to fear my Christ brother and continue to distance myself from my Christ Self. I then realized that this vision was a gift from God.

And so, I thanked my Father for His gift to me in helping me realize that this was an example of an unconscious fearful belief that I could take to the Light and allow the Light of True Forgiveness to come forth and heal it for me. And so, I took a few moments and opened up and waited for the Light to come forth and dispel this illusion away. A minute or two later I felt the sudden shift within my body and saw white light wash through me bringing with it a gentle wave of peace that flowed through my entire being. This was a step in the direction of allowing the Light of True Forgiveness to heal this unconscious fearful part of my mind. I thank my Father for His gift of the Light of True Forgiveness that helps me to heal my mind and the minds of all my brothers with me. I thank my Father for the Light that reminds me I am One with all my brothers in Heaven right now as the Christ, the perfect Holy Son of God Himself. And I thank the Holy Spirit for helping me with this forgiveness lesson and for helping me understand what it truly means to bring the illusions of darkness to the Light.

∞∞∞∞

Journal Entry on Lesson 143

Review Lessons 125-126

In the hustle and bustle of moving from one home to another, it was easy for me to be focused on all that needed to be done to have the move go smoothly. Now that we are settled in, I realized that in the busyness I had forgotten to take more time to sit quietly and nurture myself in Spirit. The ego would have me ignore the physical aches and pains, the tiredness, etc. and this is all to keep me from the love and care needed for myself through my connection with God. Feelings of sacrifice, guilt and unworthiness come to mind. A week of fast food meals, moving, running errands, picking up supplies, slowly left its toll as yesterday for me became a day of irritation and feeling overwhelmed. From burning my fingers with hot oil while cooking, to feeling frustrated that the necessary ingredients I wanted for a specific dish were not in the cupboard, to running more errands in the morning, phone calls to the plumber, internet connection problems, and other interruptions, I had hoped to find peace, but I never really took the moment to do so.

Even in the evening at our ACIM study group, it only provided surface relief. Already feeling agitated, the background noise level at the Center that we have been meeting at for a few months, did not allow me to rest as comfortably during our meditation. My focus was not within.

During our forgiveness journaling process, I had asked the Holy Spirit specifically to help me with the overwhelming and irritable feelings that I had been feeling. I had realized while I was journaling that I had not been caring for myself in a loving manner. I had not eaten until after lunchtime so I sacrificed myself to run errands and thus leading to the irritability that crept in and lasted the day. I did not take as much time to sit in quiet, to rest with God from all the physical and mental work of the last several days. It was still go-go-go! I see how that when I am not giving to myself in a nurturing manner, I cannot truly give to others.

What I give to others in those times can be terse comments, not fully listening to a conversation, and not being fully present in my life, period. The rest that I had in this time of contemplation of reflecting on today's Lesson showed me once again how vital it is to spend the time, how precious I am, and how important it is to take care of my physical, emotional and spiritual needs. I cannot be of service to others if I cannot be of service to myself. When I am in that space, I can easily feel irritated, frustrated and resentful. I give the following advice to others but yet I forget at times to follow the same advice. It is simply to, "Be gentle with yourself." And now it is my turn to embrace. I am grateful for these realizations and insights. I am grateful for the quiet enjoyment I can have when I step back and meet with the Holy Spirit in the Sanctuary of Peace. I am grateful for the willingness to forgive myself and the world. All is perfect in my life's curriculum. I have elected to pursue these lessons and I bless them and welcome them all warmly into my life. Appreciation is all that is needed.

Thank You Father. Amen.

ᴏᴏᴏᴏᴏ

Journal Entry on Lesson 144

Review Lessons 127-128

When I got home from work yesterday afternoon, I decided to sit down and spend some time with Holy Spirit to let go of some of the stress from my day. Before I randomly opened the Course to a page, I quietly asked Jesus to select something fun for me to read. The Course opened to "The Appointed Friend" in Chapter 26 titled "The Transition". I asked Jesus if I should start at the beginning of the chapter. I thought I heard in my thoughts, "No. This is it right here.", so I began reading the section.

After reading the section, some of the sentences that seemed to stand out to me included, "*Without Him you are friendless. Seek not another friend to take His place. There is no other friend...And it is He Who is your only Friend in truth.*" Realizing that Jesus was talking about the Holy Spirit, I started to have this feeling that I wanted to get to know my Friend better. This desire was coming from the feeling of being disconnected from Him because of the business of my day. I wanted that feeling of being connected and not alone to come back to me, so I decided to talk to Him about it in meditation.

I closed my eyes and became silent for a few minutes. The thought then came to me to tell Him how I perceived friends in my life and that I wished I could experience Him the same way. I shared with Him that I thought it would be easier and that I would appreciate it if I could see Him in some way. I told Him that the Course is telling us that He is invisible. He seemed to remind me about the Light that He shows me. I said, "Oh Yeah". And then I remembered that His Voice can speak to me. I told Him that I wanted to get to know Him as my Friend even more and asked Him to help me do that. I also told Him that I wanted His gifts and asked Him to help me make room on His throne for Him. (*"He brings you gifts that are not of this world, and only He to Whom they have been given can make sure that you receive them. He will place them on your throne, when you make room for Him on His."*)

Just before I woke this morning I had a dream with three distinct visions. I dreamt that I had to wake up early to beat a storm that was coming, I saw meaningless sheets of white paper with type written word on them, and I saw a blank white door access card that reminded me of the one I use to get into work. I didn't understand these visions after I woke and let them go as I began my day. After doing today's lesson, Deb looked out the window and said, "You better get going. It looks like it's going to rain." I was planning to ride my bike because our only car was in the shop for repairs. I began to feel afraid and tried to come up with a solution; I would call a friend from work and have him pick me up on the way.

Deb and I scrambled to find his phone number through meaningless paperwork and computer files without success. As the fear rose, I practiced telling myself, "Trust Him, Trust Him". It began to sprinkle while I took a quick shower, I kept praying, "Trust Him, Trust Him". By the time I got dressed the sprinkles stopped and I surrendered to riding my bike the two and a half miles.

As I pulled out of the garage, I smiled at Deb and said, "Ching Ching", pretending I had a bell on my bike. The dark gloomy clouds were getting close. Needless to say I pedaled a little faster today. Just as I began coasting the last 25 meters to the door at work the rain started. Someone just happened to be at the door and held it open for me. Not needing to use my door access card, I coasted right into the building. "Thanks!" I yelled. I then understood that my Friend really did hear my requests to show me that He is with me and that He is my Friend. I was reminded once again that I am not alone and friendless, and that He will help me if I ask Him. Thank you Holy Spirit! I love You!

∞∞∞∞

Journal Entry on Lesson 145

Review Lessons 129-130

Today's lesson brings only peace when I come to know which world I truly want. It is the world of God; it is Heaven itself. Through my forgiveness I lay guilt aside and *"bring the darkness to the light, and guilt to holiness."* T-18.IX.9:1. The Holy Spirit is my dearest Companion correcting all errors in my mind. It is up to me to make the choice of where to place my trust as each voice calls out to me. Is it fear that I meet today, or love. It is up to me. I will remember and the memory of God will come to me when I forgive. In forgiveness the false is removed from what is true and the trueness being only God. To which voice do I listen? Even today, as I contemplate all that I need to accomplish, are my accomplishments, my to-do's as important as my "to-be's"? Be in the Real World, not of the illusory world. Be at peace. Be in the space of True Forgiveness. Be in God's Love. Simply Be.

TWO WORLDS

Two worlds, No in-between
One is real, one make believe
One my prison, one my release
Two worlds, no in-between

Two worlds, each within me
One a nightmare,
one a happy dream
Whichever I choose,
will play upon the screen
Two worlds, no in-between

Two Worlds, each is calling me
Heaven or hell
No in-between
~Donna Marie Cary

Our dear friend, Donna Marie Cary writes and sings truly inspiring music. This is from Donna's "No Solid Ground" CD, to hear a sample and to order, go to: www.donnamariecary.com

∞∞∞∞

Journal Entry on Lesson 146

Review Lessons 131-132

Yesterday I experienced the Holy Spirit's work in action! Having just moved into our new home, I wanted to contact old friends and share with them our joy of the new place along with the news that my youngest daughter was coming to live with us very soon.

In one email to a friend, at the end, I added an unusual request. I didn't know why I was to include it, but felt led to do so. My friend received the email and responded right away. I perceived her to be taken aback and even angry at the request. I subsequently began to make this about her, instead of looking within to see where the problem really was which, as a Course student I know that it is within my very mind. This ensued with a few emails back and forth to further explain and respond. The tension mounted.

At one point I felt the hurt, the sense of loss, sadness and separation, even judgment towards myself and her. I felt the tears beginning to well up in my eyes. I stopped right then at the keyboard and asked for a miracle. "Holy Spirit, I give to You all that I am feeling towards my friend and myself right now. All the sadness and judgment. Everything. What is it that I need to know? I accept Your guidance and peace."

Within a few moments, I felt an enormous wave of love flow through me. It was an outpouring of gratitude and appreciation as I remembered how she had been there for me when I had gone through a family crisis years ago. All that love and care that I felt for her then and her for me came back. It was full, even overwhelming and warmed my heart. A sense of true appreciation for her was graciously received and felt. A miracle had occurred. Nothing else seemed to matter. I opened my eyes and saw that she was still on the internet. I sent her a smiley face via instant messenger. Holy Spirit then guided me to share this healing in an email, sharing the appreciation for the friendship and the healing itself. She likewise responded as she had been touched by my sharing of appreciation and had had a shift herself. All from one email, we mused. Love was still present. It had never left; a great healing taking place in the One Mind. Two had joined as One.

Later I was reminded of the quote from the Text in Chapter 12:

"Only appreciation is an appropriate response to your brother. Gratitude is due him for both his loving thoughts and his appeals for help, for both are capable of bringing love into your awareness if you perceive them truly. And all your sense of strain comes from your attempts not to do just this."

And so in my seeking for the truth, I did in fact succeed. And I thank You Holy Spirit, my Friend, Who leads me always to the truth, I love You and appreciate You. And to my dear friend here in the illusion, the part of my One Self that has provided me with such a healing, I love you and appreciate you. And to me, for having the willingness to step back and to remember peace, I love and appreciate you.

ooooo

Journal Entry on Lesson 147

Review Lessons 133-134

Let us remember that perception is anything we can see, hear or feel with the body. The ego which is everything you normally see, feel and hear with the body including the body itself is an illusion; and thus is valueless. If you have a desire to see, feel, hear or experience anything in the world of the ego it is a waste of time because it is not real. This is difficult to believe when these are the only things that you seemed to have experienced all of your life, but remember there is another world that can be perceived and experienced. It is carefully hidden but truly there. Hidden within your mind you have spiritual eyes, hearing, feeling and experiences that are available to you. These are gifts that come from the Holy Spirit to help you to perceive the truth. The other world that He would show you is a world of Light.

The Light of the other world can be perceived within your mind if you allow the Holy Spirit to show it to you. The Light you see and the Voice you will hear is the bridge that will help you to transition smoothly from this world to the other world which is your Home in God. It takes a lot of practice and willingness to let go of the world you now perceive in order to perceive the other world. When you begin to perceive the Light of the other world and hear the Voice of God speak to you, you are beginning to perceive forgiveness as it is. You will know it when you see it and hear it because it always brings with it the gifts of joy and peace.

This is the beginning of the removal of the blocks of the awareness of Love's presence. Love which is Who you really are, always brings with it glad tidings from your Father to His Son, Who you are; and from you, His Son, back to His Father. We are all in Heaven in perfect Love right now that lasts and grows forever. We are all eternally happy and joyful in Him Who created us and we share it together with each other in everlasting Love. Let us remember to thank Him for His gifts to us. They help us to remember what is valueless through the perception of the Light of Truth as it is now in Heaven. Praise God. Amen.

∞∞∞∞

Journal Entry on Lesson 148

Review Lessons 135-136

Do not draw a line in the sand that keeps you separated from your brothers. This is not what your heart desires. It seems that way when others do not fulfill the function that you had planned for them. Each time a brother seems to let you down, you defend yourself by forgetting the truth and digging deeper into your fortress of unforgiveness. Use forgiveness as the saving grace that brings down the walls of pain and leads you to the Holy Grail of Light. You know if you check within your heart that this is what you truly want. You want peace, not conflict. You want love, not fear. Rely on Me to lead you out of the fortified walls of fear and into the valley of serenity. This is where you will find and remember the Oneness that you share. Know that you are Love. Teach that you are Love. Remember that you are Love.

oooooo

Journal Entry on Lesson 149

Review Lessons 137-138

As we practice the lessons in the Workbook for Students let us remember that Jesus is helping us to restore our gift of Spiritual sight. He is helping us to remember that there is another way of seeing. We can learn how to see through the other part of our mind that has been kept hidden from us by the ego thought system. Everything we see through the body's eyes is part of the ego thought system. When we see a person we are not seeing what God created, we are seeing what the ego thought system made, an image of a body. The body is not really there but we think it is because we think we can see it, feel it, smell it, etc. Imagine that, the ego thought system seems to have manifested thoughts into physical reality that gives us the illusion of seeing, feeling, smelling and hearing things that really aren't showing the truth about who we really are and where we came from. And then to make things a little more difficult, the ego thought system gives us the illusion that we have forgotten who we are and where we are right now in Reality.

Jesus knows that our minds are caught in this ego thought system trap. It is an illusory prison for our minds. In Reality right now we are completely surrounded by Heaven and are Heaven Itself. We are God. We have a Creator Who Created us exactly like Himself and we share His existence as God with Him in Heaven right now. In Reality we are a Spiritual Being. Think about that for a moment, we are not a body, but instead, a Spiritual Being of Light.

Jesus: Close your eyes and pause for a moment and let Me help you imagine what it would feel like to be without our body. Do you see how free you are beginning to feel? Now multiply this feeling into eternity to give your self a glimmer of what it would be like. This memory and experience has never really left you but in the illusion it has. This is why the Holy Spirit was created; to help the Son of God restore the memory of Who He really is. That's you!

The Holy Spirit sees us exactly as we are in Heaven right now and He has a Spiritual Gift for us to see. It is the gift of the Vision of Christ. The Vision of Christ is a vision of white light that He is waiting to show us in our minds. It looks very similar to the famous Bethlehem Star seen during our season of Christmas. It is a symbol in the world for the Vision of Christ which can actually be seen very clearly within our minds if we focus all of our attention on trying to see it. Ask the Holy Spirit to help you and He will.

Our first glimmerings of the Light of Christ may be experienced as sparks of white light. It may feel a little scary to try to see the Light at first but once we do, we will recognize that we actually love the Light and will naturally want to see more of it. These are glimmerings of the Light of our True Self. These are Holy Instants. In the flash of an instant, we catch glimpses of Heaven, the reality of our brothers and of ourselves in Heaven right now with God. How wonderful it is to be reminded from brother Jesus and from each other that this can be done.

Thank you Father for your gifts to us and for helping us to find our way Home.

∞∞∞∞

Journal Entry on Lesson 150

Review Lessons 139-140

"Monday Morning Blues" - something we all have experienced at one time or another in our lives. Paul and I talked about this today as we rose and began our day with the Workbook Lesson. He was able to relate the feeling back to his childhood and the wonderful Sundays he would have at this grandparents' farm, the joy and happiness and freedom of exploring and having no cares in the world. Back home again Sunday night and through the week, he would experience a great deal of pain in his family with his father's alcoholism and situations that resulted in fear. It was a burden to return to the regular week, a week that consisted of no hope, limits, and a feeling of unworthiness.

As we shared about the idea of the "Monday or After Holiday Morning Blues" several ideas came to mind for me. And yes, I have experienced those myself over the years. What came to me in meditation was first an 80's rock song "Everybody's Working for the Weekend." To me, the title of that song speaks volumes. We are not present in what we are doing on a daily, even moment by moment basis. I recall my past employment experiences. I put in my time, all just for my pay, just so I can try to enjoy myself on the weekends. It never happened. Each Sunday night/Monday morning I would have rather call in sick than face the day ahead. The job is not what fulfills me. It is simply a means of getting something that really gets me nothing. I had placed all happiness outside of me. And so, I do not truly focus on the work while I am at my job because I would rather be somewhere else in my mind.

The other insight I had came as Paul shared more about his childhood experiences. In this world we have made, we have divided out time to five days of "work" and two days of "play, rest and worship." And so, we do not rest until we have completed our work. Mmmm...that sounds familiar. Not only that we give

God one day, maybe not an entire day, but an hour of our time. And then we wonder why we feel so disconnected. And so, here I am living in limits that I have placed upon myself, always searching for what will be the next solution to my happiness. A vacation perhaps....ah...but we still don't want to go back to work after that too. Why not vacation or weekend in your mind?

In relation to this whole talk on the 7 days of the week, what also came to me was the Course quote, "*Make this year different by making it all the same.*" To me, the Holy Spirit said, "Make each day different by making them all the same. Give the time to God. Give the time to play. Give the time to work. Give the time to rest. Give the time to complete the tasks. Give the time for happiness. And this is done by giving all that you do to Me. It is very simple. Step back and allow Me to step forward in your life. You have tried to find happiness in a day or two of rest. Rest with Me throughout the moments of your day and you will know the meaning then of being in the moment. You will not feel angst or anxiousness, tiredness or the desire to be elsewhere because you will only be in one place with Me, the place of peace. There is no time like the present. That is what you need. This Now moment is your salvation and I ask you to accept it now."

∞∞∞∞

Journal Entry on Lesson 151

All things are echoes of the Voice for God.

In this morning's Lesson Jesus instructs us to give the Holy Spirit our thoughts so that they may be transfigured. This reminds me of an experience that I had with the Holy Spirit the other day. I pulled an Enlightenment Card out of Gary Renard's Enlightenment Deck and it presented me with the idea of becoming proficient at practicing forgiveness. I went into silent meditation and asked the Holy Spirit about this idea of becoming proficient at the art of forgiveness. After a few minutes of waiting in silence, I began to observe images that the Holy Spirit began to show me. He showed me an image of a hamburger and then a spark of white light flashed it away. And then He showed me another image of something that I unconsciously feared and flashed that away with a spark of white light. Another image came and that too was flashed away with a spark of white light. With each spark I felt a little more healed, a little more free, a little happier because I felt the peace come and wash away the fear and heal it.

You see, I had this unconscious fear that every time I ate a hamburger the grease within it would eventually clog my veins and arteries, give me a heart attack and take my life away from me. The ego had taught me this fearful thought and belief a long time ago when I was a child. This fearful belief was planted in my unconscious mind and recently started to come to the surface to bug me every time I tried to enjoy a hamburger. This may seem a little silly, but if I compound this with all the fearful thoughts and beliefs that the ego has planted in my unconscious mind over the years, it feels quite wearing indeed.

The other day I truly experienced the miracle of the Light of Forgiveness. The Light has come and healed my mind ever so little, and has freed me a little more from the untruth of the illusions of fear. The Light has reminded me of the truth that lies beyond all illusions. There is nothing in this world that will harm neither me nor anyone, because the world is an illusion of fear and sickness and death. I am truly grateful for the Light because it shows us the truth of what lies beyond it all, and frees our minds from the unholy thoughts we learned from the ego thought system.

Thank You Father for the Holy Spirit Who helps us to transform our thoughts of fear into the Light of Reality and Truth. Amen.

Journal Entry on Lesson 152

The power of decision is my own.

This morning while I waited in silent meditation I humbly asked the holy Son of God to reveal Himself to me. I spent a few moments talking to Him with thoughts of encouragement to show Himself to me and to speak to me. (I recognize that I was really giving myself words of encouragement to help me feel more open to seeing my true self again.) I told Him that I wanted to be his Friend forever. I said to Him that You are dreaming a dream and that it was like being stuck in a dream that was hard to awaken from. But it's going to be okay because we are going to awaken from our dream, and we are going to do it together gently. It's okay to show me how beautiful and innocent You are and I would really appreciate having an opportunity to see and to hear You talk with me again.

I've seen Your light before and I know You are there. I've heard You speak to me very clearly in an audible voice before, and so I know that Your Voice for God is there too. So right now, I wish to see and hear You speak to me once again so that I can know You as my Friend a little more. Please reveal Yourself to me. And then I waited in silence expecting Him to show himself to me. All of a sudden He did. I saw the Light of Christ. A pure solid white light about the size of a water drop illuminated in the center of my mind's eye and rays of white light radiated from it illuminating the rest of my mind's peripheral vision. I felt the Light of Healing and Peace shoot forth from my chest when my mind illuminated. I believe this is an experience of the Vision of Christ. And I believe this vision waits in store for each and every one of us because the power of decision truly is our own. As we continue to practice opening our minds to Him, not only will we perceive the Light of Christ but we will also hear His holy Voice speak clearly to us. And then, because of these miracles, we begin to understand and see a glimmering of how our Father really created us. We begin to recognize and personally experience a glimmering of Who We Really Are.

∞∞∞∞

Journal Entry on Lesson 153

In my defenselessness my safety lies.

It is important to remember that no matter how much planning we do to surround ourselves with things that help us feel safe; we will never really truly feel safe until we find the strength of Christ within ourselves. The way the ego thought system works is that we are led to believe everything is okay for awhile, then suddenly there is a rude awakening and something seems to go wrong, things seem to be taken away. This is the endless cycle of the ego's shenanigans. There is nothing in the ego thought system that we can ever place your reliance upon. There are no guarantees except one, the illusion that our inner peace will be taken away from us time and time again. This is what the ego thought system was designed to do, to block our awareness of love's presence and to keep our minds trapped in the state of fear and hell for as long as it can. Fortunately, the Light of Christ that resides within us can never be truly abolished. For the Light comes from our Source and our Source, our Father, is eternal.

Out of His Eternalness He created Us, His perfect Son. In Reality, we are a perfect creation of our Father. In all aspects we were created exactly like Himself with one exception, we did not create ourselves. He created Us and therefore we could never abolish ourselves no matter how hard we seem to try in our dream of illusions. The Holy Spirit is with each and every one of us. He is the Friend that was assigned by our Father Himself to help us awaken from our dream of hell. He will help us to recognize the strength of Christ within ourselves. The Light we see and feel will help us to understand our sinlessness and our defenselessness. He helps us to understand that all things beyond the illusion of separation are perfect; that everything and everyone we see is holy and resides in the Light of Perfection right now. Let's be silent and remember to let Him show us the gifts of Light He has in store for us and let His Voice speak to us in remembrance of Him Who created Us. We thank the Holy Spirit for His gifts to us, for they free us from our dreams of insanity and set us free indeed.

ooooo

Journal Entry on Lesson 154

I am among the ministers of God.

To be in service to others.....to attend to others.....this is the meaning of ministering. We do not need to have a distinction or accreditation. We are here simply to fulfill our special function for others. In the world, it may be as an accountant, artist or even formal minister. It is for me to listen to the Voice for God and accept His Word for myself and to share it with my brothers. That is how I am in service and an as an attendant to them. That is part of my function; it is to bring my brothers in union as One through my forgiveness. The messages of the ego will speak to me of separation in its various forms through feelings of competition, jealousy, judgment, gathering material surroundings, etc.

Only the Voice for God will speak of communion with all. This is my freedom. This is the message that I receive to know my true nature, to know that I am as God created me, and to know that my brothers however they may seem in the world to me are really reflections of myself here to help me recognize my True Self. My brothers may seem to frustrate me, anger me, hurt me but they are only images of the aspects of myself that need to come to the healing sanctuary. If I am in the space of upset, then I minister to myself with unconditional love, knowing that I am doing the best that I can and as I am ready to listen to the message of the Holy Spirit about the situation or person, I will. It is a divine gift when I accept it. I have to be attentive to my spiritual needs as they arise. Sometimes the message I receive is to contemplate alone in silence, sometimes it is to join in joy with others, at other times it may be a combination. All is perfect because God is perfect, and I am God's Son. I am grateful for the messages that I receive to carry forth to the world. I never know what the message will be until it is received and accepted in my heart. It is always a blessing to know when another mind has been lit, even though that fact does not matter.

Holy Spirit, let my mind be lit by your Eternal Love and allow me to carry forth all that You would have me share. I am Your holy vessel today. Amen.

ooooo

Journal Entry on Lesson 155

I will step back and let Him lead the way.

The Holy Spirit is always walking with me. Whatever path I take, to the left or the right, He is there with me. It is my decision then to either allow Him to lead or allow the ego to lead. And I am aware that there have been times in my life when I have allowed Him to lead and many times in the past where I allowed the ego to lead. In those times of the ego's leadership, the Holy Spirit was still beside me every step of the way. He knows that it is my decision on who I am following. Any decision that I have made is not lost. The Holy Spirit can use every choice that I have made to be used for my healing process. It is as I am ready to review those and accept the healing. The lessons continue with or without my knowledge.

Now that I am on the path with Him, dedicated to that journey with Him, I am well aware that there are times that I have been *"tempted still to walk ahead of truth, and let illusions be my guide."* This is when fear has taken hold in my mind and I feel that I can lead much better, sorry Holy Spirit You just cannot handle this one and so I'll take care of this one myself.

An example with this would be with finances or abundance. This occurred last year when we moved to Madison, WI and even though I was confident that Holy Spirit's plan for me was to minister full-time, when we sat down to determine the income and the expenses, fear took over. Because of this fear, I promptly looked for a part-time job under the guise that I could still devote some time to the ministry. Since I allowed the fearful part of me, the ego, to take the guiding steps, I did indeed manifest a perfect job. However, I was not happy, fulfilled and it was obviously not what I was called to do.

After a few weeks of pain and contemplation, I decided that the Holy Spirit had directed me truly. It was for me to simply trust and allow Him to show me the limitless Love that He has for me. It was to trust and know that He would not abandon us and that all would be taken care of. And so, I resigned from the position and accepted my position with the Holy Spirit. Within a very short period of time, I was illuminated with inner strength and a certainty that He goes with me. It was revealed with each trusting belief how He does indeed support me. More students for me to work with appeared in my life, our Illumination Journal was completed and published, spiritual counseling clients, website design for other ministers, all this in allowing the Holy Spirit to lead and all that was needed found its way to us.

I am grateful to look at this even now, to have this reminder Holy Spirit, this reminder to allow You to step forward in my life because I know that You know the fears that I have. The ego can bring up the fears that surrounded those outflows of monies with our recent move in addition to the trip that will occur later in the month to bring my daughter home to live with us. More expenses, Holy Spirit. I know that I have been tempted to fix the problem myself. I know if I attempt to fix the problem, it will not work. Holy Spirit, You know that I falter at times with this, but always You outstretch Your hand to me, ever encouraging me to place my hand in Yours and know that Your Loving Presence will always support me in security and safety. True Abundance is in You. The Truth goes before me and I will not look behind me and allow the past to steer me astray. I seem to have traveled a long way, but it is ever shorter with You. Thank You for journeying with me, walking the way to my True Self, walking the way to God. Amen.

∞∞∞

Journal Entry on Lesson 156

I walk with God in perfect holiness.

Walk with Me a while and let Me tell you of your holiness. Let Me tell you of the Light that you carry deep within you. Let this Light step forward and shine away the fog of illusions that have held your mind. See now the Truth that you behold. It is there right in front of you. Let It guide your ways now. Let the Light within you always sing to you of your greatness in My Eyes. This Light you carry, all your brothers carry as well. As you recognize It in yourself you will recognize It in them as well. Listen well to what I tell you. This Light, this Love is Who you are. You have covered It over by pretending that you are something else. You made this world to hide from the Truth for it scared you so. Do not be afraid to let your Light shine. Cherish the Love that you are for that is only how I see you.

There is not a thing that you could do or say that would change that precious Love that I have for you. You are My Holy Child. Unwrap the gift of potential, put away the toys of madness, embrace and join the song of Life. What you have made here is only to be forgiven. Place each thought, each belief, each situation, all that troubles you, all that you see, take it now and place it on the holy altar of forgiveness. As you do so, let Me be the Beacon of Truth. You will see now beyond it all. You will see the radiance of Perfect Love. At times it may seem hard to believe that you could be loved so much by Me. It is true! When you can accept My Love for your very self, you will accept the greatness that you are. You will accept your worthiness. No more tears but tears of Joy will be had. Come now and walk with me, embrace the Light, and embrace your brothers. Bask in the Light that joins us all as One. You are Loved.

ooooo

Journal Entry on Lesson 157

Into His Presence would I enter now.

The rain softly taps against the window this morning, as I contemplate on today's Lesson. The healing waters purifying the pollen in the air, yet also nurturing the ground for the harvest of healing that continues to grow; this is what it is for me as I enter into the Sanctuary with the Holy Spirit. I am here today to purify and nurture myself once again. Coming in silence and in trust, knowing that I am touched ever so gently by His Love with my hands are open, ready to receive the illuminations of my mind. All that had troubled me as I fell asleep last night has now been regulated to the dream world. Today, I can trust in Him. Today I can start afresh and leave any discomfort in my mind on His holy altar. This is where I find peace.

I do not have to carry around the judgment and angers of the past for they are simply unneeded and truly unwanted baggage. I may find that I do this many, many times. It does not matter. Holy Spirit knows that everything is here for my learning and for the remembrance of Him Who walks with me. It is freedom to travel lightly, releasing the burdens that I cling on to and insist on carrying in my mind. Be they little or large, it is certainly time to release them all. I have gone through periods where I have been able to do so consistently which resulted in great peace. Then other times, I have allowed the world to step in and define my feelings. It is through this recognition that I can decide to change my mind, to accept another way of being. That is what I do today as the rain falls gently from the sky reminding me to go within, go into the Holy Shelter and wait awhile. Stop and listen to His Voice and receive His peace. No need to go anywhere just yet, but to simply wait with Him in the stillness. All questions are answered here. All burdens released and all peace is restored. Thank You Holy Spirit. Amen.

∞∞∞

Journal Entry on Lesson 158

Today I learn to give as I receive.

Today, greet the day with open arms of gratitude. In the mirror, see your True Self reflected. As you walk about your day in your various travels, look upon the further reflections of your True Self revealed in your neighbors, your friends, your family and even the seeming strangers you come across. They are all Christ to you. Which do you want to see? The Light or the darkness? Behold the Light today by forgiving all that has darkened your mind. Travel with holiness. Travel with Me and I will continue to show you what is meaningful and what is meaningless. I will show you with each step how to see yourself and others. Use My Eyes, the Eyes of Love to see truly today. Walk the way of Love.

∞∞∞

Journal Entry on Lesson 159

I give the miracles I have received.

There's an old song that goes, "Love is nothing 'til you give it away....you end up having more. Love is like a magic penny, hold on tight and you won't have any. Lend it, spend it. You'll have so many; they'll be rolling all over the floor." And so is true with miracles today. What I focus on increases and expands, so be it love, miracles, forgiveness, healing, light, it all will become abundant and all my brothers can reap the harvest.

The more I try to control in my life, the less I will truly be happy. I am grateful for having received that lesson years ago. I know others who are going through this very lesson now. One does not see that the same way they keep handling situations is bringing the same results and of course resulting in unhappiness. Yet, when are we ready to experience another way?

Fear is what keeps us guarded from allowing love in. I may lose something. I may be abandoned. But by switching into a loving mode and giving the love away, loving freely, allowing others to do so, one will find that they will have more love than they ever imagined. We do not want to give because of our own insecurities caused by our own past of pain. And so we continue to live our lives seeking for happiness outside of ourselves, controlling and managing each situation so all is perfect in our eyes. But it never is. Situations are always outside our control. We cannot control others. We can decide in our mind on which voice to listen to, the Voice of Love or the voice of fear.

In this decision, I will remember the truth. I will love as God would have me love. I will offer forgiveness. I will offer healing. I will offer miracles. In truly knowing my abundance in all, I can give what I have received because I have received all from the Father. This is the lesson to teach. It is a simple lesson of love. You will smile more. You will be truly happy. You will experience a lightness in your body. You will walk with certainty and trust. You will experience peace. All because you have accepted the treasure that is already yours. You have accepted your worthiness. You have accepted your True Self. You have remembered God.

∞∞∞∞

Journal Entry on Lesson 160

I am at home. Fear is the stranger here.

I have wandered around believing that I was homeless. Even in my day to day life there have been times when living in this world just has not seemed right. "Stop the world I want to get off," is quite the feeling indeed. When I see the injustices, the wars, the conflicts between family members, the actions done in the name of righteousness, I truly wonder "Is this really the world God created as told to me as a child?" I always knew somehow deep down that it was not.

At 16, I questioned all that I was taught. I found meditation and the deep connection to the Divine. I found that God truly was only Love and All-Loving and not full of damnation and punishment and hell. And then as I became older, I forgot, as the world tempted me with its glittery trinkets. "This is love," it called out. And then I came to remember again when the Course entered my life in 1994. Reading its pages, I truly believed that I was now home. My home is not of this world. This is not what God created. I have placed my own fearful sullied image upon God and what He created in truth. But now the light had dawned. Fear is the stranger, it is not my friend. Wanting to control anything in my life is based in fear. Seeking for happiness in material or other things is based in fear. It is not accepting who I truly am. I am as God created me. I had simply forgotten and at times I still do if I get distracted by images in the world. But I can remember and I do. That is what the Holy Spirit is here to do. He is here to help me remember as I am willing to do so. The Holy Spirit will reveal my true Home to me and I will be comfortable, cared for and carried as I recognize Heaven as my only home. Love welcomes me because It only recognizes Itself. I gladly embrace the Love that has never left for I am recognizing my Self.

∞∞∞∞

Journal Entry on Lesson 161

Give me your blessing, holy Son of God.

As I recall someone to my mind, it is only the reflection of myself that I am bringing forward to practice this lesson. It may appear that there is another individual who spites me so. This person may be dishonest, argumentative, deceitful, bull-headed, controlling, self-centered, selfish and the list may continue at arm's length. However, these qualities that I believe are held within another are something for me to look at as well since I project all these upon another probably because I possess the same qualities. I wouldn't want to see myself that way now would I? With this lesson then, I am choosing to see with the eyes of Christ and thus see my brother as innocent and pure, and so I am truly willing to see myself the same. What are the lessons that I can take from this? Where are the places within myself that I can begin to release? To heal?

If a brother troubles me by their consistent lack of respect, where have I been disrespectful myself to others? Am I willing to see and change and forgive it in both of us? Am I willing to let go of the anger that has possessed me so? Am I willing to now listen to the Holy Spirit's perception of us both? It is shifting my focus from what I perceive as negative and wrong to that of what is God's truth. We can see beyond the behaviors to the essence of who we are, of who they are. The essence is that we are God's children. So by asking for a blessing, I am asking it for myself. I am already blessed and so is my brother. This allows me to accept it within both of us. This takes willingness to see differently, to see that this person is not what they appear to be. They are just another angel there to assist us in letting go a little more of the fear that has permeated our lives. This person does not have to continue to be in our lives, such in the case of abuse or the like but I can withdraw my grievances and offer miracles instead, offer blessings instead to both of us. With that I can move on to a more peaceful life. It is my choice in what I offer. I choose to offer blessings today.

ᴏᴏᴏᴏᴏ

Journal Entry on Lesson 162

I am as God created me.

"I am as God created me".....over and over as a mantra or focal point while I sat quietly in solitude with the Divine. Today it is my honor to accept once and for all. My Father does not see what I see. He does not see the grief and misery, loss, the sin and guilt that I have concluded for myself. He sees only perfection. And, if He sees only perfection in me, why not experience that for myself? *"I am as God created me,"* is a breath of fresh air. It is the rainbow after the storm. It is the covenant of Creator to His Son. The light has come to bless my holy mind and accept His will for me.

Each time today if I am reminded otherwise, if the ego insists that it is my creator, I will silently say to myself in confidence and trust, *"I am as God created me."* I fool not myself in this for this is the absolute truth. Applying the idea for the day is my joyful task. Sometimes it is forgotten, but oh when it is remembered, the light dawns brightly and the choirs of angels sing. It is a gentle shift into my awakening, stretching and yawning from the slumber of illusion. I am yoked with the Father in true relationship and as in yoga, I gently "come back to center," as I return Home, not as a prodigal son, but as His glorious Son that He so dearly loves.

ထတတ

Journal Entry on Lesson 163

There is no death. The Son of God is free.

In meditation on today's Lesson, the first paragraph continued to intrigue my mind. Death appears in many forms, all that it may deny the Eternal Life of God. I was also then guided to the Manual for Teachers, Section 27. "What is Death?" This section reminded me that *"Death is the symbol of the fear of God."* and *"Without the idea of death there is no world."* and *"There is either a god of fear or One of Love."* and finally, *"He did not make death because He did not make fear."* Any forms of death, the sadness, fear, anger and the like all deny the truth of God's existence and thus deny who I am as well. These forms of death strengthen the ego's strange world. My practice for today is to extend all these forms to the Holy Spirit. Give Him each one as they would appear in my mind, the concerns, the uncertainties, all the fear, I gladly release to Him. And if after I release, I feel the same feelings arise, then again will I offer the fears to the Holy Spirit's altar. More and more the peace will fill my mind, the miracles will enlighten me. But what of others, what if they are feeling loss, grief or anger, do I tell them to not feel that way for they are wrong?

It is not for me to judge another where they are nor to force them into the awakening process. The Holy Spirit is there within each one awaiting the willingness to see differently and experience the miracle. I can hold the sacred space for the other person, just as the Holy Spirit does for me when I am lost in the wastelands of fear. I can be a comforting friend, a holy companion that continues to hold the truth. I know when I am going through this gamut of emotions; it feels very real and dark to me. I cannot see the light. It is only through my willingness then I place my hand in the Holy Spirit's and trust to be led out and into the light. Trust that my brothers will do the same; I may even be Holy Spirit's channel in speaking to them. That is when I stop and ask, "What would be helpful in this situation right now? What would you have me say or do?" And then I stay in the flow with Him. I am the messenger of God and my eyes will see the reflection of His Love in my brothers and myself. This is the flow of life. This is aliveness and joy, to be One with all.

∞∞∞

Journal Entry on Lesson 164

Now are we one with Him Who is our Source.

In meditation, I began to hear a song we used to sing for the folk mass at my Catholic High School. The first two lines of this message are similar to the lines in that song.

Sing to the Lord a new song, let your song be sung from the mountaintops for He has turned your sorrow into joy, your darkness into light. Sing with Him now the sweet melody of Home. You hear it ever so faintly as you stir from your night's slumber. As you come to awaken you hear it more clearly; its meaning is known to you. It is what your heart as longed for, to remember the Father and the Son as one. Each time you give the openness and silent space for Him, He will enter fully into your mind. It is a gift gladly given and joyously received. I am here to help you strengthen the connection with your Father. It is what you want. Release all that crosses your mind that holds you joined to this world. Accept freedom in the limitless, formless love that you are. There are no chains to bind you. Walk away and into the Light of His Love. Each link of the chain you believe holds you, you have forged out of fear and so the chain is nothing, simply a holographic image. Release your belief in the image of fear and you open up to a world that has been given you. In this, you will see your innocence. In this, you will see your great worth. Christ is here. See through the eyes of Christ and accept salvation as your own.

∞∞∞

Journal Entry on Lesson 165

Let not my mind deny the Thought of God.

In the world the last few days I seemed to be experiencing communication problems, whether it was issues with the old traditional phone company as we switch to the new VoIP company, or not being able to contact Paul at certain times while he has been away these last 2 weeks for military training. I also found that other folks were experiencing similar situations, miscommunications with "the boss", friends or family members. The ego certainly does like chaos.

And as it says in Chapter 4, Section VII, "*The ego is thus against communication, except insofar as it is utilized to establish separateness rather than to abolish it.*" So the ego being quite "*literally a fearful thought*" does not want me to have a direct link to the Father. This reminds me of the "Telephone" game that probably most of us have played as children. We allow the ego to filter and divide the information over and over again and thus not listening to the True Source speak directly to us. It is fear that keeps me from the direct communication with God. And it is fear that keeps me separated from my brothers. And so this is how I deny the Thought of God, through the filters of fear that the ego has made. The ego sees the direct communication as a threat, since its existence depends on my belief in it. If I accept the Thought of God in my mind the ego disappears. The Thought of God is always present, and it is for me to focus upon It.

As the seeming frustration mounted with each is communication occurrence, I knew that through forgiveness I would clear the channel or "clean my ears" so to speak, and hear the guidance, love and support that is there for me from God. With forgiveness, it is my asking to hear only His Voice speak to me. This brings me to a more peaceful place in dealing with whomever and whatever I need to deal with. It takes me out of reactionary mode and allows a calmness and clear-headedness to step forward. With forgiveness, it is denying the ego and accepting the Thought of God that "protects me, cares for me, makes soft my resting place and smoothes my way, lighting my mind with happiness and love." Ah...that certainly feels much better.

Thank You Father for the Holy Spirit Who is ever present in my mind assisting me in all situations, and all I need do is ask and be willing to receive. Amen.

∞∞∞∞

Journal Entry on Lesson 166

I am entrusted with the gifts of God.

"Christ's hand has touched your shoulder, and you feel that you are not alone."

Your reassuring touch assures me that I am safe at Home. Indeed I have wandered in the wastelands, alone and afraid. But You were there with me the entire time. With my eyes lowered to see the depths of darkness I did not see upward towards the Light that was always present. I thank You Spirit for continuing the journey with me, consistent in Your care and direction. Today, I feel Your presence and rejoice knowing that I have all that I have been searching for. The abundance has been mine, I just needed to have lifted my eyes and look into Christ's face. This home that I have made here in the world has never felt like my home for I have never felt welcome. In my heart, You have welcomed me and shown me the places in which to dwell. Coming into my own, coming into my brilliance, I gladly share and extend the same Light to my brothers. This assures them that all they need do is raise their eyes and see the Truth of the Father.

We need not walk as homeless and without cause. I, along with all of my brothers, have a mighty purpose now. My purpose is to remember the richness of Eternal Life. Here, am I safe and secure. Here, am I confident and certain. The reassuring touch I place on others, encourages them, loves them, and brings them also to their radiant Self. And so what more can there be, letting go of my poverty, to accept my gifts, the gifts that have been entrusted to me. Gladly do I give up what never was mine, and accept what is. I remember, Father, I remember.
Thank You. Amen.

ooooo

Journal Entry on Lesson 167

There is one life, and that I share with God.

Some random thoughts on today's Lesson:

...I have made many decisions in my life that opposed God. Because of this I have brought fear, anger, abuse and depression into my life. As I live my life now on the path that seems right for me, the ego wants to tell me that I do not deserve to do so, that I do not deserve happiness that I should sacrifice and suffer like everyone else seems to be doing. Listening to the ego's voice will bring the same pain. Is that what I really want? No, I want to be happy! When I listen to Holy Spirit I know that I am ok, and I know that to experience true happiness all I need do is follow God's Will. This world will never understand God's Will...

...It is my unwillingness that prevents me from my true joy. If I would allow myself to let go of all that I do not need - fear thoughts, angry feelings, being right - I could experience the gift of life that is within my soul. It is important for me to take the time to relax, be still and listen instead of getting caught up in the world and all the judgments it brings. This is death. By utilizing my time wisely with the Holy Spirit, He brings me peace and a reminder of my living connection to Love. I choose to follow the Holy Spirit and not my ego self. Following Spirit's lead will ensure supreme happiness. Thank You Spirit. Thank You God. Thank me...

∞∞∞∞

Journal Entry on Lesson 168

Your grace is given me. I claim it now.

Thank You Father for the Divine Gift of the Holy Spirit Who assists me in lay downing all my burdens of fear before the holy altar. As I lay them down, I recognize my freedom and come to state the truth of the grace that has been given to me by You. Father, my mind is open and I know that as I open to You, You will come to me. And now in quiet, I wait to listen to Your Word of Love to be spoken to me. It is a silent space to come into communion with You. In this stillness, I find my resting place. I find my Home. I come to You and You take me the rest of the holy way. That is what I desire today, to go Home to You and to forget about all that I have made in this world, if even for a moment's peace.

Gratitude is mine this day for this experience. And now I can continue to walk through my day bringing with me the knowledge of all that is mine in You. If I stumble, I need not grumble, but merely remember to choose once again the truth. Mistakes are just that, a miss-take and so I go on with Take 2, 10,

100, whatever it may be. It does not matter, for You dear Father do not even count those takes. It is only the ego that counts and keeps record. You see me as perfect for there was only one take when You extended Your Love to me. It is all for me to remember and in the end the One Son is the winner who takes all because the One Son has had it all along.

∞∞∞

Journal Entry on Lesson 169

By grace I live. By grace I am released.

I started today's meditation with the prayer, "*By grace I live. By grace I am released. By grace I give. By grace I will release,*" praying it several times as a mantra. Then, silence. A soft Voice said, "*God is...*" I then remembered the next line, "*...and then we cease to speak...*" At that point each thought or word that came to mind in relation to God's attributes was released as I repeated again, "God is...and then I cease to speak." How could I put boundaries and limits on what my Creator is? How could I then put limits on me, His Son?" Or on my brothers? How can I write anymore this day in relation to my Father when it is so elegantly summed up in two words, "God is,"? I began to feel the power and strength in these simple words. If all this be true, and it is, then there is no reason for me to judge, to fear, to hide, to mistrust, to do anything but accept what is. If "God is" then the ego "is not." At this realization, I felt the light pour forth and fill my mind. Illumination had returned to my holy mind. I am released. And with this knowledge I release the Sonship. "God is," is a present, living moment. It is eternal. It is now. God is...

∞∞∞

Journal Entry on Lesson 170

There is no cruelty in God and none in me.

It does not matter what you think you did or failed to do, you are always a beloved Son or Daughter in your Father's eyes. Your Father loves you and nothing else matters. Nothing else exists and nothing else is true. Anytime you feel concerned that you have done something that warrants forgiveness in your Father's eyes, the ego is at play. Anytime there is a feeling of guilt or shame, remember that it is the ego thought system that believes this and the ego thought system is designed to keep you separated from the awareness of God. It is designed to keep you afraid of opening up to the experience of God Himself. The Light of God is always with you. It is inside of you and it surrounds you at all times. It is the reality of who you really are.

The darkness of the ego thought system blocks your awareness of the healing Light of Love by focusing your attention on things that you believe are not appropriate for Love's acceptance. These are merely distractions and delaying maneuvers from having you focus your attention on opening up to the Light that you really are. Your Light is always shining, always radiating Love outward. It doesn't matter what you think you are doing now. Your Light still shines whether you see it or not. Waste no more time dwelling on the darkness that you think you are experiencing and try something new for a change. Try dropping whatever it is you may be concerned about and completely bypassing it to focus on experiencing the vision of Christ within you instead. The Light is there hidden within your mind. Let the Holy Spirit show it to you. Let Him illuminate your mind and heal all that you thought was there. You will then understand that everything else was merely just a waste of time. Amen.

∞∞∞∞

Journal Entry on Lesson 171

Review Lessons 151-152

Direct communication with God requires openness and a willingness to allow the Light of God to flow through you and out into the world. Channeling love in silence and in gratitude to your Father is a beautiful experience indeed. Letting go of all things you think you know now and allowing Him to come to you and work through you into the world is a healing and glorious experience indeed. Allowing yourself to be filled with light makes you one of the saviors who walks the world with your brothers. Do not be afraid to allow the light to begin to flow through you.

As you allow the Holy Spirit to channel the Light of Christ through you, your life and your world will begin to change indeed. All things you perceive and touch will begin to heal instantly because that is what Love does. It heals. The Light collapses time and arranges all things for your holy blessing. It lays out a carpet before you to walk upon where the lilies bloom upon each footstep you take because they recognize the Son of God, the Light of the world is walking their way. All things you touch as a Son of God begins to heal. All things and all people, all misery, sadness and pain is replaced with joy and glad tidings as the Son of God begins to awaken to the reality of Who He Really Is.

This is the experience I began to have as I awakened and allowed the fear within me to be abolished by the Light of God. The Light heals all things and all times including yourself. It is a joyous and glorious time indeed to truly let go and open up to allow the Light to flow through you like a faucet of Love, flowing from the Source of Love to Love Itself through you. The many gifts the flow of Love brings with It to you and to the world is glorious indeed. How happy are the Sons who begin to awaken and allow the Light of Love to flow through them in gratitude and thanks to their Father Who created them and Who share their Oneness with Him. It is an acceptance of the Atonement, their Oneness with Him in Reality is beginning to manifest Itself at last. Hallelujah, Hallelujah, Hallelujah! Praise God for His Son is awakening at last!

Thank You Father for Your gifts to us.

Let us be still now that we may hear Your Voice speak to us.

Thank You. Amen.

∞∞∞∞

Journal Entry on Lesson 172

Review Lessons 153-154

It's real easy to get caught up in the illusions of the world. The ego thought system likes to keep us busy with planning future events and worrying about what may or may not happen. When we walk with the Holy Spirit by our side, we do not have to worry about these things. The Holy Spirit is with us all the time and He is available to assist us upon our asking, every moment of everyday. We forget to ask Him for help with everything we do because we think we cannot see Him or His effects, but this is not true. As we continue to develop the habit of asking Holy Spirit what we should do and how we should respond to various situations that develop in our lives, we will truly begin to see that He does indeed answer us and help us every time. This is a wonderful habit to develop, this asking of the Holy Spirit, for this is how we begin to recognize that we are not alone and that we truly have a Friend Who goes with us wherever we go.

Remember to call upon Him in times of uncertainty which is every time for you who forget to ask. Remember you do not know how to respond in any given situation and therefore you cannot plan. Only the Holy Spirit knows the whole plan that has been established to help God's Son awaken from his dreaming. The

Holy Spirit has the power to collapse time and rearrange situations and events for your accelerated learning and awakening each time you ask of Him for His help. In time you will learn that you need to nothing but trust Him in everything He does. You will begin to recognize that He has already arranged everything for you and for your awakening.

Once you realize this, your walk in life becomes much easier because it becomes a complete walk in trust with Him Who leads the way for you. There is a sense of being provided for and carried through the dream and all you need do is be happy and joyful in the recognition that you are being completely provided for by Him Who loves you. He is your Friend. See that He is taking care of you always and rejoice in the gifts of happiness and joy that He gives to you upon seeing this. Remember to practice thanking your Father for His gifts to you and sending Him your love for He has already given you the Kingdom of Heaven indeed. You are One with Him in His Kingdom that you share with Him in everlasting love forever. Amen.

∞∞∞

Journal Entry on Lesson 173

Review Lessons 155-156

Anger is always one of the ego's fiercest weapons. Subtle anger may come out in the form of childish play but it is always used to separate, attack and isolate. There is no such thing as subtle anger. It is a devious decoy to lead God's Son astray. Childish anger can become an idol that can be pulled out and placed upon the altar so as to crucify the Son of God and make manifest what is simply not true. We are not separate from our Father nor are we separate from each other. Our brothers and sisters share complete Oneness with us in the Kingdom of Heaven with our Father right now. We are not isolated. And we are not separate from each other. We are friends, the best of friends always. There is no separation in Heaven and this idea we must make manifest in the world to free us from the chains of hell.

Always remember to choose to practice seeing and remembering our oneness with each other. Ask the Holy Spirit to help you in times when you are tempted to pull out the idol of anger and place it on the altar of Christ instead of seeing the Christ Himself. Defile the temple of Christ no more. Remember to choose to see the Light of Christ that dwells within yourself and within your brothers each time you are tempted to use subtle anger to crucify yourself.

Ask the Holy Spirit to help you to remember the truth always when you are tempted to respond with anger. Remember to respond immediately with *"My brother is the Christ, the Holy Son of God Himself, and so am I."* And ask the Holy Spirit how you should respond to the situation at hand. Remembering to ask the Holy Spirit for help in every situation is the key to forgiveness and the way out of hell for you. It is the key to happiness. Your willingness to turn to Him for help and ask in time of need will begin to free you at last. Follow His guidance, whatever it may be, with complete trust and thank Him for His gifts of Love to you and to your brother. Amen.

∞∞∞∞

Journal Entry on Lesson 174

Review Lessons 157-158

"Into the Light would I enter now," is the practice we are trying to develop today. Learning how to open up to the spark of white Light within yourself is the beginning of the release from hell for you. Think of how you would normally deal with stress, anxiety, worry and strife in your life. Perhaps you would find some food to comfort yourself with, call a friend, or even take a pill. These are all magic thoughts and they do not lead you to the solution which you seek. The next time you feel worry and fear rising within your being, try something new for a change. Try to sit down and learn how to access the Light within yourself. It is the answer that Father has given to you for every problem and situation that you will encounter in your life indeed.

When the spark of white Light flashes in your mind you will notice that it suddenly replaces all of the worry within your being with a fresh wash of Love that brings Joy, Peace and a sense of well-being. You will immediately begin to relax and have this feeling of contentment and that everything is ok. This is the work of the miracle worker. This is the practice of being miracle worker in the world. We learn how to access and use the Light to heal ourselves and in turn the world around us begins to heal as well because we are beginning to heal ourselves at the level of the mind where everything started. The awareness of the Light of Christ within ourselves is what we seek in all problems and in all situations as we learn and remember how to move into the Light of His Presence once again. We are also learning at the same time that we are giving and receiving at the same time.

When we open up to receive the awareness of the Light within our minds, we recognize at the same time that we are giving the Light to ourselves. This is because we are the Light. We are the spirit of the Light. We are the Light that we see. The Light is a reflection of our Oneness with each other and with Father Who created us and when we see the Light, we will thank Him indeed for the recognition that joy is at hand. We begin to recognize that we can practice doing this anytime we want, in any place, any time or circumstance. We can heal ourselves and our minds with the Light in a holy instant. It is our choice and it is a choice that we can choose to practice and make anytime we want.

Ask the Holy Spirit for help with moving into the perception of this vision of the Light of Christ within you. You come only partway because of your lack of willingness. He and the strength of Heaven that He brings with Him will carry you the rest of the way in a holy instant. He will help you each time you ask Him for help. Ask Him from the heart and He will respond from the Heart of God Himself. He will help you and you will begin to see this as you practice this helping that He gives to you. You will thank Him each time for the Hand that He has given you to help carry you to the experience of the Light within yourself. Thank You Father for Your gifts to us. Amen.

∞∞∞∞

Journal Entry on Lesson 175

Review Lessons 159-160

Have faith in the Light that leads you Home. Have faith in nothing else. When you place your faith in what is outside of you, you will never be led to the truth. You will only be led to darkness and sadness. That is not what you truly want. You want to feel alive. You want to experience true joy and happiness. Be as a child. Be in the moment. Remember your innocence.

Thank You Holy Spirit for these reminders of where I am always. Thank You for holding the door open wide to my Home. This world is strange to me. I am not welcome here. But you offer me so much more. I learn each day that the more I give, the more that I receive. Withholding love from anyone does not really bring me anything but internal pain. Thank You for reminding me of my real Joy in my Father.

Dear One, you are loved in such a way that you could never possibly imagine the depth and magnitude. The Love You Father has for you is beyond all words, all songs, all light, all the angels in Heaven. It expands and grows even now as I speak to you. Each moment your inner Light of radiance wants to shine, wants to extend to all. You cannot keep it hidden, keep it covered. Let it shine. Let it shine to all your brothers and sisters. They are indeed one with you. Be one with them in peace.

Spirit, sometimes I find it hard to do so when I see and experience situations that are other than love. I hear Your Word and I know that it is true within my being. At times I feel lost and alone, but now feel reassured in Your Gentle Care. You do love and care for me even at the times when I do not. I rest in You. I can feel you caressing my forehead, soothing me into a relaxed state of mind. Your peace is welcome in my heart and mind. Thank You for Who You are. Amen.

∞∞∞∞

Journal Entry on Lesson 176

Review Lessons 161-162

Whenever a brother that I see seems to act out behaviorally in one way or another, it is always a call for love. It does not matter what the actions may be. It is for me to see beyond the behavior to the Christ within. When someone is acting out, it is because they have forgotten the truth of who they really are. Their actions may seem to protect them in some way, a shield in defense. Deep down they are tormented by rage and fear. They do not remember their Source of Love. It is easy to want to take their actions personally, to even desire to retaliate, however, that is the not the solution. See them only for the truth that they are, the love that they are, your brother in their time of need. Remember for him. He needs you and you need him. You are connected. You need this connection for it is only Oneness that you share.

When a bully bullies, it is only to cover the insecurity and self-hatred that they have for themselves from the world. That is all.

Do not respond with anger. Do not recoil in distaste. Love them. Simply love them. There is nothing else that you need do. Forgive them for they do not know what they do. They are reaching out, reaching out to you, their savior. Release the chains from them and you release them from your very self. You enter then into the Kingdom of Heaven, joining hands and sharing God's Love. Remember this always when someone does not appear to be in their right mind, for they are not. They are "possessed" by the ego mind and they are miserable. Even if their actions bring them momentary glee, there is always underlying guilt that they carry. The anger they project is only to cover and hide it from their very self. Their actions are meaningless. But yours can be mighty when you turn to love and away from fear. Bless them. Bless them. Bless them and freedom will be yours.

∞∞∞∞

Journal Entry on Lesson 177

Review Lessons 163-164

When I read *"There is no death"* in this morning's message I noticed that the word death stood out to me. I observed an underlying fear that came up around the word and that I was afraid to take a closer look at it. I quickly attempted to turn my attention away from the word and attempted to look at some of the other words in the lesson so that I could focus on something different, more positive and happier. Almost unconsciously, I tried to sweep the fear under the carpet and pretend that it wasn't there. I then went into meditation and Jesus started showing me images of things that helped me to realize that something was going on.

As I opened up to looking at it with Him, I began to realize that the underlying fearful thought and belief was that death was going to catch up to me someday; either by getting me or by taking a loved one away from me and there was nothing that I could do about it. There was an unconscious feeling of helplessness over this belief, which is why I didn't want to look at it. Now that I was more open, Jesus started to point out that this was a common trick of the ego belief system; to scare us into not looking at it so that it can never be healed.

The truth is, it can be healed and it will eventually be healed through our willingness to be mindful of these tricks and to take them to the Holy Spirit for healing. Our job is to get into the habit of taking all of our fearful thoughts immediately to the Holy Spirit and asking Him to help us heal them. This is how we are going to move into being more peaceful inside.

Jesus also reminded me that the second greatest fear that we have is the fear of death and the first greatest fear that we have is of God. He pointed out how the ego tricks us into delaying the healing. Notice how a fear came up (fear #2) and instead of taking it to God for healing (unconscious fear #1) the ego chose to avoid it. The fear never really did get dealt with nor healed because it was never taken to the Holy Spirit for healing. See how the ego thought system works. It tries to keep us trapped in the cycle of birth and death. Now as we begin to see how this works, we can make a change, we can choose to remember to take each fearful thought to either Jesus or the Holy Sprit and ask it to be healed. Eventually we will begin to notice that the fear is gone and healed. Thank you Jesus for your help today. And thank you for *A Course in Miracles*, our handy-dandy tool kit for getting Home. I love you. Love, Paul

∞∞∞∞

Journal Entry on Lesson 178

Review Lessons 165-166

Everything we perceive now is an experience of the denial of the Thought of God. Anything that is not of the experience of Heaven can only be an experience of hell. The memory of God still resides hidden within our minds and can be recalled anytime we choose to do so. It is not easy to recall the memory of God, but with practice it can become easier to look beyond the resistance of the ego in remembering your True Identity. The memory of God can be perceived as a white light within your mind.

When you come to a place where you have a desire to see nothing else but the Light of God within yourself, then the light will come and free you at last. When we perceive the light within ourselves, we begin to perceive the gifts that our Father has entrusted us with. The gifts are many indeed for the One Gift heals all illusions.

When we begin to perceive the Light of Christ within our minds, we begin to recognize our Oneness and that all things have been given to us. We begin to recognize that light and joy truly abide within us, for the experience of pure joy comes with the release of light within ourselves out into the world for the healing of all split minds.

The Light of Joy illuminates our mind and brings us happiness in all ways. It heals our mind of the worries and anxieties we would hang on to as we continue to attempt to deny the Thought of God. But this will not prevail, as we continue to practice asking the Holy Spirit or Myself with help in your times of turmoil or need. You cannot call upon Us in vain. We are always with you for We are One with you in Heaven right now. And it is Our goal, the goal of the Sonship, to heal the One Mind and restore all the Sons of God to their rightful place in the Kingdom of Heaven where We share eternal joy and everlasting peace with each other and our Father.

This is a joyous time indeed for all of us. For the One Mind that We share is continuing to awaken at last, and our complete wholeness and oneness is continuing to be realized at last. The Kingdom of Heaven is at hand, for ye who carry the light within themselves, the light of their Source, our Creator, could never be abolished. Hallelujah! Hallelujah! Hallelujah! Praise God! The Creator of All That Is. God Is. We sing with Our hearts in unison with Him our love for Him and all that We are and for His mighty creation of Us and His mighty gift of Creation to Us to share and extend with Him forever and ever. Amen.

ooooo

Journal Entry on Lesson 179

Review Lessons 167-168

As we continue to practice moving into the Light with God, we will find that all of our aspirations will be met in our lives. This is how Love works. Love gives all to all. All has been given to His Son. The extension of creation of Love Itself was given to Him, His Son that He may extend it for His own joy. The extension of Love is the most fulfilling experience in the Sonship.

Developing the habit of extending unconditional love in the world of form will be the most fulfilling and joyful experience for those who truly practice doing just that. It emulates the process of creation in Heaven, and through the practice of this emulation in the world of form, one begins to remember and awaken to his or her reality in the Sonship as Spirit now.

Glimpses of the experience of being in Spirit will be given to you as you practice remembering that you are God. There is no other way to do this other than actually putting your mind to it to practice. Mindfulness and willingness to let go of the dream you now behold in exchange for the gifts given to you by God is the only way to begin to awaken from the dream. This letting go of everything you behold now is the process of forgiveness.

Asking the Holy Spirit for help will accelerate your awakening to joy. Ask Him and ask Him and ask Him again whether or not you believe you are perceiving the results. Have faith my brother and trust in Him. Send out your requests over and over again for your call to joy; for He answers each and every one. It is His job to help you to awaken to joy and He will gladly do so upon your asking. "Thank You Holy Spirit for helping me to awaken to the Light and Joy that abides in me", is your response to all fearful thoughts the ego would present to you. Deny all forms of fear, how subtle they may be, and ask the Holy Spirit to exchange them with joy instead, and it is done. How holy is His Son who begins to recognize his Oneness with his Creator in Heaven. "Holy Spirit, give me joy, give me joy, give me joy", is our mantra for today.

Thank You Father for Your gifts to us. Amen.

ꝏꝏ

Journal Entry on Lesson 180

Review Lessons 169-170

At work, I often find myself distancing myself or avoiding interpersonal contact with my supervisors because I am afraid of their perception of me. When I do communicate with my supervisors, I notice I am more comfortable communicating with them via email as opposed to face-to-face. The reason for this is that there is an underlying feeling of guilt and self-judgment that I could always be doing a better job. The ego thought system tends to attack with thoughts about how I could be doing a better job or I'm not as skilled or as intelligent as some of my peers. The ego always tends to tell me that if I do not stand out in some way, or if I have inadvertently rubbed with another, that down the road I will be punished by having something taken away from me such as my job. The ego belief system likes to tell you that you are guilty and that you are going to be punished and you need to hide in order to avoid this punishment.

As I meditated upon this with Jesus and the Holy Spirit, Jesus pointed out that this is an example of a reflection in our belief in the separation from God. When the tiny mad idea seemed to come about within the mind of the Sonship, and the split mind seemed to happen, the Son of God seemed to come to a belief that he had done something wrong and was separated from God and that he needed to hide from God or else he would be punished. Jesus reminded me that my supervisors really weren't there. The images of my supervisors and my own body within the illusion and the interaction between these bodies are just that, an illusion. The images we see are being projected from the unconscious part of the mind, the ego thought system. They are not really there and this is not really happening. These are made-up stories by the ego thought system that we think we are seeing, feeling and hearing.

We do not live because we have a job, money and can feed and shelter ourselves. We live by the grace of God. Our worldly supervisors have no cruelty in them because the Light we perceive beyond their images is the Light of our True Selves. Upon this reminder and recognition, we can now take these stories and practice the process of forgiveness with them.

Dear Holy Spirit, I have been believing in these false stories and now I wish to heal them with your help so that I may restore my mind to a place of true inner peace. I forgive myself for believing that I am separate from my brothers and that I am not whole. And I release these beliefs in this situation to You for healing of my mind. Thank You Holy Spirit. I trust that our One Will has been done and the reality of that One Will will come into my awareness soon. Thank You again. I love You. Amen.

∞∞∞

Journal Entry on Lesson 181

I trust my brothers, who are one with me.

As I sat in the waiting room while Paul was having a minor surgery procedure today, I saw many others waiting for their loved ones. In some faces, there was tension, some fear, some relief as the attending physician came to discuss the results. For me, even though I had been at first a little nervous, I found solace in connecting with Holy Spirit by reading the Course and taking time to be silent in my mind. I knew that I trusted the doctor because I trust Holy Spirit. The doctor is my brother. The others in the waiting room are my brothers. They are one with me because they are me.

If I put barriers in any form, it is simply a distancing device from that Oneness that we all share. Some of the people in the waiting room were interesting characters, some even exhibiting anger toward their spouse in public. It is for me to release judgment of what I think I see for I do not know. I do not know what lies beyond these characters lives. This is all a story, a story that I have made up in my mind to keep me separate from the Divine Parts of My Self and to keep myself apart from the Divine Itself. If I focus on the stories of anger, fear, distancing and pain, then that is what I attract into my life. If I focus on the truth, on trust, on forgiveness, on the Love of God, then that will definitely expand and grow. My brothers are my mirrors. This reminds me of a sign outside the church down the street, "Have you been mugged by your mirror?" or something to that effect. So the message for me is to smile at my brother mirrors, for I am smiling at Divine Itself, Me.

Thank You Father for Your Direction and Love. Amen.

००००००

Journal Entry on Lesson 182

I will be still an instant and go home.

Thank you Jeshua for today's Lesson because I feel that it answers the question I was raising to you and Holy Spirit not too long ago. I recall that I kept having this feeling that I was missing something and I couldn't quite put my finger on it. I seemed to be ok but no matter what I did that particular day, what activity I engaged myself with, I kept feeling that there was a question being asked within my mind but I couldn't figure out what the question was. All there was, was this underlying feeling that I was missing something. The Lesson that you share with us today reminded me of the simple answer to the question. The question being, "What am I missing here?"

And the answer is, "I have forgotten the experience of Heaven." The awareness of the experience of Heaven which is my Home seems to be missing right now. The answer and the solution to this problem, which I am truly grateful to have found, is hidden within my mind. The bridge to the experience of Heaven can be crossed by stilling our minds and opening up to the Light of our Home in Heaven. I am so grateful for the Rock of Light that Father placed in our minds for us. I now know without a doubt that the solution to all of my problems is to simply be still and find the Rock of Light amidst the stormy seas of the world. It does not matter whatever may trouble me, there is only one simple solution and one simple place to go to solve the problem, and that is within.

Each day as I practice allowing the awareness of Heaven to glimmer in and illuminate my mind for just a moment, I find that my daily experience in the world becomes happier indeed. Thank you Jeshua! Thank you! As I continue to practice raising my awareness to the Light and Love of Heaven that surrounds me always, I find that my experience of the world takes a tiny step closer each time to the transformation of becoming Heaven on earth for me. I am so grateful for this precious gift of healing that lies within my mind and I thank you for Your help in learning how to use it. Thank You for reminding me that this is the secret to happiness and for helping me to realize that it can all be done from the quietness within my home. I need do nothing but continue to practice being still an instant and letting my mind open up to Home.

Thank You Father for Your gifts to us. We love You. Amen.

∞∞∞

Journal Entry on Lesson 183

I call upon God's Name and on my own.

Brother Jeshua, I am really excited about today's Lesson and I thank you for sharing it with us. I already know that if we practice your lessons as you suggest that we can have personal experiences with God Himself. I am so grateful that you have shared these secrets to happiness for us. For I was lost in darkness for a long time, and now, because of your help and my willingness to practice your lessons, I have begun to find my True Self. Thank You Holy Spirit for Your gifts to us.

Today, I ask You to help me remember to make the word "God" my mantra for today with every breath I take. I know that You will help me to accomplish this goal, for with all my heart, I want to have another personal experience with God so that my faith in His Love for me and for all of us may be bolstered even more. Thank You Father for Your gifts to us, for Your Name and my name is the only One I would hold in my mind today, that I may raise my awareness to our Oneness with You and each other once again.

Father, I long to hear Your Voice speak to me once again as my own. Thank You Father for Your gifts to me. I love You Father, and I love the gifts You have given to all of us which help us to remember the truth about ourselves and our Oneness with You and with each other. I know that proof will be in the pudding today, for I trust that if I follow the instructions given to me today by Brother Jeshua that You will come and answer me personally. You will come and show me that the sick and the dead can be raised and healed indeed. Thank You Father for Your gifts of life to us for we are One with You in Heaven forever. We love You Father, so now I will turn my mind to only one thing today, one word, and that is to call upon Your Name and on my own. Amen.

In joining together this day in calling upon God's Name and our own, my mind was filled with an arc of golden Light. Peace surrounded me. I rested in this peace, this knowing of the Oneness that encompassed me. I then saw an image of a glorious garden, lush and green, flowering and fragrant. An outdoor banquet was set and all were beckoned to come and take part of the abundant richness laid before us. Many happy souls were there, laughing and enjoying the moment. My mind then flashed to last evening when we had our Course friends stop by seemingly to park their vehicle to walk over to Madison's "Rhythm and Booms" fireworks celebration. A threatening storm cancelled the event just as they pulled into our driveway. Earlier in the day we had our own immediate family cookout, and so much food was leftover. We were guided to offer to share it with our friends as they waited for the traffic jam to dissipate.

The senses were alive with children playing, adults interacting, food on the grill and love and laughter at the table. All unexpected, all brought about by love. With joy in our hearts, all embraced upon the end of our impromptu sharing.

In calling upon God's Name today, I am calling upon myself and the Oneness that I share with my brothers. It is accepting the truth and extending that truth. It is aligning my mind with Holy Wisdom and following that guidance. It is being in the space of silence and receiving the gifts of God that are already there. The banquet is indeed prepared, the cups overflowing, and I am anointed, as we all are, by the Most High as His Holy Son indeed.

Today Father, I embrace the abundant Life in You. Amen.

∞∞∞∞

Journal Entry on Lesson 184

The Name of God is my inheritance.

There are other sights and sounds that are available to us besides the ones we have already experienced within the world. The sights and sounds that Father has given to us, to behold with the help of the Holy Spirit, are reminders of a place long forgotten by His Son. The sights and sounds of Heaven are gifts indeed because they remind us of a Home long forgotten. They show us that the world that we perceive now with our eyes and ears is not real and that there is something else much greater.

These are miracles of love indeed because when we perceive with the Holy Spirit we receive joy and love and healing at the same time that we see and hear His gifts. These are His reminders of where we came from and where we truly belong. These are calls from Heaven Itself, and once the calls are perceived, the heart yearns to return to these True Perceptions more and more over time until time comes to an end. This Answer, God gave to you when you forgot who you were. Each time you hear the Voice for

God call to you and you perceive His Light, you are reminded of another world to which you must return and will want to return as your mind is healed from the darkness it once held. The gifts of the Holy Spirit are the same for everyone. Each is a reminder that you are not who you think you are, but instead, you are a part of something else much greater.

What a relief it is to begin to discover these gifts within yourself. Remember to ask the Holy Spirit to help you to remember the truth about yourself. Ask Him to show you who you really are over and over again until your mind has become willing enough to receive the treasure house of gifts He has for you. Each pearl He gives to you will be used to frame the new picture of yourself as the reflections of Heaven remind you of Who you really are. You are God's Holy Son! He loves you and you love Him. Together you share your love for each other which is beyond all measure, all comprehension of the world, forever and ever. Thank You Father for Your gifts to us. We love You. Amen.

∞∞∞

Journal Entry on Lesson 185

I want the peace of God.

Today we work on truly desiring the peace of God. You are already aware that you have chosen many other things over this. Whenever you start to feel restless or bored you turn to the ego for a solution to help yourself come to a place where you feel better. When you turn to the ego for a solution it will not last. It will always end with a feeling of unfulfillment and sadness. The ego will busy you with a change in activity that may seem fun for awhile but in the end you will be left empty-handed once again. Your salvation will have seemingly been held off a little longer once again.

The next time you begin to feel discontented or bored, try remembering to turn to the Holy Spirit and asking Him for some help with the situation. It only takes a few minutes to go into silent conversation with Him within your mind. It is there where He will help to bring clarity and understanding to the situation at hand for you and if you could ask Him what you could do to be truly helpful to both yourself and those around you, He will gladly give you guidance that will lead all of you to a feeling of joy, peace, and fulfillment. He alone knows best for the situation at hand. Remember He wants to talk with you. He wants to help you. He wants you to be a happy person within the dream while you awaken. He needs His happy teachers to help reach all of Father's children who seem to be lost within dreams of dreams. They are looking for Him, though they may not realize it.

He needs your help in reaching them in a manner in which they can understand, and learn from you through your demonstration in how they too can learn to turn to Him for their own guidance to joy as well. As you turn to Him for His counsel in everything you do your light becomes brighter within the world. As your light becomes brighter the others will be naturally drawn to it for they will recognize the call of Love, the Light of Love within themselves which they have temporarily forgotten.

All lights must touch all lights once again within the Mind of God to illuminate the world with Heaven once again; to bring it back to the place before time began. You know now how to turn to your Friend for help. Thank you for your willingness to continue to practice and grow in this area. You are beginning to understand the peace and joy that comes with it each time you have the willingness to ask for peace in your life. Thank you my dear brother for your help in this area. Thank you for taking my hand as I gladly take yours and together we take our brothers' hands and we join together as One to find our way Home. In Innocence we will all gather together and proclaim our joy, happiness and love for each other and for our Father Who is One with us forever in Heaven. Amen.

∞∞∞

Journal Entry on Lesson 186

Salvation of the world depends on me.

"We can laugh or weep, and greet the day with welcome or tears. Our very being seems to change as we experience a thousand shifts in mood, and our emotions raise us high indeed, or dash us to the ground in hopelessness."

These few sentences stood out to me today as I experienced just as it describes. Upon awaking, I felt happy having had some amusing, happy dreams. As Paul and I got up and entered into the living room for the Lesson reading and our meditation, I felt peaceful yet still a little drowsy. No message was instantly received by either of us, and at times that does occur. At times just beginning the day provides for insights to enter into the mind. Such is the case today.

As the day began after our quiet time, a sense of sadness came over me. Was it that Paul was returning to work after 5 days off? Or was it the PMS? The mind searched for what the key point was. As I sat on the bed as Paul readied for work, the house was still quiet as my daughters were still sleeping, Paul could see that I was not quite myself. Depressed, it seemed he said. What a difference from the way I had woke up. You would think some time with the Course and a good meditation would have carried through the next half hour, but no, it didn't. But that's me then judging what's good or bad.

As I started to share with him, I got it touch with huge feelings of self-doubt, like I had lost the magic formula. Tears began to well up. Perhaps even a sense was there of not feeling important or as appreciated or acknowledged as I would like. Interesting feelings, indeed. After he left for work, I readied myself for my appointment with a ministerial student. Taking the time to shower with the Holy Spirit and renew and cleanse myself. Well, the darnest thing, the same topic arose again as she talked about how sometimes she wakes up in the morning with negative feelings, not truly wanting to feel that way, and feeling disappointed that it keeps happening from time to time.

So we shared together the reminders, the choices that we can make. The focus upon appreciation for self and our significant others in our lives versus the "blame game" that seems so second nature. My student commented, "I think we don't share the appreciations because it is not something that needs changed. It is what we want changed that we share." And rather negatively, we added. So after our meeting this brought me to reading today's Lesson again. Reading it like I had not read it before, even though I know I had many, many times over the years. But, that's the Course for you, always a new meaning coming to light.

And so, yes, there may be times that I do not feel up to par, feel the greatest Miracles Teacher or Student, feel the greatest person in the world even, but it doesn't mean that my greatness has disappeared. It is simply that I have forgotten. This can happen to anyone here in the world because if I am here in the world then somehow I am still believing in the ego and thus I am not in the true complete experience of Heaven. And the ego likes instability. So as I tune in again to the Voice for God, I can see that all the feelings are really nothing of course, and this understanding comes with my true willingness to receive it. And as I receive it, I do as this Lesson says, "Let it go." Forgive it and forgive it again if I have to. That is my function. That is why I am here. The peace that comes from letting go feels full and freeing. No tension, no sense of burdening, no limits. I am free. I am certain, sure and confident in the One. If I listen, really take the time to listen, I will hear the comforting song of Heaven always reminding me of the Light of Truth, the Love of God. And so salvation depends on me to remember that I have all I need within me to help me remember and I am grateful that it is so.

ooooo

Journal Entry on Lesson 187

I bless the world because I bless myself.

When I began to think about what stood out to me in this Lesson, it was the word "sacrifice." I even reread the lesson, but kept stopping at "sacrifice." I knew that this was a clue for me to tune in with Holy Spirit for insight. So as I spoke with Holy Spirit about this word "sacrifice" and what it symbolized at this moment in time, what returned to me was the following.

Sacrifice contains the essence of guilt. Sacrifice means that the giver is not truly giving out of love, but rather a sense of "I'm doing this for you and you *better* appreciate it." It is not true giving. True giving is done from one's sacred heart of love with a complete knowing that both the giver and the receiver are wholly blessed by the act and the giving itself is the return. In sacrifice, it is always "Look what *I've* done for you." It is an unloving stance. There is anger and there is judgment involved.

If I truly want to give to another, including giving to myself, then I release all attachments, all cords, all ties, all conditions from the gift. That is what sacrifice is, it is giving with conditions, emotional or other reciprocal conditions. It is giving with expectation which then always leads to resentment. There is also a sense of superiority and inferiority, and I can hear in my mind the words, "You owe me." There is a fear that I will be lost, that I have lost, never to recover again what I have given. I will end up with nothing, alone and abandoned in the darkness and so I better be sure that I get and retain what is mine.

I understand that traditionally by the church (and others) that I had been taught this concept. Jesus died for you so what do you do? You give to God and others with hidden resentment and guilt. But Jesus did not give with blame and guilt. He says in the Course that the crucifixion was the *"last useless journey the Sonship need take, and that it represents release from fear to anyone who understands it."* Thus, this idea of sacrifice comes from a place of fear. I am afraid that I will not receive anything in return and so I will make the other person, myself, God, whoever, feel guilty about it, my own guilt.

Instead I can remember the message of *"Teach only love for that is what you are."* Give only love for that is what I am. Be only love for that is what I am. I let go of the chains that bind me to conditional love. I release all to the Holy Spirit for clarity and understanding. With God within me, I have all that I need and so I can give and give again freely knowing that I am replenished with an unending supply. I am truly giving to myself.

And so I lay aside the crown of thorns I have used and remember the lilies through their purity of love's forgiveness. I remember that I am whole and complete and that I am shining in the grace of God. As I shine, I encourage others to shine their most precious light. We are all blessed, every one of us.

∞∞∞∞

Journal Entry on Lesson 188

The peace of God is shining in me now.

Last night before retiring I was inspired to share in a children's guided meditation with Paul and the girls (at the time, 9 and 15.)

"A Journey to the World of Light" was the name and it was relaxing. And in receiving and remembering the Light, we are then extending that Light, Love and Peace to the planet, our family and friends, and to everyone in the world. During the meditation we were surrounded by angels who shared in our song of joy with us. When we asked for a message, or imagined what a message might be for us, we received it gladly. This was a wonderful practice to do together to close our day.

All were happy to share in the experience and all felt extremely relaxed and ready for bed. I know that earlier in the day the girls had a little conflict occur after being here together for almost 2 weeks. Neither had wanted the conflict and felt bad about it. This was their time together, as they hadn't lived together the last 2 years, and were enjoying the closeness once again. Through a gentle sharing with each of them, both felt heard and understood and later they were back to laughing and having fun together again.

In the past, I know it was easier for me to get caught up in all three of my daughters' conflicts and squabbles. And even though I had practiced and shared with them ACIM principles, including the Book of Virtues and the like through the years, there were times that I had felt frustrated in their seeming lack of cooperation. Of course, the realization was there of holding an expectation in my mind. Ah, but you know how the ego works. I always did know that they had their own individual journey and I allowed them the freedom to explore whatever it was, Christianity, Buddhism, Wicca, etc. although my mainstay was the Course.

These two years that I have been apart from raising them has matured all of us. My youngest (9) is now back from her grandmother's and living with us permanently while the 15 and 16 year olds live with their father, stepmother and 2 year old sister. At times in that household there is conflict. That is why my daughter was upset to have a conflict with her 9 year old sister here, she didn't want the conflict that she experiences back home. She felt saddened that it happened, that somehow she got it wrong, again. She didn't want the conflict; she enjoys visiting with us and the peace and quiet that is here in our presence. I assured her that all was okay. It is normal to not agree with another; even Paul and I don't agree at times too. It is what we do with the feelings that come up is what is important.

We talked about journaling, talking to a friend and even taking time to be in solitude with the Divine within to share those disturbing thoughts. Soon she felt better and ready to come back inside. She then shared her thanks for our talk and at our "gratitude sharing" at the dinner table. In all, we are always teaching ourselves, whether I share it with my children, students, counselees, or friends, I am always reminding myself of Heaven's Help, the Light that shines within me.

My process of releasing attachments to everything, started rather profoundly over 2 years ago when Paul and I were guided to leave our home and family. Of course actually before that but I really see that the last two years was a time of sabbatical, of further spiritual awakening, of refining our ministry and of the remembering of True Connections. As I have said earlier, it was a traveling ministry not in form, but to the places of the heart that needed healing.

Even though I was not physically present with my three girls, and believe me I had many judgments hurled in my direction about that fact, we always knew our deep connectedness of Love would always be there, would never change. It is truly a deep trust in God that allowed me to make the steps that I did and He spoke to me many times about it. It was not for others to understand for they were not asked to do so, we were. We are only asked to do what God knows we can do for Him. I also believe because of my loving stance, and not one of guilt, it contributed to the deepness and closeness of our souls now, their maturity, as I always held the Truth.

In the world, the older girls are high school honor students and the youngest has been a straight-A student, meaningless of course because I know their worth is not dependent on their achievements in school. Their Inner Light is the most valuable, but the other is nice to see. The young women that they are becoming of grace, faith, thoughtfulness and strength is profound indeed. And so, we never know, we just never know the gifts that we bestow upon others in their lives by our awakening to the presence of Love.

My message to me: Release all attachments to outcomes as it may turn out more beautiful that even imagined. Jerry Jampolsky reminded me of this about 6 years ago in a personal phone conversation. Thanks Jerry!

And today's Lesson reminds me of the Light of Peace shining within us all, no matter where we may be, what experiences we may have, the Light does not dim. I may choose not to see it but when I step back and give the Holy Spirit all my wandering thoughts, the stray thoughts of doubt and fear, the Light will always guide me where I need to be. I am never lost. I always have a home in God.

See the Light shining today, let go of the past and all mistakes, and simply feel the blessing.

∞∞∞∞

Journal Entry on Lesson 189

I feel the Love of God within me now.

How wonderful it is to be told that there is a way to allow the awareness of God's World to shift into our perception. The Light of God and His World can be seen, the sound of His Voice can be heard and the Love of His World can be felt in an instant right now. In order to allow His Dimension to be revealed to us, we must be willing to rest in silence and let go of everything within our minds that would distract us from being open and ready to receive His experience. Recognize, that if we are not in a state where we are continuously experiencing the sights, sounds and feelings present in Heaven, then we are in a constant state of sacrifice.

At an unconscious level within our minds, we are choosing to block the awareness of God's Light from our experience. The Light of God is truly there, hidden very carefully within our minds. His World is waiting to be revealed to us through our sincere desire to see and experience His Light and His Light alone. Anytime we allow our wandering minds to pay attention to anything that is not solely of His Light, then we are continuing to choose the idols of sacrifice instead of salvation. We are choosing not to be healed.

Let us remember the importance of what it is we are trying to accomplish here. We are training our minds to meet God. As we truly learn to open up and allow His blazing Light to reveal Itself within our minds, we will simultaneously feel His Love pouring out of our hearts and into the world. We will also experience a sudden healing, a release of fear and tension within our bodies at the same time. Once the Light of Salvation is experienced, it can never be forgotten and we will never be the same again. With the Light, we receive a gift of recognition, a recognition that we have a choice to allow His Light in, or not. Remember, that each and everyone of us are innocent, there is no need to dwell on sins committed for there is no such thing as sin in God's World. God's World is the only thing worth pursuing because that is all there really is.

∞∞∞∞

Journal Entry on Lesson 190

I choose the joy of God instead of pain.

The Light of Joy, or Heaven can wait, are our only two choices within the world and one of them is not real. Every moment we hold the world within our perception, we seemingly hold off the joy of Heaven a little longer. How wonderful it is to recognize that *"it is our thoughts alone that cause us pain."* With this recognition, we begin to understand that we have a choice, that we have the power within ourselves to change our perception of the world around us and our personal experiences to one of a Christ experience. We are the Christ, the holy Son of God Himself and we can learn and train our minds to allow the awareness of that truth to be realized. There is no one or any circumstance outside of us that causes us pain, or worry, or anxiety, or fear. We are making all of these illusions up at an unconscious level and then projecting them out into the world and blaming everyone else for causing us those experiences.

They are not true, we are doing it to ourselves. We are responsible for everything that we see. We choose the feelings we experience and everything that seems to happen to us, we ask for and receive as we have asked. This is the truth in accepting full responsibility for our part of the split mind. The mind that never really was split from God. We do not have to take anyone's word for this except God's. And God says to be open and to take time to prove this Eternal Truth to yourself through the practice of being still with a calm and open mind. It is here where you will meet the Light of your Friend Who will become your Teacher. He is like no other Friend you have ever met before in your worldly experience for He comes from the Eternal Himself. He is your Friend, your Counselor, your Guide Who will light the way for you and illuminate your mind with knowledge and understanding that exceeds the limitations of the world. These are the gifts He has for you. Accept them and receive His abundance. His Joy will become your joy and light the way as two become One and joyfully walk the path back Home where all is One. Happy faces and smiles, light footsteps and dances will be the way of the ones who choose joy instead of pain in their returning to Him Who created them.

∞∞∞∞

Journal Entry on Lesson 191

I am the holy Son of God Himself.

Join with Me today. Accept your Identity in the One. I have blessed your sleeping eyes with a Light more radiant than you could imagine. Feel it now upon you. This Light will not blind you for it will only heal you. Turn to the Light. Do not be afraid. Accept Who you are. You are as I created you to be. Holy, holy, holy are you. Breeze past the insane whispers of the ego calling to tell you of its gifts of pain, loss and despair. All disguised in your sight. I placed the call to Joy within you, listen to its glad refrain and it will carry you. I presented the gift of Forgiveness to you and it will help you see all things unseeable, hear all things inaudible, and experience so much more than the body's senses permit you to experience.

At times you feel the chains of anxiousness upon you as you wake in the morning. Anxiety is simply fear, fear that is about a future not even here based upon your past ideas. Sometimes this anxiety for you takes the form of feeling overwhelmed, or feeling that there is just not enough time to rest and to work, or even in areas of scarcity and lack, or in areas of bodily aches and pains. All to fetter you to this insane world. Lay down these attachments that you have to the world of form and time. You will benefit greatly by trusting in Eternity and formless Love. These are Who you are. They are your attributes just as they are Mine. Wake up to a new world, My World, Heaven. Place all your gifts (your fear thoughts) upon the altar of Forgiveness, and accept the greatest gift in return, My Peace. Peace I give to you, my dear One. You are free. You are saved. It is already done because you are loved.

∞∞∞

Journal Entry on Lesson 192

I have a function God would have me fill.

Why would you continue to hide under the umbrella of darkness when you can choose to come out into the Light? You have been given a very wonderful gift. The Light of Forgiveness will heal all of your problems and bring you to a state of joy and happiness all the time. You can seem to stay in hell and deny the Light within for as long as you wish but it is only hell that you ask for. The darkness of your habitual fearful thoughts can keep the Light hidden from your awareness but never truly abolished.

It takes great willingness to learn how to break through the dark veils within your mind to find the Light of Salvation but it is truly there. It will free you from every fear you to take to It and gladly replace it with joy. It takes practice and a willingness to try and see the Light of Freedom within yourself. Willingness to allow yourself to begin the practice of forgiving the things you now cherish are one of your biggest obstacles to opening up to the Light of Forgiveness. Take each one of these dark things that your mind clings to as you go about your day and give them over to the Light for healing. Let the Light abolish each and every one of these heavy dark things within your mind. You recognize the darkness because it feels heavy, because it weighs your mind down with fear, anxiety and a chattery mind.

The ego is very persistent in insisting that there is another way to salvation. It can be very convincing in having you hang on to the heavy things of darkness within your mind, shifting them from one form to another. But you are beginning to see this game of hell that the ego has been playing with your mind. It is now our time of awakening, our time of practicing a willingness to forgive these temptations as they come up, one at a time. Salvation is simple, your response to any temptation can be to call the memory of God into your awareness each time a temptation seems to confront you. Pausing a moment to remember the Lesson for the day will also serve the same purpose.

Whether you believe it will ultimately free you and bring you to happiness or not, practice forgiving anyway. Trust Me on this. Remember you are the one who is dealing with insanity, I am not. Take my hand and give me the willingness to help you out of your pain and into the joyful world Father has created for you. It will help you transition out of your dream of hell and back into the peace and joy of Heaven. It is a sweet transition indeed. Our walk together will be a joyful one. That is my promise to you. How many times must one practice forgiveness? I tell you, a thousand times a thousand times, until it is done. For the goal of forgiveness is both your true desire and God's Will for you. It is the recognition of Who you really are, the Christ, the Holy Son of God Himself. You are innocent, holy and free as God Himself. You are eternal. You remain exactly as God created you. You are Love Itself.

ooooo

Journal Entry on Lesson 193

All things are lessons God would have me learn.

During meditation, I found myself sinking into quiet peace for the first few minutes with various thoughts coming out to play in my mind, all with related images before me: The plumber arriving early this morning to do work in our home, the $300 "surprise" health provider invoice, the work that I needed to complete today, and errands to the library and bank.

As each one entered my mind, I saw it clearly, then repeated today's prayer, "I will forgive and this will disappear." As I did, each image dissolved as on a movie screen and I was renewed again with peace. These are all illusions that I have placed some attachment of fear. This attachment of fear could be a belief in lack of time or money. In God, there is no lack, only His abundant power.

So as I forgive each one with my complete honesty of where I am in the moment, then I will see through the illusion to the Light beyond. I will see differently. I just need to focus on the Now moment that's before me and Holy Spirit will lead me the rest of the way. If it is an insight to a problem, it will be there. If it is the means to pay a bill, it will be there. I simply trust and allow. I am always guided by the Holy Spirit as I work with Him throughout my day. There are no problems, no concerns, no worries, not in the sense and realm of Heaven. It is my fear that holds these heavily chained in my mind. I will forgive and this will disappear. All judgments that I hold, all emotions, everything will be dismissed. I will feel a knowing that I can accept all that approaches me for I do not walk alone.

Thank You Holy Spirit for assisting me along the path to You. As I ask to see differently it will be shown to me; when I knock, the door shall be open; and having sought the truth, I certainly will make it mine by my acceptance. It is in my practical application of what You teach me that I will succeed. Learning all the "right" words to say, the espousing of my knowledge does not truly get me what I seek and even if I see this in others, there is a part of me that I need to forgive when I make a judgment against them. It does not matter if one is perceived as intelligent by the world, for what is the world but an insane place. All of it is a separation device against the Son of God. All held in to place by fear to keep the merry-go-round of insanity spinning. It is time for me to get off the ride and simply sail off to the Light of Peace and look upon our Oneness.

My Dear One,

More and more you are leading a life of simplicity in Me. I applaud you each time you still your mind and ask ever so quietly for Me to guide your life. All that you write, do or say, you ask of Me and I surely answer and gratefully you act upon My sure guidance. You do have it within you to dispel the darkness of lies you have told yourself because the Light of Knowledge is there with you. Know that it is there. Know always that there is a purpose under Heaven. Turn to the Light, be strong, and you will be successful in all that you do. God's Will is yours. He is Love. He is the fragrance of your life. The roses outside your door are a symbol of His Love for you. Each time you stop to smell them, know that you are breathing a reminder of Eternal Love. Use this as a symbol to assist you.

As you bring the roses in to delight your home with their fragrance and beauty, know that you are the lasting fragrance too of the Father. You are never severed from your roots for you live and grow only in Him. What can be more sweeter than the sweetness of harvest of the Divine Fruits of the Spirit. Be in Love, Joy, Peace, Patience, Kindness, Goodness, Faithfulness, and Gentleness each and every day, each place you walk, and with each person you meet. The saying "Be fruitful and multiply" I give to you this new meaning; it is for you to extend the love and all these attributes unto the world. They are gifts of the harvest. Share the abundance because you are ever more radiant now than always. Undo the world with your forgiveness and you will see unravel and be no more. Thank you for accepting the Truth, for accepting Who you are, for remembering to forgive, and for your honesty and authenticity when you come to Me. It is welcomed in Heaven.

Bless you as you go about your day, dear sweet Light of God. Shine on!

Journal Entry on Lesson 194

I place the future in the Hands of God.

As we have said before, the illusion of time is already over. In an instant everything that happened within the realm of time was over. The linear progression of time that you seem to be experiencing now, is really just like replaying the scenes within a movie from your memory after having gone to a theatre and watching the movie. The mind even has the ability to change the scenes on the fly in the movie you are replaying. In any moment of replaying the movie in your mind, you have a choice, you can choose the outcome of the next scene as well. All variations of the scenes have been played out already. You are just experiencing the illusion that you are playing out one particular stream of scenes.

The ego thought system would have you bouncing back and forth between scenes that go around in circles and never come to an end. The ego's scripts always lead you to a scene of death in the end, and then it erases your memory and starts over again with the progression of serial lives. The ego will keep you trapped in the illusion as long as it can. If it were not for the Answer of Forgiveness given to you by your Father in the moment the tiny mad idea seemed to occur, your mind would have been trapped in the illusion forever.

Fortunately, this is not really possible in God's World. The Holy Spirit, the Helper, the Guide that Father gave to you when you came up with the mad idea of the dream of life and death, was given to you to help you awaken from your nightmare. Only He knows the way out of the dream and you must continue to learn how to work with Him, listen to Him and to follow His guidance in order to awaken from the dream.

This is His purpose; this is why Father created Him. He created Him specifically for you, to help you gently awaken from your dreaming. Otherwise, your mind would have been trapped in an endless cycle of the dream of life and death. How thankful we are that Father gave us the Answer Who will show us the way out of our dream of illusions. The past never happened nor is the future really there. As we practice today's lesson, it helps us to loosen the chains on our mind a little more and allows us the opportunity to learn how to shift our perception to the awareness of *Now*.

The present Now is all there is and I do not mean what you see presently in the room with you right now. What you see in the room with you right now is *not* the present moment to which I am referring. In order to truly experience the present moment, you must learn how to open up your mind and let go of everything you think you are perceiving right now. The beginning of the practice of this type of mind training is done by closing your eyes, letting go of all your thoughts and being still with an open mind. It is here where the Holy Spirit will help your mind to shift into a new perception, a true perception of the World beyond the one you now encounter. You will immediately recognize the shift because the the New World is a world of Light.

It has beautiful sights and sounds, songs and melodies, which are designed to help you in your awakening. It is a peaceful world, a happy world. It is the borderland between earth and Heaven. It is a gift that the Father has given to you through the Holy Spirit to help you make a sweet transition from the world of darkness to the lawns of Heaven; these lawns will bring you to the gates of Heaven Itself. When you reach the gates of Heaven within your mind and have accepted Atonement for yourself, the world you now know will be long forgotten and God Himself will take the final step as He lifts you back up into Oneness with Him.

∞∞∞

Journal Entry on Lesson 195

Love is the way I walk in gratitude.

Holy Spirit,

In walking your Way of Love and Gratitude, it is for me to be a demonstration of that Love and Gratitude You so embody because I embody it as well. And how can I not teach such? Your Presence shines throughout all that I do. I know that previous learning has taught me to be thankful for what I have because there are others who have less. This reminds me Spirit, of hearing when I was a child, "Eat everything on your plate because there are starving people in China." I am rather amused by this statement now because a few months ago a friend in Hong Kong stated that in China it is more noble to leave food on the plate as a sign of abundance. Perception, perception. All has all.

In my teaching, Holy Spirit, I want to be as You are with me, a Gentle Guide. In working with my brothers here in the world, it is for me to experience them as equals. All doing the best that they can. No one is better or greater than another. No Course teacher is better or greater than another. There are no winners nor losers. We are all teachers, ministers, and students. We are here to love, simply love and remember our Father.

Holy Spirit, I continue to come to You in the silent times that we have together to share with You all unforgiving thoughts. My desire is always to have these transformed with Your Well of Peace. I am refreshed and renewed when I am in Your Presence. I carry this all with me, and remember to tune in to You in all that I say or do. As judgments arise, and they do if I am to be honest with myself, I will raise them to You in a loving cup of gratitude for I know that as each is placed within Your Holy Hands, I am one step closer to God making the final step.

What is comparison but a judgment of inequality? Does it matter what my words say? Are they from the heart? Is this not my process? All that I do in the work with You, Spirit is to come with my integrity. I am not here to prove anything. I am here to extend Love to my brothers. They are my reflections of me, each aspect that I choose or do not choose to see so in fact I am either extending or withdrawing Love to my Self.

As I embrace each brother, each aspect, each lesson, I know that Heaven is smiling for it means that each fragmented part is joining unto the Wholeness of God. I need each brother, it is for me to overlook the differences that I perceive. The opinions, the philosophies, the theologies, all are devices of the ego thought system to continue the illusion of separation. If I behold the Oneness and allow that to be the only Light that guides my awareness, then I will behold the Christ.

I am grateful for this openness and willingness that I have to come to You with each thought and I know that there are no minor thoughts. Each can be disturbing to my peace. Equality with all is my mindset for today.

I can release attachments to being right, to acquiring knowledge, to appreciation, to all that may bind me to polar positions. I choose happiness. I choose gratitude for all that enters into my mind. Let me be now the holy vessel to share the Love of the Father. My heart is so grateful for this opportunity of learning. My mind is thankful for the clear Light of Peace.

May It shine forevermore.

Thank You Spirit. Amen.

ooooo

Journal Entry on Lesson 196

It can be but myself I crucify.

Be mindful of the attacks the ego can direct towards your brother for they can be concealed behind a facade of laughter and joy at the expense of true inner peace. You are quite aware when these slips into insanity occur because there is always an underlying feeling that something is not quite right. The guilt you unconsciously feel during these times comes from an unconscious awareness that you are attacking but yourself and then turning it around and laughing about it as if no harm were done. This is a great deception of the ego.

Behind the laughter the ego hides its true agenda from your awareness which is the sword of death. It is the ego's goal to keep the Son of God's mind trapped within the illusion and to crucify him and kill him over and over again. That is the only gift, the only goal that the ego has for you. It is pain and suffering and misery and death. You have allowed the ego to use the strength and power of your own holy mind against yourself because you believe in what you are seeing and experiencing. You believe that you are trapped in a world of misery and at times joy. There is a higher state of joy that can be achieved. It is the joy that comes with allowing the Holy Spirit to help you to heal your mind with the Light of Forgiveness within.

As you learn how to access the Light of God within yourself, each time your mind will be healed a little bit more. Each time inner peace within the mind will settle in a little bit more. Thousands of years are saved each time you access the little spark. In the darkness there is a light that Father has given to you that will heal everything for you. Every single problem you now behold and will behold in the future can be healed by this Light. It is within your ability to learn how to open up to the Light of Christ within yourself and to allow It to begin to heal you a day at a time. The Light of God within yourself is gentle. It will not overpower you and heal you all at once for it recognizes the fear of God which you have. Your unconscious fear and lack of willingness has delayed your healing but not for much longer for the illumination of your mind is beginning to accelerate at last.

The Holy Spirit will help you to learn how to access the Light and He will give you the much needed help in accessing It in the first place. He knows the perfect moment to give you that little nudge, that little shift you need to help your mind shift into the gap where you perceive a clear channel, a clear connection to the Holy One Himself for an instant.

Once these connections are experienced, there is a part of you that will begin to recognize that the Light you perceive is a part of you. Knowledge and understanding will begin to come with repeated exposures to the Light for the Light is pure, and God is pure, and only perfection comes with the Light. Perfection, heals all things of darkness and imperfection that the ego mind attempts to hang onto. The darkness is untruth. The Light is Truth. The Light you find is your salvation. It will pave the road for you and hasten your steps back to Him Who created you. You will understand this inherently when you first begin to perceive the Grace of healing that touches your mind when you see It.

Praise God and praise His Holy Son. This is a time of celebration indeed! For the Christ, the Holy Son of God Himself has begun to awaken at last.

Alleluia! Alleluia! Alleluia!

∞∞∞∞

Journal Entry on Lesson 197

It can be but my gratitude I earn.

The praise and accolades of others will have empty meaning if I do not appreciate myself. If I am doing what I am doing to seek approval, and do not have my own, it is meaningless. It is up to me to love and appreciate the Divine gift that I am. If I give appreciation to others for seeking something in return, then I truly am not giving at all. There are conditions attached to my gift. It is not given freely with pure intention.

Today, I will be mindful of the gifts that I give, to myself and to others. Where is my heart? What purpose do they serve? As I continue to embrace the Holy Spirit into each moment in my life, I will walk with Him, talk with Him and He will show me all the treasures that are mine as I remember God.

Today, I appreciate Who I am. I am as God created me. This cannot be repeated more than enough. The goodness and the kindness of Heaven lies past all the aspects that I have made.

Today, I give with a pure heart and clear mind. Today, I will receive an abundance because it is only an abundance I give. No one else is here. It is just me. That is not a selfish thought; it is only the Truth. There is One Son. And I can either curse or bless. What shall I choose today?

Perhaps you are having experiences where you seem to be suffering from depression, bouts with anger and frustration, or addictive and compulsive behaviors. Perhaps you have sought counseling and therapy from your brothers in an attempt to deal with these problems of the ego mind. Perhaps you feel that some of the theories, practices and medications that they have given to you have been helpful on some level.

However, most of these worldly solutions will not bring you to an ultimate place of true inner healing and peace. There will still be this underlying feeling that the root of the problem is not quite being resolved or healed. It feels like one of those elusive things as if the solution were right there but you haven't been able to quite get your hands on it. It's always just out of reach and you just can't seem to figure out why. I would like to introduce you to a new Therapist in your life.

This Therapist has the ability to heal everything within your mind and body. He happens to be hidden inside of you. You have a tremendous healing gift hidden inside of you. It is in the form of a Light. Your inner Light when raised into the perception of your mind and into your awareness will begin to heal all of the problems you perceive within your life a little bit each time. The miracle here is that once the healing is received, it is complete and never needs redone. Peace is left in its wake. Peace of mind and peace of being grows within yourself.

The Light begins to heal all things in time, past, present and future, each time you raise it into your awareness. This is the process of forgiveness and accepting the Atonement for yourself. For when you perceive the Light within yourself you have let go a little bit more and have perceived the Light of Oneness. Release and peace are always replaced within the mind and the body when the Light comes forth. Each time this is practiced and accomplished, an inner sense of gratitude and love for God and for yourself it always experienced. For you begin to recognize that you have always held the key within yourself to begin to awaken from your dream of fear and pain. Thank You Father for Your gift of healing Light that dwells within each and every one of us. Let us practice being still now that we may find His gift.

∞∞∞

Journal Entry on Lesson 198

Only my condemnation injures me.

"Only my condemnation injures me.
Only my own forgiveness sets me free."

Condemn - "To impose a penalty upon"

With my thoughts I have imposed many punishments over the years upon myself and upon others who really are myself. I penalize myself for not being good enough, worthy enough, not having enough money or status, not pretty enough, or just not enough, period.

What enters into my mind is a song by Lew Doty that he sings about being "Good Enough For God."

> *Sometimes I get to work early*
> *Sometimes a little bit late*
> *Boss don't say nothing when I get there early*
> *When I'm late, he's waiting at the gate*
> *Don't think I'm good enough to talk to me human*
> *Don't think I'm good enough to make my pay*
> *Not long ago I would have thought this true and*
> *Now I repeat these words and go about my day.*
>
> *I am good enough, good enough for God*
> *And that's good enough for me.*
>
> *Bring in the judge and the jury*
> *I used to prosecute myself real good*
> *Then God and I came up with this conclusion*
> *I was just doing the best that I could*
>
> *I am good enough, good enough for God*

And that's good enough for me. (Lew Doty)

It is my own thoughts that cause me the pain that I seem to experience. If I am down on myself, I am doing it. It doesn't matter what someone else has said, no matter what the framing of the words. If I let it effect me then somewhere deep down I am believing that what they are telling me is the truth. I have forgotten my own Truth and I have judged against myself and found myself guilty and impart severe punishment upon myself in the form of depression, anger, sadness, misery, whatever.

If I forgive all that is coming into my mind whether it seems that it is coming from outside of me or from inside, then I will simply go about my way in peace. The importance is to take everything in as information. That's all it is. Information. It is up to me what I will do with that information. Do I judge it? May what someone be saying to me be true? Am I stubborn? Is there a lesson for me to look at?

If I take the emotion out of it, the judgment, then I can turn this into a perfect opportunity for my learning. Forgiveness does set me free. Forgiveness is an illusion set aside to release all others. Forgiveness reminds me of pure Love, all that I am and all that I do. It reminds me that I am "good enough" for God because I am God's Son. The stories of the past can be let go for they are all false memories anyway. The true present memory is of God and that is what forgiveness helps me to attain.

And so I will repeat these words, "*Only my condemnation injures me. Only my own forgiveness sets me free.*" and go about my day.

Visit Lew Doty's website at www.lewdoty.com.

∞∞∞∞∞

Journal Entry on Lesson 199

I am not a body. I am free.

Jesus shares with us in the Course that the last lesson he learned before he left was hearing only the Voice of the Holy Spirit speak to him all the time. In today's lesson, and in many other lessons, he is reminding us and helping us to realize that each and everyone of us has this same Voice from God inside of us. He is also trying to help us realize that it is actually possible for us to learn how to hear the Voice of the Holy Spirit speak to us directly right now. This would be an example of spiritual hearing that he mentions in the Course. This is a gift for us in the dream from God Himself. It will help us to awaken, realize our True Friend and find our way Home. How exciting it is to learn that this is possible! To actually hear the Voice of God speak to us. Hurray! Thank you Father! Thank you! Let us realize that this is one of the major goals of the Course as we joyfully practice our listening in silence today.

I let go of the limits today and sail high above the illusion, the battleground, the world. The body has been transformed from the vexing device the ego has used to keep me bound, to the learning and communication device, the vessel of the Holy Spirit.

Holy Spirit, May I continue to release all aspects of the body that keep me tied to the ego and may I only serve Your purpose here. I willingly listen to Your Voice and Your Voice only for It is the only One that will sing of sweet Home to me.

Thank You Holy Spirit for the Love that replaces all fear. Amen.

∞∞∞∞

Journal Entry on Lesson 200

There is no peace except the peace of God.

When I got home from work yesterday I was feeling tired, stressed and worried. I felt tired because I hadn't slept well the night before and I felt stressed because the day was unusually chaotic and busy for me. My "to-do" list at work was growing faster than I could solve the problems. I was feeling worried because my contract for employment is due to expire soon and I hadn't heard about any opportunities to be hired on as a permanent employee come up yet. Of course, the ego part of my mind felt free to analyze my performance over the last year and point out all of my deficiencies and shortcomings. Needless to say, all of these attacks and judgments churning in the back of my mind through the day managed to dampen my spirit and my desire to feel happy and playful.

I decided it would be a good idea to sit down and lay back in my resting chair and practice stopping all the thoughts in my mind for awhile. I closed my eyes, tilted the chair back so that I could feel comfortable and began to turn my mind inward and relax my body. As I sunk into a more peaceful place, I practiced being very still and stopping my thoughts. I hadn't tried stopping my thoughts for a long time for a while and decided to see how long I could do this right now. I felt rather determined as I started to do this. I wanted to see if I could go for several minutes without thinking or listening to any of my thoughts.

And so I did. And as I did and actually succeeded in not listening to any thoughts or words for about a minute, I noticed an ego resistance rising within myself, a tension, an anxiousness attempted to rise within my chest. Apparently, the habitual chatter of the ego voice that the ego mind has become accustomed to listening to, felt uncomfortable listening to the peace of silence. It was something new. I instructed my mind to relax and let this anxiousness go and to focus once again on having no thoughts, no words, for as long as I could. Again, I practiced listening to silence, stillness.

This time I was able to go a little longer, perhaps two minutes. Then to my surprise something began to happen to my body as if it were coming from another source. I felt as if the Light of Peace had moved into and illuminated the room around me and my body. It was as if I had transitioned from a feeling of darkness around me, into light. The black screen of my mind's eye greyed a little as if I were getting closer to a light beyond it. I began to feel more peaceful.

It filled in the seeming void of silence and stress with peace in my body. I smiled quietly to myself and thought, "Hey, I'm on to something here." So I stayed with it. I continued to relax and have no thoughts within my mind some more, holding it longer to see if the Light of Peace would come some more, and It did.

Suddenly, I perceived the white Light behind the veil pierce through the dark screen in my mind's eye as two stars. It was as if the Light behind the veil poked two holes through the darkness and the Light was able to shine through the holes for an instant into my perception. Peace poured through toward me, from my heart, and into my mind when this happened. It felt like my mind and heart and being were suddenly being filled with the Light of Peace.

Although the stars only flashed for a moment, I laid there and allowed the peaceful feeling to soak in; I realized that I was beginning to feel happy and okay again. I felt refreshed, rested and like living life again. Although I hadn't realized it yet, in those few moments the rest of my day had made a turn for a better, happier experience. I felt quietly happy and peaceful inside again. My playful side started to feel like coming out again. I ended up having a fun dinner with my wife and two daughters that I had prepared. Afterward my two daughters asked if I would go for a bike ride with them. We did and we had a great time.

I am so grateful for these gifts that Father has given to us, to access and receive any time we want and whenever we are truly ready to receive them. I am so grateful that I know where to go now when my life feels like it's becoming a mess and unpeaceful. There truly is no peace like the peace of God, and I am glad and thankful that this is so.

∞∞∞

Journal Entry on Lesson 201

Review Lesson 181

Holy Spirit,

I have been bombarded with verbal and written information of Course brothers seemingly attacking others in little subtle ways and even in overt ways. I know that it is for me to go within with You if I have allowed this to disturb my peace. It does not matter who wants to play "King of the Hill" and in what way. It is only the ego that wants to climb that mountain to separate and divide in the varying forms that I have witnessed. It can be from making one seem more intelligent or more versed than another, to who has more integrity than another, to one's organization is better than this other organization, to this one charges for services and this one believes in Divine Providence, to this one has lied, that one hasn't, oh, how it goes on. Anything that I seem to be experiencing outside of my mind is really going on inside my mind. If I experience conflict in the world, it is the conflict in my mind.

This is what I take to you this day Holy Spirit. It is the conflict of my mind in seeing the differences, the one-upmanships, and all of the seeming conflicts between my brothers.

And so *"This thought I do not want. I choose instead 'I trust my brothers who are one with me.' "*

I know that I am only here to be truly helpful and that You are my Divine Source. I am not here to point out errors in another for that is not my job. The ego would love to make it my job especially if I had felt slighted or rebuffed in some way. This would not be owning responsibility for my own perceptions. And so I do take responsibility for all that I see as it comes from within me.

Holy Spirit, What ways can "I trust my brothers who are one with me"?

My Dear One,

See all *as* One. The Son has been asleep in this dream of separation and despair. Your brothers want to volley for the position of THE Son of God when they need to remember that they ALL are the Son of God. They have simply forgotten. I tell you to forgive, forgive and forgive again. Let it go and come into the awareness of the One. None of the fear-based platitudes or attitudes will bring anyone anything. It is only through the heart of gratitude for all that will bring the brothers as One and into the Peace of God. You sleep but for a moment longer; use the dream of forgiveness to assist you in seeing the truth.

Everyone is doing the very best that they can, even the self-pronounced Teachers of God. They are not immune to the ego and its vain imaginings. It is ego pride that comes out in the game of ego comparison. Do not fall for this game yourself. Loose instead of bind. Release the blindfold and let it fall away and truly see with My Eyes. In equality will the Son truly know Itself. You receive your power from the Light of God; use it with the intention of co-creating Love.

When you see these occurrences in the world remember that they come from your own mind. Bring them all to Me and I will dispel the darkness that surrounds them and return to you only the Light of Truth. It is merely a distraction from your own path if you listen and believe the tales that others tell. It is a distraction for them as well but it is not for you to point that error out. You know already that you are responsible for your own mind. Take that responsibility seriously and with Love.

Do not be distracted by attachments to being right. Be happy. That is all I ask of you is to be happy. You already know the key to happiness; it is through your forgiveness. Your mind has long believed in the separation as you have the witnesses surrounding you all the time in the world from your body and other bodies, to these conflicts you are witnessing, to every item that you see before you. I give you now a new belief that is the belief in the oneness of the universe. Be blessed this day. You are indeed worthy to be the Son of God for you *are* the Son of God. Allow your mind to be open to seeing this and seeing all as One. Continue your practice for you are on the right path for you are with Me. Be you blessed.

○○○○○

Journal Entry on Lesson 202

Review Lesson 182

The ego very easily could turn this review lesson around if I am feeling down or out of sorts in some way. It can beckon me to escape the world by ending the life of the body which of course it would just recycle anyway. The ego thinks the solution to the problem lies in death in some form. With God, there is no other solution but to look within and see the Life worth living, the one that I share with God. With the knowledge of God's truth, I can sweep away the cobwebs of sadness and look towards the Light. Heaven is my True Home; it is where I want to be. Not in a matter of escape but in a matter of that's where I have always been and will forever be. I am safe at home, no matter where my mind may take me.

And so now I go within to the still waters of peace and gently bring my attention to listening to the song of freedom that sings me Home to the Father. There is real peace there. Not what the ego would offer me. I gladly accept that this world is an illusion made up of my own fearful thoughts of separation from the Father for I now fully accept that I have never left the Garden of Heaven.

Thank You Holy Spirit for Your Wisdom when I have been listening to my own.

Today, *"I will be still an instant and go home."* Amen.

ooooo

Journal Entry on Lesson 203

Review Lesson 183

The ego mind delivers us temptation after temptation to continue to hold the House of God away from our awareness. These temptations must not be allowed to go unchallenged if we are to awaken from our dream of hell. The conditions for peace are quite specific. Make the choice for Spirit within your mind and being and nothing else. In your heart be with Spirit throughout the day. Make Him your Friend in your heart and He will be your Friend. The Holy Spirit will gladly help you throughout the day.

He wants to be your Friend and He wants to show you a life of highest joy in living and being in Him.

You pretend that you can ignore Him and do whatever it is you want but you know that this will only bring you pain, this foolish game. Surrender and forgiveness is the path of peace and joy. How happy are those that walk with Him and hold His Hand. Those who trust in Him and believe in Him and allow Him to lead the way find joyful lives indeed. The Holy Spirit is your Friend; take everything to Him especially the temptations that plague your mind. Every worry, every fear, every concern that clutters your mind should be taken to your Friend for discussion, insight and healing. It is not that difficult. You either choose to talk with Him about the things that flow through your mind or not. He is not going to make you do anything you do not want to do. You will always have the final choice.

However you will find that you are giving up nothing in exchange for everything. There is no sacrifice with the Holy Spirit. He is wise enough to help you to understand easily enough why you would want to let go of your chains of bondage in exchange for freedom so vast that the mind cannot comprehend. Freedom from the limits of the body is one of the goals of the Holy Spirit. There is so much joy and freedom beyond the body you will hardly believe it when you begin to discover it. There is so much joy and happiness and freedom beyond the body that you would leap there now in an instant if you truly understood where we are going with this curriculum.

Give Him your willingness, merely talk with Him and be with Him and ask Him to help you to look at all sides. Ask Him for His perspective on the thoughts that dwell within your mind. If you are going to have the thoughts running through your mind, you might as well share them with Him. At least then you would be making some significant progress in your mind healing and awakening from your dream. Otherwise you are just delaying the process. Use time for what time was meant to be used for. Forgive all of your thoughts and experiences and let them go. Choose instead to call upon the name of God and on your own. And it will be so.

∞∞∞∞

Journal Entry on Lesson 204

Review Lesson 184

The Holy Spirit is reminding me about completely trusting Him with managing my life. Over the years I thought I had learned how to take care of myself and those around me. These were only lessons from the ego. Jesus reminds us in the Course that we have been poorly taught. It is evident that this is true because every time we have followed the ways of the ego thought system it has only led us to disappointment and pain. This is not the way of the Holy Spirit. The Holy Spirit is happiness and His Will for us is to have His happiness in our lives.

Developing the habit of merely stepping back and asking Him to guide our lives for us is one of the keys to truly having a happy and peaceful experience as we awaken from our dream. We have developed many habit patterns and idiosyncrasies in the way we live our lives and see the world that we think is helping us to feel happier. But surely by now we are able to see and, more importantly, feel the pattern of disappointment and pain. This cycle is the cycle of pain and fear that only the ego knows how to do. These cycles are cycles within cycles that lead to nowhere. In order to begin to break free of them and to free our minds, we must begin to remember Who we really are and Where we came from.

The Holy Spirit is our appointed Guide, our appointed Friend to help us to do this; to help us accomplish this goal. He has been given all power in Heaven and on earth to help us, and when we call upon Him for help, He will help us. Let us remember to specifically ask Him to help us to heal the cycles that the ego mind attempts to keep us bound with and have faith that it is done. Thank Him for His help, for it is done. And He will bring it to your awareness that it is done, if you but give Him a chance. Loosen your grip on the world around you and the things you hold dear in your mind. Let them all go, just for a few minutes each day. That is all We ask of you and salvation will be surely yours. Let go of the clutter within your mind and be open to the gifts the Holy Spirit will bless you with through your mind and into your experience of the world.

Miracles are abundant to the one who lays down all idols he values within his mind and allows it to be open in exchange for his gifts from God. Your inheritance from God has already been received. You do not have to wait for it any longer. You can begin to open up your mind and accept these gifts now through the forgiveness process. And what is the forgiveness process? It is merely letting go of everything you behold now in exchange for what is true.

Allow the Light of Truth to shine into your mind and wash away all that you thought was real. There is no truth except this, you are God's Son. You were created exactly like Him. You are holy. You are perfection at its best. There are no flaws laid upon you. You are innocent. You are pure. You are sinless. You are the Holy Son of God, the Christ Himself. Let us be with that truth for a few moments now and wait for this blessing, this Divine promise and gift from God to dawn upon our minds and illuminate us with this eternal truth.

∞∞∞∞

Journal Entry on Lesson 205

Review Lesson 185

The peace of God is everything I want. The peace of God is my one goal; the aim of all my living here, the end I seek, my purpose and my function and my life, while I abide where I am not at home.

Thank You Holy Spirit for the peace that passeth understanding. This quote is a Godsend. It *is* what I truly want in this world. It can only be experienced when I am willing to let go of all that I think defines me, has been my purpose or function and my so-called life. It is not me. It is not Who I am. And so in each encounter of the day, each situation, each seeming glitch, I will remember that it is only the peace of God that I desire this day and everyday. In the quiet of the Now moment will I find what I have been seeking. Today, letting go of the distractions that take me far away from my focus on God will bring me peace. I am centered and grounded in Your peace Father. The restlessness of the night, the seeming back pain, all are now a distant memory as I remember that I am not a body, I am free for I am still as You created me to be. I will live in the shining Light of Peace and allow It to flow through me and outward into the world. Amen.

∞∞∞∞

Journal Entry on Lesson 206

Review Lesson 186

Salvation of the world depends upon you because you are making all of it up. At a higher level of the unconscious ego mind you became the director of a play that you wrote. And you decided to pretend that you were an actor in that play. Just like

Mr. Rogers Neighborhood of make-believe, you made up a world of time, space and fear and decided to pretend that it was really out there and that it was happening to you. Everything you see, hear, feel and experience within your make-believe world was designed to convince you that you are everything that you are not.

In this make-believe dream that you made up, you believe you are a body that is frail and weak, but in reality you are a spirit that is invulnerable and is the strength of love Itself. In your dream, you believe you can be born and die, where in reality as spirit you are eternal. In your dream, you believe that you are contained in darkness, where in reality you are a light. It is very possible to learn how to train your mind to let go and begin to forgive the world you made. It is possible to begin to have experiential glimpses of your true reality as the Light and Spirit of God's Son now while you are in the dream. This is accomplished by developing a true willingness to let go of everything you perceive now and to open up to the perception of the Light of Christ within yourself.

It is quite possible to see the light of the other world within yourself, the world of who you really are through the practice of stilling all of your thoughts and attempting to perceive the Light within your mind. Ask the Holy Spirit to help you do this. When the light comes, your mind will begin to be healed very quickly from the grasp that the dream of hell has had bound upon it for so long. Finding the light within yourself is discovering salvation for both yourself and the world along with you. Bring the darkness to the light and the light will dispel the darkness with the peace of God, healing all that it touches within the mind and saving the world at last. You are the light of the world and because of this salvation of the world truly depends on you.

Just before I awoke this morning, I had a rather lengthy and vivid dream. The dream was informational because the symbols and situations in the dream brought to my awareness memories of things that I am afraid of or will happen. When I first reflected on the dream and the series of fearful thoughts that it arose for me, the overall peaceful state that I was feeling began to shift into an unpeaceful state. I began to become concerned that the Holy Spirit was attempting to give me messages through the dream to help me to brace myself for an outcome to a situation that I am afraid might be happening in my life right now. After a few minutes of looking at this I then began to realize that the ego must be involved here because each of the symbolic situations in the dream included something that I was afraid was going to happen as a result of past behavior. I began to recognize how Holy Spirit was helping me with these things because today's Lesson is the perfect lesson for me to apply to each of the fearful ideas that came up in the dream and so I did. I welcome this dream now and I feel grateful to the Holy Spirit because I feel that I have given the tools to help me to heal and let go of these unconscious fears that I have been harboring in my mind.

I intend to continue to work with these attack thoughts by applying the ideas in today's Lesson toward them because I really do want to exchange the unconscious fear for peace. The fear is very subtle, a little worry here, a little concern there, little things just enough to put little ripples into the stillness of peace. Each attack thought adds another ripple to the surface of the calm waters and it is each of these ripples that I want to heal forever in exchange for perfect peace with the Holy Spirit's help. Thank You Holy Spirit for this opportunity to work with You today. You truly are my personal Friend and I am coming to know that now. I appreciate the little nudges that You give me throughout the day. I appreciate the waves of peace that You give me when I see the flashes of Light. I appreciate the little promptings You give me to help me to extend Love to others. I feel like You are really helping me and I want You to know that I really appreciate it. Thank You for helping me. I love You and I love the feeling of getting to know my Friend. Amen.

Journal Entry on Lesson 207

Review Lesson 187

I was blank early this morning in receiving a message, which didn't mean that one wouldn't arrive. Sometimes it just comes a little later. The message moves forward, just as a pebble dropped into a still pond ripples forward. The Holy Spirit had placed that infinite wisdom pebble within my mind and now it was ready to ripple forth and be felt.

I decided to sit down again for quiet meditation after realizing how much back pain I was having. It appeared all of a sudden. The girls and I had walked over to the library on this beautiful day and upon returning I stopped once again at the computer to do more work. Perhaps the pain was a reminder to stop and go within and feel the calm. All projects can wait. All phone calls can be put on hold. Simply slip into peace.

And so I shall…

(After 30 minutes of silent meditation)

With this time, it was obvious that what was needed was for me to rest. When I am still, I can remember the blessing that is mine from God already, shining ever so brilliantly from my heart. That is the image that I received. The rays of this Light I saw within my mind, golden rays emanating forth from a heart centered in my mind. It was a heart at rest, still for a moment. It was then the rays turned into gorgeous, pure white feathery wings. A signal for me to remember, that it is freedom from my thoughts that brings me the peace of God. The heart always is constant in its rhythm of life just as is my Father's Love for me.

Ahh.....to rest, to feel blessed. That is indeed a gift today.

Journal Entry on Lesson 208

Review Lesson 188

"Grounded in Spirit" - Those were the words that Paul used to describe his first impressions of me when we first met at the ACIM Center that I had founded back in Pittsburgh. This came in a conversation last night as we enjoyed our "date night" out, seeing a movie and then retreating to a fast-food restaurant parking lot for some conversation.

It was nice to have a little laughter, a little touching remembrances of where we were and where we are now on the path. It gave me time to really reflect on my actions and my words and how they influence others. Am I walking my talk? He also mentioned how much he appreciated my unconditional love and non-judgmental stance.

At times I don't feel that I am just that and it's something that I know I work with Holy Spirit on. Well, I am still believing that I live in this world so forgiveness lessons always present themselves. And of course, we shared last night, we are always our own worst critic and that inner critic is very quick to dismiss an appreciation when it is shown.

This conversation started when we were sharing about our Sunday Meditation Service and how two visiting women had commented on how peaceful we seemed. We laughed about that remark as we knew differently, or thought we did. The inner critic strikes again with its fearful response.

I reminded Paul that truly if we look at our lives over the last year, 5 years, 10 years, etc., we would see a difference, a forward motion of serenity in our lives. That's being honest with myself, I know that my life in the way of peace has increased dramatically with the Course in 1994. Meditation was one thing for many years before that, but the addition of a "new" thought system based on love and forgiveness surely has brought me to a deeper level of peace.

That desire for healing continues to be the focal point in my life. I shared with Paul, as I have many times, that my first impressions of him was of someone who deeply desired to make significant changes in his life, to follow the path of God, who was excited at having found "another way." That spark of excitement, blessed me at the time as a facilitator. It is always a great blessing to watch someone blossom in their spiritual journey. And I am witness to that all the time, with each student, each study group member, each counselee that has crossed my path over the years.

I have blossomed too, and continue to bud and grow even more glorious blooms. "Blooming where one is planted," that saying goes. Being planted, rooted, grounded in God is what brings me my joy and my peace. I have a deeper appreciation for the foundation of working with Holy Spirit in every aspect of my life, particularly in my relationship with Paul. Having given our relationship solely (soul-ly) to God has made all the difference in the world of any other relationship I have ever had.

Hearing the Holy Spirit speak to me all through the day is another benefit that I have received gladly. Allowing Him to gently lead is certainly a better way to live than I had in the past.

Grounded...Centered...At peace...

In the deep connection with Holy Spirit, I can be unconditionally loving and non-judgmental. I can bloom and extend my essence of Love to others. I can shine the peace of God ever forth.

Grounded in Spirit is trusting Spirit with all of my life, my work, my ministry, my finances, my play, my chores, my fun, my parenting, my everything!

Grounded in Spirit is centered in the peace of the still waters of my Holy Mind.

And I am thankful that it is so.

∞∞∞

Journal Entry on Lesson 209

Review Lesson 189

In meditation, I found myself completely focusing on feeling the Love of God within me. The message I received came as single words or phrases with each one being deeply felt for some time and then lifted up into moments of peace until the next would appear. You may wish to add your own as you reflect on feeling the Love of God within you.

-The Love of God-

Expansive
Mine
Inherited
Provides Freedom
Sustains me
There is nothing else I could want
It is what I want, yet I fear
Deep well of Love
Unending Supply
Blessed
Blessing
Complete
Whole
Every Son's desire
Deep connection to Who I am
Innocent
Free

Pure
Heart open wide
Light, sparkling Light
Warm Embrace
Comfort
Non-judging and Unconditional
Here I am
Here I will stay
Accept
Oneness with All
Extend
Ribbons of Joy
Homecoming

Godspeed

Amen.

∞∞∞

Journal Entry on Lesson 210

Review Lesson 190

The way to have a happy day today is to recognize that of all the choices that will presented to you, there is only one to choose from. That choice is to join with Holy Spirit in your mind and ask Him, "What would You have me do now?" The ego thought system has you believing that you know which choices will lead you to joy. Observe the clutter within your mind with the Holy Spirit and you will recognize that the ego does not truly know how to lead you to constant peace and a tranquil mind. In fact, it has become a habit to follow the ego's urges and desires that it thinks is leading it to a feeling of fulfillment and happiness. But surely by now you recognize that this is short-lived.

The mind-training we undertake is about developing new habits within the ego mind to help lead you out of the ego mind and into a state of perfect peace where you belong. You are aware that your ego mind comes up with thoughts and ideas, activities that it can engage in in the near future to help it to feel happy and satisfied. At the same time you are aware that there is an underlying feeling of dis-ease, conflict and lack of peace. These feelings should be your warning flag to help you to remember this, "I am not feeling perfectly happy and at peace right now. If I want to truly feel happy, at peace and have a tranquil mind then I must remember to ask the Holy Spirit to help me with my thoughts right now."

This little prayer that I give to you will help you to remember to step back and have the willingness to ask Him for help when you seem to forget that you do know the way. You do know the way which is to have the willingness to step back and be with the Holy Spirit in your mind and to ask Him which choice will truly lead you to joy instead of pain. His answers and His guidance will always come to those who are truly asking in the moment and being willing to follow the answer when it comes. Many will receive the answer but will still choose to follow their own made-up pain instead of joy. This is ok. It has no effect on reality at all. It is merely just a delaying maneuver, a belief in the ability to resist the will of the Kingdom within your heart and to be something else instead.

Dear Son of God,

Lay down your foolish dreams and weapons of the mind that bring you pain and anguish. Lay them down and receive the gifts of joy, true joy that your Father in Heaven has given to you already. Allow your mind to let go of everything you behold now. Let Him show you what the taste of the true Light of Joy feels like now. Be still and let the Light come and heal your mind.

Journal Entry on Lesson 211

Review Lesson 191

This Review Lesson helps me to remember the truth of Who I am. It is easy to fall into the trap of comparison especially when one is away from home and in the midst of the summer waterpark crowds. So easily the ego whispers how many younger, prettier, thinner and better bodies there are out there and you are not that. "You're getting old. The weight is not coming off fast enough. You're a failure." All this the ego taunts with. All built up from the day of "birth" into the body. There's always someone better or worse than you and you better keep the competition going because you will lose and then be abandoned and alone and die in the dark.

Thank goodness there is an escape from this insane thought system! Thank goodness for the Holy Spirit. With today's Review Lesson, I affirm that I am the Son of God, that I am not a body and that I am only spirit, who is One with God. This frees me from believing that I am anything but. In the body, specialness is wanted and sought after. It is the desire of wanting God to notice and love me and not abandon me.

But I don't need to do anything to receive His Love. I am the Son He loves. My brothers who are One with me are the same Son He loves. I don't have to change who I am or what I am or what I look like. He loves me for me and that is enough. The ego would have me keep searching for the magic combination, be it self-sacrifice, self-denial, lies, lack of authenticity, all to satisfy some other projection of ego that does not accept the truth of who I am.

God loves me for me. Period. End of ego story. All He wants me to do is remember who I am. What more could there be but the precious Love of Heaven? I'll never find it anywhere else but in Him.

Journal Entry on Lesson 212

Review Lesson 192

Forgiveness is my function. And through forgiveness I embrace the tenderness, the kindness and the true happiness of Heaven. I experience Love. All the world is a trap. It is a trap to keep me away from having the deep knowledge of the Love of God, the Love that I am. And so I remove the triggering mechanisms of the trap by releasing those to the Holy Spirit. He can dismantle the trap of hell that the ego has set and show me that it does not exist and the peace of God that does really exist.

Sometimes the traps are hidden beneath the brush and leaves on the path that I walk. With my constant connection to Holy Spirit, following His lead, listening to His Voice and sure guidance, I will know that a trap is within my footsteps and I will know in which direction to sidestep. Too many times I have stepped into the traps and been caught up in the trap writhing in pain. But I know that those times I have allowed the Holy Spirit to show me that the trap will disintegrate before me as I remove my fear from it.

Be confident and sure today in your walk with Me. Allow Me to assist you in steering in the right direction of Home. You will see golden treasures before you where once you saw traps of pain. Each now is a remembrance of forgiveness and Love.

Let your mind be free today.

∞∞∞∞

Journal Entry on Lesson 213

Review Lesson 193

Yesterday I went through an experience at work where I became very frustrated and angry with the situation at hand. I had it in my mind from the outset that I was going to solve the problem within a certain amount of time. I had set an expectation on the outcome as if I knew when the outcome was going to happen. This was an example of allowing the ego part of the split mind to lead the way.

When the time came for the problem to be resolved and it wasn't, I began to feel stressed, irritated and angry. I wasn't meeting my expectations and so I began to believe in my own inadequacies and shortcomings. I began to feel angrier and a self-hatred. I felt trapped not knowing which way to go to solve the problem. I felt more and more disconnected from Inner Wisdom. Blinders were put on within my mind and I was unable to focus clearly. My mind became closed instead of open to possible alternatives in solving the problem.

I became so wrapped up and frustrated on this situation that I became absolutely miserable and useless in a way. I eventually stepped away from the situation and carried the anger and the fear with me for a long time. I felt like I had failed a very simple task and was afraid that my co-workers would look down upon me and criticize me for failing. This was a very unpleasant experience. It was my own little hell within the illusion of hell. It wasn't until I began to completely resurrender myself to God that I began to feel a letting go and feel free again.

This is an example of how the ego part of the split mind keeps our mind wrapped up in a cycle of anger and fear. When our minds are so focused on such things, it is used to hurt ourselves. We forget that this is unnecessary and that our plans are unimportant because we do not know God's plan. We forget to completely surrender ourselves to the journey we are on and to trust God completely. We forget not to make judgments on when and how things should be done. We forget that we truly do not know the answers to any given situation at any time and what their purpose is.

Our lives become much more peaceful if we surrender completely to God's plan not knowing what it is from moment to moment and accept where we are, wherever we are. It is helpful to realize that we do not know where we are supposed to be and when and so it is helpful to not let ourselves be concerned with what we think others' expectations are of us.

We are God's servants while we walk here. We are here only to be truly helpful in every situation that is presented to us at hand. We are here to represent Him Who sent us and we do not know the way unless He has directed us. We do not have to worry about what to say or what to do in any situation but merely trust that whatever is happening is in complete perfection and in accordance with His plan that we have accepted for ourselves. And it is helpful to remember that we will be healed as we have an openness, a mindfulness and a willingness to be taught and healed at the same time. "Here, I am Lord," is our prayer, our mantra. What is it You would have me do? And say? And to whom? I am Your servant. I am Your follower and it is Your lead that I would follow, Your plan and not my own in anything. I do not know the way but You do and I am happy that this is so. I relinquish all of my plans in exchange for Your peace, Your peace of mind, body and spirit.

∞∞∞∞

Journal Entry on Lesson 214

Review Lesson 194

This morning I awoke feeling the illusion of illness having dissipated. The last 3 days had been difficult with various cold/flu-like symptoms. It was indeed a blessing to have the pain in my ear, head and throat having subsided. But as I sat in meditation on today's Lesson, the mind began to chatter about how now I had the opportunity to accomplish this task, call that person back, reschedule that appointment, etc. Gently I released the chatter to remember *"I place the future in the Hands of God."*

It does not matter if chores get done or phone calls returned. Those worrisome thoughts are just anticipation, expectation and guilt, all fear, driving the chatter. What does matter is to stay present with Him. It is knowing that all needs will be taken care of as I trust the Holy Spirit. All the timing will be absolutely perfect.

As I reminded myself of the Lesson's message, a shift occurred throughout my being. I felt lighter and more peaceful. The anxiety for those few minutes had ceased. The tension had lifted from the body, and I felt free.

The last few days of physical symptoms had tied me into the body. Most of the time I felt mentally well until about mid-day yesterday when I felt it was all wearing on me. The strain of the subtle judgment of cancelling appointments, putting projects aside, and not returning calls got the best of me. At that point I knew that I needed to rest in Him. I took the time yesterday to do just that. All things could wait. Going to peace was most important.

And so was the lesson presented again this morning. Resting in God is all that is needed. As I keep in communication with the Holy Spirit, I will know when it is time to do something else. I can bring this sense of quiet and peace with me and extend it out into the world in all my experiences. Forgetting to do so brought me the weariness.

No guilt needed. No fear needed. No judgment needed. What happened yesterday is gone. My anxiety about tomorrow, or even hours from now will not add any time to my life. So, why worry.

Thank You Holy Spirit for another perfect reminder at a perfect moment in my life. It is through You that I can apply each Lesson, each Course principle into my daily life. I truly appreciate this time with You for it deepens even more the relationship with You. I will continue to listen to Your Voice throughout the day for You will guide me in what to do and when to do it.

Thank You for Your Peace.
Amen.

∞∞∞

Journal Entry on Lesson 215

Review Lesson 195

The Holy Spirit goes with you wherever you go. He is present in your mind. The question is, "Are you walking and talking with Him in your mind wherever you go?" Your Friend is with you but are you being with Him and listening to Him? You are very adept at carrying on many conversations in your mind with the ego and being with him, but what about the Holy Spirit? You have a choice; you can walk with fear and anxiety within your mind and a lack of certainty, or you can walk with a calmness and a peace as you talk with Him Who is your Friend and your only true Guide.

Practice being with Him today in your mind wherever you go, in whatever you do. Although you may believe that you may not be able to hear Him fully, pretend that He is there anyways and talk with Him throughout the day. For example, you might say, "Holy Spirit, what do You think about this?" or "Holy Spirit, this is how I am feeling, what do You think?" or "Holy Spirit, how do You think I should handle this situation?"

Talk to Him as a child would talk with an imaginary friend. Although you will discover very quickly that He is no imagination. He is truly there to guide you, to help you, to be with you as your Eternal Friend. Think about that for a moment. You have an Eternal Friend Who goes with you wherever you go, forever. This Friend will help you to feel happy and secure and confident. He will give you wisdom always. It's merely to practice walking with Him and being with Him as you go about your day that you will discover these many gifts that your Friend has for you. He will comfort you in your time of worry.

Turn to Him with every conversation in your mind and pause and listen in silence for His inspirations. Step back from situations that concern you and let the Voice for God show you the way. Let your Friend truly be with you in spirit, mind and body. Be aware and feel His Presence with you. See with Him as you look about your surroundings throughout your day. Hear with Him as you speak to others and listen to them. Hear His Spirit, see His Spirit communicating through you as you see and observe the world about you. Observe with Him and let Him talk with you about all that you are seeing, feeling and hearing. It is about stepping back and observing with Him and letting Him show you what He sees, what He thinks and what He would have you hear for Him.

You will find that this Friend is like no other and you will come to love this personal companionship, this personal relationship, that you begin to remember that you have with Him. He is such a comforting companion indeed! A warm blanket you would never want to give up again. What a wonderful gift your Father has given to you; your Friend, your Companion, your Holy Guide. Be thankful for Him and thankful for everything He and your Father has given to you. Walk with Him today in peace, in joy, in gratitude and in love.

∞∞∞

Journal Entry on Lesson 216

Review Lesson 196

Holy Spirit, I have a memory from when I was an adolescent of believing that Father condemned me to a body, and abandoned me to this place of hell where I would someday die. This was a terrible and fearful thought for me to believe in. At the time, I did not realize that everything I was experiencing was an illusion. I did not realize on some level I had forgotten who I really was, and somehow chosen to crucify myself by believing in this illusion of separation from my Father.

You have shared with me in the Course that there is "secret guilt" hidden behind this belief that I am not even aware of, and because of this I am experiencing a darkened mind.

Holy Spirit, All of these fearful dark thoughts and beliefs I wish to give to You now. I ask You for Your healing Light to come now and illuminate my mind and heart with a flash to wash this pain away from my mind forever.

Holy Spirit, On some level I have chosen to crucify my holy Self in this way. I do not understand how this could have seemed to happen but I do not want it anymore. And so I give all of this to You in exchange for Your healing Light. I ask You to help me accept Atonement for myself in exchange for this world I made. Help me to forgive myself that the Light of Love may be restored to my mind. I turn this over to You now and I wait in silence for

Your Light to come and wash me clean, showing me my sinlessness and my innocence as my holy Self.

Thank You Holy Spirit and thank You Father for Your gifts to me. I love You. Amen.

∞∞∞∞

Journal Entry on Lesson 217

Review Lesson 197

"Who should give thanks for my salvation by myself?"

It is from my willingness to see the world and myself differently that I come into my own, come into my salvation, and come into my gratitude.

Holy Spirit, I know that my decision for peace is vital to my receiving of Your peace. In each moment that passes by, each situation, each occurrence, I can decide for the peace of God.

It is a reminder for me again about walking the middle road, the path of non-judgment, the road to You. With You leading, this path is clear and free of any obstacles. When I veer to the left or veer to the right through my judgments, fears or attachments the way can be thorny and overgrown.

Your way is a steady way. The strength in me from You allows my footsteps to be light but sure. And it is really only myself that I can thank. I did this! I chose peace! I chose You Holy Spirit!

Thank You God.
Thank You Holy Spirit.
Thank Me.

Journal Entry on Lesson 218

Review Lesson 198

Darkness into Light.

Release the self-criticisms, the self-judgments, the self-images of pain. They do not serve you. They are dark clouds that surround the Son of God's Holy Mind.

As clouds, they can easily drift away with the willingness to see truly. These dark clouds and storms, much like you are observing outside your window this morning, are not you. They may crash with thunder and lightning strikes, but they only hide the sun's light from you.

Soon they will pass away.

The storm clouds hovering around your mind can pass away to, with my assistance. you made these clouds out of fear either of God, yourself or another. Let them dissipate and their fury will cease.

In their place you will see a rainbow of glory. It is the symbol of the covenant, the promise that I have made with you. Let the Light shine forth as One, no separation of the Holy Rays touching all minds and hearts with the Love of the Father. Feel the warmth of the Light and see the clarity beyond the horizon.

And today, behold your glory and be glad.

Note: I had written this early this morning during a fierce thunderstorm. I did not know what it meant to me at the time, because I was feeling pretty peaceful in the moment, no clouds of fear hanging about. A little later when I went to upload yesterday's message reflection to the web, I saw that our database had somehow been corrupted. The clouds of self-judgment began to form and then I knew that the Holy Spirit was preparing me for what was to come. Right away I remembered the message from Spirit and was able to come to a place of peace. Although I do not have our database fixed as of yet, I am able to be in a place of Light. I am grateful for our Sunday ACIM Meditation Circle theme of "Wake Up to Who You Really Are" for it was a time for me to go deeper with Spirit in allowing His Answer to come forth. It seems He has given me another insight of what He wants me to do with the site. Such gratitude to Him and to me for remembering the truth of Who I am.

∞∞∞∞

Journal Entry on Lesson 219

Review Lesson 199

There is one goal in all that you do while you walk upon this earth and that is to find the Light of Christ within yourself. The Holy Spirit has a perception of a new world for you to behold and it is beyond the world you see now. In the other world there is no day and night that passes as time seems to go by. There are no cities of buildings and roadways interconnecting them. There are no oceans and bodies of water separating the plains of fields and land.

In the Real World which you are capable of seeing right now within your mind, there is only Light. It is the Holy Spirit's goal, it is His mission to help you lead you unto the Light of Christ within yourself. All that you see now is a reflection of imperfection. The Light that the Holy Spirit would have you behold within yourself is the Light of perfection and sinlessness. It is the Light of your True Self, of your True Home in God. The Light you see comes from you. It is *your* Holy Light that you see.

This perception of perfection is the bridge that leads you to the gates of Heaven. It is here where your perception of Light will be exchanged for knowledge when God Himself takes the final step in your redemption. The world you behold now is the world of guilt that you behold within your unconscious mind. You secretly desire the world of guilt to bring about more guilt within your mind. This unconscious guilt keeps your perception trapped within the world of perception, blocking your sight from True Perception. Darkness clouds your mind from your desire to value what is valueless within the world.

Each time you are tempted to value something within the world. Remember to turn those thoughts over to the Holy Spirit for forgiveness. Remember to say:

"The Holy Spirit leads me unto Christ, and where else would I go? What need have I but to awake in Him?"

Remember that a sense of inner peace is your true goal. Allow the Holy Spirit to heal your dark thoughts by letting Him show you the Light of Christ within yourself. The Christ will touch your mind and heal your heart with peace each time you remember a glimpse of God. His Light kisses your soul and washes away all pain for a few moments. And then you return to earth having remembered for a moment Who You Really Are, the Christ, the Holy Son of God Himself.

ooooo

Journal Entry on Lesson 220

Review Lesson 200

Peace is impossible to those who look on war. Peace is inevitable to those who offer peace. How easily, then, is your judgment of the world escaped! It is not the world that makes peace seem impossible. It is the world you see that is impossible. Yet has God's Judgment on this distorted world redeemed it and made it fit to welcome peace. And peace descends on it in joyous answer. Peace now belongs here, because a Thought of God has entered. What else but a Thought of God turns hell to Heaven merely by being what it is? The earth bows down before its gracious Presence, and it leans down in answer, to raise it up again. Now is the question different. It is no longer, "Can peace be possible in this world?" but instead, "Is it not impossible that peace be absent here?" M-11.4

Thank You Holy Spirit for directing me to this quote in the Manual for Teachers. Although I do not watch the news very much, I do stay in touch by using international news websites. And so I recall in my mind the essence of today's Lesson, "There is no peace except the peace of God." The conflict that I see in the world, whether it be in the Middle East or between brothers is all conflict within my mind.

Holy Spirit, I enter into your holy sanctuary today to steady my footsteps on Your road to Peace. Through Your sure Guidance, I am carried and do not wander away from You. It is easy to be distracted by the images that I see on my screen of vision. These images can seem frightening with explosions, gunfire, people dying, hurt and crying out in pain.

In my mind, I can feel Your comfort and Your sure Words. I am not what I think I see. This world is not my true Home. Yet, I still believe that I am living here. These images of war can become images of peace. Peace can be present in the midst of chaos. As I go within to You, I can be still and know the Peace of the Father. The Peace that surpasses the illusions of death that I have made. Peace is present. It is here. When I come to remember the Truth in these moments of fear thoughts, and these fear thoughts are present if I have any reaction big or small to the crisis, I have brought peace into my soul.

Peace quenches the thirst of the conflicted mind. I do not really want to be in turmoil. Somehow the ego enjoys the turmoil, the conflict, the chaos for it keeps me distracted from knowing the

Peace of God. The ego doesn't care for me to find and remember that Peace, that Love of God. The more I focus on what is going on outside of me, the happier the ego is. It has done its duty; it has kept me away from God.

In my memory is the Love of the Father. I can recall it anytime and I choose to remember the Love of God as often as possible. There is no other way to live but to live in Peace.

Thank You Holy Spirit for making this so.

∞∞∞

Journal Entry on Lesson 221

Peace to my mind. Let all my thoughts be still.

The white wizard came galloping on a white horse in my mind. I imagined that it might be Gandalf from "The Lord of the Rings." I saw him dismount and take his white staff and while tapping it on the ground, he made the command, *"Peace to my mind. Let all my thoughts be still."* A radiant, brilliant, almost blinding light shone from the precious jewel at the head of his staff. This Light then filled my entire mind.

I see with this image (or dream, not sure, as I fell asleep during meditation) how it can help me to remember that I am in charge of my mind. I was reminded of an upcoming lesson, Lesson 236, *"I rule my mind, which I alone must rule. I have a kingdom I must rule. At times, it does not seem I am its king at all. It seems to triumph over me, and tell me what to think, and what to do and feel."*

I have the power to think what I choose; to follow the stream of thoughts that lead me to Heaven or hell. I guess you could say you can lead a horse to water but you can't make him drink. And so too with my mind, I can allow the ego to lead my down the path to hell but I don't have to stay there.

I do not want to follow the ego's stream. I can forgive and let go. It doesn't matter how far I follow the stream I can always refuse to drink of its poison and invite sanity in through the Holy Spirit. His Words will quench my thirst; His Guidance will lead me Home.

I stop and rest awhile here on the journey, surrounded by the living waters. It is here in the sanctuary that I find what I need. It is a haven of hope for it is the haven of forgiveness, the haven of Love, whereby I let go of the heavy mail of pain and into the shining garments of the Holy One.

It is pure. It is ever clear where I am to turn. The Voice is present if I am willing to bid my ears welcome to It. The Voice is kind with a quiet power of peace. It judges not, yet tells me the ancient truth.

I listen awhile as I rest. The day passes by me until it is time to travel once again. I take the Wisdom with me, the Peace and Love of God with me, carefully bundling it all in my heart and mind so as I meet my brothers along the road, I can then too share with them this parcel of truth.

When we meet, together we will make merry, in song and in laughter, as we forget what we thought we were in this illusion. But together remember the True Kingdom where we all are royalty of the Father; where we all must be.

And thanks to the "Wizard of Wisdom" Who assists us on this journey wherever we may go, through the fields, through the meadows, through the raging river and through the jagged rocks. We are not alone. The Light of His Strength always guides.

Today, I command my mind, "Peace....be still....and listen to the Voice of God."

∞∞∞∞

Journal Entry on Lesson 222

God is with me. I live and move in Him.

Holy Spirit, This morning I am having trouble keeping still and listening for God's Voice to speak to me. I start off by listening only for His Voice and then a few moments later I notice that my mind has wandered off from that focus and has begun to think about other things going on in my life. Would You please help me to still my mind this morning to settle down into that peaceful place where I focus solely on waiting to hear His Voice speak to me?

Son of God, This is merely an underlying ego resistance to truly having an experience of meeting your Creator. This is why it is necessary to devote yourself to frequent practicing throughout the day. In your dreaming of having a split mind apart from your Creator, you have been practicing that you are split from Him since time began. This is not really true but in your seeming experience in the split part of the mind, it seems to be unfolding for you in a linear fashion.

You will find it helpful to pause frequently throughout the day and practice stilling your thoughts and waiting for Father to speak to you. Start in little steps. Listen only for His Voice for perhaps five seconds. Then practice being completely still and listening only for His Voice for perhaps ten seconds. Continue to increment the time and your practicing of resting completely silent in peace and waiting for His Voice to speak to you until you have reached several minutes.

In this gap of peace He will answer you. It will bring you much joy indeed to hear His Voice speak clearly to you. His Voice is His Word given to you and His Words always heal. His Words are eternal because they were spoken by the Eternal. His Words spoken are His Will and His Will are promises that will be kept.

Be thankful for the Words He speaks to you for they are a reminder of His remembrance of His Son and His Son's remembrance of Him. Thank the Holy Spirit for His intercession and His help with your awakening. He holds your hand. He is your appointed Guide and Teacher in all that you say and think and do. Let Him be your Guide and let Him be your Teacher. Let Him instruct you in everything you do. He will always answer you and His answers always lead you to joy.

∞∞∞∞

Journal Entry on Lesson 223

God is my life. I have no life but His.

Everything that we seem to do and experience as we go through our day is nothing more than just a dream. It is a dream that we believe is really happening but it is not. We have decided to preoccupy a part of our mind with this fantasyland called fear that we seem to journey through.

This fantasyland is the split part of the mind we call the ego. It gives us the illusion that we are bodies isolated within a dimension of a universe that contains space and time and physical things. These are merely perceptions of projections made by the ego mind. They are not really real and only seem to be solid because the mind appears to make them solid.

As we continue to awaken to the reality of the Christ that we are, our Light will begin to soften and dissolve this seeming physical reality. The illusion will start to become like a veil of mist that seems to dissolve away with the Light beyond. Although we are not aware of it right now, we are surrounded and are the Light of God Himself.

Our Light is being blocked by the projections of the ego mind, however, it is possible to see the reflection of our Holy Light. Having a complete desire to see the Light of Christ within our minds and only the Light of Christ is the key to success. The Light of Christ will reveal Himself to us in our minds when we find that space where sinlessness is all we wish to see. We will recognize for a moment Who we really are when the Light comes and illuminates our mind. It will appear as a beacon from beyond reminding us of Who we really are and the way that it our Home.

The Light shines forth bringing with it peace and joy and happiness in that holy instant that It is perceived. This is the face of Christ we seek. It is our holy Self and a reflection of our Oneness with each other and with Him Who created us. It is a true perception of our perfection and sinlessness. It is a momentary remembrance of our Home and then we come back again, recognizing that we are not alone, isolated and friendless, but instead, we are the Christ, the Holy Son of God Himself.

oooooo

Journal Entry on Lesson 224

God is my Father, and He loves His Son.

In today's Lesson Jesus is reminding us that our True Identity is a Light, not a body. He is reminding us that the Light that we are is a gift that Father gave to us. He is also reminding us that it is possible to see ourselves as the Light of God right now. It is possible to see and experience ourselves as the Light right now.

Merely close your eyes and be very still, quietly observe the dark screen of your mind's eye and desire with all your will to see the Light of Christ illuminate your mind. Ask the Holy Spirit to show you the Light at the center of your mind's eye where you observe the darkness, and wait for His response. The beacon of white light, the Light of Christ will suddenly turn on and illuminate your mind revealing your Holy Self to you. Peace and joy are gifts that come with this perception.

In the beginning you may only perceive sparks of white light for a moment but rest assured, when this begins to happen the way and the path will be understood. Your heart's desire to see and know your Self as the Light of Christ will beckon the way from this time forth. The Light of Salvation has begun to come and illuminate the mind at last. You have taken the Holy Spirit's hand and He has taken yours and the journey Home will begin to hasten at last. All of Heaven sings and rejoices in these moments, for the Son of God is beginning to awaken at last.

∞∞∞∞

Journal Entry on Lesson 225

God is my Father, and His Son loves Him.

I received Mark Stanton Welch's CD "You Have the Power" the other day. As I placed the CD in the tray, I was prepared to be inspired by his music, I always am by his rhythms and chants. As I listened deeply to the lyrics, this particular song reminded me of yesterday's and today's Lessons. It also had a wispy, mystical, yet Native-American ambience.

"Father of the Living"

Father of the Living
Father of the ancient

Father of all things to come
Father, how I love thee
Father how I love thee
Father, you and I are one.
~Mark Stanton Welch - www.markstantonwelch.com

So simple the words, yet how elegant, how powerful and how true! Our nine year old daughter Autumn just sat down beside me as I am typing this message. As I read today's Lesson out loud to her, we talked about what could these words mean to us. A few phrases that stood out to her were, *"We are one,"* and *"How still the way Your loving Son is lead along to You!"*

The other day the four of us walked in downtown Madison for Allison's last night here with us before returning home to Pittsburgh. As Autumn and I shared about that time just now, we were reminded that as we crossed the busy streets, Autumn would take my hand. She said that she felt safe and connected with me at these times.

And that is what this lesson shares with us as well, that Jesus is there clasping our hand, and making the promise that he will always be beside us no matter what "ego traffic" comes our way. He will stop with us and wait awhile as we go to peace. He reminds us that we are already safe and secure and connected to our Father.

We do not have to be focused on the traffic jam in our mind but on the path that he has made open for us to see clearly to our true Home. It also reminded us of the mopeds that get around so easily through the traffic on the busy streets downtown. Nothing bars their way, and that's how Jesus and the Holy Spirit works with us, easily maneuvering us away from the traffic of our mind as we are open and willing to do so.

Father, thank You for this message today. I never know what to expect and You always bring it to me in a way that is perfect for me to accept right now. My words may not always be flowery but instead plain and simple gets the point across all the same. I appreciate the loving connection with You just as I appreciate the loving connection with my daughter. This is truly giving and receiving. Thank You for Your Everlasting Light of Love. Amen.

∞∞∞∞

Journal Entry on Lesson 226

My home awaits me. I will hasten there.

I received a phone call from a friend last night and this morning we spoke again. She had been distraught about some recent events in her life. These events that transpired were quite the opposite of what she had expected. She had pinned her hopes and aspirations on being fulfilled, feeling complete through her husband and a spiritual center and its' activities. Even though she knew the principles of the Course, it was devastating to her that yet again she placed her salvation on circumstances and people in the world.

During this conversation some lines in the Course were brought to my awareness:

> *Seek not outside yourself. For it will fail, and you will weep each time an idol falls. Heaven cannot be found where it is not, and there can be no peace excepting there. Each idol that you worship when God calls will never answer in His place. There is no other answer you can substitute, and find the happiness His answer brings. Seek not outside yourself. For all your pain comes simply from a futile search for what you want, insisting where it must be found. What if it is not there? Do you prefer that you be right or happy? Be you glad that you are told where happiness abides,*

and seek no longer elsewhere. You will fail. But it is given you to know the truth, and not to seek for it outside yourself.

No one who comes here but must still have hope, some lingering illusion, or some dream that there is something outside of himself that will bring happiness and peace to him. If everything is in him this cannot be so. T-29.VII. Paragraphs 1 & 2.

With today's Lesson I am reminded that this world is not where to place my trust. There is no value in this world. With the ego, this world is ever-changing and always changeable. The ego desires conflict; it feeds on distraction. The ego does not want me to remember where my true Home is. For if I recognize it, the ego knows that its demise will be soon.

This is why the further distractions and attachments that seem to creep in and to take hold of us appear. We buy into it. We place an attachment to an outcome for a situation. It must be thus! And when it isn't, we are sad and depressed. We weep each time one of these idols, these people or places, do not serve their function as we have placed upon them.

And then we are thrown into a cyclone of fear.

But then as we are ready we remember. We remember that Home is where the heart is..... and that is with God. Not in this world. Not in that someone who opens their door to me in just the way that I want it to be opened. Not in a spouse or family member. Not in a friend. Not in a spiritual center. That is all looking outside to find where happiness abides. It will never be found outside of who I am.

And so the question is this: "*What need have I to linger in a place of vain desires and of shattered dreams, when Heaven can so easily be mine?*"

I go within, uniting with God and welcoming Him just as He has welcomed me.

∞∞∞

Journal Entry on Lesson 227

This is my holy instant of release.

From moment to moment within the illusion we have a choice, we can choose to be happy or to listen to the voice of fear. Each moment has the potential to be a holy instant where the reality of the Christ that is within each and every one of us is revealed to you.

"This holy instant would I give to You. Be You in charge. For I would follow You, certain that Your direction gives me peace," from Workbook Lessons 361-365, should become our response to anything that comes up that seems to disturb our peace. It is your call to Holy Spirit for help for when fear has entered your mind you have forgotten Who you really are and Who your brother really is.

The Light of Christ within yourself will heal your mind from your dark illusions of fear. These are not the thoughts your Father would have you dwell upon. See the light of sinlessness within yourself and within your brother instead. This is your choice from moment to moment, to perceive reality with the Holy Spirit instead of this. This is your gift from God Himself. The Light will show you the way and the truth. It is your holy instant of release and the restoration of the memory of God. It will help you to find your rightful place in the mind of God where your thoughts are His and His thoughts are yours and this is but truth alone.

Thank You Father for Your gifts of freedom and salvation to us.
~Jesus

Journal Entry on Lesson 228

God has condemned me not. No more do I.

Before Allison left for her travels back to Pittsburgh, we showed her the "What the Bleep Do We Know?" movie. It was the first time that she had viewed it and what stood out to her most was how Amanda was able to change her mind.

And today's Lesson reminds me of this changed mind at the end of the movie where Amanda is so beside herself with self-anger and self-hatred, condemning who and what she is. She stops for a moment, and we see an image in the mirror of the man from the subway who says to her, "If those thoughts do that to water, imagine what they can do to us." *This refers to Dr. Masaru Emoto's experiments using labels with words such as Love, Gratitude, and "You Make Me Sick" placed on containers of water and then photographing the water crystals after some time. The photographs were stunning as they differed based upon the words or thoughts used.*

As she remembers his statement, she knows now what it means, and then she remembers to laugh at the absurdity. She begins a purifying and loving ritual of bathing herself along with loving every inch of herself through the simple act of decorating herself with hearts of love all about her skin.

God has not condemned me. It is time for me to let go of the self-flogging that I have been doing for so long. Even the subtle ways that I may do this. I may drop a pencil on the floor, or spill milk, or stub my toe. Immediately the tongue may go to a curse, cursing the pencil, the milk, my toe or (and the ego loves this) my stupidity in doing so.

It's all a mistake, an error in my judgment.

If God knows who I am, shall I not believe Him? After all He created me. I can change my mind in an instant and know my brilliant self. And this is the choice that I make today.

oooooo

Journal Entry on Lesson 229

Love, which created me, is what I am.

Yes, Dear One, you do hear these words I speak to you. I know it is not what you expected in a message for today, but I am well aware that you were thinking about someone's perceived problems, but imagine Me speaking these words to you and to them.

"Love, which created you, is what you are."

Repeat them as often as you can this day, say it now to yourself, out loud at first and silently within your holy mind. *"Love, which created me, is what I am."*

Too soon you forget from where you have come. Know within that holy place, that place of brilliant light, that you are loved and carried. There are times that you feel that you are not. Perhaps you feel that you are not heard or your feelings validated. Come to me with each splinter in your mind and I will assist you in plucking it out. I offer you only a gentle and loving process. It is forgiveness.

No need to sacrifice any longer. No need to seek approval and acceptance outside of you. Validation will never be found in the world. For within the core of your being, your holiness was placed. It has no name but One, it is your God Self, the connection to Your Father.

You are too quick to assume that everyone outside of you is here to injure you in some way. You are too quick to assume that judgment is seen in their eyes. It is in your eyes where the judgment reflects. You have called out in fear to the far-reaching ends of the earth asking to return the messengers to you. They arrive and are placed strategically in your daily life. You may feel victimized and alone, yet I assure you that you have allowed your mind to believe all of what you are experiencing.

This pain can be eliminated in an instant, a willing instant. Come to Me now as you observe your senseless fear thoughts rambling away in your mind. They are in a cage of doubt. As you free each one to Me, you will know true freedom yourself.

Observe. Be still. Be patient. Trust in Me. I will lead you always down the path of Love. Be gentle unto yourself. Be kind. Be confident in all that you do, you do with Me.

You are the precious One. No more to cry in the darkness of the night from the depths of your soul. The Light has come. You have asked for It, and it is here to solely reflect to you that which you are. You have turned away before, but now look into the Eyes of Love. Take the hand of the One Whom loves you more dearly than anyone on this earth could.

Place your trust within to the Holy Place. You have allowed the ego to run your life. Allow it no longer. Your Identity is Innocence. You cannot be harmed.

You have now taken responsibility for your mind. You can release the box of pain that you have surrounded yourself in. Think outside the box. You can make the step to heal for you make the step with Me. I am the Comforter, the Counselor, the Holy Wisdom that you seek. I am here for you. My ears are bent to listen to your tears. My heart is open to help you to find peace.

Connect with me. Converse with me. Walk with me awhile.
And you too will know the Love which created you.
And you will know that you are Love Itself.
Whole and Complete.
Loved and Cared for.
Always and Forever.

Amen.

∞∞∞

Journal Entry on Lesson 230

Now will I seek and find the peace of God.

Sit back, close your eyes, sink down and relax, and quietly observe the dark screen in your mind's eye for the spark of Peace to come. The Light of Peace is shining in you now. It is a gift that Father gave to you to help you perceive your True Self and your Home. The white light will come sparking into your mind very clearly as you continue to practice using your spiritual sight to see the Light of Christ within yourself. You need do nothing but quietly sink down into peace as you observe the misty veil that obscures the Light beyond.

The Light of Atonement will reveal Itself to you as you allow it to come forth. It is your witness to yourself of Who you really are. The peace of God is shining in you now because you are the Light and Peace that you see and feel when the Light comes.

In the holy instant of Its coming the spark heals the mind of all illusions for a moment and peace is given instead. The spark is your friend. It is a reflection of your Holy Self. Once perceived the mind begins to heal itself of all illusions very quickly. Time is saved and time is used for what time is for, which is forgiveness through the Light you see. The Light of Forgiveness is the tool given to you by your Father to heal yourself of dreams of hell.

The Light will come and heal all things as you accept It into your awareness. Love's presence cannot be blocked by darkness forever for it is not Love's will that you hide in darkness forever. Your Father has saved you from your dreams of darkness and hell for you are His Light and His yours forever. You shine in Him forever, and He shines on you with the peace He gave to you in your creation. You share that peace He gave to you with Him in perfect union and love forever.

You are One with Him and He is One with you. The peace of God is shining in you now, seek and find it today.

∞∞∞

Journal Entry on Lesson 231

Father, I will but to remember You.

In the margin of my Course book on this Lesson I had made the notation, "addictions." This is related to the sentence, "*Perhaps I think I seek for something else; in something I have called by many names.*" Addictions can be the typical ones that I can immediately think of such as alcohol, drugs, sex, food, and gambling. Indeed it can run the gamut.

As I think about this Holy Spirit, I recall that one can be addicted to raw emotions or to the pain one experiences. "Absurd!" one may think to be addicted to "my feelings of anger" for instance.

But indeed inside there is a rush, an investment of some kind, that I, or anyone, may get of of these raw emotions time and time again. Perhaps it is as simple as attention and sympathy. Or perhaps it allows someone else to pat you on the back and reaffirm your victim status. They define me, I am justified, or so I think when I am entangled in them.

So how to break the addiction?

By replacing the thoughts that are associated with it. By bringing my thoughts to You, Holy Spirit, all my thoughts, to You. When I am caught up in the cycle of intense emotions, I have forgotten my Father.

Sometimes God seems so distant at those particular times as if God could never be felt or experienced in any way. It can seem that I am in the bowels of hell, banished there for eternity to suffer alone, afraid and abandoned. And there I stay in my victim hood.

But yet the Light is there, a ray of pure light shining upon me, shining through me. It is me. The Hands of God's Love reaches me, carries me upward. I can remember.

How can I remember at these deep dark times, when it seems that I am alone and friendless?

I may be reading these words now. I may have reached out to telephone a friend. I may have written in a journal. I may have picked up a book. I may have taken a long walk.

I have in some way remembered the spark within me, perhaps not consciously, but I have remembered my connection to the Source of Love. I begin now to take responsibility for what I see and experience, for what I think and feel. Taking responsibility of my thoughts can seem hard but it is the best step that one can make.

As I take responsibility for my mind, I can allow the remembrance of Heaven to light my mind further. Insights occur.

Instead of seeing responsibility as a further punishment, I can see it as a choice.

This I have done; this I must undo.

I am not longer the victim of the world. I become the change-maker, the peace-maker of my world. I have sought and placed my love and trust in that which changes, and now I place my love and trust in God.

Father, I will but to remember You this day. To release my fears, my thoughts, my emotions, my experiences, my situations, my outcomes, my whole life to You. It is not sacrifice but merely surrender to what is True.

Say this to yourself as sincerely as you can, remembering that the Holy Spirit will respond fully to your slightest invitation:

I must have decided wrongly, because I am not at peace.
I made the decision myself, but I can also decide otherwise.
I want to decide otherwise, because I want to be at peace.
I do not feel guilty, because the Holy Spirit will undo all the consequences of my wrong decision if I will let Him.
I choose to let Him, by allowing Him to decide for God for me.
~ Text Chapter 5, Section VII, Paragraph 6.

∞∞∞∞

Journal Entry on Lesson 232

Be in my mind, my Father, through the day.

Dear Father,
Thank You for the Light that you gave to me. When I was feeling sad and lonely I learned how to let go in exchange for Light. And

the Light came and healed the feelings, blessing me with peace and happiness instead.

Father, I'm feeling disconnected, sad and alone again. I have forgotten to practice being willing to let go of the things that I think I want or need in the world in exchange for your Light of Happiness that always brings me joy. Help me to remember that this is always what I truly want. Help me to remember that the Light is the only thing that will only truly make me feel happy.

I often allow my mind to become preoccupied with thoughts that are not of the Light and they only make me feel dismayed, worried and disconnected. I forget the importance of laying these thoughts down immediately in exchange for thoughts of You and our Light that will free my mind and make it feel happy again.

The gift of Light that You gave to us is such a wonderful gift indeed. We appreciate how simple it is to heal our minds with the Light. The Light knows the way to joy and happiness. It leads us to our Home in You where all is well. Heaven resides in our mind and we forget that so much.

I am grateful for *A Course in Miracles* and the constant reminder of the truth of Who we really are. I am grateful for the miracles and the gifts that the Course reminds us that we can experience. I am grateful for the recognition that we can perform miracles right now, miracles of healing, miracles of instant love, miracles of joy. How simple it is to allow You to come forth and do all these things for us as we learn to accept our Oneness with You and we learn to remember the Light we share with You and that You share with us. Remembering the Light is all we need do to heal all things that dismay us.

Thank You Father and may we continue to develop the habit of remembering You and Your Light that frees us more and more each day. May we remember it every moment that our minds may be made freed and released to constant joy and happiness at last. Amen.

∞∞∞

Journal Entry on Lesson 233

I give my life to God to guide today.

Father, I dedicate my day to trying something new. Today, I dedicate my day to not being a puppet of the ego thought system but instead to stepping back and following You in all that I do.

Today, I will take time to step back and frequently pray and reaffirm that I am giving all of my thoughts and actions to You. Let me remember every moment to step back and watch You lead the way and may I experience the many gifts You have for me by doing so.

If something begins to bother me, or disturb my peace in any way, help me to be mindful and to remember to turn it over to You right away in exchange for Your Thoughts instead. Help me to remember to surrender my will and desires to You today. May You guide all of my thoughts, words, and actions today. Let me practice patience and stillness as I allow You to be my Guide.

Perhaps I could just follow You as a peaceful, quiet observer and watch Your work unfold before my eyes. As I see this happen, may I remember to have thoughts of gratitude, love and appreciation for how You take care of all of us and for the ways You do Your work. Grant me quiet wisdom today as I step back and watch Your peace and joy lead the way. Amen.

∞∞∞

Journal Entry on Lesson 234

Father, today I am Your Son again.

Today Father, I did not get to do the Lesson and to this message as I had originally planned. However, I do realize that the two souls you sent to me for me to be their listening ear in counsel, was the practice of Your Holy Lesson.

The length of time for each call sailed by, 3 1/2 hours in the morning, 1 1/2 hours in the afternoon. My ego insisted that I ought to be dragging and exhausted. But yet, I know that holding the sacred space, acting as Holy Spirit's vessel does not exhaust me. It reminds me of my purpose. To work with a brother is my own invitation to heal.

I let go of all plans that I have made and strictly follow You, Holy Spirit. You guided me to be that rock, that strong oak tree where others come to rest and restore. Despite the outside world's clamoring, I stood strong in my guidance to only serve Your Will. It was perfect. Everything that occurs is perfect.

In my mind, I allowed healing as each person shared and processed. I saw past the dreams of sin and guilt to the holy meeting place of peace. Gratitude was given me by both, the ego though chimed in that I had done nothing of merit by just listening.

But You, Holy Spirit, You said that listening with an open heart and loving mind was all that was required of me. I only wish to follow Your example Spirit, of allowing the dark thoughts to surface and rise and then be released, thus allowing the shift to occur with Your blessing. This is as You do for me. This is my practice with others.

I see how words are not necessary.

Quotes from *A Course in Miracles* are not necessary.
Intellectualizing, analyzing and preaching are not necessary.
Closing my mouth and opening my ears is necessary.
Being in a space of Love is necessary.
Remembering Truth is necessary.

How can I help others but to listen and trust that I will be led to do what You would have me do?

The ego can fool me into thinking that I have to say certain things, maintain certain postures. It is only following You that I will truly be helpful.

Father, today I am Your Son again. I remember Who I am. I remember it for my brothers today. The memory within me is safe, just as it is safe in everyone. Access the memory and I access the peace that only You can bring.

∞∞∞∞∞

Journal Entry on Lesson 235

God in His mercy wills that I be saved.

It is focus, persistence and vigilance that will assist me in the goal for today's Lesson. It seems rather artificial at first, especially if I am feeling downright hurt, angry and victimized. What do you mean that all I need to do is look upon all these stupid things that hurt me and say "God wills that I be saved from this?" Who the heck are you kidding?

But yet with focus, I truly will see that He does will that I be saved from what my mind has created to disrupt my peace. The ego does not want my happiness and so it distracts and turns my attention away from the Will of God. God's Will is only happiness for me.

How do I do this when I am in the thick of the emotions? When it seems that no matter what I do I cannot shake loose these feelings of unworthiness, or inadequacy , or anger, or whatever they may be at the time?

I can call a friend, a minister, a counselor. I can write and write and write in a journal, using the concept of the "3 page rule" where I keep writing for at least 3 full pages. I can talk to Holy Spirit in my mind or through the mentioned forms.

It is bringing all the darkness to the Light. Not hiding one speck of darkness from Him Who is our Helper. Holding on to the pain will not serve me. I may know all of this intellectually and say "yeah right," but yet, I need to keep releasing, having patience with myself as best as I can until I am ready to hear His Voice speak to me and to receive His Answer and the gift of peace.

The gentle process of the Holy Spirit is there. He waits, He listens, He makes no judgment, He criticizes not. His presence is one of Love, Support, Safety, Caring and Kindness. Nothing in the world will match it.

As I let go of these thoughts that seem to hurt me, I will know that I am saved. I will know that I am loved beyond measure. I will experience peace.

∞∞∞∞

Journal Entry on Lesson 236

I rule my mind, which I alone must rule.

Just imagine if you could go through a day of complete acceptance of what the Holy Spirit brings to you. It would be a happy and peaceful day indeed. Imagine going through a day of non-judgment and relinquishment of all your ideas and plans and the way you think things should go. This would be a day of simple being and allowing to happen whatever it is that is supposed to happen. Being in this place of complete acceptance and openness allows the Holy Spirit an opportunity to reveal His presence to you.

As we practice having a completely open mind and surrendering all of our thoughts to the Holy Spirit, His Voice will be allowed to come forth and speak to us. That is the purpose for the practice of our meditation. The goal is to still our ego minds, to come to a place of complete stillness, a place where no thoughts or words are spoken within the mind, A place where we are open to receiving the miracle instead.

Our awareness will shift into perception of the Light of God. You will be able to see it very clearly. You will recognize it because this Light is not of this world and yet it can be seen. It is a gift from your Father. The Voice of God can be heard very clearly too. It will be as if He were speaking directly to you in your mind; as if someone had put a speaker there. His Voice is clear and unambiguous, calm and certain. You will know it when you hear it.

Complete stillness with an open mind is the realm of the Kingdom of God. The miracles come in little glimmerings and specks at first, and then they become more predominant over time as you become proficient in letting go of the thoughts that churn and preoccupy the ego mind.

It is true that what you ask for you will receive. If you decide that you want to feel angry about something then anger will be given to you in your perception. You have chosen to side with the ego mind when this happens. You have decided to perceive what the ego would have you perceive instead of Holy Spirit's gifts for you instead. Peace is the condition for the miracles of the Holy Spirit to come into your mind.

Lay down your thoughts and your desires for awhile, and allow the Holy Spirit an opportunity to come forth and speak to you and show you the Light of your True Self that surrounds you all the time. Your Father is with you, here and now, and you do not even realize it because you have chosen to block your awareness from Him with the world you see, perceive and feel now. It is not real. It is merely an illusion, a projection from your own unconscious ego mind. It will merely disappear when you simply practice allowing it to go and be replaced by the reality that surrounds you instead.

You will be amazed how simple this is once you get the hang of it. Indeed, it does take a lot of willingness and practice, but the gifts offered you instead of the world you made are abundant indeed. Let us practice being still now, completely still, and allowing our minds to open up to the Kingdom of God.

∞∞∞∞

Journal Entry on Lesson 237

Now would I be as God created me.

The last few days has been filled with numerous severe thunderstorms with wind and heavy downpours, even power outages. This has left me indoors, to contemplate forgoing my daily walk in the warmth of the sun.

So indeed I am indoors, going within as I "seek shelter from the storm." How true this is whenever I am going through a major mind-healing growth spurt.

The upswelling of emotions come, raining down tears or the fury of anger, emotion after emotion being felt. It is natural and it is felt as it occurs. Sometimes I may feel that I am alone as the dark clouds loom and crackle with their intensity. But as I go within to the Holy Spirit, I will be kept safe and warm and dry.

Sometimes I sit feeling disconnected from the One, the Eternal Power Supply. It seems dark but in the period of darkness I ask for Light. It comes. It always comes. It was already there. I just did not see that I had turned it off in my mind.

And soon the storm passes, perhaps in twenty minutes, or in a few days. But it always passes. A rainbow appears. The sun shines clear. I return to peace. I return to the remembrance of Who I am and what God created.

God did not create the storms that surround my mind. He created the Light of His Love.

He created me.

∞∞∞

Journal Entry on Lesson 238

On my decision all salvation rests.

This morning I woke up feeling quite uncomfortable from a cold that feels like it is beginning to peak out. My mind feels weary from being totally focused on not being able to breathe because of the congestion I have been experiencing. I have been treating my body with magic pills and magic fluids to combat the symptoms. I know that this is not the solution to my problem but in my discomfort I found it very difficult to feel like turning my attention to God and focusing on receiving some help from Him.

I think this is mainly because I do not believe yet that the Holy Spirit would truly heal me of this in an instant. I am sure that I am mistaken in this belief and feel bad that I do not seem to have the willingness to truly let this belief go and be healed by the Holy Spirit.

I found myself gazing through the Table of Contents of the Text of the Course this morning looking for something for Deb but I noticed that my eyes kept locking on to a particular section. I thought that perhaps the Holy Spirit was guiding me to read this section but wasn't sure at first and so I ignored the urge and went on to something else. A minute or so later I noticed that my eyes began to lock on to the title of this section again, "The Decision for God." (Text, Chapter 5, Section VII) So I decided to take a few minutes to read the section.

As I did, I began to recognize that the Holy Spirit was speaking very directly to me at that moment about the physical sickness that I was experiencing in my mind and body at this time. In the section, He was telling me that on some level I had made a decision to experience this sickness and that I was using it to attempt to block God's Love from my awareness. I was using the sickness to block myself from hearing the Holy Spirit's Voice speak to me. And then at the end of the section I felt like He had given me a prayer that I could use to heal myself of this sickness. I believe that if I do as He instructs that I will be healed.

At the end of the section, Jesus gives us these instructions:

> *Therefore, the first step in the undoing is to recognize that you actively decided wrongly, but can as actively decide otherwise. Be very firm with yourself in this, and keep yourself fully aware that the undoing process, which does not come from you, is nevertheless within you because God placed it there. Your part is merely to return your thinking to the point at which the error was made, and give it over to the Atonement in peace. Say this to*

*yourself as sincerely as you can, remembering that the Holy
Spirit will respond fully to your slightest invitation:*

*I must have decided wrongly, because I am not at peace.
I made the decision myself, but I can also decide otherwise.
I want to decide otherwise, because I want to be at peace.
I do not feel guilty, because the Holy Spirit will undo all the
consequences of my wrong decision if I will let Him.
I choose to let Him, by allowing Him to decide for God for me.*

And so today, I dedicate my day to practice in silent meditation
allowing the Holy Spirit to decide for God for me because on this
decision all salvation rests.

ooooo

Journal Entry on Lesson 239

The glory of my Father is my own.

Congestion in the body.
Congestion in the mind.

We both have spent the day resting from our physical symptoms
of illness. Even with the body at rest, the mind continues to
ramble on and on with guilt attached with the many waiting jobs
needing to be completed, including this message. Earlier this
morning we took a peek at Louise Hay's book, "Heal Your Body"
revealing with the symptom of Upper Respiratory Illness, "Too
much going on at once. Mental confusion, disorder."

Bingo!

Paul related very well to this with all the projects that both
his jobs have required. Oh, how does the mind chatter on about
our seeming guilt!

Ah, all of this is easy to say, but what to do.....more mental chatter.

And so we release the mental chatter to the Holy Spirit, He asks us gladly for it.

How can I listen to Him with my mind ill at ease?

I read to Paul this morning from Chapter 14, Section VI, p. 286.

> *"The Holy Spirit's function is entirely communication. He therefore must remove whatever interferes with communication in order to restore it. Therefore, keep no source of interference from His sight, for He will not attack your sentinels."*

With this I know that I am to give to You Holy Spirit, whatever congests my mind which is whatever blocks my awareness of You and Love's Presence. You will not clear away the congestion without my invitation and so I gladly share all thoughts, all worries of time and outcomes, all fears, judgments and upsets, any angry thoughts, all come to You.

You listen with unconditional Love, with acceptance and with non-judgment. I need not fear Your Love, Your kind heart.

I can take as long as I need to allow the mind congestion to follow its natural course. Soon I will feel clearer, my mind lighter, my thoughts ready to receive and know the glory that is my own.

∞∞∞∞

Journal Entry on Lesson 240

Fear is not justified in any form.

This message was received through Paul after I led him through an Accessing Inner Wisdom Counseling Session. During the session, all unpeaceful, uneasy thoughts are explored and then released to the Holy Spirit with peace and love resulting in guidance being received.

Fear is not justified in any form because you are the Light and that is all that you are. You are only Light and nothing else is true. Do not dwell on things that are not of the Light they are merely a waste of time. The Light dwells within you now. You can find It, see It and feel Its peace heal you anytime you want. It is there waiting for you to discover It.

It is your greatest gift given to you from your Father. Let go of all things that seem to trouble your mind and desire only to perceive the Light of God instead. The Light you see is the Light of God, It is the Light of Christ, the Light of the Holy Spirit, the Light of Forgiveness, and the Light of your True Self.

When you see It you will recognize It. You will feel that there is something familiar about It. It will feel like a friend that is going to free you at last and in this you will be correct. You will know that this Light is the gateway to your freedom at last. You will feel the Gateway to Joy when you see the Light. The Light is your Home! It is your Guide, your Comforter, your Teacher and your Friend.

Come and embrace Him within your mind now. Sit and be still desiring only to perceive the Light of God and when the Light comes you will know that you have found your way Home.

Thank You Father for your gifts to us.

Thank You Father for reminding us Who Your Beloved Holy Son is for we see ourselves in the Holy Light of Shining Innocence just as You created us.

∞∞∞∞

Journal Entry on Lesson 241

This holy instant is salvation come.

"The day has come when sorrows pass away and pain is gone."

I can remember quite clearly many days in the past where I did not feel that "sorrows would pass away and that the pain would be gone." Even with some clients who I have been working with as of late also seem to not see that the time of hurt will be over. I always hold the truth that it is already done.

It's hard to swallow in those moments that it is just my choice, that all I need do is change my mind. Read the Course, go to the Holy Spirit. Is it that easy? It can be but there is a state of readiness, willingness and openness that needs to be present before I can experience the holy instant of knowing all has been forgiven, all is clean and clear and pristine, and that all is an illusion.

When in the thick of emotions it certainly does not seem that this world is an illusion. Angry, unloving words seem to sting and wound, loss seems to be apparent, worry and anxiety becomes a way of life. Jesus does share with us a new life we can have. The moment of decision that I made to be in hell is the same moment that I can decide to let it all go. Should I say the "sane moment" in which I can let it all go.

In the insane moment I am not seeing the big picture, I am seeing a fragment of the picture that is colored by the past. I am seeing what I choose to see. Sure, intellectually it is easy to know this but bringing it into the feeling level is another thing. Covering it up with a facade of "Love and Light" does not work. Denial of the feelings does not work. The Holy Spirit is there, ever present, ever loving, ever caring, ever patient, and ever willing to listen to all my blocks to Love's Presence.

Who's to define an instant? Do I measure it by the world's standard of time? I come to the holy instant whenever I arrive at releasing my hands from what I am handing over to Spirit. I do not have to be as a dog playing tug of war with a chew toy. I can "drop it" as I am ready to really, really, really, really want the peace to dwell in my mind.

I had heard someone say that there's a faster way by "just going to the Light." No one can make me ready, no one can push me into the Light, not even the Holy Spirit would do that. I have to be ready to enter into the Light. And sometimes I just need to release, and release, and release. Allow tears, allow whatever feelings are there. I move naturally through the process, sometimes in a few minutes, sometimes it may take days. I am always held in safety. I am always loved through the process.

And this I do for others, holding that sacred space as they go through their own process from darkness to Light.

Is there joy in salvation? Definitely. I have watched not only myself but others as well move through the clouds and into the warmth of the Light of God. Sometimes a little rain must fall, but it nourishes the foundation with its gentle lessons. The power that I felt outside of me seeming to oppress me disappears and I stand in my own power of which is my Divine nature.

"The Holy Spirit can use all that you give to Him for your salvation. But He cannot use what you withhold, for He cannot take it from you without your willingness. For if He did, you

would believe He wrested it from you against your will. And so you would not learn it is your will to be without it. You need not give it to Him wholly willingly, for if you could you had no need of Him. But this He needs; that you prefer He take it than that you keep it for yourself alone, and recognize that what brings loss to no one you would not know. This much is necessary to add to the idea no one can lose for you to gain. And nothing more." T-25.VIII.1

"Yet what is not given to the Holy Spirit must be given to weakness, for what is withheld from love is given to fear, and will be fearful in consequence." M-25.4:9

"In the blessed instant you will let go all your past learning, and the Holy Spirit will quickly offer you the whole lesson of peace." T-15.11.1:7

∞∞∞∞

Journal Entry on Lesson 242

This day is God's. It is my gift to Him.

There are many places to go and things to do, remember to take Me along with you. I want to help you to have a happy dream, and I will, if you ask Me. Just like right now, you asked me for help. Are not the words coming to you? Yes. Are they the words you originally were thinking? No. You see, I am here with you right now and you are hearing My answer. Your faith and trust in this will grow as you continue to practice talking with Me and continue to see the results manifest.

It is so simple that the ego part of the mind does not want to believe it; it wants to question it because the ego does not understand simplicity. The ego only understands fear. Fear gives the ego life. Do not give it life. Let Me show you the Life that you are. When peace and joy enter into your mind and being through our Friendship, the ego is washed away by Our light.

I observe everything that you do without judgment and with unconditional love; just as a true friendship would be. I am with you always. Ask Me about everything, talk with Me as if I were your Friend looking over your shoulder. I am with you and will gladly talk with you and show you things that will bring us both happy laughter and joy together as we practice remembering our friendship together. I am your best friend and I am always with you, no matter what seems to happen. I will help you through your toughest times and your happiest times. My mission is to help you to be happy all the time, to help you reawaken to the peace that you are, to help you awaken to your highest Joy, to help you awaken to your True Self. You are Me and I am You. We are God and We are the best of Friends forever. I love you, My Son.

∞∞∞∞

Journal Entry on Lesson 243

Today I will judge nothing that occurs.

Brother Jeshua gave us a very helpful tool in accomplishing the goal of today's Lesson. In the Text, Chapter 5, Section VII, "The Decision for God", he instructs us to say the following in any moment that we are not feeling wholly joyous:

> *"I must have decided wrongly, because I am not at peace. I made the decision myself, but I can also decide otherwise. I want to decide otherwise, because I want to be at peace. I do not feel guilty, because the Holy Spirit will undo all the consequences of my wrong decision if I will let Him. I choose to let Him, by allowing Him to decide for God for me."*

Try to remember today to let go and respond with this prayer any moment that you notice yourself feeling impatient about whatever is occurring in that moment. Let this be a warning flag to remind you that this moment of impatience is really fear hidden behind anger and anger is hidden behind impatience. This is the facade that the ego uses to hide the fact that in that moment you made a decision by yourself, you made a judgment.

When you begin to recognize and see that this is happening, stop yourself and step back to allow peace to reassert itself within your mind. It is not this that you truly want, it is peace. You really want to feel happy and free all the time from these little surprises that the ego thought system likes to bring up to disturb your peace throughout the day. This is why we practice mind training, it is to remind ourselves that this is not so. It is merely an illusion. There is no such thing as time, and so, how can time be wasted? Why would you allow yourself to give away the experience of Heaven and joy in exchange for a belief that doesn't even exist?

Take a walk in God's time today. Judge nothing that occurs and thus free yourself from all of the beliefs the ego thought system has taught you and would have you continue to believe. Continue to talk with your Friend Who walks with you today about everything that you think you are perceiving and believing. Let Him show you new perspectives about the world you think you see. You can walk through this world quite easily with Him as your Guide. Continue to work on developing your relationship with your Friend.

Remember, He is right there with you seeing what you see, hearing what you hear, feeling what you feel, knowing what you think. Ask Him to show you how He sees this, what does He hear in this, what does He feel in this, and what does He think about this? And then be open to His many messages. Allow Him to guide your eyes as you look about. Allow Him to guide your thoughts and you will begin to recognize that He *will* communicate with you all through the day. Your Friend is a happy friend. You will learn about being joyful and happy because He is the Messenger of joyfulness and happiness. He will help you along the way in everything that you do, guiding you and giving you comfort. There is a whole other world that He would have you see, hear, feel and experience. He will help you to awaken to the perception of that world.

As you continue to open up to working with Him and allowing Him to show you these things, you will find that these are very wonderful experiences indeed; allowing the world you see now to be completely replaced with glimpses and experiences of the other world that lies beyond. His Voice that speaks to you and the Light that He shows to you will lead the way. Peace is your guide now. Would you have it any other way?

ooooo

Journal Entry on Lesson 244

I am in danger nowhere in the world.

Turn on the news and you will be sure to believe that you are in danger.

Bombings.
War.
Terrorists.
Sexual Predators.
Murder.
Hurricanes.
Recalls.
Hunger.
Bird Flu.
Accidents.
They seem to "strike fear in the heart."

As you look at these images, and they are just images that you believe in, you seem to believe that what you experiences is true. The body can be harmed and it appears to harm. Even in the world you collectively believe that your so-called "natural disasters" are an "act of God."

I assure you that what you see before you is not an act of God or even the will of God as many in your world would say. You have invented this elaborate story of the world, this place of separation from your Father. You have placed an image of pain and punishment upon your Holy Father.

He has always held you safe my Child, always in His Love and Care. No need to feel guilty about any of this. You know the truth now. That is all that matters. You have believed in the body, this shell of who you think you are. This shell cannot even contain your Essence. It tries but all it does is attempt to limit your potential as a weak substitute for God. You are unlimited beyond measure. All glory is yours.

If you witness these dark images that seem to surround you, look within your mind. You yourself prey upon your mind, you create the storm of fear, and the ravages of war against yourself. Your own dis-ease with truth has brought you to this place.

Look within.....go deeper....go past these images of fear. Go to the sanctuary where the Holy One abides. Stay focused on what is true.

I am there with you. These images, give them to Me and I will shine the Light of Truth on them, through them until you see that they are no more. Give Me your anxieties, your worries, your concerns and you will then rest in Peace truly.

You are blessed as a Son of God. The ego has tricked you into believing otherwise. The fear of death can take over but you have died a thousand times with each entertainment of the fear and judgment in your mind. What you think you experience is not life. To live in God is to remember the Oneness that you share with Him.

To live is to be happy.

When these images come, come to Me. Come into the Arms of Love. Come back to where you belong.

It was a dream. You were just asleep for a little while, but now the dawn comes and you are waking to your True Self. Stretch and yawn. Greet the day of Rebirth with Joy and Gladness. This silent space that we share now is your place of repose. Come and join me whenever you like, whenever you feel that there is danger afoot. Come within and know that you are in danger nowhere in the world because you are always in Heaven.

I love you.

My angels of Love surround you always.
Be at peace for you are loved.

∞∞∞

Journal Entry on Lesson 245

Your peace is with me, Father. I am safe.

There is a calm light of peace within me. In my mind's eye, I envision it now as a glorious, golden Eternal flame, flickering, yet burning brightly. I can see the image of a pure, solid white candle.

Those who You have sent to me, Father, share their deepest fears, their hurts and wounds, and I have been their witness that their light is still present, though it may seem dim to them. I tip my light to theirs to allow it to burn brighter, burn for eternity. I do not focus on what is going on outside in their world but yet Father I attend with very willing ears. I listen with my heart. My experiences have shown me compassion for others and for that I am grateful to use those experiences for the grace of healing. I do not have to further their illusion or join them there but yet I join them in the True Light of Your Peace. Your Holy Spirit calls to me with the Love of You.

Be present.
Be willing.

Bring My Peace to the sad and tired hearts. Those who come to you for guidance only need gentle assurance that they too have the light within and can feel My peace. They have lost their way a little while and connect with you until they remember that I am with them always. Through your trust and strength and confidence, your faith in what is true, they will move past the dark clouds of doubt that seem to conceal their radiance.

As you listen, be My vessel. Through Love, they will come to know that they are held safely in Me. Everything you do, you do for Me. Be in the space of the Will of the Father.

Be accepting. Acknowledge the Truth.
Be a beacon of strength.

Your peaceful manner, the Love you hold in your heart will be deeply felt. The healing has begun. You teach now what you need to learn for yourself as a continual reminder for yourself.

This healing is your healing.
Your healing is their healing.

Share of your experiences, yet share the healing you have experienced. In the sharing the miracle is received.

Speak now only from the Divine Heart. You are blessed. Bless all that occurs. Bless your brothers.
Bless yourself.

You are Home.

(When this message was complete in its reception, I was guided to open up the Text to Chapter 21, Section I, The Forgotten Song. The last lines follows.)

"The light in one awakens it in all. And when you see it in your brother, you are remembering for everyone." T-21.I.10:6-7

ooooo

Journal Entry on Lesson 246

To love my Father is to love His Son.

It does not matter what you seem to do within the world, it will not change the fact that you are God's Son. The cloak of darkness that you seem to wear upon yourself while you reside within the world is merely an illusion. The darkness that you surround yourself with cannot hide the Light that you are forever. Your golden light will shine away all things forever and restore the mind of God's Son to his rightful place.

You can deny the light within yourself for as long as you wish but it is not what you truly desire. Your vain imaginings within the illusion merely delays the discovery of the inevitable; that you are the Light of the world and you are God's Son. Denial of this Light within yourself can only bring you pain. Surrender and acceptance of who you really are can only bring you light and joy.

When you allow the Light to come into the awareness of your mind, you allow peace, happiness and joy to fill you at the same time. This healing Light within you will begin to restore you to your rightful place within Heaven very quickly, because the Call of God has been answered. You have forgiven the world and the Light will come and restore Heaven to Its rightful place within your mind.

Yours is the Light that you perceive. The Light of the Holy Spirit *is your Light*. He is merely showing you a reflection of the Light that you are when you perceive the Light. It is somehow familiar, a vague memory of Home that you recognize and understand that this is the way to find yourself at Home. This is the way that will help you to recognize that this is the way to awaken from the dream of hell. The Holy Spirit is your Guide now. He has the road map of light laid out before you and will show you the way to go if you will let Him.

Let him show you the light and you will understand that His path is the path of joy. His path is an easy path of Awakening. The detours into hell are not necessary. Let them go and begin to surrender to your ultimate destiny. It is here that you would join with your Friend in the Temple of Love, the Sanctuary of Love where He will guide you in all that you should do to help to accomplish His mission for the awakening of God's Son. He will not fail in His mission, nor will you because He will not let you. He has joined with you already and together you have already restored the Sonship to its Oneness. You have never left your Home in Him, Who is your Father. You have merely dreamt that you have been away but for less than a holy instant. You have never really been separated from your Father but in illusions you think you have. You have never really been separated from your Self but in illusions you think you have. Turn to the Light within your mind and let Him help you to remember that this world is not so.∞∞∞∞∞

Journal Entry on Lesson 247

Without forgiveness I will still be blind.

How will you know when you have achieved forgiveness for a moment? You will know when you have perceived the Light within your mind. When your mind is suddenly illuminated with the white light of Christ, the vision of Christ has been accomplished; true forgiveness has been accomplished for a moment.

The world that blinded you from seeing the light disappears for a moment and the Light of the Real World reveals Itself to you. In silence, practice becoming completely relaxed and focusing all of your attention solely on seeing the Light of Christ at the center of your mind's eye. Pretend that the dark screen in your mind's eye is a movie screen and just focus all of your attention on the center of the screen as you wait for the Light of Christ to reveal Himself to you.

The experience often starts out by perceiving sparks or flashes of white light; as if a flashbulb were going off from a camera there. A white star or twin stars may flash. You will know it when you see it because love, peace and healing instantly come with the Light. You will feel the deep light of Love shine strongly from your heart, flooding your body with a sudden release of tension. The tension is replaced with a deep sense and feeling that everything is okay.

As the feeling soaks, a feeling of quiet happiness and joy will sink in and begin to carry you through your day. You will just feel happy, this is what love does. It is your greatest gift hidden inside of you. It is who you really are.

∞∞∞∞

Journal Entry on Lesson 248

Whatever suffers is not part of me.

Let us remember that the part of the body that can be shocked and surprised with fear is not who you really are. The part of the body that seems to feel the discomfort of headaches or migraines is not a part of you. In fact, the whole body that you have identified with is not the real you. The body is like a cloak of darkness that you have surrounded yourself with. This darkness can experience fear, pain, worry, anxiety, sadness, death and depression.

Beneath this cloak of darkness that you seem to wear is your Light. You are really a Light. Inherent with the Light that you are, are the following qualities: joy, happiness, peace, contentment, certainty and love. All of these aspects about the Light that you are, are all experienced as one.

When you decided to put on the cloak of darkness, you decided to deny your reality as the Light. And so you came to believe in something else that became a mockery of God. You are the light of the world and the memory of the light that you are can be found hidden deep inside of you. When you begin to remember the light, you are beginning to forget the body. Try to remember today that the body that you think you are is not real. Nothing that it experiences is the real part of you but you can sink down into silence and peace and remember your True Self.

In the silence you will begin to remember your True Friend and Who you really are. You will hear your Self speak to you in certainty that, "I am okay." The Voice will tell you, "I have everything I need." This is the place where we will find and meet the memory of our True Self. Let us practice today the complete surrendering of the body and its chattery mind along with it in exchange for this memory of God within ourselves.

Journal Entry on Lesson 249

Forgiveness ends all suffering and loss.

These are random thoughts along with quotes as I was guided to different places in the Text this day in relation to our Lesson.

Forgiveness is unlimited. It can heal. It can bring me to the right mind to know my own wholeness.

> *"Be not deceived about the meaning of a fixed belief that some appearances are harder to look past than others are. It always means you think forgiveness must be limited." T-30.VI.6:4-5*

Through true forgiveness I see beyond the veil. I see beyond the anger of self-attack, the guilt that has consumed me since I believe I had been kicked out of the Garden.

I have never left. I am whole. My brothers are joined in wholeness with me. I look beyond what I believe in them, past their face, their gestures, their words, and their actions, but to the truth what lies beyond the mask of the body.

> *"Look on your brother with the willingness to see him as he is. And do not keep a part of him outside your willingness that he be healed. To heal is to make whole. And what is whole can have no missing parts that have been kept outside. Forgiveness rests on recognizing this, and being glad there cannot be some forms of sickness which the miracle must lack the power to heal." T-30.VI.8*

God's Son is perfect. And I am God's Son.

As I return my mind to You, Father, I forgive myself for what never was. I have made a world in my mind of limitation and lack, of obstacles and barriers, of judgment and fear, all to keep me away from You and Your Precious Love.

I no longer need to suffer. I can choose to be happy. It is the vigilance of the mind that brings me the peace, comfort and healing. I will remember only the love and overlook the rest.

"To forgive is merely to remember only the loving thoughts you gave in the past, and those that were given you." T-17.III.1:1

Thank You Father. Amen.

∞∞∞

Journal Entry on Lesson 250

Let me not see myself as limited.

What if one morning when you woke up and looked at yourself in the mirror, you didn't see an image of a body but instead saw a beautiful blazing white light? And as you stood there, looking at the reflection of this light, you felt yourself smiling and feeling so happy at how beautiful it was to gaze upon? What if, while you looked at this light shining away, Great Rays and all, you instinctively knew it was a reflection of your True Self?

This image is quite different from the one that we are used to seeing every morning. The image of ourselves that we are used to seeing shows us a body with all kinds of limitations. Over time the body's hair looses color and falls out, the skin grows old and becomes wrinkled, it's joints and muscles slow down and become sore. The body cannot move about freely without the aid of legs, a vehicle or an aircraft. It is susceptible to disease, starvation, dehydration, asphyxiation, hypothermia, heat, impact, pain and eventually death.

Jesus and the Holy Spirit have shared with us many times that the image of the body that we see is merely just a cloak of darkness that we have used to surrounded our light with; to block us from seeing the reflection of our True Selves. Isn't that wonderful to know? Isn't it wonderful to be given the instructions and tools we need to learn how to restore our ability to see truly instead of illusions? Jesus shares with us over and over again throughout the Course that He and the Holy Spirit have another vision for us to see, and that it can be seen! It is a vision of ourselves as a beautiful blazing white light! When we actually have an experience of seeing our light, we begin to recognize that it is unlimited in all aspects. It is endlessly beautiful to look upon. It reflects peaceful innocence that is felt within the heart when seen. Happiness fills the heart. Love is all we feel. The list goes on and on, just like our light Itself.

Thank you Father, for your gifts to us.

∞∞∞

Journal Entry on Lesson 251

I am in need of nothing but the truth.

During my morning meditation walk, Holy Spirit made me aware of the fact that it was garbage collection day here in Madison. Everything that is not needed is cast aside. The clippings, the leftovers, the dirty diapers, the broken toys and furniture, all that once served a purpose are now gladly released without another moment's thought.

I do not spend my time picking through the garbage insisting that I save that banana peel or that moldy bread now do I? Then why hang on to the old beliefs that no longer serve me as well? I needn't jump and play in the garbage in my mind any longer. And just thinking about playing with garbage, what an image! I just let it go and allow the Holy Spirit, the Great Trash Collector, to do His job by collecting it all from my mind to be disposed of forever.

I do not keep a broken chair, one with upholstery worn and tattered, with springs poking through. It is no longer useful. I instead place myself in the solid seat of the Father where I am always safe and secure, loved and at peace.

Today, I allow my thoughts to be guided to the Truth. Any thought that is not of love or held in serenity, I joyfully give to You, Holy Spirit. I will watch my mind, forgive and be free.

Amen.

∞∞∞∞

Journal Entry on Lesson 252

The Son of God is my Identity.

Who am I?
I am the Son of God.

Who am I?
I am the Son of God.

Who am I?
I am the Son of God.

Stronger now, feel it deep within your heart. Feel its essence of truth of who you are.

No ID card required.
No Driver's License, social security card, library card, ATM card, grocery store card, member's card.

I am not a minister, counselor, teacher, facilitator, student, writer, leader, web developer, wife, mother, daughter, sister, friend, neighbor, volunteer, customer, client, ex-wife, woman, Caucasian, early 40s, middle class, Democrat, citizen, American.

I am not even Deborah.
I am the Son of God.

It may appear in the world that I am all the labels and identities. But the labels do not and will not ever fit the truth. They are merely a collection of meaningless words. Only my judgment puts something on those words. That judgment comes from my past which brings to those words the meaning that they hold for me and meaning to the words that I have made for my brothers. In God, they are all meaningless. The labels have brought separation to the world I see.

Within I am complete and whole and possess only one Identity. In that Identity is simply Love, nothing but pure Love. That Identity is worth more than any other that the world could prescribe for me.

Today, I release the many identities that I have created and even have been attached to in some way. It does not matter if they carry a positive or negative connotation. They are limits all the same. I accept freedom in the brilliant, shimmering Light of Who I am. This Light gently touches me, embracing me with the Love of the Father. I am no longer who I think I am for I have accepted the limitlessness of being the Son of God who my Father created out of perfect Love. I will remember today to be as I was created to be, to extend the rays of Love outward and join with my holy brothers as One.

ooooo

Journal Entry on Lesson 253

My Self is ruler of the universe.

What I focus on I receive.
What is it that I choose to receive in my life?

Do I want a happy life? Then focus on forgiveness.
Do I want a peaceful life? Then focus on stillness.

Do I want a life of bitter disappointments? Then focus on grievances.
Do I want a life of misery? Then focus on judgment.

I am worthy of a life that supports me in my spiritual Self. I can cast aside what I do not desire and place my attention to that which I do desire from the depths of my soul.

I know that it is through determination, dedication, commitment, vigilance, practice, faith, trust and listening to the Holy Spirit that I will achieve that which my soul desires.

I desire to know God fully. I desire to know the Oneness. I desire to remember. I desire joy.
I desire peace.

∞∞∞

Journal Entry on Lesson 254

Let every voice but God's be still in me.

I direct my mind. I choose the thoughts. I can elect to escort the thoughts offstage. They do not need to dance and perform in my mind. I choose the setting of silence, thus closing the curtain and relaxing in the resulting peace.

Whether I practice this in sitting meditation or in walking meditation, I bring my mind to the focal point, in this case today's lesson, and using it as is suggested here, "to quietly step back, look at the thoughts, and then let them go."

The ego's thoughts are there to distract me with its tactics of smoke and mirrors so that I will not see the illusion that it is. The ego attempts to keep me grounded in this world by lifting those thoughts into the mind that would only make me think of the world. Such as: today's rainy weather, the chores to be done, appointments to make, phone calls to return, aches and pains, family and friends, past memories. All appearing in my mind as a distraction to settling into listening only to the Voice that brings me assurance and peace. If I choose not to keep the other voices, those demanding, commanding ones, then indeed the stillness will be mine.

It is not a chore, it is simply a labor of love, love of my Self to redirect my mind to peace and to wait for His Voice, His Will and His Love.

Thank You Holy Spirit for Your Presence in my mind in which I can release all thoughts in Your Direction. It is a glad exchange, to exchange the voices of fear for the one True Voice of Love. Amen.

∞∞∞∞

Journal Entry on Lesson 255

This day I choose to spend in perfect peace.

The word "choice" and its derivatives are mentioned 578 times in the Course. I think it is a clue that it is a decision that I must make. Whatever seems to be occurring in my world, no matter how chaotic, I can step back and choose peace instead.

I found this last evening during our study group session as we engaged in a lively, yet at times challenging and tension-filled discussion precipitated by one person who attends irregularly. Even after all these many years of doing the Course and facilitating groups, I found myself at first wanting to judge this person, even perceiving him as an angry, unpeaceful person coming to the meeting with an agenda. Others did as well.

I knew that it was for me to go within and see the angry, unpeaceful parts that I carry, that I wish to keep hidden from my sight. Plus, where and when are the times that I come to a situation with my own agenda and not desiring to surrender to the Will of God.

In these moments, do I prefer to be right or happy?

As the evening progressed, at its highest point I found myself continuing to go within and ask Holy Spirit for guidance and assistance in forgiving the situation, the person, and myself. I saw how the evening was not at all following my agenda. Ah...and here I perceived that this very person had walked in with his own agenda! More forgiveness, more guidance with Holy Spirit!

At the end of the evening as we shared embraces, he came to each person, hugging them and apologizing, sharing love. All that could be seen now was love and forgiveness. Holy Spirit showed me that this may be a pattern from his past. Challenge, conflict, tension, judgment, anger and afterwards be reassured that he has not been abandoned or that love was somehow taken away.

This was something for me to think about as well. If I see this within my brother, then I see it in me.

This day I choose to spend in perfect peace by remembering to forgive all that I see and turning my attention to God. I do have that choice, in the midst of a phone call, a grocery store line, heavy traffic, a group interaction, or sitting in a room by myself with my own thoughts. I can choose peace instead of whatever is presented before me. My peace is only disturbed because of my interpretation that I place upon whatever seems to be there. Do I give power to the situation or to God?

As always it is my choice. And if today Holy Spirit I cannot choose, I will come to You to ask You to decide for me, trusting and knowing that You will. Amen.

∞∞∞

Journal Entry on Lesson 256

God is the only goal I have today.

Here you are seemingly with your head stuck in the clouds perceiving a world around you that is but a world of illusion. Through the practice of forgiveness the world that you see around you will but give way to a world of light hidden beyond. Forgiveness is the practice of letting go of everything you see, feel, hear, and perceive with the mind now.

By sinking down into deep silence, stilling all of your thoughts and focusing all of your attention on one goal, which is to see and hear God speak to you is the way of forgiveness. You will be quite surprised when He reveals His Light to you and you hear His

Voice speak to you. They come from His World as gifts to you to help you find your way Home. Everything is done within the mind. The Light of Salvation and the Voice of Forgiveness are one and the same.

Perceiving the Light and hearing His Voice will but heal. But you must desire to see Him and hear Him with all your heart and willingness. Have an open mind and wait for Him to come to you. He will answer your call and He will gladly help you. He is right here with you right now and yet you know Him not because you believe you are alone. He has never left you. He watches with you and sees and knows everything that is going on within your mind and in your life.

Your Friend is here with you waiting for you to ask Him for His help. He responds immediately to every request you have of Him. Have an open mind for Him. He will guide your body to help you know that He is there. He will guide your eyes, your thoughts, your limbs and your movements. Allow yourself to be open and filled with the Holy Spirit of Christ today. Talk with Him, be with Him and thank Him for all His help He gives to you today. What other Friend and Teacher would you want but this one? He knows all the answers and the way to go and He is always correct. Trust in Him and allow Him to guide your life and the gifts of happiness and joy will be yours.

Let Him show you what He sees today and the vision of the Light of Christ will be yours. From deepest silence and stillness let Him speak to you today and know your Friend Who walks with you.

∞∞∞

Journal Entry on Lesson 257

Let me remember what my purpose is.

What I want.
What I am.
What ego says.
What God is.
Enter Forgiveness.

Today, I am determined to remember to unify my thoughts and actions under one goal and purpose: to forgive. I cannot serve two masters and feel completely at peace. The so-called peace that the ego brings is only one of falsity and truly is a facade. It is not true; it is not lasting. It only represents a false hope, a vanishing, vaporous image outside of me grasping yet not being able to cling on to.

Within my being is the only true Essence of Peace. As I drift past the fog of illusions that fill my experience, I am moving closer and closer to the experience of true peace in the Light of God. The Light is the beacon that brings me Home. It recognizes Itself.

In the midst of the day, I can be attuned to what is not of God, thus not of peace. I can release my petty desires for the one true desire for God. I do not need anything but this.

But yet while I am believing I am in the world with a body and with physical needs, I can stay connected to the Holy Spirit knowing that He is present with me, assisting me if I so ask.

It will be effortless and I will find that all that I need will come to me. My faith and trust in Him will remove all barriers. The obstacles that I perceive are just that, a perception. With the Holy Spirit, they vanish into thin air.

My purpose is to forgive the barriers to Love and I accept the task with joy today.

Thank You Holy Spirit. Amen.

∞∞∞∞

Journal Entry on Lesson 258

Let me remember that my goal is God.

Let us remember that the toys and trinkets of the ego include sorrow, guilt, projection, fear and anger. Through the use of these weapons the ego attempts to continue to hide the truth about yourself from your awareness. There are many forms of fear but in the end there is only one truth. You are not who you think you are and the other person is not who you think he or she is.

You are not a good father nor a bad father. You are not a good mother nor a bad mother. You are not an alcoholic, a drug addict, an overeater, nor a poor wretched soul. These beliefs and many more the ego has about you and others are simply not true. There is only love. The true essence of every person and being you see within the world is radiant love. Love created you exactly like Itself and nothing else is true.

Beyond the image of every person and being that you see within the world shines the light of their true essence. It is quite possible to see this light shining from everyone and everything. It takes a lot of practice and willingness to perceive the light that radiates from them. Everyone has the light shining within them. It shines eternally because it comes from our Source, from our Father in Heaven.

As we continue to practice the art of true forgiveness, we will begin to see the light more and more over time. In the Light we all stand in perfect innocence and holiness. Anything but the light that you see is but darkness that is utilized to conceal the Light. You can conceal the Light from your perception with the darkness of guilt and fear you hold within your mind, or you can choose to let it go and allow the Holy Spirit to show you a different vision; an image quite different from the one that you are used to seeing.

The vision of the Light of Christ stands before you each time you see a person in your life and you see it not, because you have chosen to see darkness instead. Ask the Holy Spirit, the Great Teacher Who has been assigned to you to help you find your way Home and the Light of Truth about yourself and others, to help you see this Light of Innocence shining ever so brightly within your Holy Self and others. It truly is a gift of peace and freedom from the world we see.

Let us remember today, that our goal is God.

∞∞∞

Journal Entry on Lesson 259

Let me remember that there is no sin.

I am not condemned to a life of hell.
I am not in a time and space of no hope.
There is not a black mark on my soul.
There never was; there never shall be.
In God, is everything made new.

At the end of the movie "Dogma" after all the destruction and death, God simply looks around, invokes Divine power and it is done. The scene is made anew. What had seemed to occur has now disappeared.

I am made anew in the Father. Whatever story I have written

here in the world, it will not define who I am. And, my Father will not love me any less. He does not see what I see for His sights are beyond and my innocence is held within His Heart.

I do not have to live in the self-inflicted pain. Sure, I may attempt to continue to do so, even having a cavalier attitude. However, as I realize how much serenity that I can have in embracing truth and shedding all that is not my Self, I will accept true happiness into my life. My life will change.

God does not attack, no more shall I. It is my own self-attack, this living in the fog of a past that cannot even be grasped. If I live in this state of being, only those situations, those witnesses will be called forth to support my own self-attack and thus I feel victimized. And when the channels are blocked and free expression is diverted, that is where my pain occurs.

My job is to remember to identify with the Father and to release all identifications with the father of the illusory world unto Him.

No guilt required, only forgiveness.

In releasing to the free and full expression of Love, the channels are open. The Holy Spirit is there beside me ready to facilitate the connection with the Divine. I then become secure in Who I really am.

It is always my choice.

Today, I choose sanity in remembering that there is no sin.
Today, I relinquish all self-attack and self-punishment.
Today, suffering is no more.
Today, I am born anew in Love.

Thank You Holy Spirit for this daily connection with You. In looking at my mind honestly and authentically with You, without hiding or denying any thoughts, I know that I have entered the healing sanctuary.

∞∞∞∞

Journal Entry on Lesson 260

Let me remember God created me.

Father, I accept within my being and without a doubt that You are my Source. This physical pain that has surprised me with its presence, its intensity and fluctuation, I know does not come from You or by anything that You have created. The ego mind desires to analyze from where it came and make the body real. It speculates on what guilty thoughts are hidden, thus punishing me from "hiding" from You.

A silly ego game.

It does not matter what I believe about the pain or what thoughts may be underneath the surface. What does matter is that I offer You all the pieces of it, from the actual pain, to the concern, to the mind judgments, to the analysis, to the excavating, to the research, to the Course quotes, and to whatever others have conferred about it.

It is yours.
It is now in Your Holy Hands.
I am blessed in Who I am in You.
I identify with You; the wholeness and the beauty I possess in You.
Let the walls crumble down.
Let the Creative Power of Who I am shine forth in the Light of Forgiveness.
Let me remember.
Thank You Father, Amen.

Journal Entry on Lesson 261

God is my refuge and my security.

When we begin to believe that we are God, we will begin to have experiences that we are God. The mind of the mystic relinquishes the mind of the body in exchange for his rightful mind as God. Through the practice of silent meditation and stilling all thoughts is the way of Christ and the sages that have followed Him in time.

It is quite possible to establish direct contact with God within your mind through this practice. As we continue this mind mastery we begin to tap into an abundance of power hidden within ourselves that is far beyond our understanding and expectations. Opening up to Him Who is our Guide will show us the way of peace, happiness, abundance and joy. He knows all things and He knows the way to your True Self. He is your Guide to help you find Him Who is One with you and the Prime Creator.

The sages have learned how to relinquish all of their thoughts in complete stillness of the mind in order to experience the truth of who they really are, and you will too as we continue to practice this art of silent meditation. You too will join the masters of enlightenment as you continue to work with Me in finding the Light within yourself. The Light contains all knowledge and understanding because the Light in which you perceive is God. It is your True Self.

The Light within your mind is the Light of Christ. It is the Light of your Home where your Friend will speak to you and guide you along the way. He will give you wisdom far beyond the wisdom of the world. The practice of stilling all of your thoughts and focusing intently on seeing only Him and hearing Him is the key to success.

Daily practice and surrendering with an open mind in stillness will allow the experience of the Divine and Holy within yourself to come forth and touch your mind with Love, compassion, happiness, holiness, abundance, peace and joy. The Spirit of Love is within and will come forth into your awareness with all of these gifts as you continue to practice daily sinking down and letting go of all you thought you knew before. It is here you will find your refuge, security and Home.

∞∞∞

Journal Entry on Lesson 262

Let me perceive no differences today.

Hot/Cold
Black/White
Male/Female
Cat/Dog

All distinctions, all differences. All fragmented, shattered into millions of pieces. Grasping on to none yet knowing somehow, knowing that no matter how fragmented that a golden cord of light gathers all together for it is only Light that is the Oneness connecting all.

None other.

One Son.

In the Oneness, in the wholeness I experience my Freedom. I am not alone. This pain of separateness does not exist. When I remember, I don't feel disconnected and off center. I don't feel then outside the circle. In Reality, I am not but somehow in my mind I have placed myself outside.

Is it for attention or simply insanity?

Insane am I to think that I could create something other than Love. Only Love is real. Only Oneness is real.

"What's in a name? that which we call a rose By any other name would smell as sweet"

And so are we - the Son of God.
In the fragrance of His Love I will come to know my Self.

∞∞∞

Journal Entry on Lesson 263

My holy vision sees all things as pure.

When we look upon another person, let us remember the Vision of Christ that the Holy Spirit has shown to us about that person. Should we see something other than the Holy Light of that person before our eyes, may we remember to pause for a moment to forgive the vision of darkness we see instead. Let us remember that our own projection makes perception. What we perceive is a reflection of our current state of mind. Let us remember that we are choosing what we see and we are choosing what we feel.

If we are not feeling happy and peaceful, then let that be a reminder that the ego is behind the steering wheel of our lives again. Let it be a reminder that it is time to step back and to turn inward for Holy Spirit's perspective on the particular situation. If we are unconsciously afraid of something, the Holy Spirit will bring it to your awareness. Then, it is your job to take it to the next step, which is to ask Him to help you heal the unconscious fear within your mind. It is your job to work with Him on whatever it is that is bringing you discomfort and pain.

When we turn within our minds to ask for the Holy Spirit's perception, He will remind us to be happy, He will fill us with the Light of joy in the moment to help us remember what it feels like to be happy and free of fear again. The Holy Spirit is our Friend. He always knows the perfect thing to show us in the moment to help us through difficult times and situations. He always helps us to move into a direction where we feel happier and more peaceful. Is it not nice to have such a Friend in our lives?

∞∞∞∞

Journal Entry on Lesson 264

I am surrounded by the Love of God.

As the autumn chill arrives with the frost and the leaves just beginning to clothe themselves with glorious colors I too feel the frost of the ego upon my mind. When I step inside the warmth of my Home, I step into the Truth of God.

I am protected wherever I go in my mind. I may have times that my mind is left outside its Home and experiences the frozen aspects of the ego. The ego wants to keep me frozen in time, particularly in the past. Waiting on expectations but only receiving resentments. It's solution is no solution at all.

Staying outside my Home, stomping my feet and rubbing and blowing on my hands will not beat the chill. These magic tricks will not bring me the knowledge of everlasting Love of the Father.

Go within. Go within to the place of comfort and the hearth of Love. Take your brothers with you. Sit by the fire with a soothing hot drink. Drink in the Holy Spirit's Wisdom, letting it soothe your mind and warm your soul.

You are never alone. For as much as you walk, you walk with Heaven always.

Know this and you know Love.

Know this and be happy.

∞∞∞∞

Journal Entry on Lesson 265

Creation's gentleness is all I see.

The word "kindness" has been in my mind today, along with "compassion." Let me be these towards my brother today in whatever I may think I see occurring. If I see controversy, jealousy, conflict, attacks and defenses, let me realize that it is my own self-attack. No one is the victim here. No one is the victor here. We all are insane or we are all sane.

Let me pluck the thoughts out of my mind this day. I refuse to accept these tendencies to judge all the rights and wrongs of the world. I sink down past all the effects of my ego mind and go to the sanctuary where Love abides. Within there is peace, there is gentleness.

It is whispered to me, "Experience compassion in all that you do. Be kind. See past the facades that we use to hide our fear. It is by looking truthfully at the places that need healed in the mind where peace will be felt.

Do not attack your brother today, even if you perceive that you have been attacked. Do not defend yourself. Only forgive. True forgiveness will set all of the brothers free. There are no sins, there is no need to catalog them further. No need to build a case. Rest the case. End the judgment.

All are innocent.

Observe the lion and the lamb. See them lie down together. Fear is absent; peace is their virtue.

> *"The lion and the lamb lying down together symbolize that strength and innocence are not in conflict, but naturally live in peace."* T-3.I.5:3

No matter how spiritual one professes to be, remember that whilst in a body even spiritual teachers are susceptible to the ego's dictates. See past their forgetfulness. They know not what they do. Do not lower them instead uplift them in the space of release. Bind not your brothers. Let go of your own guilt. It has merely been projected upon them.

Be at peace. Forgive. There is nothing more that I need say to you but this. Trust in Me always when you feel you do not know the response. The only response is Love to the desperate calls for Love.

Remember the blessing, *"Creation's gentleness is all I see."*

∞∞∞∞

Journal Entry on Lesson 266

My holy Self abides in you, God's Son.

<u>I Need You Brother, On the Journey Home</u>

I need you brother, on the journey Home
Discard your mask
And I'll discard mine
I need you brother, on the journey Home

Your Light does shine when I see what's pure
My Light does shine when I let go
I need you brother, on the journey Home

Each grievance, each judgment
I come now to You
Holy Spirit, Your peace is the only Truth
I need you brother, on the journey Home

Love and Peace abide in me
And so dear brother, It abides in you
The recognition of our Oneness is my call
I need you brother, on the journey Home

Gratitude is due you brother
In all that I learn
You are my teacher; I, your student
I need you brother, on the journey Home

And when the roles are reversed
It is one and the same
I need you brother, on the journey Home

The Light does shine from my mind to yours
And when embraced in Divine Accord
I need you brother, on the journey Home

We are Home
We are Home

Thank you brother for the journey Home.
As we continue to open to the possibility that we can perceive a
light within our brothers, the light will begin to reveal itself to
you. Every brother that you perceive now has a light shining from

him but you see it not because your mind is clouded with misperceptions of reality. You think you are perceiving reality now when you see your brother, but what you see you are really making up.

If you were to focus all of your attention on ignoring what you see now in your brother, but instead attempt to see only the light within him, you will be quite surprised what is revealed to you. The Light that shines from your brothers can be seen as plain as day when the mind is clear and open to the peace of the Holy Spirit. The Holy Spirit will show you the truth about everything that seems to surround you. There is only light.

Everything you see around you now is a block to the awareness of Love's presence. Love and Light are one and the same. Love and Joy and Happiness are all One and the same. You cannot experience one without experiencing the others. When you literally see the Light you will also experience joy and happiness and love at the same time.

Opening our minds to the awareness to Love's presence is the goal of the Course. It is done through the practice of forgiveness which is practiced in many forms and flavors, but in the end forgiveness really only means one thing, merely letting everything go with your mind. Whatever it is that seems to preoccupy your mind with what you perceive now, merely practice letting it go in silence with your eyes closed and sink down to open up to the world of Heaven within your mind. Focusing all of your attention on this and only this will reveal the world of Light to you. It is truly there and can be seen. The illumination of the mind is unmistakable when the Light has come. It is a gift from Heaven Itself; from the Creator unto each and every Son that is perceived within the world.

In the world there appears to be many sons but when you use your Spiritual Vision to look beyond the body to each of the sons and daughters you perceive, you will see the same Light. That is because there is only one Light, there is only one Son and one Father and all are One.

∞∞∞∞

Journal Entry on Lesson 267

My heart is beating in the peace of God.

"Out of love he was created, and in love he abides. Goodness and mercy have always followed him, for he has always extended the Love of his Father." T-13.I.6:6-7

And so in peace do I belong.

In quietness I now place my mind.
The world so still that only the beating of my heart is what my yearning ears hear.

Be still, for it beats the One Pulse of God, of all Creation.

Ah, but it is not the human heart that I alone hear but it is the collective heart of Love. Always expanding without end....beating in the rhythm of Universal Peace.

Take my own pulse of my body and it seems to tell me that I am alive. But I do not know what true living is until I have forgiven the world.

The Breath of Life carries me along. The ears attuned now to the Voice of Truth.

All collected within the Body of Christ. All as One.

Home is where my Heart of Love abides.

Journal Entry on Lesson 268

Let all things be exactly as they are.

The ego mind has a habit of deciding for us what it would like to have and do with its life. The ego is not really alive, it only thinks it is. The ego is a projection of an image and experience from the mind of God's Son. That's you! Because you have temporarily forgotten who you really are, you believe that you are something else. And because you believe that you are something else, you believe you want other experiences that are not of God. You have forgotten that what you are really looking for is the experience that you are God and that you are missing out on nothing.

From the perspective of the Mind of God, which is where you really are right now, everything is okay. In fact, it's better than okay. Child of God, you have been given everything by your Father in Heaven. You believe you are trapped in a world condemned to struggle and suffer until the day you die. This is simply not true and you have been given the keys to prove this to yourself personally, experientially. Do you not understand or see what a wonderful gift this is? You do not because if you did, you would be here no longer. Continued practice of a little willingness is all I ask of you my brother. Take my hand and I will show you much greater things than what the ego world has taught you. Let them go! They are nothing and I *am* offering you everything.

Remember as I have taught you, *Forgiveness is the key to happiness.* You are getting the right idea now. Give all thoughts and beliefs that concern you, that disturb your peace in any way, to the Light. Remember to ask the Holy Spirit to help you let the Light heal whatever it is that is concerning you. Then remember to wait in silence for the Light to come wash it away from your heart and mind with peace. It is truly that simple. Allow the Light to come and heal it for you. You need do nothing but ask and allow it to happen. The Light *will* come when you are ready. Relax and be open. The sparks will show you the way. Just stay with them when they begin to happen, they will get brighter and stronger, bringing with them corresponding strength in healing, peace and joy. The memory of God is what you are really looking for and the memory that everything is okay, just exactly as it was before the time of fear began.

∞∞

Journal Entry on Lesson 269

My sight goes forth to look upon Christ's face.

This lesson recalls a memory to mind of an experience that I received during meditation several years ago. As my mind quieted and was then completely still, I felt the sensation of lifting up above the ground as if I was levitating. I didn't open my eyes, but remained fully focused on the experience. In my minds' eye, it appeared as if there were a cloud or fog present in the room. As I allowed the experience to occur at one point I left the body and was in such a place of indescribable light. It was glorious, magnificent, radiant, marvelous, sublime, all-loving and all the adjectives that you could possibly conjure up to use. Honestly though, how could mere words, these symbols upon symbols describe this experience.

I rarely share these meditation or light experiences because of just that, that it is prohibitive to paint a picture of Heaven with inadequate equipment. Enough aside, as I continued in this experience, I felt that I had touched the face of Christ, not a physical touch but yet a distinct knowing that my inner vision had become connected with the Presence of All.

The experience seemed to last an eternity, yet when I returned to the body and it is only because of an inkling of fear that arose that I did so, it was only a few minutes in the span of time. Even coming back into the body felt very heavy and burden-laden, as such was the lightness and freedom I had felt moments before.

It is my own grievances that keep me marooned in the body. Through the practice of forgiveness with all my brothers and myself and including this world, that I will enter again into this experience. Perhaps not the same experience each time, but yet similar in Love all the same. The experience of Oneness, of truly knowing without a doubt in every fiber of my being, that we share and are connected with God.

The body is merely a fence, a limitation that I have invented that prevents me from seeing truth. The truth will be seen through my spiritual eyes as I realize. (Real Eyes) It is there I choose now to look.

My body is not who I am and never will be.
Nor is it of my brothers.
Forgive the body. Forgive what these measly eyes behold and look upon the face of Christ. Hold the Sonship in your heart and know that they are a part of you.

> *The body is a fence the Son of God imagines he has built, to separate parts of his Self from other parts. It is within this fence he thinks he lives, to die as it decays and crumbles. For within this fence he thinks that he is safe from love. Identifying with his safety, he regards himself as what his safety is. How else could he be certain he remains within the body, keeping love outside? W-pII.5.1.*

ⲟⲟⲟⲟⲟ

Journal Entry on Lesson 270

I will not use the body's eyes today.

Jeshua, What words can you give me today to help me see the light of the forgiven world? What words can I share that would be helpful for all of us?

There is a visible light that can be seen not by the body's eyes but by spiritual sight. Practice detaching yourself from the world you see today and allow yourself to become an observer for the light. Remember that everything you see is like a painting on an canvas and your mind is projecting the paint. The paint seems to create the 3-dimensional images the body sees. You can allow the Holy part of your self to project the light too, if you allow yourself to become detached from your projected images. When you let go of the past that you associate with the images the light will automatically begin to reveal Itself. Your paint projections are merely distracting your attention from the light. Your belief in the images the body sees is blocking perception of the light. Letting go of what you perceive today and becoming an observer for a new kind of light will step you in the right direction.

Is there anything else that I can do to help facilitate an experience of seeing the light today?
You are already doing it, you are asking for help and I will gladly do so. Be quiet and pay attention as you go about your day today. Be mindful and vigilant for the light of the Kingdom today. It is all around you waiting to be perceived. You can practice periodic walking meditations today while you are at work. As you start your walk remind yourself that you will not use the body's eyes today, then turn your attention away from the people and things you see. Quietly place your attention at the center of your mind and be open. Still your thoughts and quietly walk with your attention waiting in quiet expectation of perceiving the light. Do not look at anything specific. Just walk and focus quietly seeing

with the mind. It will just begin to happen as you continue to practice this type of letting go or forgiveness. An attitude of gratitude will be helpful too. Ask Me to join with you on your walks. Pay attention for My inspirations for I will be with you, giving you a helping hand. The results you experience will be your witnesses and reminder that I am truly with you. I love you brother. Thank you for asking. Let us share together a peaceful day today.

ooooo

Journal Entry on Lesson 271

Christ's is the vision I will use today.

Father, Sometimes it seems wearisome to experience the world. Each moment it may seem like the straw that has broke the camel's back. There's a puzzling notion that I know I can experience something different however why do I keep choosing the same pain again and again.

I know a brother whom I care deeply about who appears to be self-centered and selfish in the world. I see this brother with the vision of Christ today. I slip past his unthoughtfulness and unkind gestures, his harsh words, his inconsistencies and even deceit. I slip past it all and listen to Your Voice behind his words, Your Face behind his countenance and Your Light behind his darkness.

The darkness, the distractions, the addictive behaviors are all camouflaging his True Self. He doesn't see it for himself. He doesn't see the obstructions to experiencing and recognizing love in his life. The love that is right there before him. He is surrounded by other brothers that love him so dearly, but yet he does not see the love. He refuses to accept it because he refuses to accept it within himself. And if I am finding pain in watching his own seeming destruction, then I too am concealing the Light of God's Love from myself.

I extend love to my brother. I extend compassion to my brother. I extend empathy to my brother. I see beyond it all and see the connection of us both to the One Light of Heaven. It is not his unkindness's that I want to carry on in my heart, but rather save all the kindnesses and know the blessing and the beauty of the unselfishness of Eternal Love.

The mistakes are vanished. All that remains is the love and the present moment. It's a time of rebirth. A time to begin anew. Thank You Father for redeeming us from this prison house that we have made. Thank You for Your gift of the Holy Spirit, in which forgiveness is His gift and our own function.

How can you who are so holy suffer? All your past except its beauty is gone, and nothing is left but a blessing. I have saved all your kindnesses and every loving thought you ever had. I have purified them of the errors that hid their light, and kept them for you in their own perfect radiance. They are beyond destruction and beyond guilt. They came from the Holy Spirit within you, and we know what God creates is eternal. You can indeed depart in peace because I have loved you as I loved myself. You go with my blessing and for my blessing. Hold it and share it, that it may always be ours. I place the peace of God in your heart and in your hands, to hold and share. The heart is pure to hold it, and the hands are strong to give it. We cannot lose. My judgment is as strong as the wisdom of God, in Whose Heart and Hands we have our being. His quiet children are His blessed Sons. The Thoughts of God are with you. T-5.IV.8.

∞∞∞∞

Journal Entry on Lesson 272

How can illusions satisfy God's Son?

"I am surrounded by Your Love, forever still, forever gentle and forever safe."

When my eldest daughter was almost 17, she had phoned long distance to share with me an explosive argument that she had with her father which caused her to promptly leave the home retreating to a friend's house. The ego scrutinizes and pushes me to get caught up in the drama, and an almost 17 year old can be very dramatic in her depictions of the situation.

Granted, I did not agree with her father and his parenting methods, personality and other behaviors and so it always has been a consistent reminder for me to practice true forgiveness. And let's just say that I have had years of practice.

The ego loves to bait though with its attack/defense mode, screaming, "You must do something to fix this situation." But Holy Spirit's Voice is soft and gentle, reminding me that in Reality everyone is safe and in His Loving Arms.

During the course of the several conversations we had, I admit that I followed the temptation to travel the path of drama, until my request for sanity from Holy Spirit was received and answered and peace entered in. Holy Spirit reminded me that she is not a victim and not to come from that frame of mind in speaking with her.

He guided me to remind her that she has a choice. Not only does she have a choice but she has to own her responsibility in the situation and the choices that she has made. A few years before she and her sister begged me relentlessly to go live with him, then she has allowed the friction of what he says to upset her. My daughter having a quite a temper herself, then chose to continue the argument with him. All expressed gently but she of course did not like hearing this.

I know that for me it is in the acceptance of "what is" that I can then make the transformations that are necessary for my own healing.

I have to trust that Holy Spirit is working with her in His perfect timing and not mine. I cannot compare her to myself or even her sisters. I have to allow her the room to grow, to move through the dream at her own pace receiving what lessons that she needs to receive. All the while knowing that as I stay tuned in with Holy Spirit and that if He guides me to say or do something, then I will do it.

Allowing the ones we love to make mistakes and fall on their faces can seem heart-wrenching. We love and care about them so much and we certainly do not want to see them suffer. We desire the highest good for them. The real love is allowing them to make the mistakes for how else do we learn. My job is to trust, trust and trust.

Of course this is hard for people on the outside who have formulated their opinions and judgments about the situation, but honestly they do not know the situation because they are not directly involved. One does not know what they would do until they are there in that place. I am not here to please others. I am here to follow God.

As I experienced this situation, of course a kernel of guilt was flagged. A mother's lioness instincts entered. Then Holy Spirit entered. No matter how I could try to fix the situation, the illusion is still the illusion. It cannot be fixed in this illusory realm, only in the realm of God can the Answer appear. I can hold in my mind that healing has taken place. It is imperative to release any guilt to

Holy Spirit, release the situation to Holy Spirit, the feelings of being "sucked in" to the drama to Holy Spirit. Any blaming or criticism that comes my way is also to be released to Him.

The world will never agree on anything that should be done, because the world was set up by the ego. It is a world of utter conflict and confusion. Only in God's World is there clarity, peace and pureness.

My daughter did return home, just as we all will from this world, recognizing that all that I have made will never satisfy the hunger for the Reality of God's Love.

∞∞∞∞

Journal Entry on Lesson 273

The stillness of the peace of God is mine.

When our Father Who is perfect Peace created us, He created us exactly like Himself. Peace is yours because you are Peace Itself.

In Heaven you are Peace, you chose to block the awareness of Peace that you are in exchange for something else. Just as easily you can choose to change your mind and remember the Peace that you are.

In stillness and with your eyes closes, you can practice letting go of all you thought you made and allow the memory of Peace to restore Itself to your awareness.

You are using darkness and with great effort to block the awareness of Peace from Yourself. The memory of Peace that you are lies hidden in your mind with the Light as well. Perceive the Light and peace will come. Perceive Peace and the Light will come. For you, Light and Peace are truly One. They are yours, you are Them.

You are Father's Prince of Peace and aren't you glad that this is so?

I am ready for undisturbed tranquility today.
I am willing to learn to have the experience of peace.
I dismiss all disturbances from my mind as they arise as I hold and repeat in my mind, "The stillness of the peace of God is mine."
I am grateful for my determination for the experience of peace.

∞∞∞

Journal Entry on Lesson 274

Today belongs to love. Let me not fear.

Father, today I can think of all kinds of things to be afraid of. I can think of all kinds of "sins" and mistakes to feel guilty about. And certainly, there are all kinds of people out there who would gladly help me to do so.

Father, a little while ago I asked You to show me all of the things that You appreciated about me. I think that this was the first time I asked You how You see me in contrast to the way that I see myself. I was surprised at your responses. The little inspirations that came from You reminded me of the little moments of love, the little moments of choices that I made to extend my love to others in quiet ways. These little gifts of love that I gave to others, I overlooked as inconsequential and insignificant. But You helped me to see that these were little golden nuggets of investments that were going to pay off big dividends in love and joy later. I could not see this big picture but You could. But because I asked, You shared it with me so that I could see more truly as You do. This helped me to feel better about myself. Thank you. I am grateful that I took a few moments to ask and receive how You saw me. I have been afraid to do this because I have already decided for You that I was unlovable and unworthy by my actions in the past. Oh dear Father, how mistaken and blind I have been.

Dear Father, may I remember to turn the reins of my life over to You, over and over again, from moment to moment so that I may be carried by You. I can see now that You have a better way and You will show it to me, if I merely get out of the way and let You do it for me. These reins I give to You today and everyday to lead the way for me out of fear and back into Love.

Thank You Father for Your gifts to me. I love You and appreciate You too.

∞∞∞∞

Journal Entry on Lesson 275

God's healing Voice protects all things today.

Trusting in Your Voice is the only solution for me. In the past, I have trusted in the ego's voice. It has lied and betrayed me. Promising me a life of happiness and closeness with You, but yet all it has done is kept me at a distance from the True Intimacy that I can share with my Holy Father. It was in listening to this voice that numerous lessons have come my way, seemingly painful ones, lessons of loneliness and unworthiness, precipitated by the witnesses of fear that I welcomed to me. The walls were built higher and higher, walling me off from You.

This is not the voice that I want to beckon to any longer.

Your Voice sings sweetly to me of healing, of peace, of Eternal Love. I have forgotten at times to listen. Any anxiousness that I feel dissolves at the cadence of Your Voice. Trusting in You assists me in all the decisions that cross my path each moment. I remember now, yes, I remember now.

> *"For Your Voice will tell me what to do and where to go; to whom to speak and what to say to him, what thoughts to think, what words to give the world."*

I do not have to surrender to the ego's voice that insists to not work on the relationship with You. It is a call of isolation and deceit. The relationship with You Father is reflected in my brothers here. As I treat them, I treat myself and You. It is only a holy relationship with You and them that I seek. My brothers are myself; they are You. How I see them is how I see myself in relation to You.

I want to see with the eyes of Love. I want to feel with the heart of Love. I want to hear Your Voice speak through the darkness, lifting my eyes up to the Light, recognizing and holding It as my very own.

I join with You now. May I know Your Voice and accept the healing now. Amen.

ᴏᴏᴏᴏᴏ

Journal Entry on Lesson 276

The Word of God is given me to speak.

After meditating with the Lesson, I was guided to this section in the Manual for Teachers, regarding the use of words:

> *Is the teacher of God, then, to avoid the use of words in his teaching? No, indeed! There are many who must be reached through words, being as yet unable to hear in silence. The teacher of God must, however, learn to use words in a new way.*

Gradually, he learns how to let his words be chosen for him by ceasing to decide for himself what he will say. This process is merely a special case of the lesson in the workbook that says, "I will step back and let Him lead the way." The teacher of God accepts the words which are offered him, and gives as he receives. He does not control the direction of his speaking. He listens and hears and speaks. - M-21.4

How perfect in relation to the Lesson! Thank You Father for this reminder of allowing You to be in the forefront of my mind and life. You will give me all the words that I need, I trust and rely on that. Relying on my own strength does not achieve anything but the goal of pain. Relying on You assures me of my holiness and my innocence.

I am pure and holy as God Himself.

It is this that I repeat today. It is this that I treasure within my heart. I am reborn in Truth! Reborn in Love!

Father, it is You Who created us to be the Divine Beings that we are. All that You are has been amplified in me. And I duly accept my role and honor my Self and You by magnifying the Love to my brothers. I do this through my forgiveness of forgetting all grievances, all judgments, all opinions, all needs to be right, all side-taking, all of it all.

I know that without a doubt, I am here to represent Him Who sent me. I do not have to worry about what to say or do for He Who sent me will direct me.

And direction arrives when I take a step backward bowing to the Divine Direction.

ooooo

Journal Entry on Lesson 277

Let me not bind Your Son with laws I made.

Jeshua, What are some examples of laws that I have made in an attempt to bind God's Son?

You believe that you are a body condemned to wither and die. Death would be an example of an idol in this case. Guilt would be another example of an idol. If you believe that you have done something wrong then you have followed the voice of the ego. For only the voice of the ego would lead you to a feeling of fear and guilt. There is always a fundamental truth about every choice you seem to make.

When you have a choice to make, always choose the path that will lead you to peace of mind. If you are not sure because of the habits of the ego then ask the Holy Spirit, "What will lead me to more peace?" Remember that peace is your one goal, always, and peace always leads to a sense of inner joy and love. Love is simple; the ego makes it complicated. Life is simple. There are no plans that you need to make. Everything is laid out before you by the Holy Spirit. You just need to continue to practice your willingness to accept His plan, His path of peace and joy for you; to allow yourself to be carried through a happy and peaceful dream.

The Son of God is bound by nothing and yet you try with great effort to bind him with everything you have made. This is blasphemy. You're trying to make something of the Son of God that He is not. How silly this is! Remember that forgiveness is the key to happiness. If you feel irritated or disturbed or anxious, then this is a time for forgiveness; if you would make peace your friend. The governing Law of Love is laid out. There is no other law. The Law of Love is simple. Choose love for that is all there is. Choose love and peace will be given you. Choose love and the joy of the Kingdom is yours. The Law of Love is bound by nothing. Now ponder that awhile.

Okay. Thanks.

ooooo

Journal Entry on Lesson 278

If I am bound, my Father is not free.

My Dear Brother,

Let us practice lying down all thoughts and aspirations today, and practice remembering Him Who created you. You have your flash cards that you use to help you remember things of the world. But these will not help you to experience the flashes of the memory of God within your mind. Each time you pick up your flash cards now, may they be a reminder to you of a holy purpose; to practice remembering and freeing the Light of your Father within your mind.

When the Light of your Father is allowed to freely express Himself and creation through you, you will experience His freedom and joy. Allow your mind to open up to the Light within it. True perception will give you all the gifts of the Kingdom.

How wonderful it is when your perception shifts for a moment to the Light. How friendly the healing of Truth is when you perceive it. The vision of the Light within your mind frees all things and you along with it, showing you the path and the way back to the memory of your Father.

Forgiveness is in order and desiring to perceive only the Light is the way to freedom and joy. The Light delivers happiness and peace and a sense of well-being; that everything is okay. This is because the Light you perceive is the Light of Love Itself. It truly is a wonderful gift to perceive It, for It *is* the gift of salvation from the Father to His Son. It is the remaining call of creation, the echo of God's Son perceived as his True Self. It is here that he will find his peace and freedom at last.

Forgiveness is in order, let all things go and perceive only the Light within your mind instead. This gift God has given to you Himself is the answer and the way to freedom at last. Freedom from the laws that you thought bound God's Son.

∞∞∞

Journal Entry on Lesson 279

Creation's freedom promises my own.

SIMPLE FORGIVENESS

Several years ago, as I awoke just before 3 am, two words were clear in my mind...

Simple Forgiveness.

3 am, a time of silence in the world. But it wasn't silent in my thoughts. Many ideas came to mind as I realized that Paul hadn't arrived home yet from his weekly helicopter training flight. 3 hours late yet. Of course the ego brings gloom and doom shouting, "Something has gone wrong!"

Holy Spirit whispered, "Simple Forgiveness."

Paul arrived 15 minutes later.

I had been following the story of the Amish schoolchildren on the news websites. I lived in the Harrisburg/Lancaster area in the 1980s for a few years so I felt a resonance in my heart with the Amish folk. In all that occurred, the Holy Spirit continues to whisper, "Simple Forgiveness." And that is what I am hearing from the Amish in these news stories, that they have forgiven the gunman, and have given everything to God, showed love and compassion to the gunman's wife and family, and it is time to move forward. Their plain and simple life of peace practices....

Simple Forgiveness.

In roughly 1993, I came across the book "Plain and Simple" by Sue Bender. Sue had left her home, husband and two sons to spend a couple of years living with the Amish. She found a sense of inner quiet in their daily rituals. The old clutter of her life now giving over to the life of simplicity and clarity. A life of freedom was found. I rather enjoyed this moving book that appeared just before *A Course in Miracles* did in my life. It coming to mind just now is a reminder for me again of the simple life, a life of practicing....

Simple Forgiveness.

The recent situation with the conflict between ACIM Teachers has also alerted me to this practice. It is for me to continue to practice forgiveness more and more with everything that I read, hear, see and experience in this world. It is for me to go to Holy Spirit with everything and let Him shine the Light of Truth. The only side to take is IN-side with Him. That is where the truth is found. I can never agree with everyone as the world is set up that way.

I know that the Course tells me that I "weep each time an idol falls." Each time that I set up an expectation in relation to someone or something, I will always be disappointed and resentful. The answer is never found outside of me, not in a physical teacher, nor a book, not a certain outcome of a situation, no-thing. The only

Answer is found with the Holy Spirit and His Answer is one of Love, one of Peace, and one of the recognition of Innocence in all.

Freedom is promised. Dreams will end.
I am released.

And Holy Spirit whispers once again, "Simple Forgiveness."

ᴏᴏᴏᴏᴏ

Journal Entry on Lesson 280

What limits can I lay upon God's Son?

Imprisonment.

I am imprisoned by my thoughts of unforgiveness. I imprison my brothers with my thoughts of judgment.

Let me loose the tight and rusty chains that bind so that I and my brother may walk free and into the Light of Truth. My brother and I are the same. It is the ego that devises ways to make separation real. It hides behind truth in exchange for its own "truth" which are only lies of deception. Lies that I believe. Lies about my brothers when in truth my brother is sinless.

I walk in sinlessness.

If I see sin in my brother, then I see it in me. If I see guilt, then it is merely the mirror of my own creation. The thoughts that keep me limited in.

Forgiveness releases the walls of fear. And it is the walls of fear that I want crumbled into dust.

Holy Spirit, this day I cast loose my fears, my judgments, my grievances unto you for I would exonerate myself from the pain of the chains that I myself have made. I no longer desire to sit in the ashes of my projections. I surrender all to you willingly. It is freedom that I seek and it is through my forgiveness that I and my brothers are set free.

Freedom.

∞∞∞

Journal Entry on Lesson 281

I can be hurt by nothing but my thoughts.

When we have fallen into the habit of listening to the ego's critical voice, we will always be dragged down in spirit. The ego thought system that we have decided to join with will always bring us pain in some form. It takes willingness and a mindfulness to change our minds to join with the thoughts of God.

Your Father has given you a gift. It is the gift of Light that is hidden within your mind. Merely choosing to let everything go with your mind and turning all of your desire to allow the Light to come through, will heal all of the thoughts that were hurting you and causing you pain.

The critical thoughts of the ego are used to judge and perceive the sinfulness of everyone and everything including yourself. These thoughts tear down and separate. None of them are true and it is you who allows them to be made up. It is a habit to believe in them. And like all things in the world, your belief in them and your habits can be changed by merely changing your mind about them. The easiest way to do this and the only way in reality, is to turn your attention to the memory of God hidden behind the veils of darkness within your mind. Recognizing that His Light truly exists and can be perceived is the first step in salvation.

Your desire to let everything go that you perceive now, which is forgiveness of the world, in exchange to allow the perception of the Light to illuminate your mind is the gift that will instantly begin to heal all your pain and woes. Practice laying everything down with your mind and only perceive your Father's Light within you. It is by His Grace, His Light, His Gift that all happiness and joy will be instantly restored to you. You need do nothing else but this, let it go and see His Light. The Light brings the gift of knowledge. The Light brings the gift of joy, healing and contentment. It brings a knowing that everything is okay and all is well.

These gifts of the Kingdom are yours to behold and to have right now. The Light reveals the Truth to you that you already are the Kingdom of Heaven. It is your light, your reflection, your sinlessness, your holiness that the Holy Spirit will show you as you allow Him to show you your Light that resides within you. It blazes away shining in eternal glory. O what a beautiful sight to remember and to behold within yourself. What a beautiful gift your Father has given to you, for He has created you pure and holy as Himself.

You are sinless as Himself. In reality, you are Love like Love Itself. Block the vision of His Light and the sound of His Voice no more, for the holy perception that He has given to you will restore the memory of Him at last. His are the gifts that you desire; there is nothing else.

∞∞∞∞

Journal Entry on Lesson 282

I will not be afraid of love today.

Dear Father,

Today, through Your Holy Spirit, You helped me to remember how I have been afraid of love. You helped me to remember how I have habitually held back from expressing love to others because of fearful feelings in the moment. I have often felt ashamed for feeling afraid to do simple little loving things for another, such as giving someone a heartfelt and meaningful hug within my own family.

As I reflected on this today, I realized that I usually held back because I didn't feel safe. For some reason, I came to believe in my unconscious mind that love was going to hurt me somehow. Somewhere along the line, probably from my childhood, I learned the lessons of love from the ego's perspective. All these years, without even really realizing it, I have been listening to the voice of the ego; the voice of fear. I have been holding back from what my heart really wanted to do. I really do not understand all of the things that I do or why I do them, but I do want to learn how to be free and happy again.

Father, I want to learn how to be truly free of fear. I am tired of feeling afraid for one reason or another. I am tired of feeling afraid to be joyful and happy more of the time. I am tired of worrying about what I could be doing or should be doing.

Father, I would really like to try something new for a change. Would You please teach and show me how to be truly happy and joyful all the time? I realize that it means that I have to be willing to let go of old ideas and beliefs that I have about myself and about the world. I am ready to do that more and more now. In fact, I am going to make a commitment to You right now.

Father, I am going to practice giving others, especially those closest to me, more meaningful hugs each day. I have to admit, the thought of committing to that is scary for me even now. But I know I can call upon Your strength to heal these fearful feelings within me. In fact, I would like to pause for a moment to call upon You now to heal this fear. I do not want to be afraid of love anymore.

(pause; going within)

Father, as I reflected on this in silence I became aware of my fear of commitment. I do not know or understand why, but I have had a deep fear of making a commitment to anyone else but myself.

Father, I feel deeply ashamed of myself for this. I am sorry. Please heal this for me. Please help me to forgive myself, to change my perception, to change my beliefs and ways. I do not want to be right anymore. I just want to learn how to be free and happy again, all the time. I want to remember what it was like to be with You again.

(pause; going within)

Father, I am glad to know that You are within me. I am glad that I can see and feel Your healing light when I call upon You. Thank You for Your gift. I feel bad for my lack of willingness to try to listen more. I will work on that. Whenever I start to feel the temptation of negative thinking or feelings of being afraid to act or do something, I am going to practice calling upon You within my mind more and more for help in those moments. Thank you Father for being there. I really do appreciate You too.

∞∞∞

Journal Entry on Lesson 283

My true Identity abides in You.

If you believe in your true Identity, you believe in the power of Love. You are Love my Child, you are everything that I am. In the Light of Oneness you will accept the knowledge of the shining essence of your birthright. Remember how your group member shared the process that she uses, seeing the outer shell of the body crumble to dust allowing the light and innocent essence of the person to radiate through. Remember this when you look at yourself or anyone. See beyond the outside shell of who they think they are, who you think you are.

See the Pure Joy.

Take a sip from the healing waters here in My Garden. Let my Love rejuvenate you, bring you to a higher plane of existence. Rise my Child, rise and walk with Me. Know that your beauty is changeless, eternal and free. Break away from the exterior you have encased yourself in. Break free of limits and limited thinking. All the limitations, judgments, despairs are now dust.

You can laugh now.

You can laugh at what never was and rejoice in what shall ever be.

∞∞∞∞

Journal Entry on Lesson 284

I can elect to change all thoughts that hurt.

Most of the time we spend our day listening to a stream of

thoughts that come from the ego part of the mind. These thoughts tend to wear us down emotionally, physically, mentally and spiritually. We have become accustomed to listening to this inner ego voice for a long time now. Hanging on to these thoughts busies the mind and blocks out the peace and tranquility that lies beyond. Each thought we think with the ego mind makes pain in some form. As we continue to practice our mind training in the letting go of these thoughts, we learn to allow the thoughts of the higher mind of God into our awareness.

Each day we are choosing to see what we see. When we choose to see with the ego, we perceive a world of pain. When we choose to listen to the ego, we hear a critical world that brings pain. When we choose to feel with the ego, we feel a world of pain. Each thought we think is creative. Our thoughts create our experience of reality.

As we learn how to let go of listening to the ego thoughts that habitually stream into our mind, we begin to learn how to receive the thoughts of God. As God's thoughts are allowed to stream into our mind, a new reality will begin to be perceived and experienced around us. God's thoughts are pure and perfect; they heal all things we perceive now with love and joy. Everything is okay in God's world which is where our true inner mind is right now. And in God's world there is no pain, there are no problems, there is nothing to worry about, there is only an eternal feeling of peace, joy, love, contentment and everlasting happiness. This is the world you seek to find now, hidden deep within your mind. It is a choice to find and experience this world.

Let us continue to develop the habit of remembering and accepting the world that Father created for us now. Let us continue to practice letting go of everything we see and perceive now, and allow God some silent space within our minds so that He may come through with His Light, His Voice, and His

Thoughts of Joy for us. When His Light is allowed and accepted into our awareness, His Joy is accepted and immediately experienced. His happiness and our Oneness with Him begins to be accepted and realized. Our joy in receiving the awareness of Him begins to fill us and make us feel whole and complete. We begin to have a knowing that we are not alone and friendless, but instead, we truly have One Who walks with us that is much greater and mightier than any friend we thought we made in this world.

∞∞∞∞

Journal Entry on Lesson 285

My holiness shines bright and clear today.

I did not wake in joy initially as the lesson suggests. Yet, even with a migraine, I realized it was an opportunity to forgive the migraine and simply rest in my holiness and I did so as Paul read today's reading. I fell dreamily back to sleep with happy expectation of waking to a day filled with peace instead of pain.

A little later that morning, awake and feeling clearer, I began my communion time with Holy Spirit. As I drifted off in meditation, I began to hear the song "On a Clear Day." I remembered the song vaguely as one that we sang in Glee Club back in high school many years ago. Recalling all the lyrics was escaping me but I could hear in my mind the haunting line of "On a clear day you can see forever." Then all of a sudden I recalled something to the effect of rising and looking about and remembering who you really are.

With great excitement then, of course I just had to do a search for the lyrics on the internet. And my goodness how beautiful the lyrics are! Tears began to stream down my face. Thank You Holy

Spirit for reminding me of my radiance and holiness in such a glorious yet simple, unexpected form.

On a clear day
Rise and look around you
And you'll see who you are
On a clear day
How it will astound you
That the glow of your being
Outshines every star
You'll feel part of every mountain sea and shore
You can hear
From far and near
A word you've never, never heard before...
And on a clear day...On a clear day...
You can see forever...
And ever...
And ever...
And ever more. . .

~From the musical On A Clear Day You Can See Forever

And so for me...

As I release all the bothersome thoughts to You, Holy Spirit, my mind is clear and bright. I ascend above the battleground of the world and all its seeming destruction, pain and misery. I rise to truly embrace my glory in the Father, the Creator of the Son, the Creator of me.

With this clarity of purpose, I am joyous, even giddy, at the discovery of the truth of Who I really am. I am the Light of Love, the Word of Love. I glow, I radiate, I extend the Rays of Salvation to all, for I am part of all. My healing is their healing. My miracles are their miracles. My Light is their Light. Joyously we sing, "We are One."

I can see forever, endlessly, eternally each time I lay aside the clouds of doubt, the fog of fear. Your Light beams through as a dazzling beacon inviting and bidding me Home to You. Yes, it is a clear day, a crystal, clear day of fear removed, forgiveness given, and Love realized.

What a glorious day indeed!

Amen!

ooooo

Journal Entry on Lesson 286

The hush of Heaven holds my heart today.

Today we practice being mindful around our hearts. We allow our hearts to be open and at peace. We allow the Light of Christ to shine through into the awareness of our minds, and at the same time, feel the Light of Peace flowing through our hearts and out into the world.

In quiet stillness we practice this today. Remembering to allow our minds to be still of all thoughts and to rest in quietness is the key to finding peace within yourself. It is here where you will find a deep peace and tranquil mind that is perfectly still and rests in God. This is where the holy altar is found; where the Son meets his Father and recognizes They are one.

Your holy altar is found within, in the place of deep silence and peace. It is here you will come to meet the Light of your Father and of your Self, and to hear Him speak to you. This is your place of Communion. This is the holiest of holy grounds. The sanctuary where all is forgiven and the new world of the Christ is revealed to you. This is the place where the resurrection of the Son of God is realized. This is the place where all things have been healed through forgiveness and the recognition that you are the Son of God comes into your awareness. It is here that the Holy Spirit takes your hand and leads the way to the hush of Heaven, your rightful place and Home.

∞∞∞

Journal Entry on Lesson 287

You are my goal, my Father. Only You.

Lay aside the meanderings of this fictional world. Come and be enveloped and robed in Truth. Your Father now calls to you, do you not hear His Voice? The goal is simple, it is Home. I repeat, your goal as you are willing to accept it is the Love of Home.

Carry nothing on your journey but your desire for God. It is only this that your lonely heart pursues. Filling your heart with the trappings of the outside world will never satisfy your craving for true Love. Do not seek it there in the world, in the body, in others, in what is not real. Put in mind the purpose of Heaven. It softly calls you, listen awhile.

Reach no more for the deceiving tactics of the ego. It is like a magician's sleight of hand, the ego makes it appear that your happiness is found there in the world, there in the smoke and mirrors. And it seems to work for awhile, but yet deep within you a churning, an unrest and unsettling is felt. Unhappiness rising to the surface and you know that it needs to be released.

Release it to Me and you will see through the grayness and poverty of the ego. See through into the abundance of the Light of

Heaven. It is Here where you belong. Set your sights now on the Light and be fooled no longer.

My Child,

Your Father deeply loves you and see you in total wholeness. See yourself in this wholeness and holiness. He sees you as the glorious extension of Him Who is Love.

Recognize Love. Recognize your Father. Recognize your Self. Be not afraid of Love today.

Recognize the one and only True Source. It comes from far beyond what your petty eyes behold. The body will never show you the Light of Heaven. Within you is all that is required for connecting to and remembering your dear Home.

Relax now and let go. The tension clouds your judgments and the tension is your judgments. In a relaxed state, your natural state, you can receive the wisdom that you need to journey forward.

Make your goal today of that of your Father and of His Love.

You want no other.

Accept this and freedom is yours now and forever.

∞∞∞∞

Journal Entry on Lesson 288

Let me forget my brother's past today.

An unkind word is spoken, and then another.
A thought of hate, a gesture of contempt, a stance of anger.

Grievances and judgment mortar these bricks of pain together, one by one.

Another wall built between a brother and I.

And so it continues. Each nuance of my brother's voice, each gesture he makes, each word unsaid, I make assumptions and then fill my mind with resentments.

More bricks.

This can continue for a long time, perhaps a lifetime, building the wall higher and higher. What does this all do for me but keep me imprisoned behind the wall of fear. Keeping me away from my brother when I think I am keeping him away from me.

Could there truly be happiness here behind these cold, stone walls?

Could there be another way?

Indeed.

Through my forgiveness the walls can come crumbling down. These walls that seem impenetrable and solid are now to be seen as a mere wall of dust as I chuckle at the mistake that I have made. It is madness that kept me apart from you dear brother. Sheer madness. I was insane to think that you and I would be better off alone, but I was wrong for I need you dear one to hold my hand, to join with me and other brothers as we journey Home.

No one is left behind the walls of fear.

Sound the trumpet again and again and the walls turn into dust and rubble. Nothing there but my own thoughts that have held it in place and it is my own thoughts of Love that remove it from its space.

There is a now built upon the dust a garden filled with the glory of the Father, robed in colors so rich and deep, and ah... the fragrance of life. It is sweet. It is lush and green. It is a loving place, a place of rest, a place of peace. A place where I shall let go of all that occurred before this time of joining and stay forever here. Nowhere to go but into the garden of Love.

It is quiet here and this is where we shall be, quenching our thirst from the living water here. Eating from the fruits of the Spirit that truly nurture us.

We are Home.

Thank You Holy Spirit for this holy instant in which I leave behind all insanity and come into the joy of the Kingdom.

> *"Only a little wall of dust still stands between you and your brother. Blow on it lightly and with happy laughter, and it will fall away. And walk into the garden love has prepared for both of you."* T-18.VIII.13:6-8

∞∞∞∞

Journal Entry on Lesson 289

The past is over. It can touch me not.

Dear Father,

What peace would I have if I let slip from my fingers all the moments that came before this moment in time. I cannot truly hold them, they are but vapors of something that I have placed all value in that really means nothing; a yesterday barely remembered. Only those moments that I gleam from it that I hold within, and even those are not even true to the moment as it was occurring. Judgment has been in my mind, either good or bad, it is still judgment that I behold with my sight.

With judgment I cannot journey forward and into the freshness and wholeness of the lush garden that is before me. In the past, it is but dust and sand, no oasis of water. Mirages all the same. Even the future is something that I only behold in my mind based upon what I know about the past. I truly do not know. I only pretend to know what I think the outcome will be to any situation.

Today, I let go of the grip that I have held on the past, its pains and hurts, even its happy days. They are not the reflection of the shining Love that is held with Your Eyes, dear Father and never could be. Your peace is only what I seek and brushing aside the past, laying it down on the side of the road will answer my call for serenity in my life.

The past is merely a dream that I dreamed at one time. I truly cannot touch it, or feel it or relive it. It is all in my thoughts that I bring into my weary mind.

The past prevents me from living in the present moment. How can I dance in happiness if I dwell on the past. Dwelling on the past robs me of my own happiness. It is my choice!

I seek differently today. I seek a different present moment, one of the holy instant of Love. I choose to remain in Eternity with You.

Amen! Hallelujah!

∞∞∞∞

Journal Entry on Lesson 290

My present happiness is all I see.

The world that we see with our eyes is not real. It is difficult for us to believe this because we seem to be seeing and doing things everyday. The world seems to offer us many things to do and places to go where we can play. Mail-order catalogs and advertisements entice us with things to buy and do. The colorful ads and the descriptive writings give us the illusion that we need to have these things in order to gain happiness. And we come to believe these things over and over again but only to find in the end that true happiness really wasn't delivered. It was just a temporary illusion offered by the ego to deceive the Son of God once again.

There is another form of seeing that is available to each and every one of us. There is a light within each and everyone's mind that we can learn how to see. It is the Light of God and of His world that He will show us if we but desire to see Him with our hearts.

Quiet your mind of all your busy thoughts, close your eyes and observe the dark screen of your mind's eye for Father to show you the Light of His world. When you wholly desire to see His Light within your mind He will begin to show it to you. First the little sparks, then the stars and the stars begin to blend together into one light, and in the perception of the light happiness is seen and felt. You begin to see and know your Friend in the Light. The Light begins to show you your way Home for miracles are seen in the light.

As you remember to forgive and let go and desire only to see His Light, it will be shown to you by the illumination of your mind. This visible light is as clear as day and is perceived more clearly than the lights you now perceive in your world. At this holy meeting place with your Father you will begin to hear His Voice speak to you very clearly. You will come to cherish this holy meeting place within yourself more and more as you come to know your Friend Who resides there with you.

As you learn to open up and commune and communicate with Father in your mind in open silence, it is here that you will receive healing and direction in your life. His Light and direction always provides healing and happiness and joy if you but follow His will. Take all of your perceived problems and concerns to Him and learn to commune with Him, learn to set them aside at the holy altar and be with Him in silence. His Light will come and flow through you.

You are a channel of His Light in the world in which you walk. Learn to allow It to flow through you as you go through your day. You can allow yourself to open up to a constant flow of the Light of Healing and Love. You will feel It flowing through you and out into the world from your heart and as you open up to this, you will see the Light too. This is your joy, this is your happiness, this is your holiness flowing through you and being reflected back to you in the world you now perceive.

This is your present happiness that you are learning to see and feel each day with the vision of Christ within your mind. This is your joy, this is your Love.

ooooo

Journal Entry on Lesson 291

This is a day of stillness and of peace.

Father, thank you for all of the help that You have given to me. I especially appreciate how helpful the light is when I get into the space where I am feeling troubled and worried about something. I am so glad that I have learned how to open up and receive the light Jesus talks about in the Course. It has changed my life so much I can hardly believe it. Perhaps I can hardly believe it is because I am still learning to accept the fact that I too was worthy of receiving Your light. I spent many years believing that I was not a very good person. I still struggle with those beliefs even now but with Jesus' help I now have found the way out.

Yeah! Thank you Father, thank you Jesus and thank you Holy Spirit! I really do appreciate all of the help that You have given to me all along the way. The little nudges, the synchronicities, the gifts, the Voices and of course the Lights, the Lights, the Lights! Thank you for the Lights, Father! I am so glad that everything He (Jesus) said is true. There really is another world and we can see it! Yeah! I know that I am still learning how but I am ready Father! Let us keep going, keep forgiving with the Light! I want to see! I want to see it all! I want to fly with you again, Father! I want to fly! Thank You, Father! I love You too!

Let me reflect Your Light Father as I enter into the hush of Heaven, this day spent in stillness and of peace. There is only loveliness here as there is no "evil" in Your name. There is only Love, only Oneness. My forgiveness returns me to the vision of purity and innocence. And I must be holy for everywhere I go You are there with me always and forever.

Thank You for the path of forgiveness that I journey hand in hand with my Friend, my Teacher and my Guide. Amen.

∞∞∞∞

Journal Entry on Lesson 292

A happy outcome to all things is sure.

Release the outcome.
That phrase has been uttered many times not only by me but by others that I know.

Let go and let God.
Ah, another wisdom morsel.

This lesson reminds me of the freedom I experience when I

release all preconceived notions on what "should" be. The ego has a way of presenting every good reasoning behind the worry, the planning, the attempt at controlling. "Sorry God this one You cannot handle." My fear is too great if I let go. Funny what comes to mind. It's like planning a first time trip to Disney World but arriving and finding it closed. If I don't control the outcome, who will? What? Leave it up to God? What if I do not like what He has planned? What if it hurts? What if His Kingdom, His Heavenly World is not what I expect?

And so the ego goes on to make something else, more elaborate and intricate, yet all with false backdrops to conceal the truth of its illusory nature.

Do I want joy?
Indeed I do.
I accept that I know nothing. I accept God's will for me, after all His will for me is perfect happiness. Perfect happiness, how perfect!

Can my plans brings me perfect happiness?

Perhaps seeming happiness, but perfect happiness?
No, never shall it be for only in God is there true perfection in His Will.

I have no problems as I rest in peace. I can sense the flow and ride the current and witness the enfoldment of something that I could never expect or predict. In releasing the outcome I can experience something much grander.

Simple, yet elegant. The concepts, the words become simpler and simpler, easier and easier to understand. Who needs elaborate explorations and explanations, stances of rightness of knowledge, applause for mere words?

It is not needed. It is a trap, it is yet another device of specialness and separation. Thank You Holy Spirit for that reminder. And so I put forth these words only out of communion with You Holy Spirit. May they remind me of God's covenant and assurance that a happy outcome to all things is sure.

∞∞∞∞

Journal Entry on Lesson 293

All fear is past and only love is here.

There are two parts to your mind. The one part which is the one that you are used to paying attention to and listening to is the ego part of the mind. The ego part of the mind has memories of your seeming past. It is critical and judgmental and sees the negative part of things in the world around you see all the time. The ego part of the mind is used to block your awareness of the other part of your mind which is the mind that you share with the Light of God.

When we learn how to ignore the ego part of the mind and tune in to the God part of our mind we begin to see things in a whole different light, literally. We start to have experiences of the other part of our mind as we practice trying to perceive its Light from a place of meditative silence and stillness. As we practice stilling our minds we're also allowing an opportunity for the God part of our mind to come through the ego part of the mind and speak to us. The Voice come through the darkness illuminating as it speaks to us.

The ego part of the mind is only able to present to us memories of our illusory past within the world and assumptions and projections into the future. But the God part of our mind shows us the world we came from before the illusion of time and physical reality began (the tiny mad idea).

Keep in mind that we are really One Spirit, we are not these physical bodies that we seem to be perceiving right now. We have only forgotten temporarily who we really are as the One Spirit Being.

As that One there is an aspect of it where we are having a dream. And, the dream and the experience of the dream is that we are not a spiritual being but instead we are a physical being, limited by a physical body with all kinds of limitations.

Through the daily practice of stilling our minds in the silence of meditation we can allow ourselves to become open to experiencing the reality of our True Selves as a spiritual being in Heaven right now. And through that practice and the experiences of our spiritual self we will come to know personally that this world isn't really true. We will begin to recognize that there is another world and that it is a Heavenly joyful world that we can choose to experience anytime we want. What a wonderful gift this is from our Father Who has given us the ability to remember our Reality as it is in the Heaven right now. The Light will come and His Voice will come and speak to us as our desire to see and hear Him grows within our hearts and in our minds.

This is a course in practical application and demonstration. As I have said before it is not a course in theories and ideas. It is a course in sitting down and doing the work with me and the Holy Spirit. Let go of the small talk in your mind and let me talk for a change. I will show you the way out; the ego only shows you the way to disaster. The ego leads you to death where I and the Holy Spirit lead you to life.

Thank you brother Jesus for this message. Amen.

Journal Entry on Lesson 294

My body is a wholly neutral thing.

We just love how Holy Spirit guides us to just the perfect sections in the Course to expand on the Workbook Lesson. The theme He has given us is sinlessness within one's self and our brothers.

> To see a sinless body is impossible, for holiness is positive and the body is merely neutral. It is not sinful, but neither is it sinless. As nothing, which it is, the body cannot meaningfully be invested with attributes of Christ or of the ego. Either must be an error, for both would place the attributes where they cannot be. And both must be undone for purposes of truth. T-20.VII.4:4-8

> Your question should not be, "How can I see my brother without the body?" Ask only, "Do I really wish to see him sinless?" And as you ask, forget not that his sinlessness is <your> escape from fear. T-20.VII.9: 1-3

I can only be the Son of God. And what God created is wholly perfect and innocent. My charge is to see beyond this limitation I have made and have made for my brother. I perceive guilt and so I perceive the walls of separation between us. But the body can move beyond that thought, it can be used as a device for me to communicate the sinlessness that truly exists from brother to brother, from us to God.

> Your function is to show your brother sin can have no cause. How futile must it be to see yourself a picture of the proof that what your function is can never be! The Holy Spirit's picture changes not the body into something it is not. It only takes away from it all signs of accusation and of blamefulness. Pictured without a purpose, it is seen as neither sick nor well, nor bad nor good. No grounds are offered that it may be judged in any way at

all. It has no life, but neither is it dead. It stands apart from all experience of love or fear. For now it witnesses to nothing yet, its purpose being open, and the mind made free again to choose what it is for. Now is it not condemned, but waiting for a purpose to be given, that it may fulfill the function that it will receive. T-27.I.9: 1-10

And so with shining sight, the head filled with Light I can look upon that which is the truth, that which is life. I need nothing else, I want nothing else but the commitment to the one goal of God. Commitment to truly live and breathe in Him. I do this when I share the wholeness with my brothers. I do this when I look beyond the gestures, the nuances in my brothers voice, the body language, the physical judgments that I have previously made. I look deep within the eyes, those glorious windows to the soul, and see even beyond the physical eyes to the Eyes of God. This is the loving purity of who we are. We live and move together my brother, let us live.

Into this empty space, from which the goal of sin has been removed, is Heaven free to be remembered. Here its peace can come, and perfect healing take the place of death. The body can become a sign of life, a promise of redemption, and a breath of immortality to those grown sick of breathing in the fetid scent of death. Let it have healing as its purpose. Then will it send forth the message it received, and by its health and loveliness proclaim the truth and value that it represents. Let it receive the power to represent an endless life, forever unattacked. And to your brother let its message be, "Behold me, brother, at your hand I live." T-27.I.10:1-7

I release now all that I ever thought the body was, release all guilt and self-judgment that has been placed there. I release all thoughts of having to change the body to match an ideal that in reality can never be reached. I allow the body to be nothing, to be in its neutral state as it always was. My meaning upon it is only what keeps it as it is. It is nothing. Let me use this body today for

Your service Father, to join instead of part, to enfold instead of destroy. Let me love my brothers and myself as One today.

> *The simple way to let this be achieved is merely this; to let the body have no purpose from the past, when you were sure you knew its purpose was to foster guilt. For this insists your crippled picture is a lasting sign of what it represents. This leaves no space in which a different view, another purpose, can be given it. You do <not> know its purpose. You but gave illusions of a purpose to a thing you made to hide your function from yourself. This thing without a purpose cannot hide the function that the Holy Spirit gave. Let, then, its purpose and your function both be reconciled at last and seen as one. T-27.I.11:1-7*

∞∞∞∞

Journal Entry on Lesson 295

The Holy Spirit looks through me today.

When I went to the 2005 ACIM Conference held in Salt Lake City, UT, I had a miracle experience that I believe touches upon the experience Jesus is talking about in today's lesson. I remember when I first arrived at the conference hotel, like everyone else, I got into line to check-in at the front counter. While I waited for my turn, I noticed that I was feeling unusually happy, open and peaceful. I felt very light in my heart; the burdens of the world did not seem to be weighing me down as usual. When it was my turn to check-in, I quietly stepped up to the counter and introduced myself to the clerk. When the gentleman turned away to retrieve my paperwork and room key, I suddenly began to observe stars of white lights randomly popping up into my field of view and begin streaking across my vision like little comets. I just quietly stood there with a smile on my face and observed them for several moments. I felt delighted to see them. The white streaks of lights almost seemed to be revealing to me the world of light that really lies beyond the world we normally see with our eyes.

As I spent time tuning into Jesus and the Holy Spirit this morning, talking with them about today's lesson, the memory of the experience above came to me. I believe that in those moments at the hotel front desk I was experiencing an example of what it is like to see what the Holy Spirit sees. I think it is an example of how we can allow the Holy Spirit to look through us. Normally, when we see, we see a world full of distortions, depths, colors, shades, movement, change, shift and separation. But the Holy Spirit sees beyond our world and only sees a world of oneness. All the Holy Spirit sees is a world of one light. It does not change. It is just one continuous eternal light. If the unforgiven world is the world of distortion that we see, then the forgiven world must be something that shows us something else like oneness. And it does! Jesus tells us in the Course that the light that we can see is the symbol for Love. He also tells us that when we see the light we can feel it too; we can feel Love at the same time. It is our way home. If we forget about all the things that we normally worry about or preoccupy our minds with and offer our openness and eyes to the Holy Spirit, He will give gifts back to us in the form of these types of light experiences. He will give us gifts of perceiving the light of the real world, the light of our true home, the light of our true reality, the light of our true Selves. What a wonderful gift our Father has given to us. Thank you Jesus for *A Course in Miracles*, thank you Holy Spirit for helping us and thank you Father for Your gifts to us.

∞∞∞∞

Journal Entry on Lesson 296

The Holy Spirit speaks through me today.

In each conversation that I have today, each person that I touch, each student, each one I counsel, each unexpected friendly 'hello', let me know myself as healed. Let my voice be Your Voice of all that I want to learn. Those voices that I experience outside of me are merely aspects of me. Let me love each one wholly and completely and in complete joy.

If I am aware of someone's voice not coming from truth or seems to be abusive in some way, let me know forgiveness. Let forgiveness sing in my heart and let me harmonize with the peace that is returned to me.

All that I give today, I give through You, Dear Spirit. Let my words be of Love, as a healing balm to any soul that feels the sting of pain of unworthiness or fear. Let it soothe me as well.

Holy Spirit, be in my mind, on my lips and in my heart this day. Amen.

∞∞∞

Journal Entry on Lesson 297

Forgiveness is the only gift I give.

In 2006, as I was preparing for my weekly radio show at the time, "Tuesdays with Spirit", I was gifted with insightful material to share. It seemed that Holy Spirit guided my hand to the perfect pages. First, a letter I had received from someone here in Madison on their forgiveness of self, to being specifically guided to sections in the Text, and then guiding me within to release and cleanse even more my own psyche right in the moment of the live sharing. The following is some of what I shared that day.

If you would like to listen to the recording of the show, go to our archives: www.miraclesonelightuniversity.org

It is the file, October 24, 2006 - Topic: Healing and Forgiveness

Go to peace for a moment.

Holy Spirit, today I make the commitment to let you be in charge of my mind. I let all private thoughts step back and I keep opening myself to You, opening to You my Inner Teacher. You are my Inner Teacher of Life, of Love, of Joy, of Peace.

As I keep opening up, I open up to Love. I open up to God. So I imagine now blending into the ocean of Universal Love. Its healing waters is cleansing away all dead thoughts, shedding all perception of limitation and lack and I let these thoughts gently be dissolved into forgiveness.

My willingness is growing stronger and stronger. I let go of perceptions and I am aware of the healing waters of forgiveness washing through the places in my mind. I let my mind be healed today.

I received a photocopy of an email from a friend's friend who was allowing the healing waters to cleanse and purify her. She has been emailing this to so many people. She wrote in this letter, "I'm sorry" to herself, and then listed many things that she was sorry about not only about herself but towards others in her life.

I'm sorry that I didn't make better choices for myself. I'm sorry that I didn't take the time to make sure I was safe. I'm sorry that I stepped over my intuition and refused to listen to the messages of the universe. I'm sorry that I couldn't make everyone understand my perspective. I'm sorry that I let others influence my decisions. I am sorry to all the people that I have hurt directly or indirectly....And with this, I ask all the sweet, innocent parts of myself to forgive me.....give me the courage now to forgive myself.

Some thoughts that came to mind with this letter.

Tears not only cleanses the eyes, but the psyche. Saying "I'm sorry" moves me to the place of Love. Forgiveness is my function. How can I help others if I need the help (unhealed healer).

> *Healing is a sign that you want to make whole. p. 197, Text*
> *Healing thus becomes a lesson in understanding and the more you practice it the better teacher and learner you become. p. 197, Text*
> *Can you imagine how beautiful those you forgive will look to you? p. 352, Text*

How beautiful you will look to yourself when you look in the mirror? When you see through the eyes of Love?

> *Nothing in boundless love could need forgiveness. p. 548, Text*

Love is never having to say you're sorry. What does that mean, Spirit? Nothing in unconditional love needs forgiveness. Guilt free. Apologizing helps me to get into that place of love. What is it for me? I can look at different areas over my last 43 years and see where were those places I needed to forgive myself and others. Seeing the beauty in all that has occurred. Whatever has occurred, whatever turn I have taken either to the left or right, Holy Spirit, you are there with me. You travel with me even if it seems that I have taken the wrong turn. You use everything to assist me and I gladly accept the lessons and the subsequent healing.

It is time to let go of the tiny spot of sin that holds me back. Release the guilt instead of piling it on. Know truly in my heart that I am connected in perfect love. In the mind I am joined with all.

And so....

I forgive myself for entering into situations that did not serve me.
I forgive myself for being afraid of love.
I forgive myself for the feelings of unworthiness.

I forgive myself for searching outside of myself for completion.

I forgive myself for the abuse that occurred in my life and in the lives of my children.
I forgive myself for doubting.
I forgive myself for not knowing the difference.
I forgive myself for not knowing how in the past to appropriately express my emotions (anger, sadness, fear).
I forgive myself for believing in the ego self.
I forgive myself for not meeting my expectations or anyone else's.

LOVE IS FOR GIVING.....

I forgive my parents who only did what they knew how to do. I see you as the innocent children that you are.
I forgive the men who have been in my life and other relationships who didn't know the truth of who they were or the truth of who I was. I see us all now as One for I now know the truth, the truth of who I am.
I forgive the abusers and anyone else who I have blamed for squelching or stifling me.
I know that it was me that blocked me from happiness.

And it's ok. And it's ok, because forgiveness is the only gift that I give. It is healing me.

I can now look in the mirror and look into those eyes and see beyond those eyes. See beyond the face, the past, everything that has occurred and know the truth of Who I am. That I am perfect love. And that I am worthy and deserving of God's unconditional love. And that is a joyful thing. To now to be able to look in that mirror and love that person when in the past I hated that person. Not only did I hate that person, but I hated all those witnesses around me. And I called those witnesses to me because of the self-hatred that I had.

And so now with the self-love I am surrounding myself with a spiritual family of love. Thanksgiving for when we step into our own and embrace our radiance and we forgive and love.

Thank you Holy Spirit for leading me today to the perfect places not only in the Course, but in my mind for healing. Thank You for the cleansing waters of LOVE.

The music on the recording is by our friend Sean Mulcahy at www.expressthelove.org.

∞∞∞

Journal Entry on Lesson 298

I love You, Father, and I love Your Son.

While I meditated on this morning's lesson the Holy Spirit guided me to turn to page 235 of the Text. When I did, I discovered that it fell within the section titled, *The Attraction of Love for Love.* After reading it, I realized it was a perfect selection to go along with today's lesson.

In this section Jesus reminds us that it is possible to have an experience of actually remembering God. We can see His light and we can hear His voice speak to us. "Because of your Father's Love you can never forget him, for no one can forget what God himself placed in his memory. You can deny it, but you cannot lose it. A Voice will answer every question you ask, and a vision will correct the perception of everything you see...his memory shines in your mind and cannot be obliterated."

So today I pray, "I love you, Father, and I love your Son. Please restore the memory of God to me today."

He also reminds us that everything we see, hear and experience in the world around us is used to attack our true reality. We are unconsciously holding into our awareness the world around us in an attempt to block the experience of actually seeing God. "The Father has hidden his Son safely within himself, and kept him far away from your destructive thoughts, but you know neither the Father nor the Son because of them. You attack the real world every day and every hour and every minute, and yet you are surprised that you cannot see it."

And so today I pray, "I love you, Father, and I love your Son. Please restore the memory of God to me today."

Despite our attempts to attack God with our unconscious thoughts, Jesus explains to us that it is okay because it is not real, it is only an illusion and Father has taken care of everything. Father saved us the instant that a slight problem was detected. He assures us that we have been totally protected from all of this and that we are completely safe and okay at Home in Heaven right now with Father. "God's Son is as safe as his Father, for the Son knows his Father's protection and cannot fear. His Father's Love holds him in perfect peace, and needing nothing, he asks for nothing. Yet he is far from you whose Self he is, for you chose to attack him and he disappeared from your sight into his Father. He did not change, but you did. For a split mind and all its works were not created by the Father, and could not live in the knowledge of him."

And so today I pray, "I love you, Father, and I love your Son. Please restore the memory of God to me today."

Now that we are reminded that it is possible to see and hear our real world, Jesus tells us that all we need to do is to ask for the experience to be given to us. "You have but to ask for this memory, and you will remember. Yet the memory of God cannot shine in a mind that has obliterated it and wants to keep it so. For the memory of God can dawn only in a mind that chooses to remember, and that has relinquished the insane desire to control reality."

And so today I pray, "I love you, Father, and I love your Son. Please restore the memory of God to me today."

In closing, He reminds us again of what is possible right now. He asks us to practice looking upon the Vision of Christ within our minds right now, because it is all that we really want. "The real world was given you by God in loving exchange for the world you made and the world you see. Only take it from the hand of Christ and look upon it. Its reality will make everything else invisible, for beholding it is total perception. And as you look upon it you will remember that it was always so. Nothingness will become invisible, for you will at last have seen truly...Your Father could not cease to love his Son."

And so today I pray, "I love you, Father, and I love your Son. Please restore the memory of God to me today."

∞∞∞∞

Journal Entry on Lesson 299

Eternal holiness abides in me.

"Eternal holiness abides in me."
Repeating these words assures me of the truth.

Feel each word and know inside what it means. Know that it means that you are eternally holy.
This is a gift to you this day. Accept it gladly.
You are aware now of the Essence from which you came. In the heart of your Father, a Word was whispered and it was you, My

Son. Life was breathed into It and the whisper grew to an applause of Joy.

When I say that you are forever perfect and untouched, it means exactly as I say. No more stories, loved One. No need for them. For you abide in Me, and in Me you abide in the purest and clearest Light. It is a light beyond what you even could imagine. No sparks here, but a mind illuminated and a continual extension outwardly to the unending depths of the Light of Holiness. You have seen this Light many times.

This is you. Know that it illuminates your mind always. Your task is to remove those heavy drapes that you have used to veil each shining Essence of Truth. Stretch out now, go beyond what you know and let the rays gently kiss each shining face with quiet joy.

The Light of Peace is there within.

How do I know when I have reached Heaven?

You will know. You will know without a doubt when revelation has been met. It is undeniable. Remember the experience that you had some time ago. It was beyond words. And it is even beyond these words that you write here. Have you noticed that you find it harder and harder to put into words these experiences? How can the limitations of mere words express the Love of Heaven? They cannot. You may think all of it simplistic now and it is. You are moving beyond the need for symbols. Let others do as they may but know that communion with God is felt, not just conversed about. I assure you all is perfect.

What of these additional experiences?

Allow. Simply allow them to be what they are. You have been practicing this for a very long time. Each time it becomes a little deeper and more profound. All that you experience is used for your understanding and learning. Do not fret over the format of the questions, merely know the One Answer. Know Love. Know your Eternal Holiness that goes with to the core of your soul being. Mere garments, the body, possessions, money, and the like do not bring anyone such happiness. They are but tools. Walk in to the garden that Love has prepared for you.

You are blessed My Child in every way. Celebrate with others in Joy at this awakening that has been occurring in the witnesses of your brothers that you have joined with recently. You know not what it is for yet, but I do and all will be revealed. Trust Me. Trust Me with every opinion or second guesses. Let Me Guide. Let me bring the calm to your busy mind.

Thank You Holy Spirit. I accept all that You have shared from the Sanctuary of Love of which It was intended. I step gladly into the NOW moment and welcome what is here.

I embrace my eternal holiness that so abides in the Father. I have accepted the Will of the Father for it is also my will to accept. In Oneness do I share all the abundance of Eternal Life.

Thank You Holy Spirit. Amen.

○○○○○

Journal Entry on Lesson 300

Only an instant does this world endure.

Let us remember today to not be grasped by our perceptions of the world. The world only contains illusions; illusions designed to grasp and hold our attention away from the awareness of God. Remember to have a mindfulness about your marveling at an illusion. Your attraction to illusions will only bring about pain and death in the end. The attraction to illusions is a delaying maneuver and an act of dishonesty to one's self. When you embrace an illusion within your mind you are embracing death masked in a facade of joy. Be vigilant for your addictions to illusions.

Fortunately for you they only last an instant for the world you perceive now but came and went in an instant in the mind of God. The world you perceive now was hardly even noticed by the Father and He answered with the gift of the Holy Spirit for His Beloved Son. Nothing has ever changed His Beloved Son. He sent you a Voice and a Light that will help you to find your way Home. The Voice will speak to you very clearly as you open up to it and He will tell you all that you need to say and do for He has only one goal, to help the Father's Son awaken to the reality of the Love that He is. The Light of the other world will show you the way, may you find it now hidden within your mind. Ask the Holy Spirit for help and He will gladly help you. Ask the Holy Spirit to speak to you and His Holy Words are yours. What does your heart desire? Is it the illusions of a world long forgotten? Or, the remembrance of your Eternal Oneness with Love that created you?

∞∞∞∞

Journal Entry on Lesson 301

And God Himself shall wipe away all tears.

When I remember You, Father all sighs of doubt vanish. The heaviness of sadness of my perceived guilt is gone. I am with You Father. There is nothing more that I could desire and so now I leave behind the cloak of darkness, this manipulative tool that I have used to deceive myself that Your world was not perfect. This world that I have made, I have made out of a foundation of hurts, teardrops of pain, bricks of guilt and they will never weather the true test of Your Love. They are false, mere dust in my hands.

But, ah, Your Love is stronger than the strongest. It goes beyond the depths of my very soul and into the heart of me. I want this Father. I want the life that I share with You. This life that I have believed in, took credence in, I know that I do not have to weep over what I thought I had done because in fact I have never left You. Guilt is gone as I embrace You. I am in Heaven, NOW! I am with You always and you have assured me that You have been with me every step of the way, even as I seemingly stepped away from Your Heart. Your Love has never left. I merely covered it up with my judgments and opinions, my desires for specialness. All these blanketed my perception. But now the Light dawns and dawns brightly in my mind. The sunrise of Your Love touches all the separated ones and joins us as One. What but gratitude could be within me.

Thank You for wiping away my tears of shame and doubt and helping me to see that all is forgiven, all is simply Love. My eyes look upon now a world of joy and perhaps now only tears of joy will moist my eyes forevermore. Amen.

∞∞∞∞

Journal Entry on Lesson 302

Where darkness was I look upon the light.

Father, thank You for the light that You have given us to look upon. It is a most wonderful gift indeed. The light we see reminds us of Who we really are. When we look upon the light it also wipes our tears away and replaces them with a feeling of hope. The light we see reminds us that this world is not our home. When it comes forth from the darkness within our minds it shows us the way that is our home. It shows us that we are One at last and that all things will come to a happy ending. It shows us that we are beginning to awaken. It allows us to see that the end of the dream of exile is coming to an end at last.

Thank You Father for Your gentle light that touches the eyes of our mind and heals it. The stars of lights, soon to blend as one, will heal all minds and restore them to peace at last. Thank You Father for Your Holy Spirit Who gives us the gift of Christ's Vision to see a forgiven world at last. Thank You Father for the gift of forgiveness that allow us to behold the vision of our holy light; the vision of our True Self. The eternal light we look upon reflects our true purity and holiness back to us.

Our sinlessness and purity shines away steadily and eternally shows us our Holy Selves. May we take this final step into the holy land of light and accept our remembrance of our Holy Selves and our oneness with You the Master of all creation.

Thank You Father for creating us as one light, the same light that extends from You and to all things eternally. Your Light is the light of life itself and so we too are the light of life itself. We thank You Father for creating us and we love You . Thank You for our holy Light that we can gaze upon; where there was darkness I now look upon the Light.

ooooo

Journal Entry on Lesson 303

The holy Christ is born in me today.

Soft.
Gentle.
Peaceful.
Angelic.
Innocent.
Precious.
Embraced.
Loved.

All words used to describe the beauty of a newborn babe in one's arms. Yet, these are words that describe the Essence of your True Self. There is a connection of Love, a golden cord of Light that extends between the Parent and the Child. They sleep for just a little while longer soon to awaken into the dawning day. Rub the sleep from your eyes, let go of all your dreams. Let the warm rays of the sun touch your sweet face. You are reborn this day, reborn into Love. Amen.

∞∞∞∞

Journal Entry on Lesson 304

Let not my world obscure the sight of Christ.

What Jesus is referring to here is the shift in perception that we can experience when we practice stilling our minds during meditation on the daily lesson. When we practice settling down and stilling our minds and observing the dark screen of our mind's eye we wait for Holy Spirit to shift our perception to an experience of seeing the white Light of Christ. We will see It as clear as day as soon as it happens. We need do nothing to make it happen but sit still and observe the dark screen of our mind's eye and wait for Him to change the channel.

If you could imagine that you are just observing a dark movie screen and Holy Spirit has the remote control, in an instant, a holy instant, at precisely the perfect moment He'll press the button on the remote control and the spark or the flash from the white Light of Christ will be perceived. This is the shift we're talking about here, this is the beginning of the restoration of True Vision, True Seeing. With practice the flashes become brighter and last longer. During the longer experiences other sights will be given. The Light is a gift from Father because It shows us the way Home. It is one of the primary goals of the Course which is why Jesus spends so much time in the Workbook Lessons having us practice getting to the experience.

As I look upon this lesson today, I see how I allow the world I made to block from my sight the Truth. What I am believing in my thoughts and mind I am simply seeing it projected on the screen. If I begin today to change my mind by looking at my thoughts along with the guidance of the Holy Spirit, my world will reflect the changed perspective. I will begin to see the Light of Christ in all my brothers and the world. The illusion melts away and only the Light of God is seen. I thank you today Father for this gift of Christ Vision and also the gift of forgiveness that I give to myself each time I choose to see as You would have me see. Today, I will see only Love for I will see the Love that is reflected in me through God.

∞∞∞∞

Journal Entry on Lesson 305

There is a peace that Christ bestows on us.

Today I see that it is Your will that I am saved and so I choose peace instead of what I think this world contains for me. Your peace Father is truly a gift and today I accept it within my heart. I allow the Holy Spirit to judge truly for me all I see, think and feel. I know that when I make judgments on anyone, the world or myself, I am not making the True Judgment of Your Peace. Thus, I withhold the precious gift of You from my awareness. And so today, I will practice stepping into the space of stillness and be silent to receive Your holy Word. The Word that tells me that I am Unlimited Eternal Love as You created me. In this, I am blessed.

Father, there is a peace that Christ bestows on us. Let us dedicate today to the practice of receiving Your gift. Let us practice several times today sinking quietly down and inward to rest in that place of peace where peace will come in the holy flash of an instant. Father, we rest and wait in this place of silence for You to come to heal our minds of unholy sights and to replace them with the vision of Your Son, the reflection of our True Selves. We thank You Father for Christ has come. Let us forgive ourselves today and let everything go that would withhold us from the experience of the peace of Your Son. We thank You for Your gift to us, Father. Amen.

∞∞∞∞

Journal Entry on Lesson 306

The gift of Christ is all I seek today.

Today, we can choose to forget the world we made. The gift of Christ's vision can be given to us today if we but try. Father, help us to let go of all things that would disturb our peace today. Father, help us to remember You. Let us practice being still today with our minds quietly resting in the peace of God. Waiting for the vision of Christ to be quietly restored to us from Him Who sent us. Let today be the day that we see and experience the white Light within and hear Your holy Voice speak to us. Thank You Father for Your gift to us. Amen.

Today I come in gratitude for how else can I be as the recipient of such wondrous gifts. When I allow His Love within my heart, I am opening to a glorious treasure trove. I accept this new day, this sunrise into Heaven. As my True Self dawns, the world as I know it now simply falls away and peace fills my mind. Thank You Father for the gift of forgiveness and Your Holy Spirit that assists me to see truly.

∞∞∞∞

Journal Entry on Lesson 307

Conflicting wishes cannot be my will.

I do not desire to follow an uneasy road with twists and turns and obstacles keeping me from the peace that I truly want. The path of God is smooth and I step lightly. I cannot be on both paths at the same time. Even to attempt to do so brings me confusion. And so today, I make the clear choice to follow the Will of God. Following His Will is what He wants for me for He sees me as His holy Son. He wants my happiness, do I not want to be happy as well? Choosing happiness is choosing the Will of God. Today, I surrender to peace and allow it to enter into my ready and waiting mind. All thoughts have been given to the Holy Spirit and as peace washes over me, I accept that I am free.

Father, every time a conflicting thought or wish comes up in my mind today, help me to remember to step back and pause for a moment to let Your peace return. Give me the willingness Father to let go of all my conflicting wishes and thoughts today and allow Your peace to be restored to me, Your Holy Son. Help me to remember that all I want is Your peace. I walk with You wherever You go because You walk with me. Let's walk together today in the peace that is Your will for me. May I let go of all things that disturb my peace today in exchange for Your holy Love. Thank you Father for helping me today. Amen.

ooooo

Journal Entry on Lesson 308

This instant is the only time there is.

If we pause for a moment and look around the room that we seem to be present in now, we may see a chair or a table or a picture on the wall or a clock on the shelf. As we gaze upon these objects, the ego thought system would have us believe that we are perceiving in the moment of Now. This is a mistake in both thought and perception. What we are perceiving is interval of time and time does not exist. If we were to get a glass and a pitcher of water and carefully observe water pouring from the pitcher into the glass.

Once again the ego thought system would have us believe that we are observing something in the present moment of Now. We are not. Again, this is a mistake in thought and perception. To truly experience the moment of Now, the moment of timelessness itself, we must be still. Close your eyes, turn inward, settle down within yourself, within your mind. Let all things go, let all activities of your mind go, sink down and inward and settle into that peaceful place of rest. Seek to see the Light of Christ. Rest in this peaceful place and observe the dark screen of your mind's eye and wait for the Light of Christ to flash into your awareness. It is there waiting for you to reveal it to yourself from Him Who sent you. Ask the Holy Spirit to help with this process or if you feel more comfortable invite Jesus to help you with this process. They are here, I assure you of this and will help you if you truly seek to find the Light within yourself.

I have been in a state of gratitude as of late. Being in gratitude is being in the moment. It is letting go or forgiving all that came before and all that I think is yet to come. Time is merely an illusion. Sometimes I do not recognize that fact when I get involved and attached to all that is going on around me. But as I remember, I can see that being in the NOW moment brings the blessing of eternity. I am grateful that I can accept what is right now and that is that I am God's Son in grace with His precious Love. This holy instant releases me and releases all the world. For that I can be thankful for it is freedom, for it is my happiness. Thank You Father, for this holy instant and the peace that You share with me. Amen.

Journal Entry on Lesson 309

I will not fear to look within today.

In sitting in holy silence today, I can feel the strength of God. This is what I fear, the strength of His Love. The ego tells me that if I join with God, then I am losing who I am, this separate self-identity. However, that is not true. I am gaining so much more in union with God. I will not fear to look within today because it is what I truly desire. I want to recognize and remember my innocence, my holiness, my wholeness... my unlimited Being. I no longer choose to make a separate world from Him. I have fooled myself with all that I have placed before me as idols. Idols of everything in this world and even idols within of guilt, fear, anger or upset. I have worshipped all in one way or another, not remembering that they are false gods to me. By my reflection today in the space of quiet, I release all the thoughts of the will that I have made and gladly give those thoughts to the Holy Spirit. He purifies them and peace is restored to me. That is my will today Father, to follow Your will in serenity and quiet. All is well because I remember You.

∞∞∞∞

Journal Entry on Lesson 310

In fearlessness and love I spend today.

Today, I am reminded to release fear from my life and to accept God's Love in its' place. At times in my life, I do not feel the Love but instead I am entrenched in fear. It is perfect to be where I am, when I am. As I am ready, I can sit in communion with the Holy Spirit. He offers me peace and freedom each time I turn my attention to Him. Heaven sings each time I release thoughts of fear and pain for I have indeed welcomed love into my heart. In complete honesty, I communicate with Holy Spirit of all that is disturbing my peace. Sometimes I do this in quiet meditation and other times through the process of journaling. Either way it is important that I am turning all thoughts over to Him in a holy exchange. He listens to every word, seeing only the innocence behind the holographic wall that I created. In His presence, the wall is removed and peace floods in. The practice of coming to Him always is so vital in my life. I want each thought to be a thought only of Love. I choose to extend that love and peace to all. Today Father, You have called and it is for me to answer Your Loving Voice in fearlessness and love.

∞∞∞∞

Journal Entry on Lesson 311

I judge all things as I would have them be.

As we continue our daily practice of stilling our minds and waiting for the Light of Christ to reveal Himself in our mind's eye, we wait and listen for His Holy Voice to speak to us. The Light is pure and white. The Voice is heard clearer than the voice I use to speak. In the reading, "What is the Last Judgment?" Jesus describes to us what we will experience as we begin to make the transition Home. Experiencing the white Light of Christ and hearing the Voice for God speak to us is the beginning of the end of the dream.

Jesus tells us that we will hear the Voice for God proclaim that "what is false is false, and what is true has never changed." He's telling us very specifically we will hear the Voice for God say something to us. We will experience this. We will hear this. He also tells us that we will see something related to the Light. "*At first you see a world that has accepted this as true, projected from a now corrected mind.*"

He tells us that after we have worked with the Light enough our minds will be corrected. Our minds will be healed. We will be given a new perception of the Real World. "And with this holy sight, perception gives a silent blessing then disappears, its goal accomplished and its mission done." We will see the world as totally forgiven in the holy Light of Christ and then it will slip away into nothingness. "And all the figures in the dream in which the world began go with it......Bodies now are useless, and will therefore fade away, because the Son of God is limitless." In this moment, we finally will have realized and accepted the truth of Who we really are.

In meditation on today's lesson, the first idea that came to mind was that when I judge, I judge everything as guilty. I do not always do this consciously. As I look closely at this thought though, I can see that it is the opposite of what God sees and God sees only purity and innocence. When I judge, I am attached to the idea, person, place, thing, situation and therefore put an expectation and control upon them. This expectation leads to resentment and pain. If I walk about my day detached, then peace is surely mine. So, today I see the nothingness that the world is and see only the Love and innocence that God would have me see.

∞∞∞∞

Journal Entry on Lesson 312

I see all things as I would have them be.

As soon as I closed my eyes this morning in meditation on today's lesson, the word "forgiveness" came in very strongly. Forgiveness is the way I release the world and come into my Wholeness. As the Course tells us, "forgiveness is the key to happiness." And I do want my life to be a happy experience. Forgiveness offers me all of this and more. So today I choose to see all things through forgiving eyes, through the eyes of love. As the second half of today's lesson suggests, as I set my intention on God and the gift that forgiveness brings to me, I will realize that I am free and that is the world that I will look upon. A world that is now free of judgments that I have made. Today, let me walk the middle path, the one that keeps me on the journey to God. It is this road that will bring me Home. I forgive and the world as I know it will disappear.

Forgiveness is the way that we heal all things. The way that we look upon ourselves and our lives now is often used as a means to reinforce our belief in separation from God. How many times have we attempted to sabotage ourselves using the things within the illusion to reinforce our unconscious belief in our unworthiness of union with our Father? We look upon ourselves and our bodies with disgust, hatred and disdain believing that it is who we really are. This could be nothing further from the truth. Attack upon attack we make upon ourselves in attempt to make true what could never be true. Our holy Selves remain as God created us. We are perfect and pure and holy forever. It is impossible to change this holy Truth. We remain as God created us eternally now and forever. Amen.

∞∞∞∞

Journal Entry on Lesson 313

Now let a new perception come to me.

There are two types of visions that the Holy Spirit uses to help us while we dream. The first type of vision includes images of people, places and things either from our past, present or future. These images are not images of reality or experiences of true perception. But they are images that Holy Spirit uses to help us to understand what is going on within ourselves within the dream. He uses these images to help us see the things that we are afraid of within ourselves. He helps us to realize how these things we fear within ourselves are projected out into the world thus giving us the experience of that fearful thought through people, places, circumstances and things. With the help of the Holy Spirit we eventually begin to recognize that there is another vision that He has to bless us with. It is the vision of our True Selves in Reality. It is the Vision of the Christ. It is the experience of true perception.

The beginning of the experience of true perception starts by seeing sparks of white Light during meditation and can be seen as you go about your day. These little holy instants is a time of celebration for you because it is an indication of your time of awakening.

As we continue to open up to Holy Spirit's gift of true perception, the sparks of white Light become larger and stronger like stars. As the Light episodes become stronger and larger, visions of the Christ will bless your mind's eye and profound peace and delightful joy will instantly permeate your body bringing blessings of healing and joy with each episode. This is the gift that Holy Spirit has for us available to each and everyone of us now. All we need do is ask and wait for Him to give it to us. This is the new perception that we want to come to us today. Thank You Father for Your gift to us. Amen.

When I am ready to let go of all that I have placed my faith in, I will sit in contemplation with the Holy Spirit. As I release each thought of fear to Him, peace floods into my awareness. I have given Him the chains that have bound me. He returns ever so gently with His Love. Indeed in this very instant of release, "*Now let a new perception come to me.*" I am ready to see myself and my brothers with the Vision of Christ. I am radiant in this knowing that I can now see a forgiven world, for it is through my willingness to let go of old perceptions that the miracles are experienced. Forgiveness once again, is the focal point for it is the key to my happiness. Through forgiveness I can see the truth and return to the richness of a life in God. It is important for me to remember today that forgiveness works as I am ready to work with Holy Spirit with my thoughts. I affirm that today, I will offer all thoughts to the Holy Spirit for His true perception and that I will accept His peace gladly.

∞∞∞

Journal Entry on Lesson 314

I seek a future different from the past.

Today, I will not allow fear to freeze me in my tracks. These petty judgments that I have made against myself is the punishment that I think I so deserve for everything I think I have done. This specifically is the belief about my separation from God. And so, I allow those thoughts to paralyze me from moving forward in my life. I choose now to release those thoughts for they only bring me pain. Instead, I choose the freedom of NOW. When I decide for the present moment, I can see that the past can truly touch me not and all I have to live for is provided me by God. My future will be different because it will be the same as the NOW moment. My future will be that of complete and everlasting peace. Thank You, Father, for this holy instant where I can know Your Word for me. The Word from You is "innocent." I am innocent for I am Your Son in Whom You are well pleased.

In the dream, we are like the layers of an onion. At the core of our being is a very holy and perfect, True Self that is a creation of God, the Father, Himself. This holy Self is fully capable of guiding us through the treacherous paths in the dream. But we have chosen to layer ourselves with different voices from the dream making them our new guides. These "ego" voices have no way of knowing how to guide us through the dream but we often fall into the pitfall of listening to them anyways. They will always bring us pain. Sometimes these guides come in the form of supervisors at work, loved ones in our lives, and our own ego fantasies within our minds. These are not the guides that Holy Spirit would have you follow. He asks that we turn to Him and ask Him to guide us in everything we do within the dream. He alone knows the way. He alone knows the smooth and joyful path through the illusion. He knows the shortcuts to directly bring us Home. His path is an easy one. Our footsteps will be light and full of joy if you take His hand in everything we do and walk with Him as Our Guide. He loves us more than we know and will happily lay out the carpet of a happy dream for us. Thank You Holy Spirit for this message. We love You. Amen.

ᴏᴏᴏᴏᴏ

Journal Entry on Lesson 315

All gifts my brothers give belong to me.

Thank you brother for your many gifts to me: a heartfelt smile, a gesture of peace, a helping hand and a loving thought. Father, help me to see all these things in my brother and more today. Help me to see his Light that showers me with blessings all through the day. I thank my brother for the blessings he gives to me and I ask You Father to help me remember the blessings I give to him. Help me Father to remember to choose today to fill his table with my love. Help me to remember today the Light that shines within me and extends to him through a loving thought, a helping hand, a gesture of peace and a moment of service. I thank my brother for his gifts to me and I thank myself for my gifts to him. We thank our Father for His gifts to us for we are all One. Thank You Father for our One Light. Amen.

One day, I had the opportunity of facilitating four different students over the course of the day. Each unique person seeming to have their own unique circumstances whether in this country or abroad; yet each phone call was a blessing for me. Each miracle, or shift in perception, that was experienced and then shared in the conversation was experienced for my benefit as well. I am the receiver of all the miracles of my brothers. The same is true of my brothers in the moments that I spend with Holy Spirit releasing thoughts of separation. In this joining, I am reminded of the unity that we do indeed share. And these gifts are not limited to those four brilliant Lights that I conversed with yesterday, the gifts extend to each of you. Each one that reads this message and even those that do not. All in their own way are smiling upon the world and coming to Him for healing. Of course gratitude is in my heart for all that we share together in God. We do not heal alone; we do indeed heal together, you and I. And so, I thank you dear friends for Who You Are. And I thank You Holy Spirit for the Presence that You are in my life. Amen.

∞∞∞∞

Journal Entry on Lesson 316

All gifts I give my brothers are my own.

As I meditated on this lesson, I received an image of a very still, calm lake. In the vision, it was a gorgeous day and because of the stillness of the water, I could see my reflection perfectly. When my mind is quiet, it is like this image of the lake. When my mind is in chaos, there is turmoil in the water and the images are not clear. By remembering to still my mind in all circumstances, I am proceeding to give a precious gift to all the Sonship including myself. And so this day Father, I accept the quiet of mind that I receive when I turn all attention to You. I am worthy of a quiet mind and a peaceful heart. Today, I will follow this journey, for it is the journey Home to You. Amen.

Hidden deep within our minds is a treasure store house of Light. The Light is a reflection of Who we really are. The Light is available to be seen within the mind whenever we wish but it takes a lot of practice and mind training to find it. Once it is found you will have found the treasure deep within yourself that will set you free. Each time you find and gaze upon the Light the world is healed for a moment and the vision of Reality is grasped for an instant. How sweet a discovery for the mind that truly seeks to heal itself! The Light of our holy presence heals all things with the joy of God. Peace then is found in all things. Thank You Father for our Radiance. Thank You Father for our Holy Light that shines now and forever in Your holy blanket of Love. Amen.

∞∞∞∞

Journal Entry on Lesson 317

I follow in the way appointed me.

Father, in silence I come to meet with You in our holy place where I can lay down my armor of fear at your altar. Father, for a few moments now I lay down all things that I use to shield myself from Your holy Light of Love. I let go of all things and freely walk through the veil of darkness within my mind until the glorious radiance of Your holy Light breaks through and blesses my eyes with a Vision of Christ. Your Son remains as You created Him and I am Your Son. Thank You for my holy Light that blesses all things with You. I love You Father and I thank You for Who I am in You. You are the Savior of all things and I walk upon the holy ground where no things ever really needed to be saved. Thank You, Father for You, for me, and for all my brothers and sisters Who are One with Us forever. Amen.

As I look upon today's lesson, I am reminded that it is Holy Spirit's Voice that I am to listen to in every moment. There have been times that I have heard the Voice ever so clearly yet I do not pay attention and decide upon my own way in the world. When I have followed my own voice, the ego voice, it has brought me to places that I really did not dare to go. The Holy Spirit however, uses every choice that I do make to assist me along the path

Home. This occurred recently in my own life when it was brought to my attention that a choice that I had made, was not truly the Plan as Holy Spirit saw it. I came to the realization on my own and when I did, I asked Holy Spirit to be with me in what step I was to take next. As He gently assisted me, I could see that in staying in the choice that I had made I was not making the way for another choice for myself. By releasing myself from the self-imposed block, I was opening up to a grander Plan that He had for me. More and more it has been revealed and more and more I see the glory of it all. And so today, I have gratitude in my heart for accepting His Plan as my own, once again.

∞∞∞∞

Journal Entry on Lesson 318

In me salvation's means and end are one.

Thank You Father for the spark of Light within me that I can use to heal all my pains. Father, I bring all my worries and anxieties, my guilts and my fears to You and offer them to the spark of white Light for healing. I wait for It to come and flash it all away. Thank You Father for the spark that is the beginning of the memory of Me. My little Friend Who helps me along the way, washing away all my "sins" and showing me that everything is ok. Thank You Father for Your Peace that comes to me and reminds me of Who we really are. Thank You for the Light that lightens my heart and gives me peace that calms me and carries me happily through the day, carefree of all worries and concerns, just like it is in Heaven now where we walk together in our loving friendship as One. Amen.

Today, I remember that I am empowered by the recognition of Who I am in God. It is for me to make the choice for Heaven and my True Self. I choose that now as I am remembering my innocence. As I remember that I am innocent, I am remembering it for all my brothers for they are indeed One with me. I offer my willingness to the Holy Spirit to let go of the misconceptions that I have had. As I offer each mistaken thought, I am surrounded by His peace. It is very simple to forgive when I remember to do so. It is my function here in this world and I accept it gladly.

∞∞∞

Journal Entry on Lesson 319

I came for the salvation of the world.

Inside each and everyone of us is the Spirit of God. The Spirit of God wills for us to have happy, successful and fulfilling lives. But in order for that to happen we must become willing through daily prayer and meditation to ask Him to help us to do that. We must become willing to let go of our personal interests in the world and to ask Him Who sent us what His will is for us. We must let go of our ego desires for persons, places and things and allow God to work through us for the salvation of the world. Great leaders of our past and present remember to ask God to help them let go of all the things that would prevent them from experiencing themselves at their fullest while they walk the earth. In the times when we feel tempted to become attracted to something other than what God's will is for us, Jesus gave us a prayer in the Text of *A Course in Miracles* on page 28 to respond with.

> *I am here only to be truly helpful. I am here to represent Him Who sent me. I do not have to worry about what to say or what to do for He Who sent me will direct me. I am content to be wherever He wishes knowing He goes there with me. I will be healed as I let Him teach me to heal.*

Or if we prefer, we can respond to temptation with the following prayer: *Father, where would You have me go? What would You have me do? What would You have me say? And to whom?*

He also asks us to remember to hand over all of our dark thoughts and temptations to the Light of the Holy Spirit and ask Him to heal it with the Holy Light. Amen.

∞∞∞∞

Journal Entry on Lesson 320

My Father gives all power unto me.

For those who have not experienced the Light of Christ within themselves, this may be a difficult statement to accept and understand indeed. Throughout the Course Jesus is trying to tell us the secret of a wonderful gift that is hidden deep within ourselves. Many others from our past and present are attempting to share the good news about this wonderful gift as well. If we were to take some time to browse our modern day bookstores we would notice that many books and tabloids are written about the Light within. Many book covers even show pictures of the Light that is hidden within. We have heard many sages from the past and present tell us about the Light within. But yet we continue to refuse and accept that it is there because we have not seen it for ourselves.

I assure you that it is there and you do want to see it. You do want to discover this most wonderful gift. It is the gift that you have been seeking all of your lives. Jesus gives us explicit instructions in the Workbook for Students in how to discover the Light hidden within yourself. Practice letting go of everything, everyday in silent meditation. Wait in anticipation of the Light that will come and illuminate your mind with the peace and joy of God in the flash of a holy instant. In that moment of illumination you will discover that it is your choice and you can choose to do this anytime you want. In that moment you will discover the cleansing peace of God, the joy of Heaven and the calm strength our Father has given us as His Son. We thank You Father for this most wonderful gift that You have given to us. We love You. Amen.

With today's lesson I accept the strength and Love that I have from my Father. I can do all things through Him and with Him because I have all that He possesses. Each attribute of God is an attribute within me. Today I am empowered with the knowledge of the Truth. This knowledge allows me to walk the middle path, the path of non-judgment, the path really only of Love. I am the recipient of such a wondrous gift in my Father and it is for me to acknowledge and to use it wisely. I have the opportunity of a clear and serene mind any time that I so choose. Today, Father, I choose to extend Your Love to the world. I put aside my agenda, the agenda of pain, and follow Your will. Amen.

∞∞∞∞

Journal Entry on Lesson 321

Father, my freedom is in You alone.

If I am feeling a twinge of sadness or a sliver of upset then I am not free. At those times I feel weighed down by the heaviness that I have made by these thoughts of fear. I may even feel it in my physical body in one way or another. When I then turn my attention to God, I am given the means in which I can lift the weight from my spiritual shoulders. Turning my attention to God assures me that I have the tools to remember the truth and allow freedom to come into my mind.

As I begin to quiet my mind, my mind may indeed chatter with all the worries and concerns that may seem to be right there. Even though I may even know intellectually that it is all fear, all from the past wanting to come into the future and present, it chatters away and I cannot seem to rest. In these situations, I can "ride the wave" so to speak. I allow the feelings and thoughts to be there, slowing rising and then falling, not resisting, but simply allowing them to be there. I am the observer. As I acknowledge, I can release them as they flow back into the nothingness from which they came. I have found that in this practice that each time the thoughts rise again they are not as strong. As I am ready and feel the willingness, I release each one to the Holy Spirit for a miracle. As each thought is released to Him, I accept the Light of peace and freedom to warm my mind. I can now breathe freely for now I breathe with the breath of God.

During silent meditation last night I asked Holy Spirit to give me some insight about my relationship with a co-worker. The Holy Spirit shared with me that this person feels agitated with me at times because I talk too much. I could almost hear the person's thoughts in their mind that they were having towards me because I tuned into this with Holy Spirit. Of course I felt bad about this and I asked Holy Spirit to help me understand more deeply what was going on in my relationship with my interactions with this person. The Holy Spirit helped me to see that I had developed a habit of engaging in conversation with others when I unconsciously felt scared a long time ago when I was a child. He pointed out that the ego had taught me that the solution to the feeling of insecurity in a relationship with another was to engage them in conversation about "nothing." The ego has taught me to fill in silence and the feeling of separation with another with the distracting noise of conversation.

As I listened to Holy Spirit share this truth with me I began to feel sick inside. My heart felt saddened because I knew that He was speaking the truth. What bothered me even more was that I knew that I had been doing this all of my life and still hadn't let it go. I mistakenly developed a habit of listening to the ego for my source of freedom. This choice is a mistake. There is only one choice, one Source Who can help me make the correct choice in every situation. That choice is to ask Holy Spirit in every moment

"What would You have me do now?" or "How would You have me respond to this situation now?" I thank Holy Spirit for helping me to see this and I thank my brothers and sisters for helping me to see this as well. And I thank myself for having the willingness to look at this with Holy Spirit and to ask Him for the help in truly letting it go once and for all. I am glad that my Father is the only place where my freedom truly lies. Amen.

∞∞∞

Journal Entry on Lesson 322

I can give up but what was never real.

I do not need the illusions that I have made. In sane moments I realize that illusions keep me veiled from the Light of Truth. Through forgiveness, an illusion itself, I am released from all illusions. Through forgiveness, illusions disappear and the Love is seen. Forgiveness is an illusion itself for in Reality it is not needed. Love is Love and nothing else is required. There is nothing then to forgive. But here in this world I made up, I need the reminder that forgiveness offers me.

It is for me to continue to practice forgiveness with everything I experience and see. Forgiving, or letting go may seem like a sacrifice as I may be attached to what a person seemingly did to me in this world. Truly recognizing love is not a sacrifice, but instead a holy gift that I give myself. When I hold on to grievances I am enslaving myself along with the other person. The other person may not even know. In letting go of the chains of grievances, I gladly receive peace within. This eases the separation that I feel with my brother and with my Father and the holy union of us all is revealed. And so today, I pray the beautiful prayer from the Course which has been likened to "The Lord's Prayer."

Forgive us our illusions, Father, and help us to accept our true relationship with You, in which there are no illusions, and where none can ever enter. Our holiness is Yours. What can there be in us that needs forgiveness when Yours is perfect? The sleep of forgetfulness is only the unwillingness to remember Your forgiveness and Your Love. Let us not wander into temptation, for the temptation of the Son of God is not Your Will. And let us receive only what You have given, and accept but this into the minds which You created and which You love. Amen. T-16.VII.12.

∞∞∞∞

Journal Entry on Lesson 323

I gladly make the "sacrifice" of fear.

Right now we can choose to close our eyes and sink down into this place within ourselves to discover these gifts that our Father has already given to us. We'll know when we have discovered the right place within the mind when we begin to experience the sparks or flashes of white Light.

As they become brighter through practice the experience of Father's gifts will become more pronounced. Peace and joy and serenity and Light will stream into our awareness bringing along with it understanding. The Holy Spirit is delighted to help us with this process to find this place within ourselves. He eagerly awaits to help Father's Son find his true home and the memory of Himself once again. Remember to ask Him for help every time you practice this process.

Ask Him to help you to find the Light within yourself. He will help you to find the blazing white Light within yourself and your eyes will gaze upon your holiness with joy. A smile will come to your face, gratitude will fill your heart and you will remember to thank Father for Who You really are. You will want to tell Father that you love Him because you will have remembered and experienced that you too are Love Itself.

I noticed that as I read and then contemplated on this lesson that I was aware of a tension held within. We had just discussed paying bills and taking care of other needed chores. This then led to the subtle tension. Any upset, no matter how seemingly small is a disturbance to my mind. In today's lesson, I am asked to give up all the thoughts that are not of truth, that bring me only fear. If I am worried; I am in fear. If I am angry, then I am in fear. Today, I release all the fear to my Father and do it with gladness and joy. It is in joy that He wishes that I live my life. I let go of the judgments that I feel towards myself or others or situations. I receive the abundance of Love that was already mine. These thoughts of fear are just dirt on my windowpanes to seeing the Light of His Love. Today, I wash them clean by forgiving each thought and receiving peace. Thank You Father for giving me the means by which I set myself free. Amen.

∞∞∞

Journal Entry on Lesson 324

I merely follow, for I would not lead.

When I lead, I am trusting in my own strength. When I lead, I am in control, or so I think. When I lead, I am attached to outcomes and hold expectations. In holding onto expectations I create hidden resentments for myself. As I have heard it said before, expectations are premeditated resentments. And so today, I release my controls and surrender to the Holy Spirit. Surrendering is not sacrificing. Surrendering is trusting in an open way to the truth. I know that when I have followed my own guidance that I have been unhappy. I cannot force happiness to occur in my life. Those times that I have been happy has been when I simply allowed the Holy Spirit to work in my life.

To me that means, that I have chosen to listen to His Voice. Listening to His Voice brings me a peace that the ego could never bring me. I never know what His guidance will bring me next, but I know that it always assures a happy outcome to all things. Today, I step back and let Him lead the way for me Home. For Heaven is my Home and today, I hasten there.

All too often we make the mistake of taking the reigns from Holy Spirit and attempt to guide our own lives under the disguise of ego's expression of joy. The ego wants us to be in pain because it's very existence depends upon it for in the reality of Heaven pain does not really exist. Pain is inconceivable in Heaven and a concept completely foreign to our Source. In today's prayer we are merely asked to have the willingness to follow Holy Spirit's guidance. The ego does not know the way out of hell for you nor would it want you to discover it if it did. The Holy Spirit does know the way and will gladly give you the guidance of which way to go in any moment which choice to make if you but have the willingness to open up and ask. The Holy Spirit will answer us. His answers are always right. They always benefit everyone and most importantly they lead you to happy experience.

Do you not want to be happy while you awaken from your sleep? Spend some time and really ask yourself this question with Me. Do you really want to be happy while you awaken from your dreams of illusions? You often respond with "yes" but your thoughts, actions and behaviors often reflect a different choice, the choice for pain. In these moments give a gift to both your brother and yourself and to Me, a gift of willingness to come to Me and hand these thoughts over to salvation's plan for healing. Just merely ask that I take them from you and heal them and I assure you that it is done my Son. You can pretend that you wander off for awhile if you like, but you are only delaying what you really want and that is to be happy with Me. Let Me guide you and I will show you so many more wonderful things in the world to experience and do, just like a loving Father would want to do for His Son to give Him nothing but pure happiness and joy. Father, thank You for Your message to us. Amen.

∞∞∞∞

Journal Entry on Lesson 325

All things I think I see reflect ideas.

Let us use the analogy of a movie projector projecting the images on a screen to explain what Jesus is talking about in today's lesson. What is really happening is that our minds are projecting everything we see, feel and hear out into the world around us, including our bodies. Everything we think we see, feel, touch, hear and taste is being projected and manifested by our minds on some level. All of it is an illusion and a dream that we are dreaming. Have you ever had the feeling as you went about your day that you were dreaming all of this?

There is a place within our minds where we can project something different and provide ourselves with a different experience. There is another part of our mind that abides with God's mind. This other part of the mind can be discovered through prayer and silent meditation. It is a place where we can have an experience of the thoughts that God would have for us. It is an experience where we experience ourselves as a Being of white Light but not with a body; more like a star. We can see and experience ourselves like a star that is radiating Light and Love and Peace and Joy in perfect sinlessness and holiness. It is the experience of the reflection of our True Selves as the Christ. It is there and a most wonderful treasure to find within ourselves. Let us ask the Holy Spirit to help us find this place today and thank Him when we are finished. And let us thank our Father for helping us to remember Who We really are. Thank you Father for this message to us today. Amen.

Today I will monitor my thoughts and hold the willingness to think what God would have me think. I will use the tool of forgiveness to help me to see truly. This lesson is a strong reminder that I make all that I see. It is from my own thoughts, the ideas in my mind of what I want, then from these ideas all that I see is made. Could I not create love with my thoughts if I align them with my Father? Indeed so. It is through my mindfulness then that I will let each thought be a thought of love. What would God have me think? What would God have me see in this world? The more I practice forgiveness; the more the gap between my brothers disappears. I will see the Oneness that we share. Oneness is the idea that I would have today so that I may look upon a world of love.

∞∞∞∞

Journal Entry on Lesson 326

I am forever an Effect of God.

Father, what can I say today except to express my gratitude for You Who created me. I am not what I seem in this world. I am not this body nor this personality. None of this exists. My true "personality" is of You. I have tried to mask all the radiant beauty that is there within. I could never extinguish the Light of Your Love, no matter how I have tried with all my "trauma drama" stories of lack and limitation and abuse.

Today, I realize that those stories are just stories. Just as an author creates a fiction novel, so I have created the biggest farce of all of being in this world. Today, I remember that I am as You created me. I am perfect Love. I am what I have been seeking for. I am part of You, You Who extended Himself in precious Love bringing forth Your Son. As I am reminded today that I am forever Your Effect, I remember that all my brothers here with me are the same. We are together; none held apart. And so it is for me to remember to hold no one separate from me today, including myself. With forgiveness in my heart I will gladly journey Home.

Have we asked ourselves, "Are we *really* ready to let go of pain today?" "Are we really ready to let go of all the little trinkets, all the activities in the world that we think will bring us happiness?" If we sit down and spend some time looking at the things we did yesterday or the day before, and truly examine them, we would find that we have developed habits of doing things that we think are making us happy.

Once the things have been accomplished, if we examine how we really feel, we would discover that most of the time we still feel unfulfilled. This is the vicious cycle that the ego mind desires to keep the Son of God's mind trapped within. These things and activities are not the Effects of our Cause. Our Cause has created an entirely different experience for us. It is an experience of perfect harmony, complete joy and a peace that expands upon itself and never ends. This experience is available to us right now.

Let us dedicate time and practice today in search of finding this place within ourselves. Let us practice hourly today the surrendering of our minds over to the Will of God. There is an accumulative effect that is experienced through practice. The more we practice and ask, the quicker we get to discovering the experience that has been given to us by our Cause. It is a glimpse of Our Reality. Father, help us today to find the Effect that is Your Will for us. We ask You for a miracle today. Thank You. Amen.

ooooo

Journal Entry on Lesson 327

I need but call and You will answer me.

Several years ago during the same time of the Thanksgiving season I had an experience with God where I learned that the words that Jesus shares with us in today's lesson are literally true. I decided to spend the day practicing every hour sitting down, closing my eyes, letting go of all of my thoughts and being very still for 10 minutes. I was attempting to get to the experience of the Vision of the Christ Light but in the 3 o'clock hour a different experience came to me instead. I heard God's Voice speak to me very clearly, "I have everything I need."

What surprised me most about hearing His Voice this time was that He used my own voice to speak these words to me. Along with this experience came an awareness of a calm certainty not of this world that everything is ok. On that day I learned that calling God to answer me is not done with thoughts or words or prayers but instead that it is done by completely stilling all of my thoughts and resting in the silence for God to answer me. I am grateful for this experience and the reminder from Holy Spirit that this is how it works.

It does not matter what I have done, judgments I may have made or guilt that I have hidden within, for all I need do is follow today's prayer. *"I need but call and You will answer me."* God has indeed promised me the Answer and He has given me the Answer to all my problems in the form of the Holy Spirit. If I want peace of mind I simply turn to Him for rest and assurance of such. Mistakes are made but the Holy Spirit sees beyond mistakes to the truth. The truth is that I am innocent. Yesterday I became angry with two different situations; one that I perceived as an attack and the other I perceived as abandonment.

As I was ready, I began to truly see these situations. They were opportunities for me to receive help from the Holy Spirit. As I turned my attention to the Holy Spirit last night and again this morning in regards to both situations, I could see that it all stemmed from my own mind. It is my own hidden thoughts of guilt and loss and separation that I project out into the world. And thus it brought me the witnesses to those beliefs. Today, I choose to be happy rather than right and ask for a miracle. My Father has given me the means by which to let go of all that I have made. The Holy Spirit is there in my mind and it is for me to be mindful of my thoughts and to turn each one to Him for His Answer. His Answer is only of peace. Today, I will choose to rest in peace with the Holy Spirit, the sure Answer to all my problems.

∞∞∞∞

Journal Entry on Lesson 328

I choose the second place to gain the first.

What is Your Will for me today Father but to step back from my petty control and allow You to lead me to my rightful Home? I have been mistaken in thinking that I could control and manipulate this world to bring me true happiness. It is not so. For me to receive the true happiness that I seek I simply allow You to be in charge of my entire life. It is Your Will that I choose to follow. It is Your Holy Spirit in which I place my trust to ever guide me where I need to be.

I know that the Holy Spirit's guidance is always sure and steady. It always leads me to peace. It is for me to remember to surrender my will to Him. It is not a sacrifice to surrender, but it is true wisdom to allow Holy Spirit's plan to be in place. Only His plan will work. My prior experience has shown me that my plans have failed too many times and now I am reminded to see the Light once again. Step back and let Him lead....so simple to say and it can indeed be simple to follow. The joy is ever present when I say "Yes" to Him.

As we go about our day today let us pay attention to that we look upon, the places we go and the things we think about. Everything we see, feel, hear and think about is the second choice. There is another choice, another alternative. It is the choice to see and experience the Kingdom of Heaven. It is the choice to see and experience our True Selves. Let us ask the Holy Spirit to help us today to find the experience of making this choice. Let us take time today to practice going to the place of silence within and asking Holy Spirit to show us the first choice. Let us rest and wait for Him to show us Who we really are. And when the experience comes to us we will feel thankful indeed. Perhaps the Voice for God will speak to us today. Perhaps we will experience the Vision of Christ. Perhaps we will capture a glimpse of reality. We thank the Holy Spirit for helping us today and we thank our Father for holding our Home secure for us in Heaven while we dream that we are away. How happy and thankful we will feel today when we find our way once again. Amen.

∞∞∞∞

Journal Entry on Lesson 329

I have already chosen what You will.

Father, we are perfectly happy and pure and holy and free just like You created us. We thank You for the Voice of the Holy Spirit Who helps us find our way Home to You. We thank You for rolling out the carpet of Light that is the path that will help us find our Home once again. We thank You for the Holy Spirit Who gives us the shifts in perception that shows us that the things of this world are not true and that there really is another place where everything is perfectly happy and free. We thank You for the Light that leads us back Home. We thank You for the truth that everything is not separate as it seems to be in this world but everything is whole and One in Heaven. We all share it with You and we all share it with each other. We thank You for the place where there is no such thing as worry, fear, anxiety or pain but instead only Oneness and wholeness, freedom, happiness, peace and joy. And we thank You for the Holy Spirit Who will happily help us find this place right now, if we but have the willingness to ask and be in silence with Him. The Light of the Voice for God will guide us Home. Thank You Father for Your gifts to us. Amen.

I seem to have choices but truly I do not. The one choice is really the truth of what is and it is simply accepting God's Will. Today, I will not make other wills above and beyond what is already there for me. God's Will is what leads me Home. Home is where I am even now while it seems that I am elsewhere. Today, I will release all that is not of God. All the fear thoughts that chatter through my mind will not bring me in alignment with remembering the truth. So as I turn my attention to the Holy Spirit, I allow each thought to become as a feather that rises to Him and is softly blown away. The breeze of peace will freshen my mind today as I accept and allow God's Will as my very own.

∞∞∞∞

Journal Entry on Lesson 330

I will not hurt myself again today.

Today's affirmation reminds me of my own responsibility for what I seem to experience. Several lessons in the Course tell me of the same. It is my own thoughts that bring me pain. It is my thoughts of the past that I carry into the present moment that make up my current circumstances. In all, the Holy Spirit tells me that I have the power to change my thoughts by simply coming to Him with each one. I do not have to continue to experience any hurt at all. I also cannot continue to blame anyone or anything outside of me for having power over me. I am indeed responsible for what I see.

One of my favorite passages that I have committed to memory is from Chapter 21, the Section entitled "The Responsibility for Sight." This passage, along with today's lesson, reassures me that nothing outside of me can cause discomfort. I can decide to be happy or I can decide for pain. In any situation that is occurring in my life, it is for me to take full ownership. And so, Jesus tells us:

> *This is the only thing that you need do for vision, happiness, release from pain and the complete escape from sin, all to be given you. Say only this, but mean it with no reservations, for here the power of salvation lies:*
>
> *I am responsible for what I see.*
> *I choose the feelings I experience, and I decide upon the goal I would achieve.*
> *And everything that seems to happen to me I ask for, and receive as I have asked.*
> *Deceive yourself no longer that you are helpless in the face of what is done to you. Acknowledge but that you have been mistaken, and all effects of your mistakes will disappear.*

It is certainly a big step in my spiritual awakening when I take this responsibility for my thoughts. I then realize that the only power that exists is the power of God. I remain a victim of the world no longer. I can indeed now live my life in joy.

Let us go within our minds today and soar with the eagles that fly with freedom within Father's Kingdom. Let us feel Father carry us through the Kingdom and show us the sights and sounds that He would have us see and hear. Let us feel Him lift us up into His loving Arms and embrace us as a mother holds her child.

Let us feel His comfort and security envelop us. Let us feel the strength of His Love warm our hearts and light our minds. Let us feel the happiness He feels for His Son. His Son has fallen down a dark hole just in his dreams. His Father holds His Son secure and safe in His arms while His Son sleeps. He whispers into His Son's thoughts while He sleeps, "I love you my Son. Everything is ok. You need worry about nothing in your dreams because I am here holding you safe and sound. I am carrying you through everything and arranging all things for you. It is ok to be happy and feel free again. When you are ready to awaken I will be right here for you waiting to receive you. All of My Kingdom will dance in delight and joy and we will celebrate together when you return. I will be the First and the Last to greet you and to receive you into My Arms while I give you the most loving hug, wrapped around you to show you how much I love you and appreciate you. You are My beautiful Son, My most precious creation."

∞∞∞∞

Journal Entry on Lesson 331

There is no conflict, for my will is Yours.

We walk and stumble around in darkness thinking we know the way. We are like a blind person without a compass trying to navigate themselves out of their dream. Only the Holy Spirit knows the way. It is His job, His task to help you awaken from your illusions. It is what He was created for. Use Him, work with Him, develop the habit of asking Him in everything you do. Before you make any choices, from moment to moment, turn your mind inward towards Him and ask Him. He will answer you. You will see He does over time and your belief will grow strong.

Every piece of guidance you receive from Him will always lead you to more and more happiness and always benefits everyone. He knows every situation that is going on with every person all at once. He knows the best choice in all circumstances, taking into account everything that seems to be going on in the universe all at the same time. He knows how to guide the blind man through the maze of darkness, back to the Home from whence he came. In the beginning you may find it difficult to work with Him because it seems that it is difficult to receive His answers. Practice, practice, practice. Have faith, He is there. He is answering you all the time. You will see this in time.

As your faith grows, His answers will grow clearer, more pronounced, more obvious and eventually you will hear the Voice for God direct you Himself. This is the road we walk together. We are here with you always and we all walk together to Home. Thank You Holy Spirit for Your help and thank You Father for Your gift to us. Amen.

I seem to think that I am conflicted in my mind of which voice to follow, but it is only the Voice of Truth that is for me. Any other voice that is not of the truth is simply an illusion, a false idea. There is no conflict with God. God is. Love is. And so for me today I let go of all other voices, all other wills that I have heard and followed. It leads me nowhere. Listening to the Holy Spirit always brings me joy, always bring me to peace, always brings me Home. The ego will not serve me as its only service is one of my destruction. It is fear personified, or at least I think so. Love is all there is. A simple statement, perhaps too simple to the ego as the ego likes complexity. Complexity is its home. Love is mine. It is really not a difficult choice if I truly think about it. Do I not want to live my life with ease? Yes, of course. A life of ease is living the life of God's Love. It is seeing with Christ Vision. It is forgiving all. There is no need for further concerns for I am Home in Love.

∞∞∞∞

Journal Entry on Lesson 332

Fear binds the world. Forgiveness sets it free.

The pain that I am feel in my head and jaw because of tension helps me to understand today's lesson. Tension in the body feels rather binding, clamping, tight and painful. This is what fear does to us in our mind as well.

As I relax, or forgive, I am releasing the grasp on what I think is right. My natural state is one of peace. When I am in fear then I am applying pressure to my natural state. The burdens in my mind can be easily set aside with the Holy Spirit's assistance. In coming into the quiet space with Him at the holy altar in my mind, I can offer all the fear thoughts that create tension in my life. He massages each thought with His Love and a sense of warmth and serenity is restored to me. The Holy Spirit's therapy is one of Love, peace and joy and it is always available, no appointment necessary.

Dear Light of Peace, let me dedicate this day to You. Let me dedicate every moment of every hour today to inviting Your Light of forgiveness into my mind to shine away each fearful image, thought, and memory that is not of God. Let me open my mind to You today to flash away every fear, anxiety and worry in exchange for Your healing peace. Today I allow the Light of forgiveness to show me the memory of God within my mind. I allow it to heal my body and set me free. This is the miracle I ask for today. Thank You Father for Your gift of healing Light to us. Amen.

∞∞∞∞

Journal Entry on Lesson 333

Forgiveness ends the dream of conflict here.

Forgiveness is the Light of God within our minds waiting to be discovered as the gift for all time. This Christmas Season let us dedicate our efforts towards finding this most wonderful gift within ourselves. The Holy Spirit within our mind will help us to find it. Let us search with Him endlessly until we find the treasure that will end the dream of dreams. The white Light is the Light without a body that radiates the Great Rays of God.

When we find it we will instantly recognize it is an aspect of our True Selves. In that instant of discovery, the illusion of the world around us will be shined away with our holiness. The release of true forgiveness in this instant heals the body of fear, anxiety and worry replacing it instantly with the experience of release and the freedom of peace and joy. This is the gift and the tool that Father gave to us to find our way Home. Thank You Father for this most wonderful gift, the gift that will help us make a sweet transition Home. Thank you Jesus for showing us the way and thank You Holy Spirit for helping us to find the way. Amen.

In true honesty do I see that conflict offers me nothing but pain and misery. With this real awareness I look on with the Holy Spirit's help and see that all conflict is meaningless. Through the practice of forgiveness I let go of all that disturbs my mind. With Holy Spirit guidance, I embrace the calm that God's peace provides. Forgiveness is the beacon that shines through all illusions showing me what is only true.

Nothing here in this world is true. This world is layers upon layers of fear that I have made up in what the ego would call "protecting" me from God. It is God's Love that I so desire; His protection is all I need. The ego likes to keep the dance of deception going in my mind through all the aggravations and fears it presents. As I am mindful of my thoughts, I partner with the Holy Spirit and allow Him to change the dance to one of forever waltzing in God's Love. Forgiveness offers me release and today I gladly accept it as my own.

∞∞∞

Journal Entry on Lesson 334

Today I claim the gifts forgiveness gives.

What gift there is but the present moment when I forgive all that I see, think and experience. Forgiveness helps me to see the way things truly are. Forgiveness helps me to let go of all that is troubling my mind. I am grateful that the Holy Spirit is there in my mind shining away all the illusions that fog my memory of Home. As He is the beacon to me, I too am the beacon to all my brothers each time I accept the gift of forgiveness in my heart. I accept it now for the recognition of the unity of our life in God. Nothing can alter or change the Truth. And when I forget, I simply remember the Holy Spirit's presence there in my mind and utilize Him to bring clarity and peace to the situation at hand. I realize that this takes practice and so I devote my day to mindfulness of my thoughts and claiming the gifts forgiveness brings to me.

Throughout the Workbook Jesus gives us the specific instructions we need to practice in order experience the gifts that Jesus is talking about here. Let us remember once again today to practice closing our eyes, and sinking down into that peaceful place where we let everything go. We wait for the waves of peace to begin to roll in to the body. They usually begin when we are on the edge of falling asleep. The shifts of peace can be felt by the body. These are waves of Light that are beginning to roll in. The Light may not be perceived at first within the mind but the effects of It are felt in the body as it feels a sudden release and shifts into a place closer to where perfect peace resides. We sink down and let go a little more and wait for the next wave of Light to come through.

Again, we may feel a sudden release in the body and a shift into deeper peace still, but the Light still may not be perceived yet. Nonetheless this is the effect of the Light that is about to dawn upon the mind. We sink down even more and let go once again and wait, and perhaps this time the wave of peace will flash into the mind as a white Light that is perceived by the mind and experienced as a larger release of peace that envelops the body. The gifts of joy, peace, contentment and healing come with these deeper levels offered given by the Light. This can go on and on and the Light will become brighter and brighter. The gifts of peace and joy and the strength of experiencing God becomes more pronounced until complete release into Reality and Atonement is accepted. Thank You Father for Your gifts to us. Amen.

∞∞∞∞

Journal Entry on Lesson 335

I choose to see my brother's sinlessness.

Sometimes we may receive little inspirations to call or talk with a loved one. Perhaps it is a parent, a brother or sister, or a friend. These are inspirations of healing prompted by the Holy Spirit. We often habitually respond to these inspirations with fearful thoughts and other distractions that ultimately convince us not to make the healing connection.

In these moments we have mistakenly made the choice of listening to the voice of the ego. The voice of the ego is very good at bringing up subtle feelings of our own past guilt around relationships and then projecting these fearful thoughts out towards something else to distract us from getting in touch with our own guilt. These are moments when it appears that we have chosen to see our brothers sinfulness but what is really happening is that we chose to see our own sinfulness. And because of the pain of seeing our seeming sinfulness within ourselves we project it away from us to relieve the pain. This all happens very quickly and unconsciously.

In order to begin to choose to see ourselves differently, to see our sin-less-ness, we need to invoke the Holy Spirit's help. Our sinlessness is the last thing our ego wants us to see. We are also unable to see our perfect sinlessness on our own. The Holy Spirit's job is to show us our perfect sinlessness for us. We need do nothing but close our eyes and choose to ask Him to show us our sinlessness and wait for it to be revealed to us. The healing flashes of Light will come and we will see and feel the perfection of our True Selves. We will behold the Light that is the reflection of our True Selves with joy and glee. Thank you Father for Your gift to us. Amen.

Today I release all judgment of what I think I want to see in my brother and even in me. I think I want to see a victimizer and a victim. If that is what I wish to see then it is only an experience through the eyes of guilt and blame. But today's lesson tells me that judgment covers the truth in us both. We are indeed guiltless.

When I cover up the truth that God created me and my brothers as whole and innocent, I make a world of misery for myself. I could never truly experience happiness in this way. As I let go of what I want to believe in, the judgments that I hold against others, I can truly see as God would have me see. I can then embrace the teaching of "love one another as I have loved you." Is that not what I really want? I want to experience love in my life and with the Holy Spirit I can release all the barriers to love in my mind. There is freedom in accepting that God has created us all as One in His Love. This belief ends all the turmoil I may ever have and for this I am grateful.

Journal Entry on Lesson 336

Forgiveness lets me know that minds are joined.

Forgiveness today is such a vital part of my life. It is through forgiveness that I am happy. It is through forgiveness that I am free. When I am wound up tightly in my emotions and have the grip on "right-ness" it is forgiveness that sets me aright. Forgiveness is simply letting go of false ideas and replacing them with the truth. I do this in my practice with the Holy Spirit. And it is through practice that I recognize the healing continually. The steps of forgiveness are outlined in the Course and many others have shared their steps to inner healing.

One such is Dan Joseph in his book "Inner Healing - A Spiritual Process." I have used this book with ACIM study groups in the past. Dan brings the information in a very easy to read format as well as many examples of his own and others' healings.

Simply, it is:

Step 1 - We acknowledge a dark thought or feeling.
Step 2 - We offer it to God to be healed.
Step 3 - We open to an inflow of love, or miracles.

To help us further with the forgiveness process, he provides us with a prayer in relation to the three steps:

1 - "When I think about _____, I feel _____ because I think/see/believe _____."
2 - "God, I am willing to release those thoughts and feelings to you."
3 - "God, I am open to an experience of your love, guidance, and comfort."

We thank You Father for providing the means by which we can

remember that we are joined with You and our brothers. Thank You for the Holy Spirit's gentle presence in our mind and His call to Joy. Amen.

∞∞∞∞

Journal Entry on Lesson 337

My sinlessness protects me from all harm.

Behold your sinlessness with the Holy Spirit and you will see that your Light is pure white as snow. The Holy Spirit wants to show you your sinlessness by giving you the gift of true perception. Everything you behold now with the body's eyes is not true perception. It is an illusion, a dream that you the Son of God are dreaming. You are dreaming that you are in exile from Your Father's Home. You are dreaming that you are in hell. You are dreaming that you are in a world of where bodies come to suffer and die. None of it is true but it is difficult to believe that when you haven't had the experience of remembering the truth.

The Holy Spirit is patiently waiting to show you the truth through His gift of true perception that He holds for you. To accept His gift go within, close your eyes, and go within and ask Him to show you your perfect sinlessness. Then wait, wait within your mind patiently, peacefully, wait for Him to light up your mind with the Light that is white as snow.

In that moment you will begin to recognize the truth of about who you really are. You will begin to recognize that you are not really a body but instead something far different. These will be the first glimmerings of the recognition of your True Self. These are the glimmerings that will begin to release you from hell. These are the steps we take in the awakening process. These are the experiences we will begin to have as our spiritual eyes begin to flutter and open to the true perception of the reality that really surrounds us. Thank You Father for the Holy Spirit, truly our Friend. Thank You Holy Spirit for Your help. Amen.

When I recognize my innocence and in turn stand strong in that belief, then the illusions of pain and suffering can no longer seem to harm me. In this acceptance of my innocence I am affirming for myself that I am as God has created me. There is nothing else for nothing exists but this very truth. My happiness is in the reflection of this fact. By continuing the forgiveness process of letting go of the false beliefs, the ones that cover the Light that I am, freedom is mine with each release. It is for me to allow my Light to shine and radiate to all. It is my illuminating gift to the world. It is my gift from God. When I can accept this fully within my holy mind then the illusion of this world will no longer be. I am innocent. I am free today. God's Love surrounds me for that is all that I am, an extension of His Love.

∞∞∞∞

Journal Entry on Lesson 338

I am affected only by my thoughts.

With this lesson, it brings the affirmation that "it is only a thought and a thought can be changed." The simplicity of this statement is the way to bring peace to my mind. I rule my mind and control all thoughts that enter in. I am responsible for those thoughts and what I then do with them. And so today, let each thought that comes into my mind be a thought of prayer. My thoughts are indeed prayers and so that it is true to say that I am always praying since my mind is always thinking.

Today I will be mindful of each thought and how it extends to not only my own experience but the experiences of my brothers here with me. What prayer do I want to share today? Will it be a prayer of love or a prayer of fear? I will choose love as my only prayer today for it is a prayer of higher consciousness, a prayer of the belief in my True Self and the Oneness that we share.

The Holy Spirit within your mind will help you to change all your thoughts to the One Thought that God wills for you to have. Whenever you feel disturbed or a sense of separation from anyone or anything within the world, go within and tell Holy Spirit about it. Tell Him what and how you are seeing the person, place or situation and ask Him to show you how He sees it. What He shares with you will always be healing for you and everyone involved.

When His answer comes you will notice a shift in perception. You may experience then an "A-ha" or an "Oh, I see." Every answer He gives you will help you to step in the direction of accepting the One Thought that Father holds for you. Ask the Holy Spirit to help you to find the One Thought He holds for you. Go within and search your mind with the Holy Spirit to find it. It is the greatest of all gifts. One that will fill you with joy, happiness and peace. The truth about Who You really are will be revealed to you in the One Thought. You will begin to experience that you are the Son of God created perfect and whole just like his Father. Thank You Father for creating me just like You. I love You, Father. Amen.

ooooo

Journal Entry on Lesson 339

I will receive whatever I request.

This is the time of the year that it is important to be vigilant for the teachings of the ego. The ego places special emphasis on the body during this time of the year. It likes to busy the body with activities of the season such as the busyness of shopping, overeating, overdrinking, and other activities. The ego's lesson is that this is salvation and that it is joy. By placing emphasis on the body the ego distracts us from the body of Christ where our true salvation and joy lies. As we go about the holiday season this year, let us practice remembering to stay tuned in within our minds with Holy Spirit's perception of persons, places and events that we may find ourselves in. Let us listen to Him speak to us and show us in those moments what He would have us see and learn about the ego's shenanigans.

After the holiday season is over, the ego likes to place more emphasis on the body through a commitment to change the body to make it look better because it believes it will bring everlasting joy and salvation. Hidden behind all of that is really a secret desire for your death because this is the gift the ego offers at the end of the dream. Let us side with the Holy Spirit and receive the gift that He has for us instead of the dream. His gift is resurrection from the dream to the awareness of everlasting life. His gift is that He will help you to gently awaken from the dream to recognize that the dream of pain really was merely just a dream. The Light within your mind will begin to show you a different reality. The little flashes and glimmers within the mind will show you the way. They will begin to reveal to you Who You really are. The body of Christ is so lovely to behold that only peace and joy could envelop the mind while we gaze upon our Light. Father, thank You for helping us to find our beauty today. Thank You for Your Voice that speaks to us and guides us Home. Amen.

It is for me to go back into the recesses of my mind with the Holy Spirit and become aware of my core beliefs. These core beliefs are hidden from my awareness. The ego has designed beliefs in unworthiness, unloveability and the like as a barrier to God. I may wonder why various situations occur and why I am brought to upset. Today's lesson tell us that the prayer of the heart is what is made manifest. As I examine these core beliefs with the Holy Spirit's gentleness, I can see that the beliefs that I seem to hold are mistaken thinking. The old beliefs are replaced by the Holy Spirit and it is known in my mind that I am a child of God, perfect in Love in every way. This is the prayer I wish to hold in my heart today and this is the request that I would have granted today.

ထတ

Journal Entry on Lesson 340

I can be free of suffering today.

The waxing and waning of the mind is what projects different experiences for you from the dream. Throughout your day you may find yourself involved with different situations, persons, or places. As you observe each of these situations, notice that each is a reflection of the state of your mind in that moment. Your mind unconsciously projects the seeming reality around you. It manifests the world you see and experience. The ego mind has spent eons developing this habit of misprojection with the mind. So much so that the experience of pain and suffering has become accepted as normal. Our minds have become complacent and do not recognize that they are responsible for projecting the world around them.

With the Holy Spirit's help, the mind can be broken free from this cycle with the practice of letting go of everything with the mind. You can allow a new experience into your perception. The mind can be moved out of the awareness of pain and suffering and into the awareness of the Love that surrounds us all the time.

While you practice closing your eyes and stilling your mind, be open to what the Holy Spirit has to show you and wait peacefully for Him to show you a higher state of the mind. He will help you to see and experience a projection of the reflection of the Light of your True Self. This in turn begins to heal the mind and free it from the illusion of fear and pain.

When we practice working with the Holy Spirit in this manner we are training our minds to opening up to the experience of our Reality and the recognition that we are responsible for projecting everything we experience. We do want to remember however that we cannot break free of the ego thought system on our own. We do need the help of the Holy Spirit. Father created Him to help us find our way Home. Call upon Him and ask Him for help in everything that you do for His only goal and everything He does is to help you to free you from the dream of illusions. And to bring you back into a state of awareness that you are in a state of pure joy. You are peace, you are Love, just like the way your Father created you. Thank You. Amen.

I choose to listen only to the Voice of Truth today. No words are needed for they just fill the empty space where His Word would be. Today, I have an openness to hear, not what I thought was my suffering but instead only of my joy in God.

∞∞∞∞

Journal Entry on Lesson 341

I can attack but my own sinlessness,
And it is only that which keeps me safe.

There are times that I feel sad and lonely, even depressed. At these times it is the voices outside of the Voice for Truth that I am listening to. These other voices demand that I am sinful, guilty, unworthy and unlovable. The Voice for Truth gently reminds me otherwise. The Voice of the Holy Spirit is the resounding call to awakening. I have been drowsy and woozy from the voices of pain. The Holy Spirit's miracle awakens me to a fresh awareness, an awareness that I am Love.

Nothing can change perfect Love. Nothing anyone says or does will change that very truth. Even all that I have used to veil myself

483

will not mask the Divineness that shines so radiantly from behind the veil. The Light indeed illuminates. The Light is Who I am. The Light is my innocence personified. Today, I will affirm for myself the snow-white purity of my Essence. I will look upon the world with new eyes, the eyes of Christ. A miracle will touch all that I do today as I connect with the Holy Spirit to be my Guide in all that I do and say. Thank You Holy Spirit for the One True Answer in my life. Amen.

∞∞∞

Journal Entry on Lesson 342

**I let forgiveness rest upon all things,
For thus forgiveness will be given me.**

Let us celebrate a new birthday today. Let us discover the blazing white Light that shines within our minds today. Let us celebrate in joy with the Holy Spirit the beginning of our resurrection to everlasting life with this discovery today. The white Light that shines within our minds will wash away all tears when we find it through our practice of silent meditation.

Patiently waiting in silence today, will bring us the gift of a lifetime. The Holy Spirit holds it out for us, waiting for us to accept the illumination of our holy minds. Let us remember the importance of what we are attempting to achieve today. This is the gift of all gifts. The one that we have been seeking for many lifetimes. The serial lives of the ego have eluded this gift from our awareness for ages, but not forever. The Light is there within our minds. Let us search and find it today. The healing and freedom it brings is beyond all things in our perception now. It is the joy we seek, the discovery of our True Selves; the discovery of the memory of Who we really are, God's one and only beloved Son. Thank You Father for Your gift to us. Amen.

Stepping through the door of forgiveness is like stepping outside after a long, cold, dead winter. The warm spring breeze of God's Love fills the air. As I step out into the Real World of no limits, I accept the freedom that is mine. I have been entombed in doubt and today is my day of resurrection. To rise above and see the Love in communion with my brothers. I trust them all for they are one with me. How long I have been asleep does not matter for now I am awake and have emerged now robed in glory of the Kingdom of God. Forgiveness offers me this freedom today and I gladly accept it. The Holy Spirit is my Guide leading me through the door of awakening and forgiveness is His golden key. It is that simple to let go and experience the Truth that I am as God created me, and so is everyone I see. I have the willingness to open my eyes today and see the innocence shining as a reflection of myself.

ooooo

Journal Entry on Lesson 343

**I am not asked to make a sacrifice
To find the mercy and the peace of God.**

In the past I was led to believe that I needed to prostrate myself and beg for forgiveness and mercy from the Lord. That is now archaic thinking for me. What I know now is that I am loved by God unconditionally. Yes, it is for me to recognize my mistakes and bring those ideas to the Holy Spirit Who purifies each one and a miracle is received. However, that is all I need do. God's mercy and peace are already mine because I am already His. I do not need to "win" His Love or affection. I need not sacrifice or even punish myself to be His own for I have never lost favor in His Holy Eyes. Father needs me as I need Him. We are One. We are complete with one another. It is for me to recognize this today. I am accepted by Him in all that I do. It is for me to forgive myself and release into the resting place of peace, my Home in Him.

Open the doorway to Heaven by having the willingness to practice searching your mind for It with Holy Spirit. I assure you that Heaven is there. You will know when you have found it when you have found the blazing white Light. Be still and open your mind up to It. Be still with an open mind and wait patiently for It to come and illuminate your mind. Set your intention solely on perceiving the Light and It will come to release you from hell. It is truly there. The miracle of the Light of Heaven will suddenly replace in your perception everything you see now with something entirely different. In the beginning of mind training it may be experienced as little sparks of white Light.

As we continue the process of training our minds to be still and open, the experiences with the Light will become more pronounced. Each experience with the Light washes the mind of darkness and replaces it with Light, peace, contentment, joy, and bliss. The experience is a glimmering of the state you are in now with your Father in Heaven. This experience can be discovered now no matter what is going on in your life. Simply practice and ask the Holy Spirit to help you to find it. He waits to give you this treasure. The treasure that will set the path back Home and free you from all misery forever. Your tears will be wiped away and be replaced with the light dance and footsteps of joy as we walk back Home hand in hand and enter the pearly gates of Heaven once again.

∞∞∞∞

Journal Entry on Lesson 344

**Today I learn the law of love;
that what I give my brother is my gift to me.**

Let me not be selfish today my Father, and let me know that when I withhold love from my brother that I am only withholding the power of Your Love from me. The spinning revolutions around my own egocentric nature will never bring me the happiness that I so seek. It is for me to get off the merry-go-round of self-indulgence and truly listen to what the Holy Spirit tells me. The Holy Spirit whispers to me that I am not alone, that not only is He here with me but so are all my brothers.

In them I will see myself, and how I think and treat them is how I think and treat myself. It is for me to remember that we are interconnected as One Light. Today, I will learn that love is for giving and receiving. It is accomplished each time I recognize my brother as myself. Let me not forget to extend myself as You extended Yourself to me. Love is all there is so why do I try to make my will and my controls above Your most holy Will? I cannot compete with Your Truth, nor will I try today. I merely accept all that You have given me as a wondrous gift. It is this gift that I gladly give, the gift of the present moment of Your purity of Love. Peace is returned to me each time I join my Will with Yours. Thank You Father for this reminder today that giving and receiving are one in truth and both I and my brothers are the beneficiaries. Amen.

Let us choose to not let anger draw blood from our brothers today. Let us choose instead to immediately turn our attention inward to Holy Spirit and ask Him for help in making a different choice. He will always help you to make the choice that leads you to happiness and freedom. Anger can be hidden in many ways by the ego. Let us remember to follow the flow of life today. We do not know what choices to make in any moment but the Holy Spirit does and His answers are always correct.

Let us remember to surrender to asking Him for help today in everything we do and for the willingness to follow His guidance. He will teach us how to extend Love. The only form of true Love in the world is forgiveness. Forgiveness is letting go of illusions. His guidance will always move you in a direction of letting go of illusions, letting go of the things we think will make us happy.

Forgiving everything with the Holy Spirit and letting go is the only way to restore peace. Let us begin to surrender to a life of peace today by letting go. The Holy Spirit will help us to do this and by letting Him help us to do this it will accelerate our awakening. Take everything to Him and let Him heal it in your mind. The Light will wash away all fear, anger and pain and replace it with peace. Thank You Holy Spirit for helping us with letting go of anger today.

∞∞∞∞

Journal Entry on Lesson 345

**I offer only miracles today,
For I would have them be returned to me.**

When the Light has come we will know that we have begun to perform the miracles that Jesus is asking us to do. When we perform the miracles we will have begun to meet ourselves as God. The flashes of white Light will show us the way that will show us the way to the Voice that will begin to speak to us from Heaven. We will soon discover that the Voice that soon speaks to us is our own.

When these things begin to happen it is a time for celebration indeed. For the Son of God has begun to accomplish the goal of the Course and has begun to awaken to the reality of his True Self. The joy that Heaven sings when this begins to happen is far beyond your imagination could grasp. The angels sing in triumphant joy. The Light that illuminates All That Is sings in joy. Father's Love for His Son sings in joy at His Son's returning to his Home. This is the time when His Son begins to recognize His Father gave him everything. His Father created him just like Himself. This is what the miracle leads to and much more.

Let us remember to practice today to discovering how miracles are truly performed. Sit still and wait for the Holy Spirit to show you the miracle of forgiveness that will illuminate your mind. Let us practice this as often as we can today until we succeed in discovering this most precious gift that the Christ has to offer us. This is the gift of Christmas that we are seeking. It is the discovery that we are the Christ, we are Christmas.

Miracles are my expressions of love in this world. As I shift my perception with the Holy Spirit's guidance, I begin to look upon a world that is forgiven and clothed in Love's glory. The Light behind the perceived edges of limitations are shown and through miracles practice I will recognize the light behind the illusions. Today, I do offer miracles, the holy shift to love; the happy place where love abides. I do not need miracles in heaven for Heaven is Love. Miracles help me to rise above and see the love while I am here. I am willing today to access Your Holy Wisdom dear Spirit and allow the eyes of Christ to bless all that I envision. The Real World lies behind it all and with forgiveness and miracles I will happily return there.

ooooo

Journal Entry on Lesson 346

Today the peace of God envelops me,
And I forget all things except His Love.

As I contemplated on today's lesson, I received an image of a time-worn box of photographs. As I began to look at each photograph, some were frozen moments of a happy time but most were snapshots of sad or painful times in my life. After seeing a few, I decided to close up the box and put them aside. These past images were no longer needed in my life as they did not define me any longer.

It was then that I could hear the Holy Spirit speak to me saying "There is no past, only Love is present now and will forever be." Today I let go of all the ghosts of the past and release the worries and concerns of the future. When I stand in the Light of the Eternal Now Moment I am resting in God's peace. What more could I want today but the peace of God? Letting go of all that I think, see or desire will most assuredly bring me that peace. And so, accepting peace is accepting Love. I honor this within my heart today. My mind is at rest as I turn each thought to the Holy Spirit. I am open to a miracle today, the miracle of peace.

Dear Holy Spirit, today we ask You to heal our minds of all past images that are not true. Images of poverty, feelings of lack, ideals of separation and differences are nothing more than bad dreams for the Son of God.

Dear Holy Spirit, we forgive ourselves for these images and we ask You for the miracle of healing to cleanse our minds. Holy Spirit, wash our minds of all things today so that the way may be cleared but the memory of Love to return to our minds. Holy Spirit help us to remember Reality today. Help us to remember the Truth that in our Home Heaven, where we truly are right now, we have no needs. Help us to remember and experience that everything is ok. That the world is nothing more than bad dreams. Help us to remember and see and experience our Father's Love for us once again. We've forgotten His Love but He has not forgotten His Love for us. We yearn to remember and experience His Love for us once again. We thank You for His mercy and His grace in restoring the memory of God's Love for His Son to His Son's mind. This is our prayer today to have the memory of God restored to our minds today. We remember that all prayers are answered and we thank You for the answer that has already come to us. That all things are certain and sure in the power of God's Love. He has not forgotten His Son and His Son will be assured of this. His Son will know that his Father has answered his call because his Father will take the final step Himself.

Journal Entry on Lesson 347

Anger must come from judgment. Judgment is
The weapon I would use against myself,
To keep the miracle away from me.

I let my mind be still today. In the quiet I will listen to His Voice and not know anger, or judgment or the basis of it all, fear. It is the belief in fear that makes the world I see and the judgments that I have placed upon it all. When I am in communion with the Holy Spirit, He looks upon all things and judges them innocent. He sees what I would not see.

Today I unite with Him in holy vision. It is important to offer my mind to Him in glad exchange of serenity and stillness. And so I will take time throughout the day to remember to come to His holy altar, lay all wandering thoughts of anger, judgment, fear and the like and sit quietly to listen to what His Voice speaks to me. I know that His Voice will speak only of the Love that I am, the Love behind the veil of illusion. This Love is the flame that continues to burn within, never to be extinguished, and always to light my way Home. For this, I am grateful today for the Eternal Love of God.

We are grateful for the message that Jesus shares with us in today's Lesson, because he gives us very specific instructions on how to have an experience of actually hearing the Voice for God speak to us. He says very specifically "Be very still." He's telling us that there is a way for us to actually hear the Voice of God speak to us. And if we really want that to happen, to have that experience, what we need to do is practice being very still. This means sinking down past all the thoughts of our ego mind and into that space where there is silence. Into the space where we do not even hear the chatter of our thoughts anymore.

Let us practice today, sinking down into that place of silence and practice listening only to the silence. Resting in this place of listening only to the silence, where no thoughts are heard, is our invitation to the Voice for God to speak to us. It is here where conversations with God truly begin. Let us remember to ask the Holy Spirit for help everytime we practice being very still today. For it is in joining with Him that our success in accomplishing today's goal is guaranteed. We thank Him for His help and we thank our Father for His gifts to us. Amen.

∞∞∞∞

Journal Entry on Lesson 348

I have no cause for anger or for fear,
For You surround me. And in every need
That I perceive, Your grace suffices me.

I am safe today Father for I know that You are with me in every moment, in every breath that I take. Your Love surrounds me as a loving embrace shielding me from the spectres of fear. I place all my trust in You today, Father. I do believe that You are with me. I affirm this now. When the moments come when I have lost faith, I know that I can come to the Answer, Your Holy Spirit, and He will restore my mind to serenity. I am grateful that I have the means to return to the shelter of Your Protection, the warmth of Your Love. I have only strayed in my mind and the gentle melody calls me Home to You.

Everything that we see surrounding us in this room right now is just a veil of illusion. We are grateful to discover in the silence the truth of the Light that is hidden behind the veil; the truth of the Voice that speaks to us from Heaven that surrounds us from behind the veil. We are grateful to discover that everything that surrounds us is just a curtain of illusion, and behind that curtian is a white Light of Love that completely envelops us. We thank you

Father for your gift of forgiveness that helps to heal the illusion that surrounds us, and allows Your gift of Light to shine through from behind the veil showing us the Way, the Light and the Truth. Thank You Holy Spirit for holding the Light for us and we ask You today to help us let go of the illusion with our minds, so that we may discover this most wonderful gift of Christmas. Thank You Father for your gift to us; the One that helps us find our way Home and restores our happiness as we find It. It is a Merry Christmas Father. We love You. Amen.

ooooo

Journal Entry on Lesson 349

> Today I let Christ's vision look upon
> All things for me and judge them not, but give
> Each one a miracle of love instead.

In today's meditation, the song "The Eyes of God" by Scott Kalechstein sang sweetly in my mind. The lyrics are: "Let me see with the eyes of God, let me love with the heart of God, let me breathe with the breath of God, let me live in the love of God." With this as a prayer today I will look upon the world with Real Eyes and realize the Truth. I will not be the determiner today, the judge and jury. Instead, I will allow the Holy One to lift the fog of illusions so that the brilliant Light of Truth is revealed. It is not sacrifice to allow the Holy Spirit to be in charge; it is merely surrender. It is surrendering to that Higher Power that will lead me through the world safely.

When I use my own strength, my own will, my own plans and control, I will always fail and I will always feel miserable. By allowing the Holy Spirit to lead and simply step back and be His vessel in this shell of a body, I will be doing the work of God. The work of God for me is to extend the miracle of Love. Today, this is my mission: to look upon all things with the Vision of Christ and see Love.

In the Text, Jesus reminds us that we are responsible for everything we see and experience in this world by giving us this prayer. "I am responsible for what I see. I choose the feelings I experience, and I decide upon the goal I would achieve. And everything that seems to happen to me I ask for, and receive as I have asked." What Jesus is sharing with us here is that we have a choice. We can continue to choose to see and experience the illusion that surrounds us day by day or we can begin to practice making a different choice. The alternative choice is to begin to practice seeing the other world through the gift of Christ Vision that is given to us by the Holy Spirit on behalf of Father. This gift is a miracle of Love. Light and Love are one and the same. When we begin to open up to the miracle of Love, we begin to open up to the miracle of Love, we begin to have experiences of perceiving the white Light of Heaven within our minds.

When this begins to happen, we are beginning to see with our spiritual vision that was given to us when we were created by Love Itself. This is the beginning of True Seeing and the beginning of the restoration of True Perception. It reveals to us that everything that we see, feel and experience in the world around us is nothing more than an illusion. The Light that flashes within our mind is the Light that leads us to our True Home in Reality with God. Thank You Father for the Holy Spirit Who holds the Light for us. And thank You Holy Spirit for Your gift of the Light of True Perception. Amen.

Scott Kalechstein's website: www.scottsongs.com

∞∞∞∞

Journal Entry on Lesson 350

Miracles mirror God's eternal Love.
To offer them is to remember Him
And through His memory to save the world.

I offer only miracles today by opening my mind to the memory of God. In God, there is only Love. Forgiveness and miracles are the means by which I return to the memory of God. Each offer of forgiveness in my mind, each shift into miracle-minded thinking brings me into alignment with God's holy purpose. My purpose is to recognize the Love that seems to hide in the dark shadows of the world. The Holy Spirit is my partner in shining the beacon of Truth to all the crevices of the darkness of illusion. Each thought of fear is brought to Him with my willingness. My willingness is all that is needed to help to heal the world. Through my gift is all that is Real then revealed. I will continue to practice today to allow miracles to mirror the Love of God. I will continue to invite forgiveness into my mind so that freedom is welcomed and peace restored. I will write all of this on my holy scroll within today, that I am God's Son and a reflection of His Holy Love.

The miracle of Love can be offered by you through the process of forgiveness. Forgiveness is the process of letting go of all thoughts, all images, and judgments about the image of the world that you think you are seeing and hearing. When you use your mind to let go of everything that you think you are seeing and hearing, the miracle of Love is allowed to reveal itself for an instant. The Light will flash into your mind replacing everything you see, for an instant, with a glimpse of reality. This flash is healing both yourself and the world at the same time because it is temporarily replacing illusions with Truth. The body feels the healing release of the illusion of fear and separation in this Holy Instant.

For a moment the mind is set free from the chains it has put upon itself. Thank You Father for these Holy Instants. The mind also becomes aware that it has a choice to offer these miracles anytime it wants through the practice of forgiveness in this manner. Miracles can be offered to save and heal the world. When the miracle is offered, everyone is affected, everyone is healed because that is the way God's Love works. Thank You Father for Your Eternal Love. Thank You Father for Your gifts to us. We love You and we are beginning to recognize that we are Love too because of the miracles You have given to us. Amen.

∞∞∞

Journal Entry on Lesson 351

My sinless brother is my guide to peace.
My sinful brother is my guide to pain.
And which I choose to see I will behold.

What choice is it that I want to make today? If I choose to see shortcomings or to hold on to grievances with a brother, I am choked in fear. I may feel justified in what I feel about them for they have "wronged" me or they have "abandoned" me. But, it is my own cold hand of fear that is gripping me and not my brother. I am not the victim at all but of my own thoughts about my brother. My brother is me. He is my savior, and I, his.

When I release my grip on fear, anger and righteousness, I open to the presence of Love in my life. I open to the gifts of God that are waiting only for my acceptance. I accept God as my Divine Source. I accept that I am His Child and so is my brother. We are innocent in the Eyes of God. I will make the choice for freedom today by relinquishing my thoughts of fear and judgment. My brother has not truly harmed me for as God's Son I cannot be harmed. It is my own thinking that has brought me to the experience of pain and it is my own thinking in alliance with the

Holy Spirit that will lead on the path of peace. Today, Holy Spirit, I will work in accordance to God's Will for me and I know that is to share in His happiness. To share in God's happiness, I simply forgive. That is what I will do with each thought, I will make the choice for Love this day. Amen.

∞∞∞

Journal Entry on Lesson 352

Judgment and love are opposites.
From one Come all the sorrows of the world. But from
The other comes the peace of God Himself.

Just as I woke up this morning, I heard the Voice whisper into my ear, "Have fun with the Course." As I reflected on this during my meditation this morning what was coming to me was that life is a course. It is a course in awakening to happiness and joy. I think the Holy Spirit is reminding me to have fun with everything I do in life, to remember to be happy and to play with life.

When I went to the store to go Christmas shopping yesterday I forgot to have fun with it. I forgot to enjoy the process. I forgot to embrace the holiday spirit. I felt conflicted and moments of irritation and impatience when all I really wanted to do was embrace the process of remembering my family and friends and wanting to extend and express my love and appreciation to them by remembering them this holiday season. The holiday season can be a joyful experience, a happy experience if we choose to let go of our judgments about it and to embrace the holiday spirit. It's the time for remembering how much we love and appreciate God in our lives and each other. It's a time to take delight and joy in knowing that truth that everything is ok and we're all in Heaven right now, forever happy with each other and with God. We are just dreaming this dream.

Knowing this, we can let go of all of our worries and just celebrate each other, love each other, remember each other and remind each other how much we love each other. That's what we all really want here in the dream is to be reminded that we exist and that we are loved. Calling someone or visiting with someone or sending someone a loving gift is a gift worth giving. Giving someone the gift of your time and attention this holiday season is a gift worth giving. Listening to them, embracing them and being with them in the moment is a gift worth giving this holiday season. It is a gift of love. It is an acknowledgement that you exist and that you are loved and you are Love Itself. It is a gift that keeps on giving long after the encounter. Tell everyone that you love them this holiday season and let them know this is true by being with them in the moment. Thank You Holy Spirit for this reminder. Amen.

∞∞∞

Journal Entry on Lesson 353

My eyes, my tongue, my hands, my feet today
Have but one purpose; to be given Christ
To use to bless the world with miracles.

Today I will not assume that I understand what it really means to give my eyes, my tongue, my hands, and my feet to Christ to bless the world with miracles. Instead, I ask Holy Spirit to show me what He really means by this today. I ask Holy Spirit to give me an experience in each of these areas today. And, to give them to me in a manner in which I realize it has happened so that I may truly understand what today's lesson means. As I go about my day today, I will remain mindful of today's lesson and my specific request to Holy Spirit and be vigilant for His responses. I thank Him for them now for I know they will come.

And when His answers come I will not judge them instead I will lay judgment and fear aside and exchange them with this response, "Thank You Holy Spirit for showing me this. And yes, I trust You and I will follow Your guidance in this area because I know that everything You do benefits me and everyone around me." I will remember that everything that Holy Spirit guides me to do leads everyone to a more joyful experience in the dream. I will remember to trust this guidance and lay aside all questioning today and to thank Him for His blessings to me. I will remember that He is my rock and He knows the way to lead me to a happy, care-free and joyful experience. When we surrender allowing Holy Spirit to guide our lives there is no need for worries or guilt because He is in charge of everything. He alone is fit to do this and we are grateful for that. His Voice will guide us, His Thoughts will guide us if we but listen. Thank You Father for Your gift to us, our Friend, the Holy Spirit. We love You, Father. Amen.

The question to ask myself today is, "Do I walk my talk?" Have I been bothered in the past by those who seemed they were on a spiritual path but their actions did not match their speech? Have I allowed myself today to be the vessel of God? Have I clothed myself with the garment of His Love? As I go about my day today, I will be conscious of my words... are they loving-speech? I will be conscious of my actions... have I asked Holy Spirit what to do, where to go and what to say?

I am His vessel. I am the eyes, the hands, the feet and the tongue of my Father. I follow His most Holy Guidance as I accept that I am here to be truly helpful. I accept that I am here as His representative. I am here to extend Love, to wipe away the dream of pain with my forgiveness. And so today, I devote myself to miracle-mindedness. I allow myself to be the extension of All That Is. My thoughts, my words, my actions will match what I now study and believe. I am confident that this is my path. I bless the world, I bless myself as I remember the holy connection that I share with my Father. Today, I will bless the world with miracles through all that I do. Let me remember that I am One with all. Amen.

ⓄⓄⓄⓄⓄⓄ

Journal Entry on Lesson 354

> **We stand together, Christ and I, in peace**
> **And certainty of purpose. And in Him**
> **Is His Creator, as He is in me.**

As the snowflakes fall so softly from the sky blanketing the land before me with snow, so too am I in that state of purity, untouched by the world. I am the Christ, the Son of God. I am innocent today and every day. Recognizing my origin is helpful to the healing of my mind. I thought I had made this world, a world that supports me not, but God supports me in all that I am. He has given me His gift of the Holy Spirit to regain peace to my mind so that all that I see is crystal clear. Many times I need to be reminded that I am as God created me and that nothing else can cover my True Existence. No words, no thoughts, no images, no situations, nothing from others will cause the denial of my perfection in Him. And so today I stand together with the Christ, my Self, and look upon the Light, the Light that sets me free.

Yesterday, I saw a story on the news of a tragedy that appeared to take lives of several people and their children. The story bothered me. It disturbed my peace and I began to question the Holy Spirit why and how this could happen. I asked Him, "Is this somehow a part of Your plan? Do people come here to go through these terrifying experiences to help others? On some level of the mind have they chosen to do this?"

This morning Holy Spirit helped me to realize that this line of thinking and questioning is nothing more than in alignment with the ego thought system. He said that only the ego would attempt to have us believe that God would ever want these kinds of experiences for His beloved Children. Nothing could be further from the truth than the illusions of tragedies that the ego uses to attack life. The Holy Spirit assured me that it is quite possible for the world to live and exist in perfect harmony.

In fact, it already does in Heaven right now. He reminded me that Heaven exists inside of us right now and is untampered. God's world lives in perfect harmony inside of us right now and we have access to that world within our minds. We forget that we have chosen on some level to block this from our awareness and to project something else out into the world for us to experience. This is the distortion of the ego-mind thought system.

On some level we have chosen to create a personal hell for ourselves. The only way to heal this is through forgiveness. Remember to forgive, forgive and forgive again until Heaven is restored to your awareness. Anytime you see, feel, hear or think something that disturbs your peace let it become a red warning flag that pops up for you and reminds you to stop and join with Me in that moment. Ask Me to help you to forgive this, whatever it is in that moment. Make it a priority in your life to heal any fearful thought or feeling that comes into your experience immediately with Me. It may feel like a rocky road but it will smooth out and it always leads to a sense of deep inner peace. The rule is this, the more you practice forgiveness; the more inner peace you will experience.

After a while, you'll come to a place where you would not give up this sense of inner peace for anything. Thank you for bringing this to Me. Thank you for having the willingness to be open to My messages. I love you. Remember that red flag. Keep practicing that forgiveness. It is the way Home and I am right here with you. I'm always here with you. And we can do it together in any moment you need. Amen.

Journal Entry on Lesson 355

**There is no end to all the peace and joy,
And all the miracles that I will give,
When I accept God's Word. Why not today?**

Why not today indeed? It is through my own determination that I can say that Heaven is the decision I must make. God has fulfilled His promises to me and now I accept them as my very own. I do desire peace and joy in my life. I do desire a new way of looking at the world. And so, I listen to the Voice of Truth which speaks to me of what I can have when I pause to remember.

In the Christmas carol, "O Holy Night", we are sung of our sweetness. Right now is the holy night as we are about to awaken to the dawning of a new life for us. It is there. It is guaranteed. We are reborn in Eternal Love. There is no sin and error as we are pure and innocent as a babe. God extended Himself to us and our soul has now recognized our worth, the Holy Treasure. Love does not ask for sacrifice, merely humbleness and surrender of the ego's thought system of fear.

If I still my mind, I will hear within the sweet melody of angels singing of my Divine nature. It is a Divine time for all of us. Joy to the world is possible, peace is possible, miracles are possible when I stop to simply listen to the Holy Spirit say, "Do you hear what I hear?" A song, an ancient melody that He sings, carrying us, cradling us to the Home within God's heart is what is heard. We are safe, we are secure, we are comfortable in His Love. It is my choice and today I answer the Call.

∞∞∞∞

Journal Entry on Lesson 356

Sickness is but another name for sin.
Healing is but another name for God.
The miracle is thus a call to Him.

Today I am assured that all I need to do is but to extend my willingness and bend my ear and indeed I will receive a clear Answer to my request. I think that I have made something else other than my Divineness in You. Father, I know that I cannot hide or cover myself in this world. The Light of Your Love always shines through, lifting the darkness up and away from me. To believe in sickness is a mistake. Only my mind can be sick.

When I bring my thoughts to the Answer You gave me, the Holy Spirit, I am healed, I am in step with the Truth. And so yes, I experience a miracle, a new perception, a healing of mistaken thinking. Today, it is for me to be vigilant of my mind. Keep a holy watch over it. I can at times seem to be caught up in the world and all its' trappings, particularly during the holiday season. Let not the tinsel and twinkling lights distract me from the One True Light that is my Friend in healing.

So as I am mindful of each thought that comes into my mind, I will pause to recognize the feeling that is coupled with it. Am I feeling tension? Am I feeling at ease? When I can be in tune with my thoughts and resulting feelings that I can gratefully work with the Holy Spirit in releasing all that is not of peace to Him. I will live a life more of peace and serenity when I do this, and this I know. Today, I remember to call to Him by accepting the miracle of Love.

ooooo

Journal Entry on Lesson 357

> Truth answers every call we make to God,
> Responding first with miracles, and then
> Returning unto us to be itself.

The sights and sounds of Heaven are carefully hidden deep inside of you by the ego thought system. This Christmas season let us spend some time with Holy Spirit and see if we can find these most precious gifts within our minds. The gifts are there and to find them we must clear our minds and sink down into silent meditation and wait patiently for them to be revealed to us.

The Holy Spirit will help us practice finding these gifts if we let Him. There is a wonderful white Light to behold within the mind. There is also a loving Voice that will speak to you that sounds clearer than the voice you hear speaking to you now. These gifts of God and many more are hidden deep inside of everyone waiting for the truth to be discovered.

When we sink down in our minds during silent meditation past all thoughts, past all images we discover the deep well of God within the seeming abyss. It is here where the Vision of Christ will be revealed to you in the flash of a beautiful white Light. It is here where you would hear My Voice speak to you saying, "Behold your sinlessness." And in that holy instant will you begin to recognize that these are glimpses of your True Identity as the Son of God.

What other Christmas gifts could you want to discover this holiday season? What other gifts could you receive this holiday season that would show you that everything you have experienced in this world, including your body and death is not true? Instead, you are the Christ, the holy Son of God Himself. These gifts inside of you are the gifts you really seek. You have been seeking them all of your life whether you realize it or not.

These are the gifts that will free you. These are the gifts that will begin to release you to the freedom and joy of flying freely and happily in life once again. It doesn't take long to practice finding these gifts within yourself. Just give the Holy Spirit a little bit of your time in practice everyday with the intention of finding these gifts, and they will show up sooner than you would expect. The surprise and delight you will feel upon discovering your gifts will surpass any other experience in the world.

Today's lesson reminds me that a healing is received when I forgive. How easy it is with the Holy Spirit's help to let go of the false beliefs that I have that my brother is not one with me. How joyous to know that he truly is. In working with the Holy Spirit, I can see the innocence in my brother and when I see it in my brother I am seeing it within myself. You quietly speak this message to me Father all throughout my day that I need just look upon the innocence and I will know my own healing. I will know the Truth.

Today that is the miracle I receive. There are some brothers in my life that at times it seems difficult to behold their beauty. Their words, their actions, their personalities really only block the Light from shining through. I do not have to like the personality but beyond that mask is what I do love, the connectedness of our lineage in God. This is what I want to be mindful of today, to look past the masks that hide the truth from myself. I will behold the gift of miracles today, those shifts in perception facilitated by You, Holy Spirit. I am thankful that I have the means for my own healing. Amen.

∞∞∞∞

Journal Entry on Lesson 358

> **No call to God can be unheard nor left**
> **Unanswered. And of this I can be sure;**
> **His answer is the one I really want.**

Very simply I will listen to Your Voice today, my Father. As I sat in silent meditation on this Lesson for a long period of time, all that came into my mind recalled only of Your Love for me. Whatever grievance would appear, I heard You softly tell me of what is true. Different situations and persons also appeared, and once again Your Holy Spirit showed me other situations in which Your Love has been evident in my life. As I reflected on the healing of my mind over the years, I could see the miracles that have indeed occurred.

My family is one situation in which I have shifted my perception. In the past, I had my judgments but as my mind has been released to the Holy Spirit's guidance I can see my family now reflects my core beliefs in God. The Holy Spirit showed me this in a flash of an instant in my mind today. Even though I wanted to be angry about what has occurred in others' families with the seeming lack of non-support and unconditional love, He reminded me that it is a lesson for all, even me. That was when He showed me the shift in perception surrounding my own family. Perhaps they do not understand all that I have done in my life, but I can now see the unconditional love that is there, the warm acceptance of my partner, the true caring that is shown. I never had seen that in the past. Is this not how I see my holy Father now? A God of unconditional Love and Acceptance? Yes, it is.

If I focus what seems to be occurring in others' relationships then I am buying into the ego's thought system of guilt, anger, blame and fear. This I will surrender all to the Holy Spirit. As I surrender all these thoughts of unworthiness to the Holy Spirit, He replaces them with God's holy peace. I am innocent in His eyes. I am His Holy Child. I rest in Him. He alone is my Guide Home. The world is not my home. The trappings are just that, a trap set by the ego to keep me enchained to pain. Today, I listen to the Voice of Truth and set myself free. I have called and He has surely answered.

A call to God is done from a place of silence. It is when we take time to practice being with God, thanking Him and loving Him with our silence. In the silence, we are telling Him we wish for nothing to be changed from what He Willed for us. In the silence, we are attempting to let go of all thoughts, feelings, and images of the past and the present. Resting in the place of peaceful silence is where we begin to experience the answers from Him Who is our Creator. This is the place where we will meet the Face of Christ and approach the gates of Heaven; where we shift from perception of our world to perception of Reality.

This is the place where we will hear the Voice for God speak to us in the silence, and see the Face of Christ revealed to us as the Light. The Light shines from Heaven and the Voice will help us to remember who we really are. We will begin to recognize and experience that we are the Christ, the Holy Son of God Himself. The Light that we see we begin to recognize as the reflection of our Holy Selves. We are the Light of the world and it is in the place of silence where we will discover that all these things are true. Thank You Father for sending us our Guide, the Holy Spirit, Who will help us discover these joyful gifts within ourselves. He holds out His hand to us, and asks us to take it, so that He may show us the way.

Thank You Father for Your gift to us. Thank You Holy Spirit for Your help. We love You and we love each other, for We are all One World without end. Amen.

∞∞∞∞

Journal Entry on Lesson 359

God's answer is some form of peace. All pain
Is healed; all misery replaced with joy.
All prison doors are opened. And all sin
Is understood as merely a mistake.

It is helpful to be reminded that God's answers always come in some form of peace. It is easy to be confused by the ego when decisions must be made. Remember to practice spending a moment of silence with God when you seek the answer to some decision you must make. Let go of all your worries and concerns and just practice being in the silence space of peace for a moment. He knows all your questions before you ask. There's no need to ask again. Just be with Him in silence for a moment and His answer will come in some form of peace.

When the answer comes, if there is a feeling of doubt or uncertainty about it, the ego is still involved. It would be wise to spend a moment of silence again and ask Holy Spirit again for the direction or choice He would have you make. How nice it is to have a Friend Who goes with you wherever you go and Whom you can call upon in any moment for the answers to all your questions. If there is still conflict in your mind about a decision that you are being guided to make, hand it over to the Holy Spirit and let Him decide for you. He has all of the power in Heaven and on earth to handle the situation for you without your intervention.

Ask and you will receive and He will always answer whether you realize it or not. Things will just happen to work out and you may look back and say, "Wow, that was neat how that worked out." Trust the Holy Spirit. He is with you wherever you go. He will answer you whether you see it or not. Let go of judgment and worries and hand them over to Him as well. It's impossible for you to judge because you are not aware of all situations.

The Holy Spirit is aware of everything and therefore can always help you to make the best choice in any situation and in any moment. Only He knows the correct answers and He will always give them to you if you but choose to listen. Ask Him with all your heart to guide you in everything you do and thank Him when you are done for it is done. He is your Friend Who holds your hand while you walk in hell, and He will guide you down the happy path through the dream of hell where the destination ends in finding your Home in Heaven. You have no other friends around you that are capable of doing this. Although they mean well, the Holy Spirit is your one and only true guide. Remember to embrace Him, to trust Him, to have faith in Him in all things and you will find your happy dream. Amen.

In contemplation on this lesson, I received a vision of my hands clamped in chains. A key was in one hand and I was able to free myself very simply through my mind recognizing that the chains were dissolvable. As the chains fell as dust, the White Dove of Peace, which I knew was the Holy Spirit, flew straight towards me carrying an olive branch in its' feet. It dropped the branch within my outstretched hands and I gladly accepted this symbol of peace. In my mind I could hear the Holy Spirit share His gratitude for my willingness to forgive my self-imposed chains of pain and misery. Soon after the Dove began to fly away, I felt myself starting to soar along with It. As we climbed higher in altitude, I was rising above the world I thought I knew. That world became smaller and more insignificant and a glorious Light beckoned me closer. The Light was inviting and warm, the message was that of unconditional Love and Peace. This is what I receive today and everyday when I let go of all thoughts that point my mind in the direction of fear. Today, I will be mindful of my thoughts and share them with the Holy Spirit. There is no need to hide these thoughts from Him. Dark thoughts are meant to be placed before Him so that the Light may be revealed. Holy Spirit, I offer all to You in glad exchange of Your gift of Peace. Thank You for showing me the Light of God's Love. And thank You Father for the Answer to all that I seek. Amen.

∞∞∞

Journal Entry on Lesson 360

Peace be to me, the holy Son of God.
Peace to my brother, who is one with me.
Let all the world be blessed with peace through us.

Peace is all I desire today. There are very few ideas to think about or words to even verbalize. Nothing seems to matter much now as I reflect simply on the peace of God. Thank You Father for Your peace and for my recognition with the Holy Spirit of my Oneness with all.

I am so grateful that Jesus shared with us specific instructions in the Workbook for Students on how to discover the truth that is hidden within ourselves. For a long time, I came to believe that I was this limited body destined for constant conflict, worry, and pain within my mind and in my life with a destination that ultimately ended up in death and possible condemnation to hell.

I'm so grateful for Jesus sharing with me how to discover the solution to all these problems; which was how to discover the truth about myself. The truth is, that I am not really a body, I am something much greater. The miracles is, that there is a way to see and experience this greater Self right now. There is a way to discover the truth that all of this is not real and that there is something else. The other wonderful thing about this discovery is that it is inside of me and it goes with me wherever I go; and I can choose to see and experience it anytime I want. We can choose to see the truth about ourselves anytime we want! We are the Christ, the Holy Son of God Himself! We can choose to see the blazing white Light of our Holy Selves whenever we want. The sight of our sinlessness is so wonderful and so peaceful and so joyful that we can't even imagine it with our minds! All we can do is open up to the experience, and wait in the silence for this truth about our Holy Selves to be reflected to us in the flash of a Holy Instant. The release of fear and acceptance of peace in that moment is so wonderful. Thank You Father for Your gift to us. Thank you Jesus for showing us the way, and for helping us to find the truth hidden inside of ourselves. Amen.

∞∞∞∞

Journal Entry on Lesson 361

This holy instant would I give to You.
Be You in charge. For I would follow You,
Certain that Your direction gives me peace.

The final lessons are an encounter in great joy for what comes is a time now for deep listening. I offer willingness with an open mind and heart to hear what the Voice for God would speak to me. I am not afraid of His Answers for His Answers will only bring me peace. All that I need will be given to me as I lay aside all the petty thoughts and dreams that I believe are mine. They are only coming from the ego mind, the haven of fear. It is Heaven that I receive today each time I forgive. Happiness is within me, I just unwrap and unravel all the ribbons of fear that have entangled it and kept it from my sight. No more will I seek to find my happiness in the world when there is only the joy of God to be had.

This is what the Holy Spirit tells me of today. Be happy by being Me, my True Self. To listen I need to release my own thoughts, my own words that fill the space where He can come. It is as the monk's bowl. How can it be filled with goodness if I keep it full of my own wanderings? My own interpretations? Today, I interpret nothing, I empty my mind and enter into the sacred space of holy silence. I wait patiently for Your Sweet Voice Holy Spirit. Sing to me Heaven's song and let the angels sing with You in Joy of Your Son Who was created like His Father. I accept the truth of who I am and let my mind be wholly healed today.

∞∞∞

Journal Entry on Lesson 362

This holy instant would I give to You.
Be You in charge. For I would follow You,
Certain that Your direction gives me peace.

Inside of us, everyone has a Friend, a Teacher, a Guide Who will comfort us and help us along our way. Let us dedicate this week to being with Him in our minds. As we go about our day, let's remember to greet and talk with Him about all of our worries and concerns and decisions that we need to make and follow in this world. Let's remember to turn to Him and let Him guide us in everything we do. Let's give Him a chance to show us what a Friend we truly have, Who goes with us wherever we go. Let's give Him a chance to show us that He is really here with us right now, and that He really wants to help us and to show us the way to a peaceful and happy life. Let's give Him a chance to give us the gifts that He has for us, and when we receive them, let's remember to thank Him for His helping hand when we are done. Let us remember to thank our Father for His gift to us, our Friend, Holy Spirit. Amen.

∞∞∞

Journal Entry on Lesson 363

> **This holy instant would I give to You.**
> **Be You in charge. For I would follow You,**
> **Certain that Your direction gives me peace.**

As I close my eyes in meditation on today's Lesson, I am aware that as I sink into silence, I am screening out the movie that I have made. Most times it has been a drama or seeming tragedy, or dare I say even horror over the years. Jesus reminds me that it all really is a comedy, an insane moment when the Son of God forgot to laugh.

When I am experiencing emotions of sadness or anger it certainly may not seem as if my feelings are not real, for in the moment they are to me. As I look at these feelings that are occurring with honesty, it is then I can begin to release them to the Holy Spirit and let Him be in charge of all my thoughts. Honesty really is the best policy.

If I quickly deny what I am feeling with thoughts of "I'm spiritual now and I shouldn't feel that way," or "All is Love and Light," when I do not really believe it, I am doing a disservice to myself in my own healing process. The Holy Spirit desires my willingness and honesty to come to Him with all the thoughts that disturb my peace. I do not have to purify my thoughts before I come to Him for He is the Purifier. With the thought in today's Lesson, "Be You in charge," I will allow Him to take all these mental rolls of film and create for me the one blockbuster hit which features the One True Self and directs me to my innocence in Heaven. Thank You Holy Spirit for being in my mind to assist me in the true direction of my thoughts. With You, I can shine as a star ever so brilliantly forever and ever. Amen.

∞∞∞∞

Journal Entry on Lesson 364

> **This holy instant would I give to You.**
> **Be You in charge. For I would follow You,**
> **Certain that Your direction gives me peace.**

What comes to mind today with this lesson that we have been doing the last few days is the idea of "Go now in peace." I accept peace as the direction, the goal in which I place my intention. As this year comes to a close, I reflect on how this year of mind training has touched my soul. Each year I follow through the Lessons and each year I feel another layer has been removed from my mind. I realize in each passing day that I have come to a place of no return. I cannot go back to the way my life had been prior to my spiritual awakening through *A Course in Miracles*. It seems that I know and comprehend much now and I say that with a smile.

Before in my life it seemed that there was no hope, no relief from the pain that I was experiencing. In my mind then, there was only hell and blame of others for my pain. Now I can see the two worlds; what's Real and what's unreal. And for me now the prospect that only Love is real has so much more substance. I can see the difference in my choices. I can realize a happier state of being and living. I can see the hope that is there and that I need not continue to suffer. Situations will still occur that need my attention whether it is a fender-bender, a bill that needs paid, a friend who has lost a loved one, or a family member who is angry or depressed. With the knowledge that I have now through my study of the Course, I can look beyond and see the truth behind all of this and not feel so lost. I can see the Love. I am indeed found in my relationship with God as I set peace as my one goal now.

Everything is given to the Holy Spirit for His clear message to be received in return and the message of Love is all there is. The Holy Spirit only supports me and all I need do is ask and then I can listen and know that He is always present. With His presence I can now go in peace and joy.

∞∞∞

Journal Entry on Lesson 365

This holy instant would I give to You.
Be You in charge. For I would follow You,
Certain that Your direction gives me peace.

Now we know that we are not alone. We know now that there is a Voice Who will speak to us and a Light within us that will heal us. We are so glad to be remembering the truth about ourselves. We are so glad to learn and discover that there is Someone Who goes with us wherever we go. We are relieved to discover that we have a Friend, a personal Friend, Who will talk with us and comfort us and tell us which way to go with all of the decisions that must be made in this world. We are glad to find our Friend Who knows all the right answers and will lead us down the right path toward a happy and joyful life experience.

At last we can sit back and rest and relax because finally we have discovered the truth about ourselves that we have a Friend within us Who will show us the way to go and show us the truth about ourselves. This is a True Friend, one Who shows you that you are not a body destined for death. Who shows us through the reflection of the shining Light of our Holy Self that we are a spiritual being who is God's one and only Creation. His only Son who He created perfect and sinless like Himself. How happy and grateful are we to discover our Friend Who is showing the truth about ourselves that we are the Son of God. We are the Christ, His Holy Son. We are the Divine just like Him Who created us. This is the only truth that there ever was, is, and will ever be forever without end. Amen. Thank You Father. We love our Holy Self and we love You.

As this year's Lessons come to a close, what thought is prevalent in my mind is the closing sentence of the Epilogue, "I will never leave you comfortless." In the past through my trials and challenges, I was led to believe that I was insignificant to God. I felt that He did not care what suffering I was experiencing. In fact, Jim Carrey's character in "Bruce Almighty" said it as I felt it then, "God is like a mean kid with a magnifying glass burning off the feelers of the ants on the ant hill."

Through my dedicated spiritual study over the years, of course I have come to know that this is not true. I am not alone. I am surrounded by the Love of God always. There is nothing that my Father wants more than for me to recognize this very fact. He has given me the gift of the Holy Spirit, the Answer, Who was instantaneously placed in my mind at the moment I had forgotten who I was.

I see an image now of the Holy Spirit holding my hand as we walk along the path of forgiveness. His hand clasped in mine, I can feel the strength and security that is there knowing He does indeed go with me wherever I go in this world. He is my Guide in these uncharted territories and together we arrive Home, where I always have been, save in Love's Arms. I can relax now in comfort and allow my mind to be soothed by the healing balm of His Love. At the fireside of Love, I am both warmed and brought into a place of stillness, of wonder, as the flames of joy dance celebrating my return. I am Home for I am Love, God's Son.

∞∞∞∞

About Revs. Paul and Deborah Phelps

Revs. Paul and Deb are both dedicated, long-time students and teachers of *A Course in Miracles*. Together, in 2005, they co-founded the not-for-profit, MiraclesOne Foundation, MiraclesOne Light University and the Miracles in Madison study groups in Madison, Wisconsin.

They have co-authored several *A Course in Miracles* inspired books and materials including: *Divine Messages, Illumination Journal for the Workbook for Students, Reflections on the Workbook for Students - Volumes I & II, Enlightenment Meditation Series audio CDs*, and the *MiraclesOne Practical Application Series* programs and *Practical Application Audio Series*, and *MiraclesOne Study Group Guide & Journal*.

In addition, Paul and Deb also produce and host several radio show podcasts: *Practical Application of A Course in Miracles, The Miracle View, Your Inner Light, Sunday Miracles, 30 Day Miracles, Divine Messages*, and *A Cuppa Miracles*, a periodical video series on the principles of *A Course in Miracles*.

Every awakening tool is co-created under Holy Spirit's guidance and designed to help others apply the principles of the Course into their daily lives. By doing so, one can embrace the personal experience of a deep and intimate relationship with the Holy Spirit and truly live the Spirit-Led life.

Through their dedicated study and practice of the lessons contained within the Workbook for Students and the principles taught in the Text of *A Course in Miracles*, Paul and Deb have learned how to accept the Gift within and become true Miracle

Workers and Teachers of God. Their lives are dedicated to helping others find, experience, know and strengthen the same Gift within themselves.

Rev. Deb Phelps - Deb's spiritual awakening began in 1980 when at the age of 16 she began practicing the discipline of meditation. She has been studying and teaching *A Course in Miracles* since 1994 and received her ordination as a ministerial counselor originally from Pathways of Light in 2000.

With an education in Community Ministry, she has served social service, ministry, church and non-profit organizations for close to 20 years with a focus on participants' personal and spiritual growth. Deb is a Doctoral Candidate in Holistic Counseling Ministry with the University of Metaphysics and a member of the spiritual counseling organization, AACC.

Deb was the Director and Founder of the *Miracles Circle of Pittsburgh*, which was an ACIM Center in Pittsburgh, PA from 2000-2004. She is currently the Director of the MiraclesOne Foundation and is available for ACIM and spiritual support during regular business hours and after hours by appointment. She is also available for spiritual counseling by appointment.

Rev. Paul Phelps - Paul's spiritual awakening began in the late 1990's when he started to ask God for the truth. He was led to Neale Donald Walsch's book, *Conversations with God*, then to *A Course in Miracles* which he began studying in 2001. Shortly after practicing the Lessons in the Workbook for Students, Paul began to learn how to perceive the visible Light of Christ within himself and others. He later began to learn how to hear the audible Voice of God speak to him with unmistakable clarity. In 2004, Paul was ordained as a ministerial counselor originally from Pathways of Light.

Paul was the Co-Director of the *Miracles Circle of Pittsburgh*, an

ACIM Center in Pittsburgh, PA. Paul is currently a Doctoral Candidate in Mystical Research with the University of Metaphysics. Paul works full-time for the Wisconsin Army National Guard as an Information Technology Specialist and part-time as a Medical Evacuation helicopter pilot.

They happily reside in Madison with two of their six children, their daughters, Allison and Autumn.

<u>To contact Revs. Paul & Deborah Phelps</u>

MiraclesOne Foundation
1949 Sachtjen St.
Madison, WI 53704

Toll-Free: 1-877-881-1433
In Madison, WI: 608-541-8000

Website: www.miraclesone.org
E-mail: revs@miraclesone.org

Divine Messages

LaVergne, TN USA
03 July 2010
188302LV00002B/144/P